Every generation needs a spokesman for its endeavors. In this respect, Frank Murphy does the young men of VIII Bomber Command proud.

—ROGER A. FREEMAN, AUTHOR AND
  EIGHTH AIR FORCE HISTORIAN

It is an honor and a privilege to be associated with the American, British, and Allied airmen who, during the Second World War, gave us much. I urge you to read Frank Murphy's truly memorable story.

—IAN L. HAWKINS, AUTHOR AND
  WORLD WAR II HISTORIAN

You fly with Frank in combat missions, cheating death more than once and witnessing death far too often. You travel with him to Stalag Luft III, witness the Great Escape, and share the joy of liberation at the sight of a white star on a battle-weary Sherman tank.

—PAUL ANDREWS, AUTHOR AND
  U.S. AIR FORCE HISTORIAN

LUCK

OF THE

DRAW

LUCK

OF THE

DRAW

MY STORY OF THE
AIR WAR IN EUROPE

FRANK MURPHY

Formerly Captain and Navigator   Crew No. 31
418th Bombardment Squadron   100th Bombardment Group (H)
United States Army Eighth Air Force
Station 139, Thorpe Abbotts, Norfolk, England (1943)

FOREWORD BY CHLOE MELAS
AND ELIZABETH MURPHY

St. Martin's Griffin
New York

Published in the United States by St. Martin's Griffin, an imprint of St. Martin's
Publishing Group

LUCK OF THE DRAW. Copyright © 2001 by Frank Murphy. Foreword copyright ©2023 by
Chloe Melas and Ann Murphy Melas. All rights reserved. Printed in the United States of
America. For information, address St. Martin's Publishing Group, 120 Broadway,
New York, NY 10271.

www.stmartins.com

The Library of Congress Cataloging-in-Publication Data is available upon request.

ISBN 978-1-250-86689-9 (trade paperback)
ISBN 978-1-250-28415-0 (hardcover)
ISBN 978-1-250-28416-7 (ebook)

Our books may be purchased in bulk for promotional, educational, or business use. Please
contact your local bookseller or the Macmillan Corporate and Premium Sales Department at
1-800-221-7945, extension 5442, or by email at MacmillanSpecialMarkets@macmillan.com.

First published in the United States by FNP Military Division

First St. Martin's Griffin Edition: 2023

10 9 8 7 6 5 4 3 2

CONTENTS

Appendices

THE CREW

Pilot—Captain Charles B. Cruikshank
  Everett, Massachusetts
Copilot—First Lieutenant Glenn E. Graham
  Freedom, Pennsylvania
Navigator—Captain Frank D. Murphy
  Atlanta, Georgia
Bombardier—First Lieutenant August H. Gaspar
  Oakland, California
Engineer / Top Turret—Tech Sergeant Leonard R. Weeks
  Elkins, West Virginia
Radio Operator—Tech Sergeant Orlando E. Vincenti
  Carbondale, Pennsylvania
Ball Turret Gunner—Staff Sergeant Robert L. Bixler
  Bisbee, Arizona
Left Waist Gunner—Staff Sergeant Donald B. Garrison
  Eldorado, Illinois
Right Waist Gunner—Staff Sergeant James M. Johnson
  Lamar, Oklahoma
Tail Gunner—Sergeant Charles A. Clark
  Highland Park, Illinois

FOREWORD TO THE 2023 EDITION
by Elizabeth Murphy and Chloe Melas

Tucked inside our den's floor-to-ceiling bookcases was a red leather-bound notebook full of my dad's World War II memorabilia. As a twelve-year-old child, I don't think I realized how special and tender these grainy, faded black-and-white photographs, Western Union telegrams, letters, and other mementos that my dad had somehow managed to save and collect from his time as a prisoner of war were.

They were covered in plastic sheets to protect the images, and I and my siblings (Frank, Patty, and Kevin) knew not to touch them directly but to handle them with care. Dad never talked much about his experiences during the war. I only knew he had been a navigator; his plane had been shot out of the air during an intense firefight, and he had remnants of shrapnel in his left arm and shoulder, which sometimes flared up.

Later, Dad would flesh out the story and describe how he parachuted for the first time on that day, October 10, 1943, and landed in a German farmer's field near Münster. The occupants quickly came to his aid and took him inside their house and held him till the German police came to arrest him. Dad did speak of the German family's kindness and that he gave a small boy a stick of chewing gum. My dad was on his twenty-first mission when his luck quite literally ran out. But he was one of the lucky ones. Forty-six members of the "Bloody Hundredth" were killed in that air battle, two of whom were members of his crew. His parents had no idea what had happened to him. They were only notified that he was missing in action. A few weeks later, they received a Western Union telegram and learned he was a prisoner of war at Stalag Luft III in Sagan, Germany.

Over the years, my dad largely kept his wartime memories to himself, rarely speaking of his harrowing experiences. But as children, we were fascinated when we learned he was held for eighteen months in the same prison camp as seen in the 1963 movie *The Great Escape.* We were completely enthralled—especially when he recounted how his own barracks had been digging a tunnel, but their efforts were unsuccessful.

In 1971, during my freshman year of college at Mercer University, I was taking a course on World War II and asked my dad if I could take his red notebook to my professor and share with my class. I remember the awe on my professor's face as he leafed through the notebook. He peppered me with questions. What squadron was Dad in? Was he injured during the battle? How did he survive the prison camp? Many of his questions I couldn't answer, as Dad had locked those memories and experiences away for decades.

One thing I always knew from an early age was how much my dad loved airplanes. He could identify almost any plane he spotted flying in the sky. His more than thirty-year career as a lawyer for the Lockheed Corporation suited him well. He traveled around the world negotiating contracts for airplanes with foreign governments. By the late '70s, Dad was assigned to manage their office in Riyadh, Saudi Arabia. At this point, my siblings and I were grown. I was completing my master's degree at Northern Arizona University. My mother, Ann, was finally able to travel with my dad. While living in Riyadh, they would frequently take vacations to neighboring countries. My mother, who was an avid reader and always traveled with a suitcase lined with paperback books, happened to be reading Len Deighton's 1982 historical novel, *Goodbye, Mickey Mouse,* while they were on a flight to London. My mom recalls turning to my dad and telling him he needed to read it immediately, because it detailed the Allied invasion of Europe. Dad finished the book before the plane touched down on the tarmac and phoned the publisher from his hotel. He knew he had to get in touch with men he had flown with and was hoping Deighton could help. Deighton contacted Dad and told him veterans were holding 100th Bomb Group reunions. My father was shocked, as he had no idea these reunions existed. This was all the spark my dad needed. According to my mother, when he went to his first reunion, they said, "Frank, we've been looking for you for years. We thought you were dead!"

In the early '90s, when I began writing my first children's book, my dad came to me and said he had been thinking of writing a memoir about his time during the war for our family and friends. I enthusiastically encouraged him, and for his birthday in 1992, I gave him a book called *How to Write Your Own Life Story.* A few years later, my family moved to Dallas, Texas, and Dad and I kept in touch with phone calls and letters, and he sent me copies of parts of manuscripts, as it seemed he was always writing about the war.

Writing *Luck of the Draw* was a labor of love and took several years to complete. When his book was published, he gave me a copy, and only then did I realize the depth of pain, isolation, and sheer endurance and resilience he had needed to withstand the horrors of war. I found myself rereading page after page, as it seemed more like a movie than real life. Finally, Dad was ready to talk about his war experiences. It was like lifting a veil. I believe it was why he so enjoyed the reunions and speaking to groups of veterans later in life.

Frank D. Murphy was my dad but also my hero. He was soft-spoken, compassionate, and a true Southern gentleman. But even the pain and agony of war could not harden his heart. It's been immensely gratifying to see his grandchildren, especially my daughter, Chloe, take a profound interest in his wartime experiences and carry the mantle. After all, it's the next generation that will make sure we never forget these brave men who sacrificed their lives for the freedoms we have today.

—*Elizabeth Murphy*

As a little girl, I spent most of my weekends at my grandparents' home in Atlanta, Georgia, where my grandfather would tell me bits and pieces about his World War II combat missions. His stories sounded like fairy tales, conjuring up images of him flying over mountains and oceans in far-off lands.

As I got older, I began to ask more questions and explore his home office, which was frozen in time with photos all over the walls and newspaper headlines from his time during the war. To this day, my grandmother has kept that room intact.

Every time I return to Atlanta from New York, where I live now, I sit in his desk chair and try to remember the sound of his soft Southern voice telling me about how he survived and that—just like the title of his book—it came down to "the luck of the draw."

There are too many memories to recount and not enough pages to do him justice. But as I sit here writing, I can still hear him telling me about the death march from Stalag Luft III to Moosburg's Stalag VIIA, a prisoner of war camp in Bavaria about twenty miles northeast of Munich. What he didn't know was that they would march for the next three days and nights in subzero temperatures with little rest and hardly any food or water. Many men did not make it, with my grandfather recounting how men would collapse in the snow from the exhaustion and freezing weather. He said they would plead with the others not to give up. He even traded his shoes with a fellow soldier, as his leather soles were soaked, and he was given a pair of wooden clogs. I have one of those shoes—we don't know what happened to the other.

My grandfather's bravery during the war earned him the Air Medal with three Oak Leaf Clusters, the Purple Heart, and the Prisoner of War Medal.

Once I reached college at Auburn University, my interest in his combat missions and experience as a POW only heightened. During the summer of 2006 after my freshman year, I was studying abroad in London—just a few hours away from Royal Air Force Station 139, where my grandfather flew his perilous missions.

That summer, I learned my grandfather was diagnosed with cancer. I decided to make the two-hour train ride from London to Thorpe Abbotts, which is now a museum.

I'll never forget the museum's caretaker, Carol Batley, walking me into the air traffic control tower on the base, which is now filled with uniforms in glass cases and some personal belongings of the men who were stationed there—including my grandfather's.

We walked in, and she said, "Hello, boys," as if they were all still standing there in the control tower. The hair on my arms stood straight up; it's a moment I'll never forget.

I then found myself on the runway, where I called my grandfather from my tiny prepaid Vodafone. At eighty-four years old, it was the first and last time I ever heard him cry.

"I'm here," I said to him.

He broke down, responding, "That's where it all began."

He died that next summer almost to the day, on June 16, 2007, at the age of eighty-five. Going there was one of the best decisions I've ever made.

I went back to England in the fall of 2021 for the chance of a lifetime. My family and I went to the set of *Masters of the Air,* the Tom Hanks– and Steven Spielberg–produced television series for Apple TV+. The show tells the stories of the 100th Bomb Group, and I can gratefully say my grandfather is a character.

After months of thinking we might not be able to go to the set due to COVID-19 travel restrictions, we finally made it, a few hours north of London not too far from my grandfather's air force base. Although this time I couldn't call my grandfather and tell him where I was standing, I felt in my heart that somehow, he knew. He would be quietly bursting with joy that his family had made the journey for this truly remarkable moment.

Aside from being a journalist, my most important job is being a mom to my two sons Leo, five, and Luke, three.

I want them to know why the men and women of World War II are rightfully called "the greatest generation" and about our hero, Frank. At bedtime, we talk about Frank and his plane flying high in the sky. Leo frequently asks me about him and tells me he wants to fly planes like Great-Grandpa.

My grandfather once told me he spent the rest of his life walking with ghosts but looking back with pride.

Our family's goal is to keep Frank's memory and that of his fellow men alive and pass on the greatness to the next generation.

—*Chloe Melas*

ACKNOWLEDGMENTS

The recounting of contemporaneous events that occurred more than fifty years ago in voluminous detail is not an easy task, even for one who was an eyewitness to many of the scenes described. This narrative, therefore, has been made possible only through the collective efforts of many individuals who generously offered their assistance and whose knowledge and insights have made it a far better story. It is as much their story as it is mine. To all of them, I extend my sincere gratitude.

There are, however, several individuals to whom I am particularly indebted:

Fellow Comrades in Arms

My crewmates *Charles "Crankshaft" Cruikshank,* pilot, and *August "Augie" Gaspar,* bombardier, of Crew No. 31, 100th Bomb Group, two of the finest and bravest men I have ever known and who shared the major portion of the journey described in this story with me, for, as always, giving me their unstinted, full support as I struggled to tell our story.

The late *John Donnelly Brady,* New York, one of the original pilots of the 418th Bomb Squadron, 100th Bomb Group, and a first-rate musician whose quick Irish wit relieved many a tense moment, for generously giving me the benefit of his vivid recollections of our days together both in training and combat.

Lieutenant General A. P. Clark, a fellow prisoner of war in Stalag

Luft III and Stalag VIIA, later superintendent of the United States Air Force Academy, Colorado Springs, Colorado, now president of the Friends of the Air Force Academy Library, for permitting me to reproduce photographs of Stalag Luft III and Stalag VIIA from the extensive academy library collection.

Joe Consolmagno, another ex-kriegie with me from Stalag Luft III and Stalag VIIA, and former editor of the *Kriegie Klarion,* the newsletter of the Association of Former Prisoners of Stalag Luft III, for his kind sharing of his information and remembrances with me over the years.

Ralph Giddish, my first cousin and himself a veteran of thirty-three combat missions as a tech sergeant and radio operator with the 44th Bomb Group of "the Mighty Eighth," for sharing his knowledge of our family background with me.

John J. O'Neil, formerly of the 482nd Bomb Group, who believed in my earlier drafts enough to decide to publish this manuscript.

Supporting Cast

Paul M. Andrews, historian, scholar, and author of several monographs on the United States Army Eighth Air Force in the Second World War, including *We're Poor Little Lambs* and *Project Bits and Pieces,* for generously sharing the fruits of his many years of research with me, for his research efforts on my behalf, for reviewing and correcting my manuscript, for the superb, comprehensive, and informative appendices he has prepared for this book to complement my story, and, most of all, for his warm friendship and support throughout the writing of this story. Paul would be quick to tell anyone that behind his many years of research there is a "small army" of those who have been extremely helpful. Paul would like to thank the special efforts of those who have assisted him directly in this effort. They are David Giordano and Walter Platt of the National Archives, Dan Hagedorn and Larry Wilson of the National Air and Space

Museum, and Mike T. Stowe and Randy Leads for researching aircraft accident reports.

Charles P. "Nick" McDowell, Springfield, Virginia, editor and publisher of the Foxfall Press, for "sanding" my often clumsy prose chapter by chapter as I completed them and for his consistent support and encouragement when I needed it most.

Suzanne Comer Bell, Pisgah Forest, North Carolina, who meticulously edited my first draft and carefully outlined for me all the basic rules I would have to observe if I intended to write an interesting story.

Joanne Davis, the Alumni Office of the Marist School in Atlanta, for diligently searching her files and supplying copies of photographs of my old school in the 1930s.

Meredith Evans, the Atlanta History Center, for her assistance in locating suitable and interesting photographs of old Atlanta.

Michael P Faley, Studio City, California, 100th Bomb Group photo archivist, for searching and sifting through his extensive collection of 100th Bomb Group photographs to select appropriate pictures for this story.

Roger A. Freeman, British historian, world authority, and author of numerous books and articles on the operations of the United States Army Eighth Air Force in Europe during the Second World War, the man who named us "the Mighty Eighth," for kindly reading my manuscript, offering much insight, and correcting errors.

Cindy Goodman, editor of *Splasher Six,* the 100th Bomb Group Association newsletter, for supplying historical information and other data in the course of this story.

Ian L. Hawkins, British historian, my dear friend for many years, and author of the classic book on the Münster raid, *The Münster Raid: Before and After,* the most comprehensive, in-depth reporting of Eighth Air Force operations during Black Week, the week of

October 8–14, 1943, in print, for reading my manuscript, correcting my mistakes, challenging my conclusions, and correcting errors.

The late *Heinz Hessling,* Beckum, Germany, a talented artist and an eyewitness to the events of October 10, 1943, who dedicated months of his time locating the sites where I and members of my crew landed and our aircraft crashed.

Karin N. Jones at the Boeing Company, for locating the illustrations of the B-17F used in the book.

Dr. James H. Kitchens III of the Air Force Historical Research Agency, who took the time from his busy life to answer some of our questions and provide the manuscript a rigorous review from a historian's perspective. His perspective on the state of the air war at the beginning of Black Week in Europe in October 1943 is outstanding.

The late *Heinz Knoke,* Bad Iburg, Germany, an Me 109 pilot and Luftwaffe fighter ace with fifty-eight air victories, for his many hours of discussion of the 1943 German air defense system with me.

Kristina Moeller, Alpharetta, Georgia, who for many years expertly translated all my German correspondence with the Berdelmann and Rawe families.

Jan Riddling, 100th Bomb Group historian, for poring through numerous historical records to provide and confirm many details about the 100th Bomb Group, as well as spending untold hours reviewing, correcting, and adding to the data contained within the appendices. These indispensable efforts have ensured that this manuscript is as historically accurate and complete as is humanly possible.

Paul West, 100th Bomb Group historian emeritus, who organized and first computerized all available information on the 100th Bomb Group, for reviewing this manuscript and sharing his immense knowledge of the 100th Bomb Group's history.

The late *Gerd Wiegand,* Munich, Germany, Fw 190 pilot who

achieved thirty-one air victories with the famous Luftwaffe JG 26 fighter group, Lille-Nord, France, 1942–1944, who kept a detailed wartime log of all his air combats, including drawings and sketches of tactics and maneuvers by both sides, which he kindly shared with me.

And finally,

Ann, my lovely wife of fifty years, for sharing her life with me, for her patience and steady encouragement during the countless hours I spent on my manuscript, and for making my life meaningful, happy, and rewarding.

Both officers and enlisted men of the Eighth Air Force earned promotions throughout the course of the war. In view of the large number of names mentioned in this book, it has not been practical to take note of promotions as they occurred. Instead, when individual names are mentioned in the text, they are given the rank they held at that point in the war. In addition, in a narrative of this kind, involving a great number of details, it is impossible to escape error. Wherever I have misperceived or misstated a fact, I will be pleased to correct the record.

FRANK D. MURPHY
Atlanta, Georgia

Acknowledgments for the 2023 Edition

Opening up Frank's manuscript has been a humbling experience, but it would not have been possible without the steadfast support of the following individuals.

Marc Resnick, our editor at St. Martin's Publishing Group. Thank you for believing in *Luck of the Draw* from day one. We are immensely grateful and know Frank would be too.

Anthony Mattero and Ali Spiesman, CAA, for years you have

guided us through this process. We want to thank you for your un-wavering support and patience on this exciting journey.

Michael P. Faley, 100th Bomb Group Historian, I've lost track of the countless phone calls and Zoom meetings. Whether it was sourcing photographs or tediously reviewing the manuscript, you were always available. We could not have done this without you. You are officially part of the Murphy family.

Matt Mabe, 100th Bomb Group Photo Archives, they say patience is a virtue and you embody that. Your feedback and knowledge of the 100th Bomb Group is incredible. Thank you for all of the count-less hours you spent on this book.

Nancy Putnam, Historian and editor, *Splasher Six,* your atten-tion to detail is unparalleled.

Val Burgess, POW Historian, thank you for all of your suggested updates. Your love of WWII runs deep and we could not have done this without your help.

Paul M. Andrews, 8th Air Force historian, author, Frank would be so pleased to know that you updated the appendices. We know it was not an easy task and we thank you for all you have done since the very beginning.

Ann Murphy, Frank's wife, you gave this your blessing from the moment we told you we wanted to republish Frank's memoir. Thank you for allowing us to share his story.

INTRODUCTION

The most momentous man-made event of the twentieth century, or of any century in history, occurred during the period from 1939 to 1945, the Second World War. All the major powers were eventually drawn into a global conflict that encompassed Europe, Africa, Russia, China, and the vastness of the Atlantic and Pacific Oceans.

Millions of young Americans, like Frank Murphy, answered that call to arms. He joined what eventually became the largest of the American overseas air commands, "the Mighty Eighth." Among the unforgettable and vivid images clearly recalled by a generation of East Anglians from late 1942 onward were the great formations of American bombers, flying to war over occupied Europe in the early morning mists.

During the perilous period in which Frank Murphy flew twenty-one daylight combat missions, the odds of returning safely were three to one against. That fact, in itself, speaks volumes.

In April 1983, distinguished Royal Air Force Bomber Command Pathfinder veteran, Group Captain Hamish Mahaddie, DSO, DFC, AFC, RAF (retired), concluded an outstanding speech at a veterans reunion in London's Grosvenor House Hotel, by quoting a fitting tribute to the men of RAF Bomber Command (fifty-five thousand killed in action), written by Noël Coward, the famous actor and playwright, who lived in wartime London.

The night bombers were occasionally routed to fly over London by their commander, Air Marshall Arthur Harris, to assure Londoners, who had suffered and endured Hitler's Blitz from 1940 to 1941, that retribution was at hand:

LIE IN THE DARK AND LISTEN
Noël Coward

> Lie in the dark, let them go.
> Theirs is a world you'll never, ever know
> There's one debt you'll for ever, ever owe.
> Lie in the dark and listen.

That moving tribute is equally applicable to the Americans of the Eighth Air Force. Between August 17, 1942, and May 8, 1945, nearly 4,300 B-17s and B-24s failed to return. The cost in aircraft alone is staggering, but the cost in young lives is incalculable— approximately 26,000 bomber aircrew made the ultimate sacrifice for our freedom.

It is an honor and a privilege to be associated with the American, British, and Allied airmen who, during the Second World War, gave so much.

I urge you to read Frank Murphy's truly memorable story.

IAN L. HAWKINS
The Münster Raid: Before and After
B-17s Over Berlin (95th Bomb Group anthology)
Twentieth-Century Crusaders (392nd Bomb Group anthology)
Bacton, Suffolk, England

The sun will not be seen today;
The sky doth frown and lower upon our army.
 —William Shakespeare, *Richard III,* act 5, scene 3

PROLOGUE

I was officially and honorably separated from active duty with the United States Army Air Forces[1] at Greensboro, North Carolina, on January 17, 1946. Life is indeed filled with curiosities and coincidences, for my discharge from military service came only two days short of the fourth anniversary of the day when, as a twenty-year-old college student, I raised my right hand and took the oath to join the Army Air Corps at the old post office in my hometown of Atlanta, Georgia. Now, in looking back to the twentieth century, the reality that almost fifty-five years have passed since I last wore my military uniform is almost inconceivable. After the Second World War, I did what most other veterans of that war did—return to civilian life. And, like so many of my comrades in arms, I was a different person, and America at times seemed a different country from the one we had left behind. Maybe it was because things really did change, or maybe it was because we, through our varied wartime experiences, had changed. Through our collective war experiences, we had seen and done things that other young men in their late teens and early twenties would not have ordinarily experienced in a peacetime world.

Memories of my wartime experiences began receding into the far corners of my mind almost immediately with the end of the war

---

1. From this point forward, I will use the abbreviation **USAAF** for *United States Army Air Forces*.

and my return to civilian life. And, like thousands, if not millions of returning servicemen, I went back to college on the GI Bill and then into the business world. As the postwar years came and went, thoughts of the war became fewer and further between. In 1949, I met Ann, my lovely wife of fifty years, and together we raised four children to adulthood. Now we have all the enjoyment and pride that go with regular visits with seven wonderful grandchildren. For several decades after the war, my professional and family responsibilities did not allow much time for me to revisit my wartime experiences. For while Ann and I, like most people, have enjoyed many personal moments of sheer joy and immeasurable happiness, we have also experienced our share of deep and dark moments of heart-wrenching despair and uncontrollable sadness—for example, the death of our charming, delightful youngest daughter, Patricia, from cancer in 1989. Eventually, I seldom thought of the war unless someone happened to mention it in passing conversation or I went to see a Hollywood rendering of the war. My four children grew to adulthood knowing virtually nothing of my military service.

It was not until February 1968 that, in connection with a business trip to the Middle East, I went back to England for the first time since the war. Even then, although I knew I would be stopping overnight in London, so much time had passed that I did not give my wartime experiences a second thought. And, as our airliner descended from its cruising altitude and began its final approach into Heathrow Airport just outside of London, it was just another landing. After breaking through a typical English overcast, however, and getting my first glimpse in nearly a quarter of a century of the lush, myriad shades of green that are perpetually a part of the lovely British landscape, I felt a strange sensation of reincarnation, a feeling that I was in the midst of a replay, a repeat performance of earlier happenings. The instant our airplane touched down at Heathrow, it all came back. I had never realized the profound effect the war had on me. Memories of the war years all at once swamped my senses. Every airman at a remote air base in England in 1943 lived for a twenty-four- or forty-eight-hour pass to London. I felt, once again, part of the great American invasion of London in 1942/43, where the center of American life in the city was the Rainbow Club overlooking the statue of Eros in Piccadilly Circus. When the Americans first arrived in England, the British were not quite sure what to make of us. Were we really allies, or were we alien infiltrators coming to undermine British institutions? Our pay was many times that of British and European soldiers, permitting American GIs to buy a few of life's luxuries for lonely women whose men were fighting far from home. We GIs were quickly, if not affectionately, referred to as "being overpaid, oversexed, and over here." The British, however, had their standards. There was the story of the American airman who asked an English girl if they could make love before both were killed. "I'd love to," the young lady replied, "but you're not the sort of man I can afford to be found dead in bed with."

By the time the 100th Bomb Group reached England in the summer of 1943, the mounting losses of American airmen in the VIII BC[2] were well known to the British public. Britons, for the most part, quickly accepted us for what we were: brash, young soldiers from a foreign land behaving like brash, young soldiers from a foreign

2. From this point forward, I will use the abbreviation **BG** for *Bomb Group*. The Eighth Air Force is generally associated with all heavy bomber operations between its first operational sortie on August 17, 1942, and the last operational sortie on May 7, 1945. Yet the Eighth Air Force did not exist until February 22, 1944, with the redesignation of the VIII Bomber Command (Eighth Bomber Command). I will use the abbreviation **BC** for *Bomber Command* and **AF** for *Air Force* where historically correct and appropriate.

land. They recognized that a soldier's life is really a series of meetings with strangers and the wartime soldier is essentially a gypsy moving about with all his worldly belongings in his kit bag. And, in the final analysis, all of us, British, members of their empire and common-wealth, as well as we Americans were alike—we had a war to win, and everybody was in the same boat.

My most telling experience, though, came the next day with my departure from Heathrow to Beirut. The moment our airliner lifted off the ground, the flutters, the butterflies, and the old anxi-eties from a quarter century earlier returned. I am not sure if any of the passengers noticed or if the airline flight attendants paid any attention, but when crossing the channel, I instinctively looked for the rest of our formation.

Where is the fighter escort, our little friends?

At the Belgian coast, I half expected to see swirling black puffs of flak from long-silenced German antiaircraft artillery bursting all around us.[3] I had a sense that the ghosts from groups of the German Air Force, the Luftwaffe, were out there somewhere behind billow-ing clouds, single- and twin-engine fighters waiting for us as they always were. Once again, I heard, through the static and crackling of a comparatively primitive interphone system, young, excited voices crying out:

There they are! Twelve o'clock high![4]
Bandits! Two of 'em, five o'clock low!

---

3. *Flak* is the term we used, which was adopted from the German word *Fliegerabwehrkannonen*.

4. See footnote on page 151 for description of system of verbal shorthand for fighter attack location.

In the years since that first postwar visit to England, I have flown out of England many times to the Continent, and always with the same haunting memories. If you were there, you never forget. Even though one may have pushed those memories to the furthest recesses of the mind, they are always there ready for something, some event to serve as a trigger to bring them to the forefront.

As a consequence, and despite my earlier lifelike reflections on the war during my first postwar visit to England in 1968, I had no further inclination to act on those memories until the spring of 1983. I was constantly occupied with my work and at that time had not been in touch with any of my old wartime comrades for more than thirty-five years. It was while I was preparing to make yet another business trip to London and the United States, this time from my office in Riyadh, Saudi Arabia, that Ann suggested I take along and read a book she had just finished—Len Deighton's marvelous story *Goodbye, Mickey Mouse.* I had read a number of Deighton's fascinating novels on espionage and the Cold War and took Ann's advice. Though I was a member of a bomber crew and *Goodbye, Mickey Mouse* was about fighter pilots and their life at a fighter base, during the flight, I eagerly read the entire book without stopping. I suspect that most people do not read the author's acknowledgments of a book, but I have been everlastingly glad I did so in this case. In his acknowledgments, tucked away in the last few pages of the book, Deighton mentioned Ian Hawkins, a British historian who was then writing a book "about the 100th BG's raid on Münster." I knew about the 100th BG of the VIII BC, and I knew about Münster, especially the October 10, 1943, mission to that city.

Upon arrival at our London hotel, I immediately telephoned the office of the publisher of *Goodbye, Mickey Mouse* and inquired as to how I could get in touch with Mr. Deighton. I was told to send them a letter addressed to him for forwarding. Using the hotel's writing paper, I wrote a note and placed it into the post that evening. In a matter of only ten days or so, at my home in Atlanta, I received a reply from Mr. Deighton giving me Ian Hawkins's address and telephone number. Calculating the time differential so that I would not wake up a household in the middle of the night, I immediately picked up the telephone and called Ian at his home. I had only just finished briefly identifying myself and mentioning the group that I flew with when Ian interjected enthusiastically: "I know who you are!" In the way that many Britons are so gracious, Ian invited Ann and me to stop by for a visit during my return trip to the Middle East.

In July 1983, forty years after arriving in England and being assigned to an air base at a place called Thorpe Abbotts, located in Norfolk County, some ninety miles northeast of London, Ann and I visited Ian, his lovely wife, Mary, and their children at their home in Bacton, Suffolk, England. Ian's study is what I would have imagined any historian's study would look like; bracketing a typewriter were shelves filled with books, photographs, and seemingly countless files with papers and documents. Ian was in the midst of writing his outstanding, exhaustively researched history of the Münster raid and the operations of the VIII BC during Black Week, the seven-day period from October 8–14, 1943.[5] During this visit, Ian handed me ten or so pages photocopied from a document called a Missing Air Crew Report (MACR). During the Second World War, a reporting system was developed to record what happened to an aircraft failing to return from an operation. The document includes the serial numbers for the aircraft, its engines, and even its machine guns. If possible, the report includes eyewitness accounts describing what happened to the aircraft or the circumstances when the aircraft was

---

5. A revised and expanded version of his original book is *The Münster Raid: Before and After* (Trumbull, CT: FNP Military Division, 1999).

last seen. Crew members, their next of kin's address, and information about their fate were also noted. After the war, a monumental effort was launched to account, to the greatest extent possible, for all of those who failed to return from operations and who were not taken prisoner or evaded capture. This effort involved the correlation of captured German records and the postwar interviews of some surviving crew members. I had never been asked about my crew, but as you will shortly learn, there was not much I could have added that others, who were in a better position, provided.

I sat down to review MACR Number 1028, and as I read the graphic postwar statements of my crewmates, Leonard Weeks, Don Garrison, and James Johnson, memories of our tumultuous war years together came rushing back. My poignant experiences on my first flight to England in 1968 seemed flights of fantasy compared to what I felt after reading the MACR. Before my visit with Ian ended, I became aware of and am forever thankful for the small army of enthusiasts on both sides of the pond and on the European continent who are deeply interested in what we Americans did in the skies over western Europe between 1942 and 1945. In early June of the following year, 1984, I traveled to Düsseldorf, Germany, where I met the warm, generous late Heinz Hessling, who as a young eighteen-year-old *Luftwaffenhelfer*,[6] watched the violent air battle over Münster through a pair of binoculars from his post with a German flak battery on the Dortmund-Ems Canal north of the city. We drove out to the Rawe farm at Holzhausen and to the Berdelmann farm near Lienen. I spoke with both Helmut and Friedheim Berdelmann, who showed me four photographs taken on October 11, 1943. I explored the area with Helmut Berdelmann, then fifty

---

6. These were teenagers, serving as auxiliaries, performing administrative duties for the German Air Force.

years of age, the only eyewitness who meticulously pointed out the exact locations where major sections and components of an aircraft fell on their farm. These names and places may not mean a great deal to you now, but I would be getting ahead of myself if I were to tell you right now why to this very day they mean so much to me.

Many of us of the so-called World War II generation find it difficult to believe that more than a full half century has passed since the end of the Second World War. Among the reminders of this seemingly ephemeral passage of time is that, more and more, I have read and been told that, before the facts have faded from the memory of living men, those who participated in dramatic battles in a great war have a duty to record their personal recollections for posterity. It is usually suggested that such remembrances breathe life into the endless volumes of dry, colorless official histories of military operations.

In my view, a more compelling reason for recording these memories is that those of us who have survived vicious battles in a major war have an obligation to speak to succeeding generations with pride of the valor, dedication, suffering, and sacrifices of our then young comrades in arms who, unknown and unheralded, fell in battle so many years ago and have long since been forgotten.

This narrative, therefore, is a memoir, a personal history of my experiences and perceptions. Nevertheless, because the world in which young American airmen went to war in 1941/42 is not the world of today, it is my belief that, where it might enhance my reader's understanding of the historical context in which the events recalled occurred, it is appropriate to set forth the overall military situation existing at the time. For example, it is crucial throughout the telling of this story to recognize that the creation of professional, dedicated, integrated aircrews for large aircraft was essentially a Second World War refinement of broad, general concepts regarding strategic bombing based on U.S. Army Air Service First World War experiences. I have, therefore, prefaced my personal recollections with a short review of the coming of age of military aircrews in the early years of the 1939–45 war. If, however, in the course of such an effort I have misstated a fact of history, it is an honest mistake that I hope will not take away from my portrayal of the character and courage of the fine men with whom I was privileged to serve.

Today, combat flying officers in the United States Air Force are usually in their late twenties to midthirties, have been flying for years, and are in a constant state of combat readiness, having trained continuously on the most sophisticated weapons systems money can buy. The young men entering the USAAF in 1941/42 were closer to twenty years of age and had joined a branch of the American armed forces with scarcely any developed traditions. They were committed to battle after a few months, to fly in aircraft that were then the most sophisticated weapons systems money could buy, but whose basic configurations and defensive systems were still undergoing final definition. United States VIII BC combat crewmen flying from England in 1942 and 1943 operated according to prewar theories of strategic bombing that, as it turned out, contained basic miscalculations. They paid a fearful price.

There was uniqueness about the time in which the events related herein occurred. Except for the eternal sameness of death, the Second World War was different from all later wars in which America has been involved. In no subsequent war has United States territory been directly attacked or invaded by an aggressive, formidable enemy capable of threatening our national survival. In the past half century, the American people have not been required to commit themselves totally and unconditionally to a war effort as was necessary during the Second World War. In every more recent conflict, with the possible exception of the Korean War, where American troops were eventually engaged by massive, well-trained, well-armed, regular Communist Chinese ground forces, American forces have gone into battle with years of peacetime training behind them and equipped with arms and weapons systems that were vastly superior to those of their enemy.

Few accounts of the events of the 1939–45 war convey to their readers a true sense of the day-to-day drama that was a part of the wartime experience. Today, as I look back to those terrible, turbulent years, I am unable to forget a distinct mood and atmosphere that I have known in no other period in my life. The war years took on a surrealistic quality; the air sparkled with a pervasive electricity. Subsequent histories have rarely fully and accurately reflected the murky, amorphous picture of what the postwar world would be like—the indisputable uncertainty of the future. For much of the World War II generation, the war years were the lost years of the twentieth century.

We saw a pervasive wartime mentality wherever we went—a resigned acceptance by people across the world of the inevitability of whatever was to come. It was impossible for anyone, anywhere, combatant or noncombatant, to ignore the war if for no reason other than the rationing of daily necessities because of shortages created by the war and the disruption of international commerce. Major battles were fought simultaneously at opposite ends of the earth on land, on the seas, and in the air.

America transitioned from a nation at peace to a nation at war quickly and without fanfare. Within weeks after the December 1941 Japanese attack on Pearl Harbor, young men who had been students, professionals, or tradesmen were disappearing from localities all across America. In their place, soldiers, sailors, marines, and airmen in uniform began to appear everywhere, for, throughout the war, uniforms were worn by military servicemen both on and off duty. Daily newspapers printed comprehensive coverage of the activities of local men in the military; as the war progressed, these columns included stories of war exploits and ever-lengthening casualty lists and obituaries on hometown men serving in far-flung combat areas.

Despite its appalling cost in death and human suffering, the Second World War was the adventure of a lifetime for the young soldier, sailor, or airman going off to war. His thoughts for the future were not about education, marriage, a family, and retirement.

When do we ship out? Will it be Europe or the Pacific?

Evenings of relaxation frequently had an eerie, false, exaggerated gaiety about them. For combat airmen, life was often for the moment; the past was gone and the future dependent upon uncertain developments fraught with danger. If a major move was impending, emotional last goodbyes were, as often as not, real last goodbyes. Kisses were exchanged with those one would never have reached the point of kissing in normal times; vows to keep in touch when peace returned were solemnly made.

My combat tour in the Second World War was in England. It lasted only four months—four months, however, in which were compressed many of the most exciting, and all the most frightening and life-threatening, experiences I have known in my entire life. Although I am often unable to recall the details of recent events, images of wartime England spill over in my storehouse of memories.

As I traveled through the countryside by train, I found England to be an undulating, cultivated, luxuriant, rich, green landscape, here and there scarred to make way for the concrete pillboxes and gun emplacements that would have been quickly manned if the bells of ancient churches had clanged a warning of an invasion. It was a panorama of preserved traditions, an amazingly small island structured in a crazy-quilt webwork of peaceful little towns and villages of ancient origin, usually built around, or close by, centuries-old Norman churches and located beside, or halved by, tree-lined streams flowing gently beneath medieval arched stone bridges. Narrow, winding village streets were routinely crammed with half-timbered and sturdy stone inns, shops, pubs, quaint cottages, colorful stacked-stone walled gardens, and wartime vegetable patches. Aloofly apart were stately manor houses with well-kept grounds and the remains of ancient stone castles with pinnacles, round or square towers, bastion-like gates, impregnable slit-windowed keeps, arcading, and crenellated walls.

Once we arrived in England, the European air war was no longer another item in the daily newspapers or simply the subject of an item on radio news broadcasts. On a clear night, particularly if the stars were glimmering in a moonless sky, we were sure to hear the steady, deep, pulsating drone of Royal Air Force (RAF) bombers passing overhead going out on another of Sir Arthur "Bomber" Harris's thousand-plane raids on Nazi Germany. There were airmen the same as us up there in those airplanes.

Would I—would we—be as brave?

Images of wartime London are inviolable queues, rubble from the Blitz, dingy streets and buildings awaiting postwar sprucing up, and temporary wartime additions, such as searchlights, sandbags, and tethered barrage balloons hovering lumpishly above docks and strategic installations like great hooked silver whales.

When I first visited London in the summer of 1943, I had the distinct sensation that I had stepped onto a live movie set. It was all still there—the Pickwickian England I had seen in MGM movies of Dickens's classics in the 1930s, in early war films such as *Mrs. Miniver* and in spectacular newsreel coverage of the Battle of Britain and the Blitz. London was to the American soldier in the Second World War what Paris was said to have been to American soldiers in France in 1918, illustrated in the lyrics of an old First World War song: *How are you going to keep them down on the farm after they've seen Paree*. The city streets seemed forever thronged with a huge floating population of classless soldiers, sailors, and airmen from throughout the world dressed in a kaleidoscopic array of khaki, navy, and RAF blue and olive uniforms with indecipherable insignia and wearing a variety of turbans, field caps, and berets—all of whom the spunky, outnumbered permanent residents of the city appeared to accept with stoicism.

Blackout regulations transformed wartime London after dark into a pitch-black skyline against a deep gray sky inhabited by shadowy figures moving about in a ghostly duskiness. Behind and below this phantomlike exterior, however, were noisy, smoke-filled, bustling, crowded pubs, basement clubs with fanciful, often witty British names doing a thriving business. In Piccadilly Circus in central London, first-run cinemas showed the latest Hollywood films; live theaters continuously ran patriotic and lighthearted variety shows. On any dark street in London, an airman might hear a soft voice out of the night cooing, "'Allo, dearie"—a Piccadilly commando in Eighth AF slang. An English satirist at the time, commenting on "off-duty airmen and on-duty tarts," once remarked that "war was made for naughty girls." Lovers and prostitutes liked the blackout rules.

For four years, from the fall of France in June 1940 until the Allied invasion of Normandy on D-day in June 1944, the Second World War in western Europe was almost exclusively an air war. The Germans occupied Poland, Denmark, Norway, the Low Countries, and France during this entire period. RAF Fighter Command had scarcely blunted an intended invasion of Britain by the Germans in the Battle of Britain when RAF Bomber Command took the offensive. The United States VIII BC joined them in the summer of 1942. By mid-1943, the combined British and American air forces considered themselves capable of systematically striking German industrial targets in force, the RAF by night, the Eighth by day—around the clock. At the same time, however, German air defenses were at peak strength. The titanic air battles in the skies over western Europe in the summer and fall of 1943 will likely forever remain the most monumental in history. Death in the sky replaced death in the trenches.

The story that follows is, in the main, a retrospective of the men of Crew No. 31 of the 100th BG flying from England in that summer and fall of 1943—who they were, where they came from, and what happened to them. It was an ordinary, everyday, first-line aircrew whose war record, along with those of the majority of their comrades in arms, is buried in impersonal tables of dull wartime operational statistics and depressing casualty lists. But it was part of the greatest air force ever assembled, and, while serving on that crew, two young American airmen gave their nation their most precious possession—all their tomorrows.

I have always considered Crew No. 31 America's armed forces in microcosm during the Second World War. We were from Yankee New England, the industrialized East, the layered, bluish, densely forested Appalachians with their irregular peaks and meandering, cascading clear, icy streams, the unhurried, sleepy Deep South, rich, productive farmlands of the Midwest, the vast, flat, wall-to-wall oil lands of Oklahoma, the pastel-hued deserts, arroyos, and mountains of the great American Southwest, and the lovely, picturesque San Francisco Bay Area. Before the war, none of us knew of the existence of the others, much less that, together, we would share the most terrifying and ill-fated day of our young lives. But, for almost one full year during some of America's darkest days of the twentieth century, we were one thing above all else—an *American bomber crew.*

I

COMBAT AIRCREWS

COMING OF AGE

Land and sea battles between organized groups using weapons in the service of military goals have been memorialized since man first began recording his history by carving pictures and writings on stone. The Sumerians, who lived in present-day Iraq in 6500 BC and who are believed to be the first people to build towns with distinguishable street patterns, had soldiers who wore similar battle dress, carried spears and shields, and fought in close formation. The seafaring Carthaginians, who inhabited present-day Tunisia in North Africa, captured every foreign ship they could east of Sardinia in the Mediterranean. The great naval battle at Ecnomus in 256 BC involved seven hundred to eight hundred ships, and in that great battle, the Roman navy defeated the Carthaginians by sinking thirty of their warships and capturing another sixty-four. In contrast with ten thousand years of conventional ground warfare, air warfare is a recent development, having next to no history. Every air battle in history has been fought within the lifetime of persons still alive, at least as of this writing.

The idea of using aircraft to drop explosives on enemy targets is almost as old as the airplane itself. In 1909, six years after the Wright brothers made the first controlled flight of a powered aircraft, Major Giulio Douhet of Italy proposed putting the airplane to military use. Two years later, on November 1, 1911, his colleague Lieutenant Giulio Gavotti made the first air raid in recorded history when he dropped bombs on Turkish positions in Tripoli. Nevertheless, before the First World War, the airplane was believed to have only limited use as a military weapon. The first opposing pilots to meet over European battlefields in 1914 flew unarmed reconnaissance missions and simply waved to one another as they passed, going their separate ways. Later, when they realized that the other pilots really *were* the enemy, they began shooting at each other with pistols and rifles. Next, they fitted their airplanes with swiveling rear-firing machine guns for the back seat observer; and finally, they fixed forward-firing machine guns that could be operated by the pilot. These machine guns were equipped with an interrupter gear, a German invention, that permitted them to be fired when the propeller blades were in a horizontal position but not when they were vertical and thereby directly in front of the guns. This is how the first single-seat fighter aircraft were born, and their only purpose was to shoot down enemy aircraft. The interrupter gear mechanism had problems now and again. The Germans discovered, for example, that one of their most famous aces, Max Immelmann, actually died because his machine gun's interrupter gear malfunctioned. He shot off his own propeller during a dogfight, causing his airplane to crash.

Being a pilot, observer, or air gunner during the First World War was hazardous. If an airplane was shot down or crashed for any reason, its occupants were usually killed—whether or not they had been hit by bullets in the air. They did not have parachutes, thus adding to the already considerable risks they took. Toward the end of the war, the Germans developed and provided their airmen with parachutes, which gave them an opportunity to escape from helpless, out-of-control, and often burning aircraft. I must add that the parachute is an invention for which I shall always be grateful!

The bombs dropped from airplanes at the beginning of the First World War were small. They only weighed fifteen to eighteen pounds and were crudely aimed and released. Surprisingly, it was czarist Russia, the least technically advanced of the warring nations, that developed the first effective four-engine bomber. It was designed in 1914 by Igor Sikorsky, whose later career brought him the stature of being a world-famous aviation pioneer. By 1917, the British, French, and Germans also designed and built an astonishing array of large bomber aircraft. The German four-engine Zeppelin-Staaken R.IV, a lumbering giant that became operational in 1917, was physically larger than the B-17. It had seven to eight hours of sustained endurance and carried 4,400 pounds of bombs. This aerial behemoth was armed with between four and seven machine guns, had a service ceiling in excess of twelve thousand feet, and was manned by a crew of seven. With an additional engine to drive the compressors for its superchargers, the operational ceiling of the R.IV was increased to over nineteen thousand feet, fully loaded. In the last year of the war, Zeppelin-Staaken R.IV aircraft flew more than fifty bombing raids on London. Not to be outdone, Britain's Royal Flying Corps struck back, attacking strategic targets in Coblenz, Cologne, and other localities in the western part of Germany, using Handley Page O/400 aircraft.

Bombers in the First World War carried a crew of three to five gunners. Late in the war, however, one crew member also operated a bombsight, and in 1917, the Zeppelin-Staaken R.IV also carried a wireless operator. The only nonpilot to attain commissioned officer status as an aviator in the U.S. Army Air Service was the observer, who operated from tethered balloons or from reconnaissance aircraft. These observers were specially trained to spot hostile troops and batteries so they could adjust artillery fire, regulate barrages, identify objects on the ground, correct maps, and take photographs. Thousands of two-seater reconnaissance and light bomber aircraft were built during the war and were operated by scores of specialized reconnaissance units in all air forces.

Following the Great War, the war to end all wars, air force leaders in Britain, Germany, and the United States agreed that *strategic bombing* was their primary mission. Strategic bombing came to be seen as being central to a nation's war-making capability, and the early proponents of airpower believed that air forces should enjoy coequal status with ground and sea forces in the military establishment. Although their sometimes romanticized vision of the future of warfare captured the attention of the public and some politicians, air force leaders ran into strong opposition from conservative ground generals and tradition-minded admirals, especially with their "independent status" argument. Brigadier General Billy Mitchell, America's principal proponent of strategic bombing and an early advocate for a dominant role for the air force in the army, was eventually court-martialed and dismissed from the army for his outspoken persistence. Moreover, during the 1920s and early 1930s, little thought was given to how this new form of aerial warfare was actually going to be accomplished. It was not until the mid-'30s, when it appeared that these new theories would be tested, that Western governments began to develop and acquire in quantity the aircraft that would ultimately fight in the Second World War.

Even so, distressingly little attention was given to the proficiency and combat readiness of aircrews. One would have supposed that, along with the design and construction of increasingly high-performance and complex bomber aircraft, training programs to qualify skilled crews would also have been established. This was particularly so with the self-defending, long-range, four-engine aircraft that were being developed by the British and Americans. Astonishingly, this was not the case. Even though the United

States and the major European countries had comprehensive pilot-training programs and, by 1937, RAF leaders were questioning the adequacy of aircrew manning and training within its Bomber Command, no tangible remedial action to correct those deficiencies was undertaken either in England or the United States before 1939. As a result, apart from radio operators and gunners, other aircrew positions were almost nonexistent before 1940.

There are, I believe, several explanations for why the Army Air Corps was slow to remedy its unsatisfactory aircrew situation. First, notwithstanding the fact that the B-17 had its genesis in 1934, as late as the beginning of 1939, there was no assurance that the Army Air Corps would be permitted to develop a strategic heavy bomber program at all. Owing to bureaucratic vacillation and continuous disagreements with the navy and other elements of the army, quantity procurement of the B-17 was delayed until the late 1930s. Throughout the '30s, the mission of General Headquarters (GHQ) Air Force, the strategic arm of the Air Corps, which operated the B-17s, was limited to supporting the "first line" of coastal defense: the navy. It was only after war broke out in Europe in September 1939 that the War Department realized the Army Air Corps possessed the only strategic bombing capability in the U.S. military. As a result, the B-17 program was given a full go-ahead. In September 1939, the Army Air Corps had only twenty-three B-17 aircraft in its inventory. All its other bombers were obsolete and saw no wartime service. Compounding this situation, the prototypes of the B-24, B-25, and B-26 aircraft, which, along with the B-17, would also become the mainstay of the USAAF heavy and medium bomber forces, had yet to make their first flights.

The Boeing B-17 was the first of a new generation of low-wing, four-engine American airplanes, and it set the style for the bombers and airliners that came later. Interestingly, however, the B-17 was the beneficiary of aeronautical technology developed for commercial rather than military aircraft. In the decade immediately preceding the Second World War, the military services were no longer the principal sponsors of research and development in American aviation. From the early days of the Wright brothers through the First World War, American aircraft manufacturers relied on military orders for their livelihood. However, by 1930, aircraft sales were mainly due to the rapidly expanding and highly competitive commercial airline industry, and the designs of the military aircraft they sold were based on commercial designs. During several long periods in the 1930s, the Boeing Company itself funded development of the B-17.

The requirements of commercial airline operators differ from those of military air forces. A commercial airliner can easily fly ten times the annual flying hours of a military airplane and must not only be more efficient than a military airplane, it must possess virtues that are more economical than technical. The development of large, all-metal, low-winged aircraft of stressed-skin construction, incorporating wing-mounted cowled engines, variable-pitch propellers, slotted flaps, retractable landing gear, and streamlined fairings was the direct result of commercial airline calls for fast, streamlined, long-range, and cost-efficient aircraft.

It should also be noted that the enormous popularity of air racing and intense international competition for the setting of aircraft speed, nonstop distance, and altitude records in the late 1920s and 1930s played a role in the development of aerodynamically efficient aircraft. These activities were particularly influential regarding the use of higher-octane fuels that permitted higher compression ratios and reduced fuel consumption in aircraft piston engines. Engine designs capable of higher supercharger pressures using improved fuels made it possible for aircraft to operate efficiently at higher altitudes. It was well-known that in the thin air at thirty thousand feet, an airplane can fly up to 40 percent faster than at sea level with the same power settings. Both American and European designers were experimenting with pressurized cabins in the early 1930s. The first pressurized substratosphere aircraft to actually fly was the Lockheed XC-35, a modified Model 10 Electra, which was delivered to the U.S. Army Air Corps in 1937. Although it experienced technical problems, the XC-35 proved that pressurization did not mean drastic changes in an airplane's structure and that it added little to the weight. In 1937, the Army Air Corps was awarded the Collier Trophy, the United States' highest aviation honor, for sponsoring development of the XC-35.

Not all of these technical innovations were invented or developed in the United States, but virtually all of them were equally desirable in military aircraft. And they were not unknown to American military airmen. It was, however, the acceptance of innovation by commercial airlines and the willingness of American designers to package and incorporate these features into new civil aircraft that made the United States the world leader in aeronautical development. From the early 1930s onward, the performance and reliability of American military aircraft, including fighter aircraft, were a direct outcome of product improvements developed to accommodate the needs of commercial airlines. With a rated speed of 221 miles per hour, the 1930 prototype Lockheed Y1C-17 command transport, adapted from the Lockheed Vega and fitted with a Pratt & Whitney R-1340-17 supercharged Wasp engine, was the fastest aircraft in the Army Air Corps fleet. It was lost while piloted by Air Corps captain Ira Eaker, who was thirty-five years old at the time and was later to become commander of the Eighth AF. He started his cross-country flight at Long Beach, California, to set a new nonstop transcontinental record. Unfortunately, he lost the Y1C-17 when he crash-landed in Ohio on March

10, 1931. When he attempted to switch from his empty fuselage fuel tanks to his main wing tanks without success, he then tried switching to his reserve tanks, but to no avail, and his engine died. He made a dead-stick landing in a meadow, went through a fence, and flipped over. No airplane had ever flown so far, so fast. He covered 1,740 miles at an average speed of 237 miles per hour, and had he completed the flight, he would have shattered the transcontinental speed record. Lockheed later determined that air had leaked into the airplane's special rigid fuel lines and had shut off the fuel flow, and the crash was not Captain Eaker's fault.

The Martin B-10 bomber of 1932, which also incorporated design features adapted from commercial aircraft, was faster than any fighter in the Army Air Corps. When Swissair introduced the Lockheed Orion into passenger service that same year, it was faster than any military aircraft in service anywhere. All transport aircraft that saw significant service with the USAAF in the Second World War were based on the design of civil airliners. The prime example is the legendary Douglas DC-3. On December 7, 1941, there were approximately 360 DC-3 aircraft in domestic airline service in the United States, many of which were immediately requisitioned for military use. The reason was that the Air Corps was only then receiving the first deliveries of its C-47, the military version of the DC-3, and the first orders for these C-47s had not been placed until 1940! The Curtiss C-46 Commando transport, the other transport aircraft procured in quantity by the Army Air Corps at the outset of the war, evolved from the Curtiss-Wright CW-20 thirty-six-passenger commercial transport designed in 1937.

The belated development of fully qualified aircrews by the Air Corps before the Second World War, a condition that was allowed to exist due in large measure to inadequate military budgets, is perhaps no better illustrated than by the story of USAAF navigators.

The experts knew that no air force could maintain sustained long-range bombing attacks unless it was reasonably capable of operating in all weather, by day and by night, and over both land and sea. A fair-weather air force operating only over land is virtually useless. In 1925, the American Aeronautical Safety Code, based on the then existing international aeronautical convention, set the U.S. standards for professional aircraft pilots, navigators, and engineers. The code required that aircraft navigators "demonstrate knowledge" of the use of maps and charts, dead reckoning, practical astronomy and celestial navigation, aeronautical navigational instruments, and basic meteorology. The U.S. Army Air Service accepted these standards and for many years after the First World War taught its lighter-than-air airship and balloon pilots, who also served as full-time navigators and observers, celestial navigation. In the 1930s, Army Air Corps fixed-wing aircraft pilots were required to be proficient in the use of aerial maps and basic dead reckoning as well as flying the aural radio-range beacon system, which was then in operation throughout the United States. However, since the time-consuming complexities and the specialized equipment required for celestial navigation were not practical for pilots of single-seat aircraft, army pilots were generally not trained in celestial navigation. This significantly limited their ability to navigate over long distances, over open water, or above 10/10 cloud cover when radio aids were not available.

At the same time, in the spring of 1938, the Air Corps saw what it believed to be the opportunity it had been searching for to prove the navigation capability of its long-range bomber force. The Italian ocean liner *Rex* was in the Atlantic Ocean, about seven hundred miles from U.S. shores. Three B-17s from the 2nd BG at Langley, Virginia, were detailed to search and locate the *Rex*. If they could find and fly over the ship, the Air Corps would thereby prove it could do its job. When the three-airplane flight took off early in the morning, the weather was poor and getting worse. As they droned on through black swirling clouds, the navigator kept refining his calculations based on the last known position, course, and speed of the luxury liner. He finally estimated his intercept at 12:25 p.m. At exactly 12:25 p.m., a crew member shouted, "There she is!" as they passed over the ship. They had proven that the Air Corps was capable of precision navigation over great distances. However, the Air Corps still had no full-time navigators. The navigator on this historic flight was Lieutenant Curtis LeMay, who, five years later, would be my bomb wing commander in England. The operating philosophy of GHQ Air Corps in 1938 was that all fliers would be pilots who would qualify in navigation and bombing as well. Lieutenant LeMay was a rated navigator, as well as a pilot, and for a while in the 1930s ran an advanced navigation school for Air Corps bomber pilots, but he was the exception rather than the rule.

Moreover, the *Rex* mission caused an uproar within the U.S. military establishment. The navy immediately complained that it was the navy's job to intercept invaders beyond one hundred miles from U.S. shores. The three B-17s had hardly returned to Langley Field when the War Department issued an order limiting air activities of the Army Air Corps to within one hundred miles of the shoreline of the United States. Later, when the U.S. entered the Second World War, this order was simply ignored.

Nevertheless, in early 1940, the Air Corps still could not carry out large-scale, overwater operations and had limited institutional expertise in navigation training. Recognizing this critical shortcoming, the army turned to Pan American Airways, the only American air carrier with extensive overwater experience. A navigation training program for the Air Corps was set up in Coral Gables, Florida, near Pan American's main operating base. The first class of specialist navigators graduated from this school in November 1940; however, it was not until July 1941 that navigators were commissioned as officers. This seems a bit surprising since observers and observer/navigators were commissioned officers in the U.S. Army Air Service from the First World War through the 1920s. My navigation instructors in early 1942 were mostly Pan American–trained army navigators. However, we had occasional lectures by experienced Pan American navigators who had crewed the glamorous Clippers, fitted out with wicker sofas and potted palms, that flew to China, New Zealand, South America, and Europe before the war.

The prewar state of aircrew training in the British RAF was equally deplorable. When the war began in 1939, the only aircrew member considered to have a full-time occupation in the RAF was the pilot. A significant percentage of crewmen classified as observer/gunners in the RAF were actually ground crew who doubled as air gunners to gain extra pay. In August 1939, Air Chief Marshal Sir Edgar Ludlow-Hewitt, commander in chief of the RAF Bomber Command, said he had to face the fact that over 40 percent of his bombers were unable to find a target in a friendly city in broad daylight. As late as August 1941, two years into the war, after studying crew reports and photographs of one hundred separate raids on forty-eight targets, one official study concluded that of all RAF bombers recorded as attacking their targets, only one in three got within five miles of the targets. To make matters worse, of the total sorties flown, only two-thirds of the attacking force was recorded as attacking the targets. It was not until after Sir Arthur "Bomber" Harris took over RAF Bomber Command in February 1942 that the crew position of navigator, whose only duties were navigation, was introduced on RAF aircrews.

America's entry into the war a little over two years later enabled it to buy precious time for the training of combat aircrews by the Army Air Corps. As a result, the specialized schools needed to teach all aircrew skills, not just those of pilots, were in place and in operation by December 1941.

It was clear to all participants from the outset of the Second World War that long-range bombing would play a major role in how the war would be fought. Every first-power air force had committed itself to the acquisition of a strategic bombing capability in the period between the wars. What could not have been predicted was the fall of France in the first year of the war with the result that, for four full years, the Second World War in western Europe was almost exclusively an air war. Moreover, before 1939, there was little empirical evidence upon which to structure a strategic bombing program in terms of weapons and tactics, particularly in the face of determined opposition by an enemy. In formulating their strategic bombing tactics and order of battle, the advocates of airpower relied almost entirely on assumptions based on speculation. Both British and German air commanders believed that massive aerial bombardment of the enemy's production, communications, and transportation centers would destroy his economy and eliminate his will to resist. American air commanders believed that armed, self-defending bomber formations could penetrate enemy-controlled airspace without escorting fighters and, with precision bombing, assure the destruction of key enemy targets without unbearable losses. All believed that airpower would shorten the war and avoid the mud, misery, and appalling casualties that had been the steady diet of the last war.

All of these assumptions were wrong. The Battle of Britain and the London Blitz in 1940 suggested early on that aerial bombing alone was unlikely to break an enemy's will to resist. Technical difficulties identified before the war, such as target-finding and bomb aiming, especially at night for the RAF, and in bad weather for everyone, would seriously hamper the bombing operations of all air forces throughout the war. At the same time, new radar and electronic communications equipment, virtually unknown before the war, would enable air defenses to quickly detect the location and flight path of incoming bombers and concentrate friendly fighters at intercept points. The Battle of Britain and RAF bombing raids on Germany early in the war had shown that air superiority over the target area was essential to sustained bombing operations. Further, by the time of the Second World War, all fighter aircraft—unlike the fighter aircraft of the early 1930s—were much faster than any bomber and posed a severe threat to bomber formations that had little or no friendly fighter escort.

The RAF did not go to saturation bombing at night because it was their preferred tactical strategy but rather because their aircraft losses in daylight operations early in the war were not sustainable. Apart from the reality that military commanders must fight with the men and resources given to them, in early 1943, VIII BC commanders truly believed in their daylight precision-bombing strategy, and they continued to dispatch American bombers over Europe with limited or inadequate fighter escort. This continued until the fall of 1943.

The moment of truth came for the VIII BC in the five-month period from June through October 1943. Although the first elements of VIII BC arrived in July 1942 to support the RAF Bomber Command in its bombing campaign, it would not be until May 1943 that American air commanders believed they had sufficient aircraft and trained crews to carry out sustained attacks on targets in Germany itself. In Germany, the appearance of large formations of American bombers over their cities in daylight, striking vital industrial installations with tight bomb patterns, could not be tolerated. The entire German available fighter force, including night fighters, would come up and fight in defense of the Fatherland. Additional fighter aircraft were pulled in from the Russian and Mediterranean fronts. By August 1943, the German Air Force—the Luftwaffe—had gathered one thousand fighter aircraft in Germany, France, and the Low Countries to oppose the daylight bombing attacks by the Eighth AF.

It must be noted, however, that the Germans could not deploy all these aircraft simultaneously against an American attacking force. The German air defenses were functionally divided into single-engine (day) fighter aircraft and twin-engine (night) fighters with essentially different equipment, tactics, and roles. Moreover, geographically, the German air defenses were divided into defense of the occupied territories in the west and the defense of Germany itself, which were controlled by two separate air commands, Luftflotte 3 with HQ in Paris and Luftflotte Mitte with HQ in Germany. Further, available German fighter defense forces had to be dispersed over all of northwestern Europe, which meant that on a good day the Luftwaffe could seldom concentrate more than four hundred to five hundred aircraft in opposition to an VIII BC mission stretched over ten, twenty, or thirty miles of sky. The Luftwaffe force usually launched was in the order of 250–300 aircraft.

Nevertheless, in the vicious air battles that took place between June 1 and the end of October 1943, both sides lost the equivalent of an entire precampaign air force. In four of those five months, VIII BC bomber crew losses exceeded 30 percent of the crews available for duty at the beginning of the month—in the one remaining month, they exceeded 20 percent. Because of these operations, the Eighth reported more than 5,600 American airmen missing in action and wrote off almost 650 heavy bombers. The Germans lost almost 1,000 aircraft. Death in the sky had replaced death in the trenches.

After a brief pause to regroup and awaiting the first arrivals of the long-overdue new, long-range P-51 escort fighter aircraft, the Eighth came back stronger than ever in 1944.[1] The Luftwaffe, however, could not recover. In the end, the Germans lost the Second World War for the same reason that they lost the first: they simply could not win a war of attrition. It was in 1943 and against this background, and in the historical setting depicted above, that the events to be described took place.

---

1. The 354th Fighter Group of the Ninth Air Force was the first unit assigned with the P-51 to arrive in the United Kingdom. The group's elements began arriving in October 1943 and flew its first heavy bomber escort mission on December 5, 1943.

2

BEFORE THE WAR

My mother was a precise chronicler of events important in her life, the birth of her children naturally being among such happenings. She wrote that there was a hint of early fall in the air when I was born at 6:45 a.m. on Friday, September 9, 1921, at St. Joseph's Infirmary. The infirmary was operated by the Catholic Sisters of Mercy and was located on the southwest corner of Courtland and Baker Streets in Atlanta, Georgia. My mother was twenty-two years old at the time, and my father was twenty-five. I was a small baby. At birth, I was twenty-two inches long, and my weight was five pounds, twelve ounces. The attending physician was Dr. Stephen Barnett, whom my mother adored. In his early fifties, Dr. Barnett was a general surgeon; he was tall, erect, elegant in appearance, and steadfastly warm and unflappable. He was the only doctor my mother completely trusted. She turned to him for advice and counsel on medical and nonmedical problems alike. For his part, I am sure Dr. Barnett saw my mother as the loving, decent, conscientious young lady she was. In her usual meticulous way, my mother also noted that the nurses in attendance at my birth were Misses Lutie Ward, Marie Davis, and Audrey Mansfield. She added that I "wore the smile that won't come off."

I was the second of three boys born to my mother and father. They had no daughters. My older brother, Michael, was named for our father and was sixteen months older. Until we were grown, we were often mistaken for twins. My younger brother, John, was born five years after I was in January 1927. In 1921, we lived near Grant Park on Atlanta Avenue in a cramped redbrick bungalow with a deep, thick row of red calla lilies across the front. We did not own a car until 1925, when my father came home one evening driving a "flivver," a black Model T Ford.

I am named for my mother's older brother, Frank Gidish, who at nineteen years of age died on August 3, 1915. He died from injuries he received when a motorcycle he was driving struck a seventy-year-old Black street sweeper by the name of Mark Cornwell, at the intersection of Washington and Fulton Streets in Atlanta. According to newspaper accounts of the incident, my uncle and a passenger on his motorcycle were riding at a moderate rate of speed on Washington Street toward downtown Atlanta when the elderly man, who apparently failed to see them, stepped off the curb in front of them. My uncle jerked his motorcycle sharply to the right to avoid a collision; as a result, he struck the curb, burst a tire, and crashed into Mr. Cornwell. Frank was seriously injured and was immediately carried to Grady Hospital by two men in a passing truck. He died the next morning. I do not know the fate of Mark Cornwell.

Father Joseph Kennedy baptized me at the Catholic Church of the Immaculate Conception in Atlanta on October 9, 1921. I spoke my first word, *da-da*, on March 15, 1922, to my father—much to the distress of my mother. I cut my first tooth on April 12, 1922, and after taking my first faltering steps, I collapsed in my mother's arms on September 1, 1922.

My recollections of my first six years are fuzzy and consist largely of fragments of ordinary experiences likely to make an impression on a small child. I played endlessly with my ever-patient brother Mike, who never teased or tormented me. We had a major crisis in our lives every time it rained on Atlanta Avenue, because when that happened, the unfinished dirt basement of our house flooded. When the basement flooded, my father and Skeet, a skinny, affable, loose-limbed, young Black man in his early twenties, who worked at my grandfather's store in downtown Atlanta, sprang into action. They pulled on rubber boots and laboriously bailed the water out of the basement with buckets. Otherwise, our coal bin and coal-fired furnace would have been swamped.

Mike and I were fascinated by the happy-go-lucky Skeet, who quite willingly put everything else aside and played any game we wanted, anytime. On the other hand, Skeet occasionally called upon my father for special help. I remember Sunday mornings when Mike and I awoke to find that Dad had gone to the police station in Atlanta to pick up Skeet, who had been a bit immoderate in his partying the previous evening. Even though we eventually lost contact with Skeet, we did not lose any of our fond memories. Years later, when reminiscing about our growing up in Atlanta in the 1920s and 1930s, one of the many stories that Father affectionately recalled was the uninhibited, irrepressible Skeet's quick-witted response about his Saturday night revelries: "Mr. Murphy, if you was ever colored on Saturday night, you would never want to be white again."

I was in Mrs. Henderson's kindergarten class at Hill Street School when Captain Charles A. Lindbergh set his high-winged, single-seat, single-engine *Spirit of St. Louis* down at Le Bourget Airport in Paris at 11:22 p.m. on Saturday, May 21, 1927. He landed in Paris thirty-three hours and thirty minutes after roaring off the ground at Roosevelt Field, New York, which was 3,600 miles away. He thus became the first person in history to fly solo, nonstop across the Atlantic Ocean. In clear weather, Lindbergh flew as high as ten thousand feet above the water; in heavy weather, at times he was only ten feet above the white-capped waves of the cold, perilous North Atlantic. As he glided to a soft landing on the brightly illuminated airdrome in Paris, twenty-five thousand Frenchmen, who had gathered in anticipation of his arrival, surged onto the airfield. For a few moments, it appeared that several people would be cut to pieces by the airplane's whirling propeller blades. Lindbergh quickly turned off the switch, and the engine died. He was pulled from the airplane and carried on the shoulders of the crowd to the airport office, where French officials and American ambassador Myron Herrick were waiting to congratulate him.

The next day, my father was observing his once-a-week Sunday morning ritual, listening to the news on radio station WSB in Atlanta through a headset attached to a small, tubeless, crystal radio receiver. I distinctly recall him jumping up abruptly and yelling to my mother, "Sib, he made it! He landed in Paris last night!" Although I am sure that airplanes circling the skies over Atlanta were a familiar sight in 1927, Lindbergh's historic solo crossing of the Atlantic is my first clear recollection of anything having to do with aviation. In the six months following his historic flight, Charles Lindbergh visited every state in the Union, which included a visit to Atlanta on October 11, 1927. He was honored in a huge downtown parade, after which he was given the keys to the city at a city hall ceremony. I am sure my father saw this parade.

Six years later, in 1933, on a hot, hazy, muggy summer day, Dad took Mike and me on our first airplane ride. We took off from Candler Field, adjacent to the small town of Hapeville, south of Atlanta. In 1909, the president of the Coca-Cola Company, Asa Candler, bought three hundred acres of land at this location for an automobile show. Since the First World War, however, it had been used as an airfield. Atlanta purchased this property for use as its municipal airport in 1929 for $94,500, and it has been the site of Atlanta's main commercial airport since then.

Our flight was a bumpy swing in warm, turbulent air high over

the trees, streets, and houses of Hapeville; a turn around the small
train station and railroad tracks running through nearby College
Park, then back to a straight-in landing at the Atlanta airport. Mike
and I were not the only ones making our first flight that day. It was
also the first time our father had ever been up in an airplane, and I
have no doubt that it was, at least in part, his own desire to see for
himself what flying was all about that led him to arrange this flight.
Our aircraft was one of several versions of the old, corrugated metal
Ford Tri-Motor transport aircraft capable of carrying a dozen or
so passengers. I do not know how my father became aware that
such rides were possible or why such a large airplane for its day
was available for this purpose. My guess, however, is that it was
probably operated by one of the hundreds of barnstorming pilots
who, during the hard times of the early '30s, traveled all across the
country selling airplane rides to the public.

It was the thrill of a lifetime. A flight in an honest-to-goodness
airplane was nothing less than an incredible, mind-boggling experience for a twelve-year-old boy in 1933. Not once in their entire lives
did any of my four grandparents ever go up in an airplane. None
of my schoolmates or friends had ever made an airplane flight, and
most of them despaired of ever doing so. The most spine-tingling
experience any of us could conceive of in those days was probably
a ride on the spindly, rickety-looking Greyhound, the roller coaster
at the Lakewood Park Fairgrounds in Atlanta, which we visited on
a school holiday for the county fair once each fall. The incontro-
vertible fact according to my friends, who professed inside knowledge of such important items, was that the Greyhound had been
condemned. Exactly who had condemned it and why was not clear.
The possibility, however, that this whole tottering wooden structure
might collapse at any moment as we swooped up and down its dips
or clattered around a tight curve only added to the excitement of

the ride. But that was nothing compared to my flight in that old Ford Tri-Motor.

Our first airplane flight in 1933 had to have been an extravagance for my father, who was then thirty-seven years old and had endured several changes in our circumstances in the years between 1927 and 1933. With a wife and three small boys to support, he was struggling financially. But he was not alone. In 1933, America as a whole was at the bottom of an economic depression that began with the collapse of the New York Stock Exchange in October 1929. By 1933, one-quarter of the country's labor force was out of work; in some heavily industrial areas, unemployment was as high as 50 percent. Thousands of banks across the country failed and closed their doors as depositors, who had lost confidence in the American economy, descended on them all at once, demanding all their money. There was no government deposit insurance covering bank accounts, and there were no credit cards. People were afraid that if they waited and allowed other bank customers to arrive at tellers' windows ahead of them, there would be no money left when they arrived. They were right.

The day President Franklin D. Roosevelt took office, March 4, 1933, all banks in New York and Pennsylvania were closed by state authorities to prevent their collapse. The president's first official act on the day of his inauguration was to issue a proclamation closing all banks in the United States for four days, thus putting all Americans, rich and poor, in the same boat for a brief breathing spell. Farm prices had fallen so drastically that farmers nationwide were unable to pay the interest on their loans and other debts and as a result were facing foreclosure. In Iowa, a group of farmers dragged a judge from his courtroom, put a rope around his neck, and threatened to lynch him if he did not stop signing farm foreclosure orders. He stopped.

During the 1920s, my father worked as a tailor in his father's men's custom tailoring shop at 2 Decatur Street, a prime location just two doors from Five Points in the center of downtown Atlanta. Business had been good for twenty years; in the mid-1920s, my grandfather employed five male tailors and fifteen seamstresses. By 1930, however, times had changed, and the family decided to close the business. This decision was made in part because of the Depression, and in part because my grandfather was then seventy years old. The principal reason, however, for the decision to terminate the business, which was well within my father's ability to operate, was that the handwriting was on the wall for men's custom tailors. They could no longer compete with the wide array of inexpensive, good-quality, ready-made men's suits in standard sizes that, with minor alterations, could be made to fit almost anyone and were by then widely available off the rack at department stores and specialty shops across the country. It is interesting to note how such small changes have had such a profound impact on how we live and how we shop.

My father was born Michael Vincent Murphy, in Norfolk, Virginia, on August 1, 1896, the youngest of four children. His father was William Patrick Murphy, born in Manchester, England, on March 4, 1861. Thanks to help from an aunt by the name of Bridget Murphy, who lived in Norfolk, Virginia, he immigrated alone in 1879 to the United States. He married my grandmother, Phoebe Ann Parsons, who had been born in Portsmouth, Virginia, on January 30, 1860. They were married at St. Mary's Catholic Church in Norfolk on a snowy, freezing night in December 1882.

My father's family moved from Norfolk to Atlanta in 1908, when my grandfather took a job as a cutter with an Atlanta tailoring firm. My father attended and finished primary school at the old Crew Street School in Atlanta, but then interrupted his education to work in the family business. He was twenty-one years old before he graduated from Tech High School in Atlanta in 1917. He then went to Georgia Tech for one year before meeting my mother. This was not a setback for him, however, for he had been blessed with a clear and logical mind—my father could sift and sort out a set of confusing facts faster than anyone I have ever known. He had a remarkable facility with numbers. While others were reaching for a pencil and paper to work out everyday math problems, my father would do the calculations in his head and provide the correct answer. He was rarely wrong.

Almost nothing is known about the background of my grandfather William Patrick Murphy, except for when and where he was born and that as a young boy he worked in the cotton mills in Manchester. We suspect that his family was among the thousands of Irish who, facing starvation, fled to England and America during the potato famine in the 1840s. My grandfather said he knew at an early age that a poor Irish mill worker had no future in class-conscious England, so he jumped at the chance to come to America.

My mother, who was not raised a Catholic, was the one who saw to it that we regularly attended Mass at Sacred Heart Church on Sunday. She was born Mary Sibyl Gidish and was delivered at home on Georgia Avenue in Atlanta on June 8, 1899. My mother graduated from Commercial High School in Atlanta and was a typist at the Lee Tire Company when she met my father in 1918. Her father was Johann Ludwig Gutig, born in Veitshöchheim, Bavaria, eight miles up the Main River from Würzburg, on August 30, 1866. Along with his brother, George, and his sister, Maria, he was brought to America by his parents in October 1883. They entered the United States through the Port of New York but went immediately to Columbia, South Carolina, where they had German friends.

My grandfather Gidish and his siblings were orphaned when

both of their parents died within three years of their arrival in America. On September 7, 1886, my grandfather, as John L. Gidish, at twenty-one years of age, was accepted by Columbia Typographical Union #34 as a trainee printer. The following year, while working for *The Columbia Register*, he was hired by the *Atlanta Newspaper Union* and moved to Atlanta. Sometime thereafter, the time and circumstances are not known, he met and married my grandmother Ida Louella Nix, who had been born in Orange, Cherokee County, Georgia on December 1, 1869. No one seems to know what brought my grandmother to Atlanta.

I have never been able to learn when or why my grandfather's German family name of *Gutig* was changed to *Gidish* or *Giddish*, both of which were used interchangeably by others for the rest of their lives. His parents, Adam and Eva Gutig, are interred in old St. Peter's Catholic Cemetery, Columbia, South Carolina, under their correct German family name. The name change to Gidish, which was made for my grandfather and both his siblings, was probably the result of an effort by someone in Columbia to phonetically Anglicize their strange-sounding German name after they were orphaned. My grandfather never took the spelling of his family name seriously. When asked if it was spelled with one *D* or two, he said, "I prefer that the last syllable of my name be *ish* and not *dish*. I decided forty years ago that one *D* was sufficient, and I don't mind if other people put in two, but I shall continue to use only one." His only surviving son, my uncle Paul, spelled the name *Giddish,* as do his succeeding generations. My grandfather's preferred spelling, however, was honored: his tombstone reads JOHN L. GIDISH. Every Gidish or Giddish in the Atlanta City directory or telephone book for over one hundred years has been a relative of mine.

My grandfather Gidish was well known in Atlanta newspaper circles as a colorful character because of his passionate love for the theater, literature, and music and for his longevity in the newspaper business. As a young printer, he was barely competent at setting type, but because of his knowledge of words, his ability to spell and punctuate, and an impressive general knowledge, his employers had him take over the proofreading desk at the *Western Newspaper Union,* successor to the *Atlanta Newspaper Union.* He held that position for the rest of his working life. For four decades, he was superintendent of the composing room and proofreader for his company. When he retired in 1951, at seventy-nine years of age, he had worked for the *Western Newspaper Union* for sixty-four years and had worked over fifty years without taking a day of vacation!

My grandfather was said by his newspaper associates to have been one of Atlanta's best amateur students of Shakespeare and classical music. He would, with little or no inducement, dramatically quote lengthy passages from Shakespeare with great accuracy. He had a humming repertoire of the major arias from fifty operas. As a child, I saw him sit by his wind-up Victrola, eyes closed, listening to stacks of classical records. Although they were never performed, he wrote and copyrighted several plays. If we had a driving rain, he was just as apt to quote to us from *King Lear*: "Thou think'st 'tis much that this contentious storm invades us to the skin." I remember opening the dictionary with him many times to stump him in spelling. I never did. I truly believed he could spell every word in the English dictionary, and to this day, I am sure he could.

My grandfather was a chronic daydreamer, never far from his world of make-believe. As a result, it was my grandmother's lot to cope with the outside world almost alone in the raising of their six children. Born a poor farm girl in north Georgia in the harsh Reconstruction Era of the 1860s, no one had ever given her anything. She was totally uncompromising and demanded that her grandchildren work hard to make something of themselves. As for marriage, she firmly believed the clichés she often quoted: "When the wolf knocks at the door, the dove flies out the window," and "Marry in haste, repent at leisure." Gardening and flowers were my grandmother's passion. She encircled her house with flower beds so that every walkway and path was lined with rocks and stones. From every crevice crept colorful thrift, verbena, sweet william, or tiny clusters of other herbaceous plants whose names only she seemed to know. Every opening on her front porch was a profusion of color from luxuriant hanging baskets.

My mother was the essence of gentleness and impeccable manners. She was constitutionally incapable of shouting or screaming; never in her entire life did she utter an off-color word or raise her voice to a living, breathing soul. Everything she did, she did well. She loved to read, especially poetry, and she could recite the poetry she had memorized as a child almost endlessly. The only recording I have of her soft, Southern voice is one that I made in 1940, and in it she is reciting a poem from memory.

The American South into which I was born was not the American South of today. By the early 1920s, the generations of Southerners who lived through the devastation of the War Between the States and the vengeful Reconstruction Era that followed were largely gone, and with them much of the bitterness that was the legacy of that war. And, in the interim, the Spanish-American and First World Wars had been fought, and Americans from all parts of the country fought in them as one nation. However, since both of my grandmothers, and many of our neighbors and friends, were the children of Confederate soldiers, there was an enduring pride in the patriotism and courage of the people of the South during the 1861–65 war. Virtually every family we knew had a picture of Robert E. Lee and his generals prominently displayed somewhere in their home. There were monuments to the Confederate soldier in every town in Georgia. Memorial Day was always celebrated on April 26, Confederate Memorial Day. The national Memorial Day in May was known as the *Yankee* Memorial Day.

Atlanta had been the scene of fierce fighting in the summer of 1864. In the 1920s, my grandfather Murphy lived on Cherokee Avenue, directly across from Grant Park. Often, when he took me along on his brisk morning walk, which went completely around the park, we would go the short distance from Boulevard down Confederate Avenue to the Confederate Soldiers' Home. We would talk to the few remaining Confederate veterans still living there; they were old and in failing health, but they would reminisce about the war with us. Fort Walker in Grant Park, a block away, was the southeastern anchor of the fortifications around Atlanta in 1864. As small boys in the 1920s, Mike and I regularly played on the old cannons ringing the earthworks at Fort Walker.

Our grandfather Gidish's home was on Dekalb Avenue across from the Georgia Railroad, one block north of Moreland Avenue. It stood squarely in the middle of the battlefield where the Battle of Atlanta was fought on July 22, 1864. In fact, his house was on the exact spot where Battery A of the 1st Illinois and Colonel Wells Jones's entrenched 53rd Ohio Infantry were overrun by the Alabama and South Carolina regiments of General Arthur Manigault's Confederate brigade. The Confederates came streaming out of the woods to the east, yelling like demons. This was the only successful Confederate attack in what was otherwise a disastrous day for the South.

The warm, largely muted affection that the people of the South and my family felt for the Confederate soldier in the first decades of the twentieth century was summed up beautifully by the eminent Georgia historian Lucian Lamar Knight over eighty-five years ago. He wrote, "If heroism alone could have prevailed, we would not have lost an unequal fight; and, around the campfire of an aftertime would have told in another key the story of Appomattox. But, an all-wise God held the scales of battle in His omnipotent hand; and while the North was elated with her laurels, the South was left to her memories."[1]

In 1933, we lived in a small two-bedroom house on Nelms Avenue in East Atlanta. It was our third home since leaving Atlanta Avenue. From November 1929 until the summer of 1931, we lived in Cleveland, Ohio, where my father took the only job he could find, as a clothing salesman at the May Company. I have pleasant memories of Cleveland: sledding in the snow, attending the second and third grades, and making my first Holy Communion at St. Rose's Church and School. Our neighbors, obviously fascinated by my Georgia accent, were forever asking me to repeat certain phrases over and over. In the spring of 1933, I finished the sixth grade at Sacred Heart School. In September, I went into the seventh grade at the Marist School, a military day school for boys, on Ivy Street next door to Sacred Heart Church in downtown Atlanta. Marist was founded in 1901 by the Marist Fathers, a teaching order of Catholic priests.

Twelve-year-old boys are rarely idle. They move effortlessly between their world as it is and the unlimited universe of fantasy and imagination where all things are possible. In 1933, I was an avid reader of dime novels and pulp magazines that published stories of the American West and the First World War. I was particularly fascinated by the exploits of the famous air aces. In addition, there were the early sound movies realistically re-creating the dramatic aerial dogfights of the First World War, among them *Wings*; Howard Hughes's *Hell's Angels*; and several years later, *The Dawn*

1. Lucian Lamar Knight, *Georgia's Landmarks, Memorials, and Legends, Vol. 2* (Atlanta, GA: Byrd Publishing Company, 1914), 166.

Patrol, starring Errol Flynn, Basil Rathbone, and David Niven. In these films, helmeted and goggled pilots in clumsy aircraft, scarves flapping in the wind, dove out of the sun at one another in close quarters. Their engines alternately sputtered and roared as their guns rattled. A jumble of planes rolled, twisted, turned, swooped, jinked, climbed, and finally escaped into the clouds or spun earthward in a dizzying spiral marked by trails of smoke.

I read the histories of all the men behind these stories: Eddie Rickenbacker, who went to France as General John J. "Black Jack" Pershing's chauffeur and became America's supreme air ace with the 94th Pursuit "Hat-in-the-Ring" Squadron; Frank Luke, the undisciplined, brash American balloon buster who would never stay with his formation and who specialized in attacking German observation balloons, which were heavily defended by antiaircraft and high-angle machine guns—he was finally shot down and landed successfully, but was killed on the ground when he foolishly drew his pistol and engaged in a shoot-out with the German troops who were attempting to capture him; and Raoul Lufbery, the fearless American who, after eighteen air victories, jumped from his burning plane at an altitude of two thousand feet, hoping to land in the Moselle River. A parachute would have saved his life.

I knew of the exploits of the British aces and Victoria Cross recipients William Avery Bishop and Albert Ball; the French ace Georges Guynemer; and the most famous of them all, the top-scoring fighter pilot of the war, Baron Manfred von Richthofen. The Baron painted all the planes in his squadron in brilliant colors, thereby giving them the name by which they were known throughout the war: "the Flying Circus." It was the master huntsman Richthofen, from a noble East Prussian family, who treated his prisoners courteously after a fight. He would drop notes on Allied airdromes telling the fate of airmen he had shot down. When Richthofen himself was later shot down behind British lines, the British gave him a Church of England burial service complete with a coffin, flowers, rifle volleys, and a bugler sounding the "Last Post." The practice of dropping notes asking and giving personal information on downed pilots became fairly routine on both sides. Once, the Germans even dropped a note protesting that it was not sporting that an American pilot had shot down a brand-new German pilot who was only practicing takeoffs and landings in an unarmed training plane. Other notes in prisoners' handwriting asked that food and other items be sent to them through the Red Cross. Finally, when the Germans dropped a note asking about two of their missing pilots, a foolish American airman called First Army Intelligence to find out, and when he was asked why he wanted the information, he told them. Orders immediately went out that communication with the enemy was a court-martial offense and the practice would be stopped.

In 1933, Mike and I shared a room. We had always shared a room and would continue to do so until Mike went to college. John slept in a single bed in the same room with our parents. The streetcar line to downtown Atlanta came down McLendon Avenue and ended at Clifton Road, two blocks from our house. Mike and I rode that whining, swaying, clattering, and clanging streetcar to and from Sacred Heart School and Marist regularly for three years. We were a close-knit family. All our grandparents lived in Atlanta, and we were at one or the other of their houses almost every weekend. If we were missing anything in life, we were not aware of it.

The center of my world throughout the 1930s was school. I was no scholar, but I believe I was a better than fair-to-middling student who, if nothing else, had fortunately inherited some of my father's facility with numbers. My teacher in the seventh grade, who taught all subjects, was Professor Edward McKeon. He was a stocky, bandy-legged, no-nonsense, fiftyish Irishman, whose once-sandy hair was graying. He wore a shirt, tie, and suit complete with vest to class every day. Each morning when we entered his classroom, Professor McKeon had a large wall calendar hanging over the middle of the blackboard in front of the class. On the board behind the calendar, he had written a column of figures in chalk, six numbers across and nine numbers down. When the school bell rang, Professor McKeon removed the calendar, thus revealing the numbers. Each boy in the room was then to add the column of figures as fast as he could. The first boy to raise his hand with the correct total received a piece of sour lemon hard candy. While we were working, Professor McKeon walked around the room checking answers. Those who appeared to exert too little effort received a sharp whack on the back of the hand with a wooden ruler to inspire them to try harder next time. It was the height of folly to try to hide one's hands to avoid this inspirational message. I can hear the professor now, roaring, "Jay-sus, Mary, and Joseph! Don't be a bigger fool than nature intended ye."

I found early on that I was consistently one of the first boys in the class to raise his hand with the right answer. Eventually, this daily exercise became a two-man contest between my classmate Bobby Baker and me. At the end of the school year, however, I had been first with the right answer to this daily problem most of the time and was given the Professor Edward McKeon Medal for Best in Rapid Calculation. It was the only scholastic medal I ever won.

At this same time, Mike and I were members of Troop 111 of the Boy Scouts of America. Our troop met at the Epworth Methodist Church on McLendon Avenue. Troop 111 had a drum and bugle corps. Mike and I were drummers. And because we were receiving military drill instruction at Marist, we were assigned the two corner posts on the front line of drummers. Under the direction of the father of one of our members who was in a drum and bugle corps himself, we practiced marching, playing endlessly after school

on the playground at Mary Lin Elementary School across from the
Candler Park golf course. We became well known in Boy Scout circles playing at Scout jamborees and marching at the head of Scout
units in parades in downtown Atlanta. Drum and bugle corps were
immensely popular in the 1930s. The highlight of every patriotic
parade in Atlanta was the splendid drum and bugle corps from Atlanta Post Number One of the American Legion. It was composed
of veterans of the First World War who, wearing silver-plated steel
helmets from that war, swung down Peachtree Street blasting and
rattling windows with their stirring rendition of "There She Goes."

The following fall, as I was entering the eighth grade and Mike
the ninth, both of us went to Mr. A. J. Garing, the bandmaster at
Marist, and asked if we could try out as drummers in the school
band. We were given an audition at the first band practice of the
year, and we were both accepted. After a few months, however, Mr.
Garing told Mike and me that if we really wanted to be in the band,
we ought to seriously think about studying music and learning to
play a musical instrument. Mr. Garing was himself a fine musician;
he had been a trombonist in John Philip Sousa's famous band and in
the 1930s was the bandmaster at Georgia Tech. After some discussion with our father, it was agreed that Mike would study the trom-
bone and I would learn to play the clarinet. Mr. Garing arranged
for me to take lessons from one of his bandsmen at Georgia Tech,
Karl Bevins, a brilliant young co-op student from Nebraska who
was a classic clarinetist. After the war, Karl was principal clarinetist
in the Atlanta Symphony Orchestra for many years. Karl took me
with him into several orchestral groups in Atlanta, including the
WSB Little Symphony Orchestra on WSB Radio. In my junior and
senior years at Marist, I was a soloist at the Georgia School Music
Festival in Milledgeville, Georgia; the judges gave me a Superior
rating both years.

I loved sports and athletic events of all kinds and enthusiastically played football, basketball, and baseball with my friends in
vacant lots and in the streets of our neighborhood. Marist had varsity teams in all sports, and as soon as I thought I might have a
chance to make a team, I tried. Although I was never more than a
competent player in any sport, I managed to win three varsity letters
in basketball and two in football. The high point of my sports career came on Friday night, October 28, 1938. The underdog Marist
football team, on which I was the starting right guard, played the
powerful Atlanta Boys High School team under the lights at Ponce
de Leon Park, the home of the Atlanta Crackers baseball team. Boys
High had won the Georgia state high school football championship
the year before. The newspapers didn't give us much of a chance,
but in writing about us, they used words like *plucky*. Marist put
twenty-six players on the field, while Boys High dressed out forty.
We were badly outplayed and pushed all over the field, but won the
game 2–0 on a safety in the fourth quarter. No one, not even we,
could believe it. In my last year at Marist, my classmates generously
voted me president of the Class of 1939. And in my last two years at
Marist, Angelyn Collins, the prettiest girl in Sacred Heart School,
with her dark eyes and golden brown hair, went to our spring proms
with me.

I entered Emory University in Atlanta the first week of September
1939, the same week in which Adolf Hitler unleashed his blitzkrieg
against Poland and thus precipitated the Second World War. The
outbreak of a major European war, even though it was prominently
covered in newspapers, radio news broadcasts, and theater news
reels, had no immediate impact on our lives. It was happening far
away, there was little military activity in the first months of the war,

and President Roosevelt assured the nation that we would not become involved.

Emory was a totally new world for me. The centerpiece of its campus was a large grass-covered quadrangle around which stood graceful, unadorned, gray-toned marble buildings and tree-lined walkways. It was a scene that spoke of tradition and education. Its students were from everywhere in Georgia and the South; many went to class in button-down oxford shirts and, seasonally, in seersucker or Harris Tweed sports jackets and slacks. There were more students in my freshman history class at Emory than there had been in the entire Marist school. I was in class only three hours a day, apart from labs twice a week. In the basement of the chemistry building, there was a co-op where we could buy a snack and a Coke, and listen to Artie Shaw and his orchestra on the jukebox with Helen Forrest singing "Deep Purple" or "A Man and His Dream."

Again, I was following in the footsteps of my brother Mike, who had entered Emory a year earlier with the specific intention of studying medicine. It was an easy school choice for me, as I had no defined goal. I went to Emory because Mike went there, because it was an excellent school, and because we could live at home and drive there in five minutes or, in good weather, walk to school. Mike had also been rushed by, and joined, the Kappa Alpha fraternity; the KAs gave me a bid and I did the same. Fraternity Row at Emory was a narrow, wooded, sun-dappled street lined with a single row of enduring stately mansions with classic porticos. The parties along Fraternity Row were fabulous: pretty girls everywhere, from nearby Agnes Scott College, or local pinks from such exclusive private schools as Washington Seminary and North Avenue Presbyterian School in Buckhead and northside Atlanta. The more popular girls arrived with their dates in roadsters with rumble seats. They were usually attired in the uniform of the time, a simple plaid skirt below the knee, solid color cashmere wool pullover sweater or a cardigan worn backward with a single strand of pearls, bobby socks, and properly scuffed penny loafers or saddle shoes. We all drank Coca-Cola. Emory was the Coca-Cola school.

A few months after I entered Emory, I heard that one of the saxophone players in the Emory Aces, the popular dance band at Emory, was about to leave school. The Aces were the equal of any professional band in Atlanta and were the band of choice by almost all college and high school fraternities, sororities, and other groups of young people in and around Atlanta when they wanted live music for their formal or other dress-up dances.

Although my music training had been traditional, by 1939, I was a devoted fan of the big band jazz music that exploded in the '30s through the rapid growth of the recording industry and the arrival of network radio with its nightly broadcasts of jazz bands from nightclubs and hotel ballrooms throughout the country. Benny Goodman, Duke Ellington, Tommy and Jimmy Dorsey, Artie Shaw, and Glenn Miller were household names across America. They were particularly popular among college students, who flocked to hear the big bands, danced to them, and stood in droves in front of bandstands just listening to the music that would forever thereafter be identified with the Second World War.

I desperately wanted an audition with the Aces and had two fraternity brothers who were in the band and who knew I played clarinet. They told me they would arrange it. I was sure I could read the music, but I had one small problem: I had never played the saxophone! I hurriedly rushed to the Ritter Music Company on Auburn Avenue and persuaded Mr. Ritter to lend me an alto saxophone. I then called Karl Bevins, who played saxophone in addition to clarinet. I was aware that a decent clarinet player could adapt to the saxophone easily, and after several days of intensive instruction and practice, I went to an Aces rehearsal. After hearing me play, I was told I could sit in with the band the following Friday night. I borrowed a tuxedo and played my first job with the band at Margaret Bryan's Dance Studio on Peachtree Street across from the Fox Theatre. That night, the Aces took me on as a permanent member of the band.

The Aces were the center of my nonacademic life for the next two years. We played tea dances after Georgia Tech football games and sock hops in fraternity houses at Emory. It was always the Aces for the Emory interfraternity dances at the Shrine Mosque in downtown Atlanta. At intermission, everyone made a mad dash for snacks at the Varsity Drive-In on North Avenue, famous for its chatty carhops. Spring formal dances were held in the staid columned ballrooms, or in the cool evening air outside on terraces softly lit by orange-colored lanterns, at the Druid Hills Golf Club, the Piedmont Driving Club, or Brookhaven Country Club. Radiant young ladies with purple orchid corsages from Betty Longley or Weinstocks florists pinned on voguish organdy or satin evening gowns, often strapless, jitterbugged and flashed satin sandals, or swayed trancelike as we played "Night and Day" or "Stardust" with no breaks while dateless stags stood along the walls looking on forlornly. If we played for a dinner, dance, and breakfast, I could make $20 a night, which was not bad when the average annual earnings of full-time working men in America at the time was $1,500.

It was also during my first year at Emory that my earlier fascination with aviation was rekindled. Bill Folsom, another friend and fraternity brother, told me that he was taking flying lessons at Candler Field and insisted that I go out there with him one day. Finally, on a Saturday, I drove to Candler Field with Bill and met his instructor, Johnny Lyons. Flying lessons did appear exciting, and I agreed to begin them at eight dollars an hour in a two-seat Piper J-3 Cub monoplane with a Lycoming O-145 sixty-horsepower engine. I went flying when I could for several months, learning about the controls, flying straight and level, banking and turning, taxiing, making takeoffs and landings, stalling, recovering from spins, and all the rest of it. My instructor was constantly reminding me, "Make all moves smoothly. Don't jerk the controls. Easy does it." On May 4, 1940, I was issued Student Pilot Certificate No. S11237 by the U.S. Civil Aeronautics Authority. On May 27, 1940, Johnny told me, "It's all yours. Take her around."

I taxied to our usual takeoff point on the grass next to a paved runway used by commercial aircraft, waited until the green light showed from the tower, advanced the throttle, and went bumping down the field and into the air. I have known no feeling exactly like the sensation I felt during my first solo flight; it is an experience that can never be repeated or duplicated. On that same day, the British government conceded defeat in the Battle of France and dispatched an armada of small vessels to help rescue the stranded and beaten remnants of the British Expeditionary Force from their trap at Dunkirk as best they could. I did not realize how close the clouds of war were coming, but when I had the money to spare, I drove out to Candler Field on weekends and went flying. Eventually, I knew that if war came to America, I wanted to go into aviation.

Although the world was largely given over to war, and the Germans were winning everywhere except Africa, my life changed little until Sunday, December 7, 1941. It was shortly after noon. We were cleaning off the dinner table following our Sunday meal of leg of lamb, roasted with new potatoes and vegetables, when my father received a phone call from a friend telling him to turn on the radio immediately. We then heard the news that Japan, by air and sea, had attacked Hawaii, the Philippines, Malaya, and Hong Kong simultaneously and without warning. At Pearl Harbor, our strongest base in the Pacific, we had two thousand to three thousand American casualties and heavy damage to ships, planes, and other property. The next day, at the request of President Roosevelt, Congress declared war on Japan. On December 11, 1941, Italy and Germany declared war on the United States. My life was soon to change dramatically.

3

THE WAR COMES TO AMERICA

The attack on Pearl Harbor on December 7, 1941, was a spectacular military success for the Japanese and a great humiliation for the United States. Perhaps the single most enduring consequence of the attack was that it brought the American people together with the common goal of utterly defeating Japan. Prominent politicians and other famous personalities who had previously been outspoken in their opposition to American involvement in another European war, and who had been critical of President Roosevelt's open support of the embattled British, promptly reversed their positions. Now they urged their fellow citizens to come to the aid of their country. Although questions were immediately raised about the reasons for the apparent failure to warn those who had been attacked, Americans knew they were embarking on what would prove to be the greatest and most critical war in their history. Potential civil or military culpability for the disaster at Pearl Harbor would play no part in America's determination to prevail over her enemies.[1]

---

1. It would be many years after the war before we would become aware of and appreciate the enormous British and American efforts to break the Japanese and German codes. The British, under the code name ULTRA, had penetrated the German Enigma encryption machine, which allowed them to decode German radio traffic, and we, under the project name of PURPLE, had the ability to read the Japanese diplomatic traffic, which also contained military information. Here is the misperception—having the ability to decode message traffic did not mean that all the traffic could be read all the time and that the information would

On the whole, my Emory classmates and other friends responded to the news of Pearl Harbor calmly, but with obvious indignation and outrage. Conversations were peppered with expressions of disbelief and contempt that "the miserable fucking Japs" were so sneaky and two-faced as to stab us in the back. They were outraged that the attack took place at the very moment when Japanese diplomatic representatives were meeting with the secretary of state in Washington to negotiate the political differences between the two nations. The question heard most often as we talked with each other was, "What are *you* going to do?" We could see that it was probably going to be a long war, a very long war against powerful, efficient, and experienced enemy forces. Some wanted to enlist immediately, while others favored watchful waiting.

The early war news was grim. When Japanese bombers struck

---

be immediately available to the intelligence analyst and the decision-makers. Rather, we could read portions of the traffic some of the time; sometimes hours, sometimes days after intercepting the message. Furthermore, we could intercept only radio traffic; information sent over landlines could not be intercepted and was thus immune to American and British decoding efforts. As for Pearl Harbor, even without the PURPLE intercepts, it was clear, as pointed out in the eminent historian Gordon Prange's *At Dawn We Slept,* that by the third week of November 1941, diplomatic negotiations with the Japanese government had deteriorated to the level that war was all but inevitable. Pearl Harbor was told of this, and in a classic catch-22, they were instructed to prepare for war but do so without alarming the local populace. Complicating the situation was the prevailing thinking within the navy that war in the Pacific would strike first at the "expendable" islands, such as Guadalcanal, and that the Japanese navy was no match for the American navy. Also at the time, there was no intelligence to give any indication that the Japanese navy had left port. Finally, many American navy strategists believed that if the Japanese and American navies were to battle, it would be a battleship-to-battleship conflict and that Japanese naval airpower would play a limited role. A Japanese aerial attack against Pearl Harbor was unthinkable, and this mindset proved to be just as fatal as the *Titanic* being "unsinkable." Thus, no matter how good the intelligence collection effort and analysis, the onus still fell on the civilian and military policy makers to effect sound judgments from all available information. For insight on ULTRA and the Eighth Air Force, see U.S. Army Air Force, *ULTRA and the History of the United States Strategic Air Force in Europe vs. the German Air Force* (Frederick, MD: University Publications of America, 1980) and Diane T. Putney, ed., *ULTRA and the Army Air Forces in World War II* (Washington, D.C.: Office of Air Force History, 1987).

Clark Field in the Philippines ten hours after attacking Pearl Harbor, the bulk of American aircraft were neatly drawn up on the ground and were easily destroyed. By the end of December 1941, the Japanese had overwhelmed the U.S. Marine garrisons on Guam and Wake Island, who, after heroic resistance, surrendered. Most of Luzon in the Philippines had been lost, and Hong Kong and much of Malaya had been overrun. In February 1942, more than eighty-five thousand battered and exhausted British troops in Singapore surrendered quietly to the Japanese.

I was the only one in my family likely to be conscripted into the armed forces. Mike had already been accepted for admission to the Emory University School of Medicine for the fall term of 1942 and would be exempt from the draft as long as he was in school. John was only fourteen at the time. In September 1940, Congress had passed—and the president promptly signed—the Selective Service Bill, drafting all men between the ages of twenty-one and thirty-six for one year's military service, the first peacetime draft law ever enacted in America. In January 1941, the government announced that one-third of the men drafted were physically unfit for service, and in August, the time of service for all men in the armed forces was extended by eighteen months. On December 19, 1941, less than two weeks after Pearl Harbor, Congress extended the draft law to men between the ages of twenty and forty-four. I turned twenty years of age three months prior to Pearl Harbor.

As the depressing military campaigns of December 1941 played themselves out around the world, they confirmed our initial apprehensions; we were in an interminable war that would be fought on faraway continents thousands of miles apart. I knew that inevitably the government was going to get around to all eligible young men my age. I decided that rather than simply sit back and wait for a call from my draft board, I would try to enlist in the Army

Air Corps and seek an appointment as an aviation cadet. My goal was to go into aviation with the possibility of becoming an officer. My only problem was when to act. The newspapers were reporting that voluntary enlistment in the armed forces, particularly the navy, was jumping by leaps and bounds. If I waited too long, would the army aviation cadet program, also much sought-after, be swamped by men applying ahead of me, leaving me exposed to the draft? I decided that after the 1941 Christmas holidays, I would tell my parents I wanted to join the Air Corps.

My mother and father took my announcement quietly and with understanding. They neither took issue with me nor tried to persuade me to change my mind; they were well aware of my status, and no matter how much they loved me, they would never suggest that I attempt to avoid military service when the United States was at war. I did not register for the winter quarter at Emory.

In early January 1942, I went to an army recruiting office in Atlanta and applied for an appointment as an aviation cadet. I filled out all the papers and was given a superficial health checkup by a visibly bored doctor who was only interested in seeing if I had some physical condition that would later result in my dismissal from the aviation cadet program. I was told that I met all Air Corps requirements and was instructed to go home and wait for a call. The call came within three weeks.

On the cold, windy afternoon of January 19, 1942, at the old post office in downtown Atlanta, I was sworn into the United States Army as a private with an appointment as an aviation cadet. I was sworn in with seven or eight other young men about my age. All of us were dressed in business suits and wearing ties. My pay was to be twenty-one dollars a month. We were immediately given orders to take the train that night at 11:00 p.m. from Atlanta's Terminal Station to Montgomery, Alabama, and to report to the Aviation

Cadet Detachment at Maxwell Field. I decided not to go back home; instead, with several other new army inductees, I went for dinner at Herren's Restaurant, on Luckie Street next to the Rialto Theater. After dinner, we walked to the Terminal Station, the grand, spacious, Spanish-style landmark on Spring Street that had been Atlanta's central train station since 1905. Just before we boarded the train, I telephoned my parents. As we talked, I knew from their voices there was no point in my telling them not to worry. I closed the conversation by simply saying, "I think I'd better go now. Goodbye, Mom. Bye, Dad. I love you." I remember my mother replying faintly, "Goodbye, Frankie."

As the train clicked, clacked, lurched, and swayed its way through the cold night, I dozed, then woke, then dozed again until finally awakening with a start when I felt us jolting and grinding to a halt. Still half asleep, I looked out the window. We were stopped alongside a sprawling complex of low-roofed, unimaginative buildings crisscrossed by a vast network of weird yellowish lights fringed by tiny halos in the cold, misty, morning air. It was dark outside. I looked at my watch; it read five o'clock. We had arrived at Maxwell Field.

Maxwell Field was an induction center. It received, processed, physically and mentally tested, organized, prepared, and dispatched groups of newly mobilized aviation cadets to various other USAAF bases for specialized training. When daylight came, it was a mob scene. There were at least several thousand new inductees at Maxwell when I arrived. We had no time to be lonely or to think of home. I was immediately put into a group of about 150 men. We were assigned quarters, marched to the barbershop to have our heads completely shorn, given a canvas bag for our civilian clothes, and then taken to the quartermaster for uniforms and personal articles. We were issued everything from overcoats and overseas caps to a razor and toothbrush. Back at our quarters, we were taught to make up our cots the army way, absolutely tight with no wrinkles or messy folds. We were admonished that we were never, ever to sit or lie down on our beds between reveille and lights out.

Our days were filled to overflowing with morning calisthenics, medical exams, personality tests, manual coordination tests such as rapidly turning pegs over in holes, classes on military etiquette and courtesy, and Morse code. We pulled guard duty at night without weapons, and we marched. Everywhere we went, we marched.

On our first day of drill instruction, the USAAF tactical officer commanding our detachment asked if any of us had any prior military training, such as ROTC. There was a long silence. Finally, a six-foot, towheaded, heavily freckled string bean of a cadet raised his hand and spoke up: "Sir, I did a hitch in the marines before joining the air force." He was then and there appointed our new cadet company commander, responsible for teaching us to look soldierly on the streets and drill fields at Maxwell. Subsequently, wherever we marched, he strode doggedly alongside our formation calling out in his best stentorian marine drill sergeant's voice: "Hup, dup, thrip, four-r-r. Hup, dup, thrip, four-r-r." Then on the beat, "Count cadence," we all shouted back in unison, "One, two, three, four, one, two, three, four!"

If it took us more than two minutes to march anywhere, we sang. Every day, the air at Maxwell Field was filled with a cacophony of discordant sounds produced by groups of cadets simultaneously marching near one another while singing different songs at the tops of their voices. The number one song was, of course, the USAAF anthem, "Off We Go into the Wild, Blue Yonder." There was another favorite that we picked up from the British RAF cadets being trained in the United States:

I've got sixpence, jolly, jolly sixpence.
I've got sixpence to last me all my life.
I've got two pence to lend, and two pence to spend,
And two pence to send home to my wife, poor wife.
I've got no one to grieve me,
No pretty little girls to deceive me.
I'm happy as a king, believe me,
As we go rolling, rolling home.
Happy is the day when an airman gets his pay,
As we go rolling, rolling home.

My cadet detachment at Maxwell Field in February 1942 consisted of a mix of enlisted men already in the military who had been accepted into the USAAF cadet program along with new recruits like me, who had been recently called into active service. We did not know what was going to happen next, except that on completion of our indoctrination and after being integrated into USAAF, we would be split into smaller groups. We would then be sent to the various USAAF primary flying schools scattered across the southeastern United States for pilot training. We were aware of a separate contingent of aviation cadets at Maxwell, composed of men who had "washed out" of pilot training. Most of them washed out for little more than some perceived lack of certain innate physical skills required of pilots. They had been sent to Maxwell for reclassification and reassignment. Since these cadets met all USAAF standards for physical and mental fitness, they were the primary source of manpower from which the USAAF was seeking volunteers to satisfy its urgent requirement for navigators and bombardiers. Although it solved an immediate problem, this approach had an unfortunate unintended consequence. Later, it produced occasional hard feelings when a tactless pilot gratuitously suggested that navigators and bombardiers were people who could not make the grade as pilots. To navigators and bombardiers, these tactless men were chickenshits whose arrogance was a menace to the safety of the rest of the crew. They were to be avoided at all costs.

The physical examination of new aviation cadets at Maxwell was performed by medical specialists who were arranged in sections. The exam was thorough and included x-rays, blood and other tests, and a complete personal health history. I had no problems until I reached the eye examination. Although I had twenty-twenty vision in both eyes and easily passed the tests for color blindness, I had difficulty with the test for depth perception. The depth perception test required the person to sit at one end of a long tunnellike box and, using manual controls, attempt to align two movable posts at the other end of the box into side-by-side positions, within a range of acceptable error. I took this test several times over about a two-week period, but I never passed.

One afternoon in late February 1942, the USAAF tactical officer in charge of my cadet unit called me to his office. He informed me that he was familiar with my depth perception predicament, and although he could assure me that no decision had yet been made regarding my suitability for pilot training, he could not predict the outcome. He said that he sent for me because the USAAF had a critical need for navigators and Maxwell Field was, at that moment, attempting to fill out a class of navigation students scheduled to go to Turner Field at Albany, Georgia, almost immediately. He explained, "Everyone wants to be a pilot, but the USAAF needs navigators as much as it needs pilots." He said the navigation course was fifteen weeks, after which, as I already knew, if I passed, I would be commissioned a second lieutenant with the same ground and flying pay as a pilot. As an afterthought, he commented that my tests showed an aptitude for the math and computational skills required of navigators and thought that I should do okay. His final bit of information was that while any decision at that point about my future was mine, I had to make up my mind quickly, as the class I would join was ready to depart for Turner Field.

I had no difficulty reaching a decision. I already had concerns for my future in the USAAF because of my previously unknown depth perception problem. Besides, it had never entered my mind that I would become a career pilot or make the military a lifetime occupation because I expected to return to college after the war. Completing navigation school would satisfy my desire to be in aviation and become an officer. I knew also, from my limited experience as a pilot on short cross-country flights, that navigation is both interesting and challenging. The following morning, I informed my tactical officer that I would volunteer for navigation training.

I never regretted my decision to become a navigator. Navigation is an art and a science with roots in time to which "the memory of man runneth not." Its life span is measured in millennia. Traces the world over of human settlements on small, remote islands five or more thousands of years ago, even in the harshest of climatic conditions, provide living testimony to the skills of long-ago navigators. The fifteenth- and sixteenth-century Portuguese, Spanish, and English geographers and cartographers who explored and mapped the world were, first of all, navigators. Going back to Aristotle and Euclid, the early thinkers, noting the hulling down of ships at sea, the curved shadow of the earth on the moon during an eclipse, and the globular shapes of both the sun and the moon, first postulated and then set out to prove the sphericity of the earth. They believed the stars were in fixed positions in relation to one another within a great celestial sphere. Although there is no such sphere, the concept is the basis for celestial navigation.

The Greeks, noting the fixed patterns of star groupings, named the key constellations for the gods, heroes, and other objects of their mythology: Andromeda, Cassiopeia, Orion, Sagittarius, and Taurus, to name but a few. They gave individual names to the brightest and best-known stars. The Latin form of these Greek names are the names by which astronomers and navigators know the recognized constellations and stars today.

Majorcan and Catalonian sailors made reliable approximations of latitude by measuring the altitude of celestial bodies above the horizon as early as the thirteenth century. The method for determining longitude using lunar tables dates to the Greek astronomer Hipparchus in the second century BC, but it was not until the nineteenth century and the development of accurate timepieces that longitude could be calculated with precision. Nonetheless, Hipparchus also devised a scale of "magnitudes" for grading the brightness of stars, a system that forms the basis for the magnitude scale used by astronomers today. Ptolemy, in the second century, devised a systematic globular geography in terms of *latitude* and *longitude* and mapped the known world in degrees north and south of the equator and east and west of a zero meridian. He also estimated that the lands and seas covering two-thirds of the earth's surface were unknown—often shown on ancient maps as terra incognita.

The magnetic compass has been in use by mariners for more than a thousand years and was probably the principal factor in the development of both mapmaking and navigation. The earliest known placing of a magnetic pole was in the fourteenth century, and navigators before Columbus were acquainted with variation of the magnetic compass needle from true north and needle dip related to latitude. Christopher Columbus, despite ego and other personality traits that did not inspire confidence in his leadership, was a competent and experienced navigator. Although his date of birth is unknown, he went to sea at about the age of fourteen and sailed with Prince Henry's Portuguese navigators exploring the west coast of Africa. He visited Iceland in 1477, where he possibly saw maps then available that showed the existence of Greenland. Columbus was particularly skillful in ascertaining the altitude of celestial bodies with the shipboard version of the astrolabe and determining his latitude by reference to the astronomical tables of Regiomontanus, published in Germany in the 1470s, which provided predictions of the positions of celestial bodies. On all his voyages across the "Sea of Darkness," as the unexplored Atlantic Ocean west of the Canaries was then known, he used astronomical observations to maintain steady headings west and east on a chosen parallel of latitude. Later reviews of his maps and writings indicate his calculations were rarely more than one degree (sixty nautical miles) in error.

The determination of longitude at sea in the fifteenth century was another matter. Columbus never knew how far he had traveled and was keenly aware of it. First, he was under the incorrect assumption that the earth was about three-fourths its actual size. Further, his dead reckoning calculations were based entirely on visual observations. He had no instruments to tell him the wind forces acting on his sails and no knowledge of the sea currents beneath him. His navigation plan, therefore, was always the same: sail north or south to the known latitude of his terminal point, then maintain a steady easterly or westerly course until he arrived at his destination. The navigation achievements of Columbus and his contemporaries were nothing short of astonishing. The longitude problem was not solved until John Harrison invented the clockwork chronometer in 1759. Fifteen years later, the British Admiralty grudgingly awarded him with the princely sum of 20,000 pounds for doing so.

Turner Field was in the flat, pecan-producing, Coastal Plain plantation country near Albany, Georgia. It could have been any one of the dozens of USAAF bases built across America during the period of "national emergency" declared by President Roosevelt on September 8, 1939. Like all new air bases, it was a spread-out complex of plain wooden barracks, offices, warehouses, aircraft repair shops, hangars, and support buildings. Turner was one of a series of flight training bases established by the Army Air Corps in the southern and southwestern United States, where the flying weather was considered favorable year-round. It was a multiengine advanced flying school for Air Corps cadets in the final phase of their pilot training. In 1941, however, the USAAF, as part of an accelerated program to train navigators, added a navigation school at Turner. And, in early 1942, we had a group of approximately 300 British RAF aviation cadets on base receiving advanced pilot training under an agreement by which the USAAF trained British pilots.

At any one time in the winter and spring of 1942, we had, in round numbers, 600 aviation cadets, divided into five classes of about 120 men each, in the navigation school at Turner. The school was graduating a class of new navigators every three weeks. The housing, classroom, and study areas for navigation students were separate from those of the pilot trainees, and we only saw them after hours at the post exchange or post theater. We were quartered three men to a room. I was fortunate in that my roommates throughout my stay at Turner Field were two easygoing Northerners, Stan Polak from Ohio and Jimmy Maniatis from Boston.

However, we were still in the USAAF. Every morning, we were

awakened by a drum and bugle corps of about ten men marching down our company street, their booming music resounding back and forth off our barracks walls. We fell out immediately in our blue pants and gray shirts, sweat suits, and running shoes for our morning exercise period, rain or shine. After exercising, we bathed, dressed, and formed up again to march to the mess hall for breakfast.

Aerial navigation differs little from marine navigation; things just happen faster. The basic instruments are the same, except that the aerial navigator has specific instruments, such as the altimeter, airspeed indicator, and drift meter that are peculiar to air navigation. Coursework for USAAF navigators involved more ground work than flying work. It was much the same as being in college, except we were in class eight hours a day. Our classrooms looked like other classrooms with blackboards, wall maps, lecterns, and an oversize globe of the earth in the front of the room. There the similarity ended. We marched to our desks and stood at attention until ordered to be seated. There was no whispering, writing of notes, or horseplay: we had a lot to learn in fifteen weeks, and there was no room for nonsense.

Our instructors explained meridians and parallels; latitude and longitude; the difference between statute miles and nautical miles; different map projections, such as the Lambert conformal conic and Mercator and their uses; great circle courses; rhumb lines;[2] and other navigation basics. We studied the magnetic compass and its

---

2. A rhumb line is an imaginary line on the earth's surface that cuts all meridians at the same angle. While it is not the shortest distance between two points, the rhumb line joining those points may be followed by flying a constant true course. The shortest distance between any two points on the earth lies along the arc of the great circle passing through two points. To fly a great circle route, an aircraft must change course at regular intervals, which is accomplished by following a series of rhumb lines approximating the great circle. However, for flights of a thousand nautical miles or less, the great circle offers no appreciable savings in time and distance.

variations and deviations, as well as other aircraft instruments used by the navigator. We were taken from pilotage navigation, the old "follow the railroad tracks" method of navigating by referring to visible landmarks on the ground, through dead reckoning, wherein the navigator determines his position by keeping an account, or reckoning, of the true course and distance flown from a known position called the *point of departure*. In the days before the extensive availability of radio and electronic navigation aids, air navigators relied heavily on dead reckoning navigation on long flights over water, at times when lowered visibility obscured landmarks, and when overcast skies made celestial navigation impossible. The navigator calculated his course and distance by reference to his onboard instrumentation, his actual compass headings corrected for magnetic variation and aircraft deviations, and his airspeed readings from his airspeed indicator, both adjusted for his best estimate of the direction and velocity of the wind at the height he was flying. Because of the effect of wind drift, from the time of the Wright brothers until today, the basic navigation problem confronting every aircraft pilot and navigator flying without visual reference to the ground is that his true course is not the direction in which the nose of his airplane is pointing or the heading indicated by his magnetic compass needle, nor is the airspeed displayed on his airspeed indicator his true airspeed or ground speed.

In moving on to the study of celestial navigation, we were introduced to a whole new terminology: sidereal time as opposed to solar time; right ascension instead of longitude; declination instead of latitude; altitude and azimuth; zenith; nadir; hour angle; and so on. We had night classes to study the patterns of the key constellations and memorized the names of the primary stars used by navigators. I learned that although there are millions of stars in the night sky, only about twenty stars were used by navigators to any practical extent. We practiced using the octant and astronomical tables for the sun, moon, planets, and stars in the *Nautical Almanac* published by the U.S. Naval Observatory to solve the astronomical triangle and determine our latitude and longitude.

Another similarity to my college days was that we had a laboratory, but it was a flying lab. The USAAF training airplane for navigators in 1942 was the Beech AT-7, a twin-engine aircraft equipped as a flying navigation classroom. It had three desks for three cadets on the right side of the airplane, each with a magnetic compass. Behind the pilot was an instrument panel accessible to all students. In the top center of the airplane was a domed glass turret for making astronomical observations. There was always an instructor navigator on board. We usually flew once, sometimes twice a week to put into practice what we learned in the classroom. The flights normally lasted three to four hours and had three legs; say from Turner to Selma, Alabama, to Rome, Georgia, and back to Turner. This provided a leg for each student to navigate.

Two other cadets in my navigation class, Hugh Summer and Doug Worley, were from Atlanta. I had known Doug since first grade at S. M. Inman grammar school. Since Atlanta was only 180 miles away, one or two of us would hitchhike from Albany to Atlanta and back almost every other weekend. Occasionally, all of us made the trip. Hitchhiking by military servicemen was never a problem during the Second World War. Almost every motorist or trucker with room in his vehicle stopped to pick up a soldier or sailor catching a ride on a highway. We never had to wait more than ten minutes before someone screeched to a stop and motioned for us to get in his car or truck. In most instances, our host told about a son, relative, or friend who was in the military, sometimes overseas. It was not a fast trip, because highways in those days were all two lanes, one for each direction, and passed through the center of every town along the way. Roads were supposed to connect towns and cities, so there were no bypasses. We might have to make two or three connections, but we were never delayed. I remember strings of Burma-Shave signs every few miles along the highway and, as we neared Atlanta, signs on large boulders and ramshackle barns alongside the highway saying, "See Rock City."

Our flight schedules at Turner were well planned and methodical, and it would be difficult to imagine less hazardous flying in wartime. We never had an accident. Nevertheless, a few of the pilots assigned to the navigation school felt, perhaps with some justification, that flying navigation students around in an AT-7 trainer was not a prestigious assignment. On the other hand, there were several serious flying mishaps in the advanced pilot training program during our time at Turner. In one instance, two British cadets and their American instructor pilot were killed when their AT-11 twin-engine pilot trainer crashed while they were in the traffic pattern coming in for a landing. We seldom saw British cadets except in groups marching from place to place with the exaggerated arm swinging that characterizes the British military marching style. I felt for the Brits at Turner. The British people had suffered greatly in two and a half years of war, and the British aviation cadets were a long way from home and did not have the changes of clothing that we had. Their uniforms often looked well worn, and it was my understanding that their pay was considerably less than ours. The American cadets were paid twenty-one dollars a month; I do not know if it is true, but I heard that the British cadets received something closer to three dollars a month. No wonder they always spoke of being broke in their songs.

I had two graduation flights from Turner Field. The first was a daylight flight from Turner to Langley Field, Virginia, part of which was over the Atlantic Ocean, and return on June 19, 1942. Navigation on that flight was by pilotage and dead reckoning only. My second was a night, all-celestial navigation mission from Turner to Barksdale Field, Louisiana, on June 25, 1942, with a return to Albany the next night, again entirely by celestial navigation. The navigator's graduation flights were intended to simulate tactical missions, to be flown in both daylight and darkness, partly over water, and included the application of all navigation techniques learned. I was somewhat anxious on my final flight. I never worried about my dead reckoning navigation, but I had little confidence in my skill with the octant when observing the altitudes of celestial bodies. Since the true horizon can seldom be seen from an aircraft in daylight and never at night, a sextant or octant substitutes its own artificial horizon by incorporating a liquid bubble mechanism into the optical system to enable the navigator to hold the instrument level when "shooting" stars, planets, the sun, or the moon. The success of the user depended on his ability to hold the instrument steady, which was not easy even in smooth air. In bumpy air, the most skilled pilots were unable to hold the airplane level. Thus, even in calm air, the moment I stood up with my octant in hand, I became very nervous. Moreover, celestial navigation requires a lot of plotting and chart work and is an acquired skill. When my last flight was over, I thought my performance had probably been unacceptable. I later learned that the USAAF was well aware that, unlike the stabler ship sextants, bubble sextants were susceptible to significant error, and a position error of five to ten miles in still air was considered good work for an experienced navigator. If our position as determined by our celestial "fixes" was within twenty-five miles of our actual position the USAAF felt we had done pretty well.

I graduated from the USAAF navigation school at Turner Field in a brief ceremony on the post parade grounds on Independence Day, July 4, 1942. Several weeks earlier, each of us had been provided formal printed invitations to our graduation for mailing to relatives and friends together with tiny, white calling cards that had our names in the center and in the lower-right-hand corner the words LIEUTENANT, AIR FORCES, UNITED STATES ARMY. My mother and father drove down from Atlanta for the ceremony and to take me home for a week's leave before reporting to my next duty station, the B-17 Combat Crew School at Hendricks Field, Sebring, Florida. As we were walking off the parade grounds after the ceremony, an older USAAF sergeant, seeing me with my mother on my first day in my officer's uniform, gave me a snappy salute. As I self-consciously returned the salute, I felt my mother gently squeeze my left arm.

4

HENDRICKS FIELD, SEBRING, FLORIDA

In the summer of 1942, the USAAF Combat Crew School at Hendricks Field, located at Sebring, Florida, was part of the Southeast USAAF Training Command. The school ran a series of intensive, four-week training courses for newly commissioned flying officers assigned to four-engine heavy bombers. Pilots, navigators, and bombardiers, fresh from their individual specialist training schools across the United States, and private pilots, commissioned directly into the USAAF from civilian life, were sent to Sebring for indoctrination. Once a crew was established, the four officers on each crew remained together as a unit. We lived together, ate together, went out together, and flew together under the supervision of an instructor pilot.

Hendricks Field was another of the air bases that had been built quickly to meet wartime needs.[1] Located in the verdant citrus-growing lake country south of Orlando and west of the meandering Kissimmee River, Hendricks was in the headwaters of the canals, cypress swamps, and glassy lakes that comprise the South Florida water system. It was sixty miles north of Lake Okeechobee, which is thirty miles or more across in any direction, but only twelve feet

---

1. This is now the site of the famous Sebring International Raceway.

deep. Lake Okeechobee feeds water to the soup-warm "river of grass," the Everglades.

With no air-conditioning except in the post theater, we sweltered in the heavy air and oppressive humidity of South Florida in July and August. The weather was quite a shock for me. Even though I was from Atlanta, where we had our share of heat and humidity, our one thousand feet above sea level did make a difference. The temperature in Atlanta was almost always ten degrees cooler than in south-central Florida. Experiencing the heat and humidity gave new meaning to the expression: "It's not the heat, it's the humidity." Our barracks were stifling around the clock. I remember tossing and turning on my damp, clammy sheets in the late evening, accompanied by the boggy scents of the tropics that drifted through our open windows. I also remember crickets singing, cicadas buzzing, frogs croaking in nearby ponds, and just before falling asleep, the distant mournful wail of the *Orange Blossom Special,* the luxury passenger train from Chicago racing down the railroad that straddled the Florida peninsula and ended in Miami.

The pilot of the training crew to which I was assigned was Captain Tony LaVier, from Ohio, who had several years of experience as a commercial pilot before the war. Tony was in his late twenties, but because of a trim figure, a full head of dark hair, and smooth skin, he looked much younger. He was married and had been commissioned as a captain in the USAAF directly from civilian life. Tony was neat, relaxed, and unmilitary. He seemed out of place in his USAAF uniform, but he was terribly conscientious. I will never forget him sitting tight-lipped in the left seat of the B-17 on takeoffs, his left hand on his control column; his right, palm up, grabbing the four engine throttles on his center control pedestal and grimly working them up toward full power.

Our copilot was a polished, suntanned, straight-backed, high-waisted, outgoing, six-foot Californian, a second lieutenant by the name of Norman Hugh Scott. He was from Los Angeles and had just graduated from the USAAF Advanced Flying School in Lubbock, Texas. Scott would eventually become a central figure in a controversial incident involving the 100th BG, which will be described later.

Try as I may, I do not recall the name of our bombardier, perhaps because, though pleasant enough, he tended to keep his business and his distance from the rest of us. We rarely saw much of him in off-duty hours. He was a laconic, lean, laid-back Texan who invariably wore dark glasses. For no particular reason, I had the impression that he may have been a fine athlete at one time. He washed out of pilot training and had been sent to bombardier school. He was competent and efficient in the air but was content to do only what was required of him and no more. His principal interest, I was to learn later, was women. He was drawn to town at every opportunity by the scent of his gentle prey.

On the one occasion that I went out on the town with my bombardier, he insisted on going to a hotel with Spanish-style architecture on a palm-fringed street. From the moment we entered the dimly lit lobby, he started eyeballing all the unaccompanied women in sight. Ignoring me, he moved quickly. He would approach his "target" and appear to forward a proposition that, I am sure, was direct and probably indecent. If his prey reacted with outrage and indignation, he immediately walked away; if she laughed at his sheer nerve and impudence, he would immediately double over with laughter, sit down, and begin regaling her with stories in a most exaggerated Texas drawl. I could not believe this was the same person I flew with; but in any event, his approach to women was more than I could handle, so I left. If he missed me, he never mentioned it, but as I said, he was never talkative with the rest of the crew.

I made my first flight in a B-17 aircraft at Hendricks Field on July 18, 1942, but it was hardly an exciting event. I did nothing but sit there as our instructor pilot put LaVier and Scott through a series of nine touch-and-go takeoffs and landings. A mixture of B-17 model aircraft were assigned to Hendricks. Our airplane for this flight was a B-17B, the first production airplane in the B-17 series. Only thirty-nine B-17B aircraft were built, and all had been delivered to the USAAF by March 1940. The B-17B was designed for a crew of six. Its defensive armament consisted of five puny .30-caliber machine guns. It had two side gun blisters, one bottom gun blister in the fuselage, and one forward-firing .30-caliber machine gun in the nose window. Mostly, however, at Sebring, we flew the B-17E, which was the first of the B-17 series aircraft to incorporate the distinctive dorsal fin beginning just aft of the radio room and sweeping up into a high vertical stabilizer.

The flying program at Hendricks was intensive, and for the first two weeks, we flew from three to five hours almost every day. It was almost entirely familiarization training for our pilots and designed to transition them into the B-17. As navigator, I did nothing but keep track of where we were. The bombardier was along for the ride. I felt I was gaining little benefit from our flying schedule and was suffering in the inescapable, unmerciful, oppressive South Florida heat for nothing. Climbing into an airplane that had been sitting for hours in the broiling sun was like touching a hot stove. Inside, it was like an oven. The extensive glazing in the nose section exposed to the sunlight was permanently sealed, and it felt as if I were working in a nursery hothouse. Even though I wore only undershorts and a light flying suit, if I bent over my navigator's table during preflight to lay out my maps and other paraphernalia, the perspiration ran down my face in rivulets and fell in torrents on everything I was trying to work on. Gazing out the window, all I could see were other B-17s shimmering under a fiery sun on a field bulldozed out of lush vegetation.

But with the arrival of August 1942, our program underwent a complete change. In his memoirs of the Second World War, Sir Winston Churchill wrote: "The only thing that ever really frightened me during the war was the U-boat peril. Invasion, I thought, even before the air battle [the Battle of Britain], would fail." The oceans, and especially the entrances to the British Isles, were Britain's lifeline to the outer world, particularly the United States. The first six months of 1942 were the toughest of the war according to Churchill. At any one time, German admiral Karl Dönitz had nearly one hundred operational U-boats in United States waters, attacking American and Allied shipping, chiefly oil tankers. The German submarines operated very effectively from Venezuela and the Gulf of Mexico all the way to Newfoundland. The American navy was hopelessly inadequate after Pearl Harbor. The USAAF, which controlled almost all shore-based military aircraft, had no training in antisubmarine warfare. Nevertheless, B-17 aircraft from Hendricks Field were brought into this problem.

In August 1942, German U-boats in the South Atlantic were concentrating on ships carrying bauxite for the United States aircraft industry and oil and other supplies to the Middle East. Most of these attacks occurred inside the Gulf of Mexico and just off the Atlantic coast of the United States. Towns along the Atlantic shores of America often heard the sounds of battle. They saw burning and sinking ships, and sometimes they even rescued survivors.

Our supposed practice missions from Hendricks Field in the first two weeks of August 1942 were, in reality, six- to eight-hour antisubmarine patrols in the Gulf of Mexico and in the Atlantic Ocean off Florida. We carried live depth charges in our bomb bays and, spaced at slightly overlapping intervals, flew low-altitude search patterns covering long stretches of the Florida peninsula from the shoreline to 150–200 miles out to sea. German submarines in the South Atlantic were painted white and rested on the sandy bottom of the ocean during the day. At night, they used their high surface speed to locate their prey. Our objective was to be on station before daylight in hopes of spotting and attacking a submarine before it could submerge for the day.

Roaring low over the Everglades en route to our assigned search areas, we often sent clouds of white egrets fluttering up from the waving saw grass and arthritic cypress trees to seek peace and quiet elsewhere. Passing over the Florida Keys in those days, I saw for the first time the talcum-white beaches and irregular patterns of the colorful coral reefs beneath the crystal-clear, turquoise waters of the Atlantic off southern Florida. It seemed so peaceful. All eyes were kept glued to the ocean's surface, and we occasionally saw the sunken hulks of cargo ships torpedoed by German submarines that had operated alarmingly close to Florida's shores. To tell the truth, we were skeptical that we would find a German sub on these missions until early one morning when one of our Sebring B-17s broke our normal radio silence and reported spotting, attacking, and sinking a German submarine in the first light of day. This successful attack was verified by other Hendricks aircraft, which, upon hearing the radio transmission from the attacking aircraft, immediately flew to the site of the reported sinking and confirmed the existence of oil slicks and considerable debris on the ocean surface. The navigator on the B-17 that sank the U-boat was Lieutenant Ray Katowski, a navigation classmate of mine at Turner Field.

We completed our training at Hendricks on August 14, 1942, and were given a week's leave, my second in just over a month. The officers on my Sebring crew, even though we were no longer considered an official USAAF crew, were all given orders to report to the

29th BG, a training unit based at Gowen Field, Boise, Idaho. I traveled to Atlanta by Greyhound bus and, after my short home leave, flew to Salt Lake City, Utah, on Delta Air Lines. In Salt Lake, I joined Tony LaVier and Norman Hugh Scott, and the three of us drove to Boise in Tony's car. It was my first trip to the American West. I was profoundly impressed by the panoramic vastness and grandeur of northern Utah and southern Idaho, not to mention the giant western jackrabbits we occasionally saw alongside the road. They were five times larger than the cottontails back home in Georgia.

5

THE 100TH BOMB GROUP

Thanksgiving Day in 1942 arrived at Gowen Field in Boise, Idaho, under an overcast sky. There was a decided autumnal nip in the air. Uncertain winds, gusting lightly across the base, created an occasional mournful wail as they swirled around the corners and under the eaves of our barracks. Along with several other second lieutenants who had recently spent time in the base hospital, I had been invited to have a holiday dinner with the nursing staff in their dining room at the hospital.

In early September, while suffering from severe nasal congestion brought on by a head cold, I had foolishly gone flying. During a rapid change of altitude, I was unable to equalize the air pressure in my ears, and the result was a spontaneous reopening of an old perforation in my left eardrum that dated back to my childhood. Although I was not physically disabled, I was hospitalized for several days for observation. On top of that, I was also grounded for the rest of the month. To my dismay, the flight surgeons told me I could have a chronic ear problem and had doubts as to whether or not I should return to regular flying status, as a healthy middle ear has always been a requirement for military aircrew. I am sure the look of horror and utter desolation on my face at the mere mention of being permanently grounded had an impact on their thinking. They finally returned me to duty without comment.

Nevertheless, I did not have any flying time at Gowen Field

during the month of October 1942, principally because the flying program at Boise, as at Sebring, was essentially focused on qualifying pilots in the B-17, and most flights were local. Consequently, there was little activity for navigators. Moreover, at that time, Gowen Field was as much a gathering point for airmen awaiting further assignment as it was a training base, so I wasn't the only person with time on his hands.

This period of light duty suited me fine. It gave me frequent opportunity to go into Boise, with its excellent restaurants and beautiful capitol building on Capitol Boulevard, which is set against a backdrop of green-tinged, golden-brown, yellow-streaked rolling hills. It was also my good fortune to have Captain Hank Henggeler as my roommate. Hank was a burly, energetic, cheerful B-17 instructor pilot from Texas. He was a keen horseman and insisted that I go riding with him every weekend, even though I do not believe I had ever been horseback riding before and never did really get the hang of it. It was all I could do to hold on for dear life when my horse, no matter what I wanted it to do, would follow Hank's horse over steep precipices, whinnying, slipping, and sliding down steep inclines, scattering stones and dirt everywhere. Along with several other Southerners then based at Gowen Field, I tried skiing for the first time on the windy, cold slopes of Sun Valley in the ragged Sawtooth Range. That was where the Union Pacific Railroad established a mountain village ski resort in 1936. By the time we arrived at Gowen Field, the resort had already become world famous.

Boise had a large Basque community, composed of immigrants and descendants of the thousands of Basque sheepherders who came to America in the late nineteenth and early twentieth centuries. They came from the rugged Pyrenees border region of France and Spain to herd open-range sheep in the lonely mountains and deserts of our Far West. Several of the lovely young ladies of Basque descent in the area would usually attend the weekend dances at the Gowen Field officers' club. They were always heavily chaperoned. We were given to understand that the Basques in Idaho still lived in the traditions of their old-country European-style clans, and these young ladies would be disowned and disinherited if they became involved with persons outside the blood. We were informed that we were expected to conduct ourselves accordingly.

Early in November 1942, I was returned to a full flying schedule and, by Thanksgiving Day, had participated in ten local training flights, including twenty-two takeoffs and landings, with no further ear problems. However, the most significant development in my entire army career occurred during the third week of November. I was transferred from the 29th BG, a training group, to the newly formed 100th BG (H) (H for *Heavy*, which indicated B-17s or B24s), which was then being staffed for overseas assignment.

Several weeks earlier, a small cadre of officers and enlisted men had been transferred from Gowen Field to Walla Walla, Washington, to form the nucleus of the 100th BG that had been authorized by the USAAF in June 1942. At Walla Walla, senior ground staff positions were filled and four squadron commanders were appointed. Four aircrews, one for each squadron, were assigned to the 100th. It so happened that the aircrew for the 350th Bomb Squadron[1] was headed by Norman Hugh Scott, the copilot from my training crew at Sebring, who had by then become a B-17 instructor pilot.

A USAAF bomb group in the Second World War consisted of four squadrons, and each squadron possessed from nine to twelve aircraft. Three of these squadrons were numbered sequentially, but the fourth was given an entirely unrelated number. In the 100th BG, for example, the numbered squadrons were the 349th, 350th,

---

1. From this point forward, I will use the abbreviation **BS** for *Bomb Squadron*.

351st, and the 418th. It was my understanding that this numbering system dated back to a time when an Army Air Corps combat air group consisted of three operational squadrons and one reconnaissance squadron. By 1942, however, this antiquated unit numbering system was meaningless, as there was no reconnaissance squadron in a heavy bomb group and all squadrons were line units.

When the crew assignments were posted on the bulletin boards, I was listed as navigator on Crew No. 31 of the 418th BS. My first official involvement with my new unit was at an assembly of all newly assigned ground and flight personnel. This meeting took place in the plain wooden auditorium-style post theater at Gowen Field on the morning of November 15, 1942. We were there to hear introductory remarks by our new commander, Colonel Darr Alkire.

The meeting began as all such meetings usually began. At the appointed hour of assembly, from amid the coughing, laughter, buzz of aimless conversation, and the shuffling of feet came a loud cry of "Ten-hut!" We leaped to our feet. Out from the right wing of the stage, a neatly dressed officer of medium height with cropped graying hair and a slightly thickening waistline strode briskly to a lectern at center stage. Colonel Alkire's message was short, sober, and straightforward. He told us that the job we had ahead of us was neither glorious nor glamorous; it was going to be difficult, dangerous, and distasteful. He told us that we should disabuse ourselves of any idea that it would be otherwise. He warned us that our survival would depend on the state of our combat readiness.

The following day, I met the other three officers on my crew in the Operations Room at Gowen Field. We were strangers. None of us had met previously, even casually, as we moved about the base. I was the only one from the South and the youngest of the four. I also was the first to have been commissioned, even though the others had been in the USAAF longer. The reason was my early departure from Maxwell Field after a minimum of preflight training and the fact that I had never been scheduled for pilot training.

The pilot, Lieutenant Charles Cruikshank, then and forever after known as "Crankshaft," was a trim, to-the-point New Englander from Everett, Massachusetts. He was several years older than me and somewhat shorter. He spoke in terse, cryptic phrases in a clipped Yankee accent and reminded me of a peppery bantam boxer. I was not sure what to make of him. Down South, we do not always come to the point quickly; we can be direct, but we can also beat around the bush for a bit if doing so seems appropriate. I was soon to learn, however, that his tart New England accent could be misleading. Charlie Cruikshank was a talented, skillful pilot. He was also calm, steady, and even-tempered under stress. I believe the only statement of disappointment I ever heard him make was that the army had seen fit to make him a bomber pilot. He had graduated from the single-engine flying school at Spence Field, Moultrie, Georgia, and had hoped to be a fighter pilot. But the army, in its usual inscrutable fashion, sent him to B-17 school. Disappointment at being assigned to bombers was common in those days. When the United States entered the Second World War, the legacy of the First World War and the more recent Battle of Britain was that fighter pilots were the daring heroes of the air. Clearly, most of the young men entering army aviation at that time wanted to be pilots first and fighter pilots second, not the drivers of what they saw as a plodding, uninteresting bomber. However, as bomber aircraft and bomber crews attained recognition, this view almost completely disappeared.

Charles Bean Cruikshank was born on February 12, 1917, in West Medford, Massachusetts, into a family of Scottish ancestry. At the age of three, he moved with his family to Everett, Massachusetts, where he attended public schools. He graduated with honors from high school in June 1935 and entered the workforce at the height of the Depression in heavily industrialized New England. The only work he could find was as a milkman. However, in 1935, he also joined the Massachusetts National Guard, where he was active as a radio operator until 1940. Having attained the rank of sergeant, he sought and was given a release from the National Guard to attend prep school on a part-time basis to prepare for the Army Air Corps exam that could qualify him an appointment as an aviation cadet. He took and passed the aviation cadet exam and was ordered to report to Maxwell Field in November for his preflight indoctrination.

In January 1942, Charlie Cruikshank was sent to a civilian primary flying school in Camden, South Carolina, where he learned to fly in a Stearman PT-17 trainer. In March 1942, he was transferred to Shaw Field, Sumter, South Carolina, for two months of basic training in BT-13 aircraft. From Sumter, he went, in May 1942, to the Air Corps Advanced Flying School at Spence Field, Moultrie, Georgia, where student pilots progressed from simply flying an airplane to becoming proficient in formation flying, military tactics, gunnery, navigation, and night operations. On August 4, 1942, Charlie graduated from the school at Moultrie and was commissioned a second lieutenant in the USAAF.

On August 15, 1942, the day after I left the USAAF Combat Crew School at Sebring, Florida, Charlie Cruikshank arrived in Sebring for B-17 training. He remained in Sebring until October 15, 1942, when he was sent to Gowen Field as a B-17 instructor pilot. When the 100th BG was activated and was being staffed in Boise in November 1942, Charlie Cruikshank volunteered to join the group.

The leadership and command responsibilities of an American bomber pilot during the Second World War can probably best be described as ephemeral in terms of history. In no war before or since have American strike aircraft carried the large, specialized aircrews that manned the strategic bombers that were so much a part of the 1941–45 war. The standard B-17 crew of ten men was similar to an infantry squad in numbers, but in no other way. The four men in the forward section of the aircraft—two pilots, the navigator, and the bombardier—were responsible for delivering bombs on target. All were commissioned officers and could, credibly, claim equal importance to the accomplishment of the mission. The six men in the rear of the aircraft were all noncommissioned officers, who, although they had technical duties, were essentially responsible for defending the aircraft against enemy attack.

The pilot, logically, and regardless of rank, was the head of the crew and, in official terminology, was the "aircraft commander." He was the person through whom senior officers officially communicated with the crew. The crew was generally referred to by the surname of the first pilot. It was only on the official group roster that we were Crew No. 31; for every other purpose we were the "Cruikshank crew." In all matters regarding operation and control of the aircraft and safety of flight, it was implicitly understood that the orders of the pilot had to be obeyed. Otherwise, his command responsibilities were perhaps something of a mixed blessing: while the pilot's duties, responsibilities, and accountability for his actions were generally clear, his command authority was not.

An American bomber pilot in the Second World War was not comparable to a ship's captain who could issue orders and retire to his quarters. The bomber pilot was a full-time, hands-on, working member of a mutually reliant team of young men operating a complex machine. He was generally unable, especially in combat, to observe the activities of the rest of the crew, much less direct and control them. In a large, tight formation of aircraft, the principal duty of the pilot was to maintain his position in the group formation; "leadership" and "commanding" happened entirely inside his airplane. It was not through leading or commanding but rather through the display of courage, competence, and levelheadedness in a crisis that the pilot gave the crew morale and infused it with a sense of duty and confidence in their performance. These were the traits that characterized the pilots who had the respect of their crews. Charlie Cruikshank had the respect of every member of his crew.

The copilot on the crew was Lieutenant Charles "Chuck" Mertz from Omaha, Nebraska, who had just graduated from pilot training in Texas. He would be with us until March 1943 when, because of circumstances I will describe later, he was sent off for first pilot training. My memories of Chuck Mertz are hazy except that before the war he had been an executive secretary for the president of the Union Pacific Railroad. I had never heard of a male secretary. Chuck explained that most of his working time was spent traveling in his employer's private railcar at a time when no respectable young lady would have considered such an arrangement.

The crew's bombardier was Lieutenant August Gaspar, who was sometimes called "Gus" and sometimes "Augie," a strikingly good-looking, black-haired, free spirit from Oakland, California, who had an irrepressible streak of unorthodoxy in him. Along with Charlie Cruikshank and me, Gus would remain with the crew until the end. Gus had what from all appearances seemed to be an uncontrollable penchant for striding through the squadron area with his overseas cap perched crosswise on his head, much to the dismay of John Egan, our squadron commander, and other senior officers. However, when reprimanded or told to correct what, in those days, was described as his "raunchy" behavior, no one could fling a "fuck you" salute in the direction of a departing superior officer better than Gus.[2] He had worked for a bakery in Oakland before the war

---

2. Augie would snap to an exaggerated version of attention, standing stiffly erect, back arched, shoulders thrown back, and chin pressed against his chest. He would bring his right

and regularly had boxes of delicious cookies sent to him by his old company, which he made available to one and all. I shall never forget how appalled I was watching him shave each morning. He would take his electric razor and go to work on his wiry, dark beard with such fierce determination that I was certain that in the end he would be a bloody mess. Gus was an unselfish friend, ever a pleasure to be with. As he later demonstrated, he was also consistently and extraordinarily courageous under fire.

Augie Gaspar first enriched the world with his presence on March 30, 1917. He grew up in Oakland and attended St. Anthony's High School and St. Mary's College, in both Berkeley and Moraga, California; at the latter, he was junior class president in 1939. Thereafter, being short of the money he needed to complete college, he went to work for the Langendorf Baking Company in Oakland and was supervising a production line when the war broke out in December 1941. Because he wanted to fly, Augie volunteered for the army's aviation cadet program and was accepted. He was sent to Hamilton Field, near San Francisco, for preflight school and to the Oxnard Flying Academy, Oxnard, California, for primary pilot training. As only Augie could relate it, he said he was dropped from the pilot program after "bouncing my instructor out of a Stearman PT-17." He was then sent to the USAAF Center at Santa Ana, California, for reassignment, and from Santa Ana he was sent to the army bombardier school at Victorville, California. He graduated and was appointed a second lieutenant on Halloween, October 31, 1942. Following his graduation, Augie was ordered to report to the Second AF at Salt Lake City, Utah.

---

hand smartly to his brow, but with the palm facing up rather than down. He would then fling his right hand with all his might in the direction of his departing superior with a twisting motion, lurching, staggering, and falling all over himself in the process.

In November 1942, he was assigned to B-17s and sent to Gowen Field, where, within days, he was posted to the 100th BG.

Until the final months of 1943, the success or failure of all USAAF strategic bombing thinking and planning depended on the Norden bombsight designed by Mr. C. L. Norden for the U.S. Navy in the early 1930s but quickly adopted by the Army Air Corps. Using this bombsight, a qualified bombardier was supposed to be capable of dropping a bomb into a pickle barrel from an airplane flying at twenty thousand feet. The Norden bombsight was highly secret and was never to be left unguarded, not even for a moment. Each bombardier, always armed, carried his bombsight in a canvas bag. The bag was to be opened only in a training center or in an airplane. The bombardier was forbidden to discuss the bombsight with unauthorized persons, and if shot down, he was to make every effort to destroy it. I have vivid recollections of standing behind Augie in the B-17, watching him on his bombardier's perch, bent over his bombsight intently twirling knobs and flipping switches on the electrical control panel to his left until "bombs away."

We were introduced to the six sergeants assigned to our crew when we all gathered at the flight line for our first flight together. Two of these men would shortly leave us as normal reassignments and personal requests for crew changes were made. The other four remained with the crew until the end.

The radio operator, who would be one of the permanent members of the crew, was Technical Sergeant Orlando Vincenti, a quiet, intelligent, soft-spoken, polite fellow from Carbondale, Pennsylvania. He possessed intelligent brown eyes and an easy smile. During our long association, I never heard him use profanity, raise his voice to anyone, or lose his self-control. His goal, he said, was to complete his combat tour, enter the army aviation cadet program, and become a pilot. He never achieved that goal because his life ended on our last mission.

The radio operator on a B-17 aircraft was one of two highly trained and specialized noncommissioned officers on the crew, the other being the flight engineer, the flying crew chief. The radio operator was the airplane's contact with the outside world. Although he principally operated the long-range HF liaison radio set, through his several radio sets came all orders, warnings, changes, and other messages; out through his radios went all messages from the ship and its crew. Orlando Vincenti had completed the USAAF rigorous eighteen-week radio school. He was first-rate in his understanding of everything from Morse code and code typing to direct and alternating current circuits, transmitters, and receivers, and he could operate and repair every piece of the extensive radio equipment on a B-17.

The ball turret gunner was a gangling, rail-thin, laconic Westerner, Sergeant Robert Bixler from Bisbee, Arizona. He was probably the crew member most devoted to sensual pleasures—every crew had one, I suppose—who never missed a chance to go to the nearest town wherever we were. I thought this was understandable. To me, he had the loneliest, most difficult position on the crew. The bottom turret on the B-17 was the devil's own device. While hanging dangerously beneath the airplane, twisting and turning, the B-17 ball turret operator had to work furiously to keep his optical, mirrored gunsights fixed on fast-closing enemy fighters. It required a contortionist to fit into this turret, which I considered impossible to climb into and out of in an emergency.

Our right waist gunner was Sergeant James Johnson of Lamar, Oklahoma. Imperturbable and never excited, he wisely listened more than he spoke. But, like most of us in those days, he did not have to identify himself over the intercom, as we all quickly learned who had the Oklahoma twang, the terse Massachusetts tones, the Southern drawl, and so on. Eventually, we would observe the time-honored custom in the military of derisively imitating conventional versions of the colloquialisms and dialects of people in the various regions of the country from which our crew members came. Being from the South, if I did not get my fair share of y'alls and y'heahs in this give-and-take banter, something was wrong. Gus never tired of aping Charlie Cruikshank's Boston accent when calling for "half flaps" from the copilot on takeoffs and landings. To Gus, it always came out "haahf flops."

The permanent member of the crew with the second-loneliest job was Sergeant Charles Clark from Highland Park, Illinois, our tail gunner. He had to crawl to his cramped station just below the trailing edge of the huge rudder, and it was in that isolated and lonely part of the airplane that he died on our last mission. Small and slender, he stood no more than five feet, six inches tall. I remember him as impish, droll, and witty; but as he looks down at me from his pictures on my wall a half century later, I see a hauntingly wistful look on his face. It is the expression of a young man destined to never grow old.

When we went to Wendover at the end of November 1943, our first replacement crew member was a reddish-blond-haired, square-jawed, neat, energetic technical sergeant by the name of Leonard Weeks. He was from Elkins, West Virginia, and he joined us as flight engineer. He wore his overseas cap at a dashing, rakish angle and was assiduously efficient. When we had a problem with an airplane, Leonard Weeks knew what to do and how to do it.

As I have said, the flight engineer on a B-17 aircraft and the radio operator were highly trained specialists; they were both technical sergeants, and although they were aerial gunners when the airplane was under attack, aerial gunnery was the least of their responsibilities. Flight engineers were selected by the USAAF for their intelligence and mechanical aptitude. They were sent to army schools for eighteen weeks to study aircraft structures, aircraft systems, propellers, engines, and aircraft inspection and maintenance. The flight engineer flew with the airplane and, apart from monitoring systems performance, was fully capable of helping the pilot and copilot in operation of the flaps and landing gear and other mechanical operations. When it was away from its home base, the engineer supervised the ground maintenance of the airplane. With Leonard Weeks, we thought we had the best.

Our second and last replacement crew member until Chuck Mertz left us several months later was our left waist gunner, Sergeant Donald Garrison from Eldorado, Illinois. He was spare of build, nimble, sure-handed, consistently competent, and unfailingly attentive and precise in the performance of his duties. Later, there would be one critical action Don never failed to perform for Gus and me. Before each combat mission, he thoroughly inspected and verified the proper functioning of the flexible .50-caliber machine guns operated by the bombardier and navigator in the forward fuselage of the B-17F. Navigators and bombardiers received instruction on loading and firing the flexible .50-caliber machine gun and the basic principles of sighting, deflection, and bullet trajectory using the ring-and-bead sight. Unlike our trained gunners, however, we were not taught to assemble and disassemble these weapons or how to rectify problems with them.

Our four aerial gunners, Bob Bixler, Charles Clark, Don Garrison, and James Johnson, were, until we were committed to combat, essentially along for the ride. I did not yet appreciate that no fighting men in military service anywhere, anytime, would be more deserving of respect than the tough, courageous aerial gunners who manned American heavy bombers during the Second World War. They were enlisted men, not officers. They were all volunteers. Their prospects for advancement or promotion were virtually nonexistent.

Although they received extra pay, the risks they took were all out of proportion to their military ratings or pay. Their job was difficult mentally and physically, and fraught with the danger of injury or death, almost always deep in enemy territory. Of these four men, one was killed in action and the other three received Purple Hearts for their wounds. The gunners were usually slender or small because of the cramped areas in which they worked, especially in the power turrets and tail gun positions of all heavy bombers. They operated flexible machine guns mounted in large open ports in unheated airplanes in the thin atmosphere up to five miles above the earth, where outside air temperatures were forty to fifty degrees below zero, where frostbite was as sinister and menacing as attacks by determined Luftwaffe fighter pilots. This was an inhospitable environment where our lifelines were the essential, uncomfortable oxygen masks we wore for hours on end. The gunners had sharp eyes. They were required to meet the same physical standards as flying officers. A pilot or navigator might be able to avoid combat by being assigned to the ferry or transport command, but the aerial gunner who successfully completed his training *was* going into combat!

Our commanders wasted no time initiating crew training. In the brief time remaining for us at Gowen Field, as November came to a close, we flew three to five hours almost daily. We spent a lot of time shooting touch-and-go takeoffs and landings, primarily for the benefit of our pilots, Charlie Cruikshank and Chuck Mertz. We also made day and night dry runs over Nampa and Pocatello, Idaho, for Augie Gaspar. A *dry run* was a bombing run using the bombsight and following all required procedures up to "bombs away," except that there were no bombs in our bomb bays. When the 100th BG began its transfer to Wendover Field on November 27, 1942, I was already experiencing a strong sense of identification with men I had met only a few days earlier and with whom I would later go into combat.

6

THE 100TH STUMBLES

The 100th BG only had four airplanes when we transferred from Gowen Field to Wendover Army Air Base, Utah, in December 1942. They were flown to our new base by the four aircrews originally assigned to the group in Walla Walla, Washington. The remaining aircrews and all ground personnel traveled by train. We rode in dilapidated, hard-riding railroad cars that had neither springs nor cushions. We were sure they had been reclaimed from some long-abandoned railroad boneyard just to make our lives miserable.

Wendover itself was a godforsaken, uninviting moonscape of a place built on the edge of the Bonneville Salt Flats and enclosed on three sides by inhospitable, dingy brown and gray hills. The base was situated just inside Utah on the Utah/Nevada state line, approximately 125 miles west of Salt Lake City. This was the perfect location for bomber crew training: there was nothing there. The only visible signs of civilization, even from the air, were thin ribbons of concrete highways running east and west from the base alongside disappearing lines of telephone poles and a small, shabby, and thoroughly disreputable bar and gambling casino on the Nevada side of the state line. It was, of course, off-limits to military personnel.

Although the base was relatively new, having opened only eight months before we arrived, it already had a run-down and neglected look. Our living quarters and all other facilities except for the hangars and shops were shabby, one-story wood-and-tarpaper shacks heated by potbellied stoves. The surrounding landscape was equally depressing because there wasn't a blade of grass, bush, or tree on the entire reservation. Except for a plainly furnished officers' club, we had no recreational facilities. To its credit, the club did have a well-stocked bar and did a booming business every night. Sometimes it did too much business. For example, on the afternoon of January 1, 1943, the base commander finally had enough and ordered the bar shut down and the club locked down to put an end to the New Year's Eve celebrating that began early the previous evening.

Some twenty additional B-17F aircraft were delivered for our use shortly after we arrived at Wendover. However, flying conditions were rarely ideal and could even be quite treacherous. The perennially slate-colored winter sky could disappear quickly when fast-moving, dark, angry, low-lying storm clouds blew in and settled among the peaks that rimmed the base. These conditions cost us; on December 23, 1942, Crew No. 32 of the 418th BS, flying B-17 serial number 42-5291, encountered deep, dense clouds and snow east of Salt Lake City and ran out of gas in an effort to find clear air.[1] The pilot, Lieutenant John Brady, was forced to make a belly landing in a field near Rock Springs, Wyoming. No one was injured, but the airplane was damaged beyond repair and had to be written off. The navigator on that crew was my colleague Lieutenant Harry Crosby, who, after the war, would become the most famous

---

1. The American serial number system involves a prefix and a suffix. For example **42-30062**, the **42** prefix notes that the contract to build the aircraft was signed in 1942, and the **30062** suffix refers to the 30,062nd airframe of all types of aircraft contracted to be built. The "serial number" **42-30062** was compressed into the "tail number" **230062**, and applied to either side of the vertical stabilizer. Historical documentation may refer to this aircraft as **42-30062, 230062,** or simply as **062**. Unless spelled out directly, "tail numbers" and not "serial numbers" will be used throughout this monograph.

air crewman in the 100th BG, if not in the Eighth AF. That same day, a second airplane from the 100th, serial number 42-5349, ran out of gas in heavy weather and undershot an emergency landing field near Mount Pleasant, Utah. This ship, however, was recovered and repaired.

Crew No. 31 had anxious moments of its own. One night in mid-December, we were in the midst of making nighttime dry bombing runs in the desert between Wendover and Salt Lake City when we unexpectedly found ourselves enveloped by thick clouds. After a few turns and changes of altitude, and after traveling short distances this way and that, we were still encased in the clouds. Crankshaft turned on his landing lights, but all we saw was an opaque fog all around us. No horizon and no reference points could be seen; we were in a deep cloud base, and we were in deep trouble. I had been keeping track of our position as best I could, and I knew that we were flying at least several thousand feet *below* the peaks of mountains that were only a few miles to the north and south of us. I told Crankshaft I believed we had enough open air around us that if we immediately commenced to climb in a reasonably tight circular pattern we could get above the mountaintops and set a course for Wendover. If the weather did not improve, he could then make an instrument letdown over the salt flats in hopes that we could make a visual landing approach. Fortunately, we broke into clear air before we reached Wendover.

Despite these weather problems, the aircrews of the 100th accomplished more effective training at Wendover Field than at any of the bases to which we were subsequently sent, particularly with respect to bombing and gunnery. The Cruikshank crew flew almost eighty two hours over nineteen separate days in December 1942, including five hours each on Christmas Eve, Christmas Day, and New Year's Eve.

The bombing ranges laid out in the nearby Bonneville Salt Flats were excellent. They were in empty, desolate desert areas. Each target consisted of three concentric circles with a bull's-eye in the center that was easily visible in clear weather from an airplane flying at any altitude. We made repeated bombing runs over these targets using the Norden bombsight, dropping one-hundred-pound practice bombs. The explosions on the ground told us immediately how close Augie came to the bull's-eye.

We also flew numerous air-to-ground gunnery missions at Wendover, firing at targets positioned on the steep sides of hills in remote areas away from the base and, on at least one occasion, had an opportunity to practice air-to-air gunnery by shooting at a towed-sleeve target pulled by another airplane. While no B-17 crew expected to engage in air-to-ground gunnery in actual combat, these missions gave navigators and bombardiers the only chance we would have to become familiar with the feel of the heavy .50-caliber machine guns on the B-17. It gave us the opportunity to learn the correct procedures for loading, charging, and firing these essentially uncontrollable guns in short bursts. We were also sent to the rifle and pistol ranges and, to give us a sense of lead and timing, to a skeet shooting facility where we were taught how to aim and how far to fire ahead of flying targets crossing in front of us, moving away, or rising or falling.

We also had our lighter moments. One morning, the 418th BS ground crews noticed a male mallard duck waddling strangely around and under our airplanes. When approached, the duck made a strenuous effort to scramble away but did not attempt to fly. When our flight line crews finally caught the duck and examined him, they found that he had a broken wing. He was immediately taken into custody for treatment by our medics. In short order, the duck became a major topic of conversation. One flight crew actually took the duck up in a B-17 and let him sit on the bombardier's perch in the Plexiglas nose of the airplane. When the duck finally appeared capable of flying again, he was released. At that point, one of our talented artists, probably Lieutenant Ernie Warsaw, the navigator on Captain Bob Knox's Crew No. 36, penned a drawing of a duck wearing a radio headset while sitting inside a cracked egg with bomb fins attached. This drawing was quickly accepted as the 418th BS insignia. The drawing was reproduced in color on the leather patches, which were sewn on the front of our A-2 flying jackets by most of the 418th flying personnel. This duck logo remained the 418th BS insignia for the rest of the war.

Colonel Alkire and our senior commanders were aware of our harsh circumstances at Wendover and were liberal with weekend passes during December 1942. We usually went in small groups to Salt Lake City. On one of these trips, I bought my mother a Christmas present from a small jeweler across the street from the Utah Hotel. It was an inexpensive rose-gold Bulova lady's watch with tiny red stones at the six and twelve o'clock positions and a chocolate-colored cloth band. I put the watch in a box of personal items I sent home by way of the Railway Express Agency. Although she had much finer jewelry, my mother wore that modest watch every day for the rest of her life.

During the first week of January 1943, the 100th BG was transferred again, lock, stock, and barrel, to the Sioux City Army Air Base, Iowa. The aircrews were briefed to use our ferry flight to Sioux City as a navigation training flight. On January 2, 1943, Crew No. 31 flew cross-country from Wendover to Davis-Monthan Field, Tucson, Arizona, where we managed to stay overnight at the plush El Conquistador Hotel. The following day, we flew to Pueblo, Colorado. During this flight, I saw for the first time Arizona's awesome, magnificent Grand Canyon, cleaved out of hard rock over a period of a billion and a half years by the relentless flow of the Colorado River. From the air, the canyon's irregular steep walls resembled the inside of a huge cake that had been carelessly broken apart, revealing that it had been created by successive thin layers of red-, purple-, orange-, and yellow-colored rock applied over the ages. The winter snow that defined its exposed ledges and blanketed the subpeaks, surrounding plateaus, and tree-covered hillsides resembled white frosting on a cake.

On January 4, 1943, we flew on to Sioux City Army Air Base.

For the aircrews of the 100th BG, Sioux City itself was heaven compared to Wendover, and its facilities were infinitely superior. Iowa's winter weather, however, was next to intolerable. I thought that Sioux City in January 1943 was, without a doubt, the coldest place on the face of the earth. High temperatures often hovered around zero or below. There were days when the temperature measured thirty degrees below zero. When walking outside, we wore our heaviest clothing and wrapped our faces with wool scarves to avoid frostbite. The ground was never clear of snow, and snowdrifts as high as twelve feet piled up against every building or standing structure on the base. There were days when it was impossible for the ground crews to service our airplanes because of the weather. On the coldest days, we were unable to start the engines on our airplanes even with the use of heaters.

But we made the most of it. Crew No. 31 logged almost fifty hours of flying time at Sioux City in January 1943, much of it, unfortunately, of little value. There were no bombing or gunnery ranges at Sioux City, and flying in unheated airplanes in subfreezing weather was a miserable experience. Although it afforded me occasional but limited opportunities to hone my navigation skills, a good part of our flying time at Sioux City was spent swooping low over snow-covered prairies in Iowa and South Dakota terrorizing herds of cows. It was simply too cold to fly at high altitudes unless there was a compelling reason for doing so. I do not recall a single occasion on which we found a compelling reason to fly above ten thousand feet, where we would have to use oxygen.

I completed my first year in the army at Sioux City in January 1943 amid speculation and predictions that this would be the last of our stateside stations before the group was processed and staged for overseas assignment. I must have given that impression in my letters and phone conversations with my mother because, private person though she was, she boarded a train in Atlanta one weekend and made the long, arduous trip to Sioux City. She came to see me and to meet my crewmates, all of whom she had come to know on a first-name basis through our various communications. She received her wish. One bitterly cold evening, all the officers and several of our noncommissioned officers on Crew No. 31 drove in from the air base and had dinner with my mom at her hotel. A few of them later sent her letters, especially Charlie Cruikshank, who wrote her regularly for the rest of the war, usually telling her, like a big brother, that he was doing his best to keep me out of trouble. When I hugged my mother and told her goodbye at the Sioux City train station at the end of her visit, both of us silently believed that it would be sometime in the indefinite future before we would see each other again. Fortunately, that was not to be the case.

We were also wrong in our speculation about an impending overseas assignment. The axe fell at the end of January when higher authorities at Second AF, under whose jurisdiction we were being trained, informed Colonel Alkire that, while the aircrews of the 100th had completed its prescribed training program, we had not been certified as "combat-ready" for overseas duty. Not only that, there was talk that the 100th would be disbanded and its crews assigned as replacement crews for bomb groups already overseas. The suggestion that the group would be split up was vigorously opposed by Colonel Alkire and our other senior commanders. Finally, in a conciliatory gesture, the USAAF agreed that the 100th BG would not be dissolved but that its aircrews would be spread over eight Second AF bases for additional training. Along with other crews of the 418th BS, Crew No. 31 would go to Casper Army Air Base, Wyoming.

I have never read or been told the reasons for the refusal of Second AF evaluators to certify the 100th BG as combat-ready in January 1943. Clearly, their findings were discussed in detail with Colonel Alkire and his staff. But the decision to fragment the group and dispatch its crews to eight different air bases for further training was not the answer to our problems, whatever they were. There was no internal dissension within the 100th, and group morale was high. The 100th aircrews uniformly liked and respected Colonel Darr "Pappy" Alkire and by January 1943 had developed a camaraderie and esprit de corps that extended across squadron lines. The 418th crews got on well with our squadron commander, Major Robert Flesher, and especially with our laid-back, approachable operations officer, the elfin Captain Albert "Bucky" Elton, a wisp of a man who was also from Atlanta, Georgia. Bucky Elton was so short, his feet would barely touch his rudder pedals when he sat in the pilot's seat of a B-17. In retrospect, it would seem axiomatic that no military unit at the core of a strike force that was designed to fight as one unit, such as a heavy bomb group, could train effectively if its component parts were spread over eight bases from Nebraska to California. Ultimately, this cure would prove to be worse than the disease.

Entirely apart from the recurring heavy snows, pitiless penetrating cold, and the harsh, inclement weather that plagued us during

the winter of 1943, neither Sioux City nor Casper had the bombing and gunnery ranges that had been available to us at Wendover.
More important, it must be added that the most urgent training
requirement for the 100th at the time, which was precluded by the
scattering of our aircrews to widely separated bases, was the need
for our pilots to practice close formation flying in a large group of
eighteen to twenty-one aircraft. It was the end goal of every heavy
bomb group commander in the USAAF to have his group maintain
the most compact formation possible in combat to achieve concentrated defensive firepower and produce tight bombing patterns.
Close formation flying required smooth, steady turns by the leader
to ease the constant, tiring jockeying of throttles and controls by
the pilots of the aircraft behind. Every wingman in a flight of three
aircraft was expected to stay so "tucked in" on his flight leader that,
in a manner of speaking, he could stick his wingtip into the open
waist gun port of his lead pilot. It was a task that demanded skill,
concentration, practice, and more practice.

During the winter of 1943, it became more and more evident
to us why the USAAF should have located its year-round training
bases in the South. On February 2, 1943, Crew No. 31 flew from
Sioux City to high, wide, and windy Casper Army Air Base, Wyoming, another deep freeze where the daily low temperatures hovered around zero and frequently went much lower. Just thirty-five
miles north of Casper was Teapot Dome, a rich oil field made no-
torious during President Warren Harding's administration in the
1920s, when the secretary of the interior accepted a $100,000 bribe
and illegally leased government oil reserves to private companies.
The Supreme Court later took Teapot Dome out of private hands
and restored it to government control. This was probably the major
American political scandal of the twentieth century up to that time.
I had read about it in school and heard my father speak of it.

We did no flying at Casper during the last three weeks of February and managed only nineteen hours in March, most of which was spent ferrying two B-17 aircraft from Casper to the air depot at Tinker Field, Oklahoma City, for modifications, and one cross-country flight to Colorado Springs, Colorado. Nevertheless, we were once again in an airman's mecca, and the aircrews loved Casper. The local population was hospitable, and the town was alive with bars, theaters, and a variety of places of entertainment. The Townsend Hotel on Center Street set aside one of its meeting rooms as an officers' club. A Wurlitzer jukebox with red, blue, and yellow neon-lighted piping blared the popular songs of the day: the Harry James Orchestra with Helen Forrest singing "I've Heard That Song Before," the Tommy Dorsey Orchestra playing Sy Oliver's driving arrangement of "Mandy," and, of course, "In The Mood," "Serenade in Blue," and "A String of Pearls" by the phenomenally successful Glenn Miller Orchestra that would go on to become one of the great legends of American popular culture.

We had our last crew change in March 1943. At that time, the USAAF Training Command realized that the copilots on 100th BG aircrews had accumulated much higher than normal flying time for copilots in B-17 aircraft and reassigned all the group's copilots, including Chuck Mertz, for training as first pilots. For replacements, they brought in forty new pilots who had recently graduated from the multiengine flight school in Class 43-B at Moody Field, Valdosta, Georgia. The new copilot assigned to Crew No. 31 was Lieutenant Glenn E. Graham, who was originally from Freedom, Pennsylvania.

At the age of twenty-four, Glenn Graham instantly became the "old man" of our crew. Not only had his dark hairline begun to recede, he had developed a small bald spot on the crown of his head and, in addition, had joined the army in 1938 and served as an en-

Frank's childhood home on Atlanta Avenue.
Murphy Collection

Brother Michael, Frank, and their mother (circa 1923).
Murphy Collection

Frank's paternal grandparents Phoebe Ann Parsons Murphy and William Patrick Murphy.
Murphy Collection

Frank's maternal grandmother Ida Nix Gidish (circa 1920s).
Murphy Collection

Frank's mother, Mary Sibyl Gidish Murphy, wearing Air Force Navigator Wings during Second World War.
Murphy Collection

Frank's father, Michael Vincent Murphy, during Second World War.
Murphy Collection

Frank's German-born maternal grandfather, John Ludwig Gidish, who immigrated to the United States in 1883. *Murphy Collection*

Frank Murphy, age 3 or 4. *Murphy Collection*

Emory University Emory Aces dance band in 1941, with Frank playing saxophone on far right. *Murphy Collection*

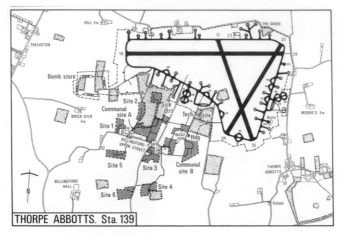

THORPE ABBOTTS. Sta. 139

Source: Roger A. Freeman with drawing by Norman Ottaway, *Mighty Eighth War Manual*, page 283.

Aviation cadet Frank standing with his mother, Maxwell Field, February 1942.
Murphy Collection

Frank with his father in home backyard, May 1942.
Murphy Collection

Lt. Frank D.
Murphy, July 1942.
Murphy Collection

Crew 31, Gowen Field, Idaho, November 1942. Standing, left to right: Lt.
Charles Mertz (copilot), Lt. Augie Gaspar (bombardier), Lt. Frank Murphy
(navigator), and Lt. Charles Cruikshank (pilot). Kneeling, left to right: T/Sgt.
Orlando Vincenti (radio operator), S/Sgt. Charles Clark (tail gunner), S/Sgt.
Robert Bixler (ball turret gunner), S/Sgt. Robert Lepper (flight engineer), S/
Sgt. Pepper and S/Sgt. James Johnson (waist gunners).
Murphy Collection

Lt. Frank Murphy at
Wendover Army Air Base,
Utah, December 1942.
Murphy Collection

Casper, Wyoming, February 1943, left to right: Lt. John Dennis, navigator on Lt. Pete Biddick's crew, unknown lady, Lt. Frank Murphy, and Lt. Charles Cruikshank. Lt. Dennis shot down on August 17, 1943 Regensburg mission.
Charles Cruikshank Collection

Standing, left to righ: S/Sgt James Johnson, S/Sgt. Don Garrison, and T/Sgt. Orlando Vincenti. Kneeling is Lt. Augie Gaspar.
Courtesy of the 100th Bomb Group Foundation

Lt. Charles Cruikshank in front of B-17.
Courtesy of the 100th Bomb Group Foundation

S/Sgt. Robert Bixler, Crew 31
tail gunner.
Charles Cruikshank Collection

Members of Crew 31 in front of
Bastard's Bungalow (230062), left
to right: T/Sgt. Orlando Vincenti,
T/Sgt. Leonard Weeks,
S/Sgt. Don Garrison,
and S/Sgt. James Johnson.
Murphy Collection

Sitting on jeep, left to right: Lt. Frank Murphy and Lt. Charles Cruikshank. Standing far right is Capt. Albert "Bucky" Elton, 418th Sq. Operations Officer. Others kneeling and sitting, left to right: Lt. Augie Gaspar, Lt. Glenn Graham, and Lt. Burr, 418th Sq. Intelligence Officer. *Murphy Collection*

Lt. Gen. James "Jimmy" Doolittle and Maj. Gen. Curtis LeMay in England. *Courtesy of the 100th Bomb Group Foundation*

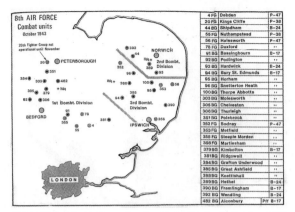

8th AIR FORCE
Combat units
October 1943

20th Fighter Group not
operational until November

4 FG	Debden	P-47
20 FG	Kings Cliffe	P-38
44 BG	Shipdham	B-24
55 FG	Nuthampsted	P-38
56 FG	Halesworth	P-47
78 FG	Duxford	''
91 BG	Bassingbourn	B-17
92 BG	Podington	''
93 BG	Hardwick	B-24
94 BG	Bury St. Edmunds	B-17
95 BG	Horham	''
96 BG	Snetterton Heath	''
100 BG	Thorpe Abbotts	''
303 BG	Molesworth	''
305 BG	Chelveston	''
306 BG	Thurleigh	''
351 BG	Polebrook	''
352 FG	Bodney	P-47
353 FG	Metfield	''
355 FG	Steeple Morden	''
356 FG	Martlesham	''
379 BG	Kimbolton	B-17
381 BG	Ridgewell	''
384 BG	Grafton Underwood	''
385 BG	Great Ashfield	''
388 BG	Knettishall	''
389 BG	Hethel	B-24
390 BG	Framlingham	B-17
392 BG	Wendling	B-24
482 BG	Alconbury	Pff B-17

USAAF Eighth Air Force Combat Units, England, October 1943.
Norman Ottaway

Photo featured in *Air Force Times*, December 1942. Clockwise from lower left: Lt. Charles Cruickshank, Lt. Frank Murphy, S/Sgt. Robert Bixler, S/Sgt. Charles Clark, T/Sgt. Leonard Weeks, T/Sgt. Orlando Vincenti, Lt. Augie Gaspar, S/Sgt. Donald Garrison, and S/Sgt. James Johnson. Lt. Glenn Graham is missing from photograph, and unknown officer pointing to map.
Murphy Collection

July 30, 1943, Kassel mission, when Frank flew with Lt. John Brady crew. Standing, left to right: S/Sgt. Joseph Hafer (radio operator), S/Sgt. James McCusker (waist gunner), S/Sgt. Adolph Blum (top turret engineer), S/Sgt. George Petrohelos (tail gunner), S/Sgt. Roland Gangwer (ball turret gunner) and S/Sgt Harold Clanton (waist gunner). Kneeling, left to right: Lt. John Hoerr (copilot), Lt. John Brady (pilot), Lt. Howard Hamilton (bombardier), and Lt. Frank Murphy (navigator).
Murphy Collection

S/Sgt. Donald Garrison, probably following the July 17, 1943 mission. *Murphy Collection*

S/Sgt. James Johnson, S/Sgt. Robert Bixler and T/Sgt. Orlando Vincenti. *Murphy Collection*

S/Sgt. Charles Clark and S/Sgt. James Johnson. *Murphy Collection*

The Robert Knox crew in front of *Picklepuss* (230063), the "legendary wheels down crew," shot down on August 17, 1943 Regensburg mission. Kneeling, left to right: Lt. Edwin Tobin, Capt. Robert Knox, Lt. Ernest Warsaw, Lt John Whitaker. Standing, left to right: S/Sgt Frank Tychewicz, T/Sgt Carl Simon, T/Sgt Walter Paulsen, Unknown, S/Sgt Malcolm Maddran, S/Sgt Joseph Laspada, S/Sgt Henry Norton, and unknown soldier. *Courtesy of the 100th Bomb Group Foundation*

B-17s on a bombing run under a heavy flak attack. *Courtesy of the 457th Bomb Group*

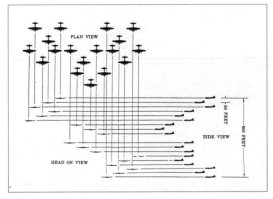

Source: Informational Intelligence Report No. 43–17, "German Fighter Tactics Against Flying Fortresses," 31 December 1943 and "Eighth Air Force Tactical Development, August 1942-May 1945," published July 1945.

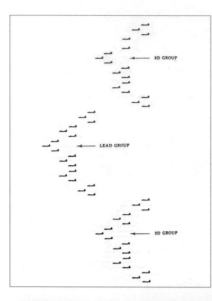

Source: Informational Intelligence Report No. 43-17, "German Fighter Tactics Against Flying Fortresses," 31 December 1943 and "Eighth Air Force Tactical Development, August 1942–May 1945," published July 1945.

Photograph Frank took of Lt. Owen "Cowboy" Roane's *Laden Maiden* (25861), foreground, and Lt. Henry Hennington's *Horny* (230611), August 17, 1943.
Murphy Collection

Photograph from Lt. Owen "Cowboy" Roane's *Laden Maiden* (25861): in the lead is Capt. Ev Blakely and Maj. John B. Kidd in *Just-A-Snappin'* (23393). On his left wing is Lt. John Brady's *Stymie* (23237) and on his right wing is Lt. Robert Wolff's *Wolff Pack* (230061). In lower left is Frank's aircraft on that day, *Mugwump* (230066).
Courtesy of the 100th Bomb Group Foundation

Photograph taken from *Just-A-Snappin'* (23393) August 17, 1943: the closest B-17 with damaged stabilizer is Lt. Robert Wolff's *Wolff Pack* (230061), above that are Lt. Owen "Cowboy" Roane's *Laden Maiden* (25861) and Lt. Henry Hennington's *Horny* (230611). The aircraft in lower right is *Mugwump* (230066) flown that day by Lt. Cruikshank crew. *Courtesy of the 100th Bomb Group Foundation*

Crew of Lt. Everett Blakely. Standing, left to right: S/Sgt William McClelland (ball turret gunner), Lt. Harry Crosby (navigator), Lt. Charles Via, Jr. (copilot), Lt. Everett Blakely (pilot) and Lt. James Douglas (bombardier). Kneeling, left to right: S/Sgt. Lester Saunders (waist gunner), T/Sgt. Monroe Thornton (top turret engineer), S/Sgt. Edward Yevich (waist gunner), S/Sgt. Lyle Nord (tail gunner) and T/Sgt. Edmund Forkner (radio operator). *Courtesy of the 100th Bomb Group Foundation*

Maj. John Egan, CO 418th Bomb Sq. and Maj. Gale Cleven, CO 350th Bomb Sq., both nicknamed "Bucky." *Courtesy of the 100th Bomb Group Foundation*

Regensburg on August 17, 1943, with the Danube River clearly visible.
Courtesy of the 100th Bomb Group Foundation

Left to right: S/Sgt. James Johnson, S/Sgt. Donald Garrison, Lt. Augie Gaspar, Lt. Frank Murphy, and Lt. Glenn Graham standing in front of *Torchy* (230035), August 24, 1943.
Courtesy of the 100th Bomb Group Foundation

Maj. John Egan and Crew 31 after the August 17, 1943, Regensburg mission. Standing, left to right: Lt. Augie Gaspar, S/Sgt. James Johnson, T/Sgt. Leonard Weeks, T/Sgt. Orlando Vincenti, S/Sgt. Donald Garrison, and Lt. Glenn Graham. Kneeling, left to right: Lt. Frank Murphy, an unknown crewman, Maj. John Egan, and Lt. Charles Cruikshank. Robert Bixler is missing from the photo.
Murphy Collection

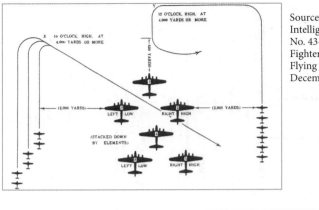

Source: Informational Intelligence Report No. 43-17, "German Fighter Tactics Against Flying Fortresses," 31 December 1943.

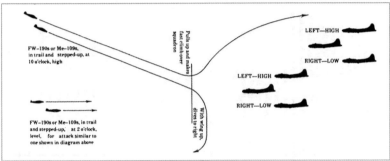

Source: Informational Intelligence Report No. 43-17, "German Fighter Tactics Against Flying Fortresses," 31 December 1943.

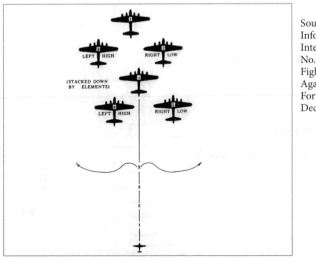

Source: Informational Intelligence Report No. 43-17, "German Fighter Tactics Against Flying Fortresses," 31 December 1943.

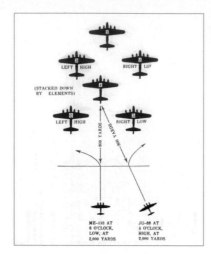

Source: Informational Intelligence Report No. 43-17, "German Fighter Tactics Against Flying Fortresses," 31 December 1943.

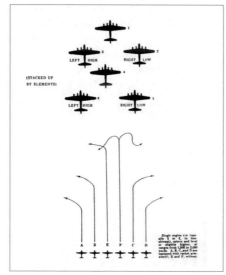

Source: Informational Intelligence Report No. 43-17, "German Fighter Tactics Against Flying Fortresses," 31 December 1943.

Source: Informational Intelligence Report No. 43-17, "German Fighter Tactics Against Flying Fortresses," 31 December 1943.

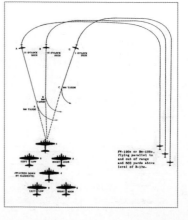

listed man in Panama and the United States before the war. He had been a radio operator on B-18 bombers and knew and had flown with many of our USAAF senior officers, including Major Curtis LeMay. When the army opened its doors to allow enlisted personnel who met the educational, mental, and physical standards for appointment as an aviation cadet, Glenn applied and was accepted.

Glenn was the only married man in the crew. His wife, Frances, was a lovely young lady from Arlington, Virginia, who visited him once after he joined our crew. If the rest of us engaged in banter, kidding around, or horseplay, Glenn would declare with feigned solemnity that the war had totally ruined the army and that he could not wait until it was over so that the army could get rid of us "college boys" and go back to being the "real army." This remark never failed to get a rise out of Augie: "The *real* army? The *real* army! Give me a break. You mean the palm tree, pineapple, and parade ground, weekend fuck-off army?" Both were smug, and the debate remained a dead heat between them.

As historian Stephen E. Ambrose has pointed out, the one obscenity that became a part of normal, everyday conversation in the USAAF, and possibly the navy, in the Second World War was the adjective form of the F-word. It was applied indiscriminately to the people and events perceived to be responsible for our problems and frustrations. It was always "the fucking Japs" or "the fucking Germans." It was even applied to things and people closer to home: "the fucking cooks," "the fucking post office," "the fucking weather," "the fucking generals," and so on.[2] Nobody noticed or even gave it a second thought.

One brilliant, starlit evening in late March 1943, some officers from the air base were invited to a cookout. Our host was an elderly gentleman who lived in a rustic home in a spectacular setting

---

2. Stephen E. Ambrose, *The Victors* (New York: Simon & Schuster, 1998), 26.

high on a mountainside overlooking Casper. At one time, he had been a United States senator from Wyoming. During the cookout, I took advantage of the only opportunity I would ever have in a topsy-turvy world to view the breathtaking scenery around Casper. I wandered away from the group until I found a spot where I could sit quietly on a rock and take it all in. Never having been west of Birmingham, Alabama, before I joined the army, I was overwhelmed by the vastness of the wide-open spaces in the western United States. Through the thin air of our high elevation I could see distant mountainsides that seemed so close I could touch them. They were bathed in moonlight and strewn with thick, dark boulders reflecting the earth's violent past. Below and to my left in the valley was a sprinkle of lights from a cluster of homes; to my right, the land was dotted with single, flickering lights identifying individual farms and ranches. I gazed up into the clean, clear night sky. They were all there, my new friends; the ones upon whom I might have to depend for my survival and that of my crew. The constellation Ursa Major, the Big Dipper, with its two bright stars away from the handle pointing to Polaris, the North Star. Tracing a slightly curved line back from the handle, I found the red star Arcturus, and farther down the curve, the next really bright star, Spica. To my right was the most brilliant and beautiful constellation in the heavens, Orion, with the three stars of its belt pointing southwest to the scintillating white Sirius, brightest star in the sky.

What had happened to me in the past year scarcely seemed real, but what was yet to come? I thought of my parents, and of my brothers, Mike and John, and all my friends and relatives back home. When would I see them again? As it turned out, I would—and it would not be long before I did. On March 30, 1943, Crew No. 31 was given a six-day leave, effective April 3, 1943. I hastily arranged to fly to Atlanta and spend three days at home. It was a fortunate visit, for I would not go home again until the summer of 1945, more than two years later. By then, I would have passed through the valley of the shadow of death and would have experienced things that were to alter my life. But on that crisp, spring evening in March 1943, as I sat on the mountain overlooking Casper, Wyoming, I could only speculate on what was yet to come.

A fateful day for the 100th came shortly thereafter. In early April, all aircrews of the 100th BG were reunited at Kearney Army Air Base, Nebraska. On April 20, all thirty-seven aircrews of the group flew a simulated combat mission from Kearney to Hamilton Field, San Francisco. The exercise ended badly. Although Crew No. 31 was among the twenty-three crews that successfully completed the mission, fourteen other aircraft in the group did not. Most had legitimate weather and mechanical problems, but several experienced "equipment malfunctions" and "discrepancies" that forced them to land in or near the hometowns of family and girlfriends. The additional training we were to receive because of the refusal of the Second AF to certify the 100th as combat-ready back in January failed to save Colonel Alkire. On April 26, 1943, he was relieved of command of the 100th and was temporarily replaced by Colonel Howard Turner, a Washington staff officer.

I believe that, in large measure, Colonel Alkire was a scapegoat. The unrealistic decision to send small groups of 100th aircrews to eight bases in six states for further training made it impossible for him to effectively manage his command, and this decision was certainly not his alone. To the extent that we failed to exercise self-discipline, his aircrews let him down. The inadequate facilities at several bases to which the crews were sent and the frequent severe weather that hampered many of our flying operations were entirely beyond Colonel Alkire's control. Only weeks after being relieved of command, Colonel Alkire was given command of the 449th BG, a B-24 unit, and served with distinction. He was shot down while flying out of Italy in 1944 and for a short period was the senior American officer in the West Compound of the prisoner of war camp at Stalag Luft III in Germany.

Under Colonel Turner, the group undertook an intensive training schedule at Kearney Army Air Base, Nebraska, during the remainder of April. The Cruikshank crew put more than thirty-seven hours in the air over five consecutive days. In early May, we learned that the 100th BG was being sent to England and began several weeks of intensive training as a group. The decision had been made that the 100th would remain intact and become a part of the VIII BC air campaign against Germany. Our time was growing near at hand, and we began to follow the progress of the war much more closely. We knew we were going into combat. We knew we would be placed in great danger. And, in the end, despite our recent history, we were told that we were considered experienced aircrews. Although I believed we *were* an experienced crew, I was still reminded of my father's standard comment regarding the value of experience: "Be careful of claims of experience. Experience is the name people give to their mistakes."

In Kearney, forty new B-17Fs were assigned to the 100th BG. All were Boeing Model 299-0 aircraft. Twenty-five of them had been built at Boeing Wichita as part of a production run of over fifteen hundred Model 299-0 B-17 aircraft. Six were built by the Douglas Aircraft Company of Long Beach, California, and nine were manufactured by the Vega Aircraft Corporation, a subsidiary of Lockheed Aircraft Corporation, located at Burbank, California. B-17F serial number 42-30062, built at Boeing Wichita, was assigned to Crew No. 31. In mid-May, all of the 100th BG aircraft were flown by their crews to the air depot at Ogden, Utah, for incorporation of extended-range Tokyo tanks in their outer wings.

I do not know when the USAAF high command accepted the practice of allowing ground and aircrews to apply nicknames to their aircraft, but the practice of naming our bombers was in place well before we received our new aircraft at Kearney. Maybe the photographs of the Flying Tigers—those American heroes in China under General Claire Chennault flying their famous Curtiss P-40E Warhawk fighter aircraft with shark's teeth and eyes painted on their noses—had something to do with it. I also suspect the application of names and even accompanying artwork to include scantily clad young women was tolerated if for no other reason than it helped build morale within the USAAF. In addition, there was also the public relations angle to consider. When in 1943 the American public saw William Wyler's *Memphis Belle,* they may have forgotten the names of the crews mentioned but no doubt could recall *Old Bill, Dame Satan,* and of course *Memphis Belle.* At a more personal level, the application of the nickname, nose art, or even your name by your crew station of the aircraft gave the individual crew member a sense of identity in what was total war where individuality was lost within the scope of the grand strategy. In the 100th BG at the time, the names and the nose art were painted either on one or both sides of the nose by one of the talented members of the air or ground crew of the squadron or group.

We in the USAAF did not lack subjects for consideration when it came to naming our aircraft. Some named their aircraft after loved ones; for example, *Judy E., Patty Ann,* or *Mary Jane.* Some used patriotic or heroic themes, such as *We the People, Tom Paine, Boston Tea Party,* or *War Eagle.* Others had catchy names, such as *Luscious Lucy, Heaven Can Wait, Flak Shack, Sad Sack, Damifino, El P'sstofo, Cock of the Sky, Piccadilly Commando,* and the famous *Piccadilly Lily.* Still others used military jargon, such as *SNAFU* or *FUBAR Express,* geographic names like *City of Natchez,* popular songs like *Moonlight Serenade,* or words or phrases with double meanings such as *Miss Minookie.* There were of course names and nose art that left little if anything to the imagination. Finally there were names known only to the crews, such as *BEBA, LONI, M'lle Zig Zig,* and the inexplicable *Aw-R-Go.* As for Crew No. 31, we by consensus named our airplane *Bastard's Bungalow,* reflecting the on-again, off-again fortune of the already star-crossed 100th BG.[3] The name was painted on both sides of the nose area by Ernie Warsaw, navigator with Crew No. 36.

Although the B-17 was a Boeing-designed aircraft, during the war, the USAAF organized a manufacturing pool whereby Boeing, Vega, and Douglas would all manufacture B-17s. The B-17F aircraft delivered to the 100th were fitted with a new single .50-caliber gun in a cheek mount on each side of the nose in addition to a single gun in the nose window, a single .50-caliber gun in the radio compartment that fired through a skylight, and, as noted above, were also modified with extra fuel cells in their outer wings called Tokyo tanks that significantly increased the combat radius of the aircraft. After being issued all manner of personal equipment, including, curiously, mosquito netting and tropical items, we departed Kearney on May 29, 1943, for Selfridge Field, Michigan. The weather across the northern United States was squally when we took off from Selfridge for Bangor, Maine, the following day, so we flew by way of Canada Red One Airway over Toronto and Ottawa, then by Canada Green One to Montreal, where we turned east to Bangor. It was the first time in my life that I had ever been outside the United States.

---

3. Wherever possible, I will integrate the aircraft's "nickname" and its tail number into the text. For example, references to our original aircraft and its tail number (serial number 42-30062 appeared on the vertical stabilizer as 230062) will appear throughout the text as *Bastard's Bungalow* (**230062**).

7

THE VIII BOMBER COMMAND

In the spring of 1943, military aircraft traveling between North America and Europe normally used two well-established transatlantic routes, both of which departed from Atlantic Canada. The destination in the United Kingdom for both routes was Prestwick, Scotland. The route selected for any given flight was essentially determined by weather conditions over the North Atlantic at the time of the aircraft's scheduled departure. The northern route included stopovers for refueling and aircraft servicing at Goose Bay, Labrador, and Meeks Field, Iceland. The southern route involved one stop at Gander Lake on the island of Newfoundland, followed by a direct flight over Ireland to Scotland. Each crew of the 100th flew its own airplane, and Crew No. 31 was assigned the northern route.

At approximately 9:00 a.m. on the cool, clear morning of May 30, 1943, following the usual preflight inspections and planning, the men of Crew No. 31 piled their assorted gray-green B-4 bags, duffel bags, parachute bags, and other personal articles on the floor of the airplane and took off for Goose Bay. We shared a general feeling of exhilaration and excitement; the uncertainties of the past were over, and we were finally on our way to do the job we had been preparing for during the last six months. From Bangor, Maine, we flew northeast across New Brunswick, the mouth of the St. Lawrence River, and then over Port-Menier at the western end of Anticosti Island, above eastern Quebec. We continued through the pure, clean air above the immense wilderness of glacier-formed, cold-bitten, sparsely populated Labrador. There were no roads or other signs of human activity for as far as the eye could see; only endless forests of black spruce trees, all of identical size, with ramrod-straight trunks standing like sentinels in the spongy caribou moss. From above, the caribou moss could easily have passed for snow. Four hours and forty-five minutes after "wheels-up" at Bangor, we touched down at Happy Valley–Goose Bay at the southern end of Hamilton Inlet.

Goose Bay was austere, and its facilities and accommodations were limited to the essentials. The base had been designed and built at the beginning of the war for only one purpose: to service transient aircraft going to and from Europe and North America. We got up in the early first light of the northern latitudes the next morning because we knew we had a long day ahead of us. While the rest of the crew, particularly Glenn Graham and Leonard Weeks, were at the flight line supervising preparation of the airplane for our flight, Charlie Cruikshank and I were in flight operations. Crankshaft meticulously worked through the items on his pilot's checklist: correlating the aircraft's gross weight with fuel and oil requirements; identifying our radio frequencies; reviewing procedures for ditching at sea; reviewing emergency landing sites in Greenland, and other important preflight details. Since time was not a factor, he traded speed for range and fuel economy. As I recall, we made our entire crossing at altitudes of less than five thousand feet and engine power settings at "long-range cruise." Meanwhile, I laid out a course on a Mercator chart taking us over Cape Farewell at the southern tip of Greenland. I would then use Cape Farewell as an intermediate fixed geographical departure point for the last leg of our flight to Iceland.

Both of us reviewed the latest weather forecasts for Goose Bay, the North Atlantic, and Iceland. Up-to-date reports on wind direction and strength were especially crucial for me as the navigator.

Flying alone in daylight and over approximately 1,400 miles of open water meant that I would have to rely for the most part on dead reckoning, the ficklest of the navigation arts. Finally, we synchronized our watches to an exact time tick on Greenwich universal time. Astronomers have been man's timekeepers ever since the Egyptians, Chinese, and American Indians constructed their calendars and determined their own gestation periods and those of their domestic animals by counting the various stages of the moon. Every geographic position determined by astronomical means requires the navigator to know the exact Greenwich time and date of his observation to develop a "line of position" using the tables in his *Nautical Almanac*. Apart from Cape Farewell, the sun would be my only navigation crutch during our flight.

As we were being trucked out to the airplane, I wondered, and not for the first time, whether the rest of the men on bomber crews considered the navigator to be an oddball. He was the only officer on the crew who had nothing whatsoever to do with operation and control of the airplane. He climbed aboard lugging a briefcase crammed with maps, Mercator charts, books, paper, pencils, drawing instruments, a handheld calculator, and strange-looking optical instruments. He was invariably hunched over his narrow shelflike table in front of which was a repeater set of basic flight instruments and radio controls. He looked at his watch constantly, drew lines, and scribbled notes to himself on the papers, maps, and charts in front of him, much like Scrooge's wretched drudge, Bob Cratchit, in Dickens's classic tale *A Christmas Carol*.

Crankshaft released his brakes, made a cautious takeoff run, and rotated the airplane off the ground at Goose Bay at about 7:00 a.m. on May 31, 1943. We turned northeast to a heading that would take us across the icy Labrador Sea south of the Davis Strait and directly toward Cape Farewell, Greenland. About an hour and a half into our flight, we began to see huge icebergs drifting southward on the Labrador Current to warmer waters, where they would melt. These icebergs reminded me of the White Star Line's luxury liner *Titanic*. She struck an iceberg in the freezing waters off Newfoundland on her maiden voyage across the Atlantic in April 1912 and went down in bitterly cold water with a loss of over 1,500 lives.

From the outset, I painstakingly monitored our compass readings against my predetermined headings, which I had carefully adjusted to compensate for wind drift, and our airspeed, particularly in bumpy air, as I continuously plotted my dead reckoning ground track. I was well aware that once my dead reckoning record of our position was broken, my efforts would be of no value until I could reestablish our position by some other means of navigation. Also, dead reckoning errors are cumulative. A 3 percent course error results in a twenty-mile position error on a flight of only 400 miles. On a flight of approximately 1,400 miles entirely over water and with only one ground checkpoint, errors of this magnitude are unacceptable. I periodically shot sun lines that gave me latitude readings suggesting that we were tracking our intended course. And, fortunately, we had the benefit of good weather and clear visibility. The cliffs, rocky shoreline, and ice-encrusted hills of Cape Farewell were impossible to miss. We made our landfall in Greenland within fifteen minutes of my expected arrival time and only a few miles south of my predicted position. I refined my dead reckoning assumptions based on our actual track course, ground speed, and the wind forces we had experienced as far as Greenland. I calculated a new heading to Iceland and gave it to Crankshaft.

At various times during this flight, I sensed that I was being watched, and I was usually right. At one time or another, I looked up and saw Leonard Weeks or one of our other sergeants crouched in the narrow catwalk below the flight deck, grinning up at me and asking the two questions that have been asked of navigators since time immemorial: "How are we doing?" and "Do you know where we are?" The automatic answers to these questions, respectively, are "Great!" and "Of course." No navigator, even if he is totally lost, will ever admit it as long as there is any possibility he can recover.

At roughly eight hours into our flight, our radio compass receiver was able to pick up a faint aural signal from the Meeks Field beacon, so we switched on the aircraft's rotatable loop antenna. As the signal increased in strength, enabling me to obtain a reliable bearing, I found that Meeks was *not* directly ahead of us but several degrees off to our left. With the use of this bearing and the wind forces it suggested, I gave Crankshaft a magnetic compass heading directly to Meeks.

Our first view of Iceland was its rocky, fjord-scalloped west coast and Mount Esja, the gray peak that dominates Reykjavik. This was the same sight that greeted Viking seamen returning home from Greenland and Vinland almost one thousand years ago, although from a different perspective.[1] We passed low over the coast south of Reykjavik and into a soft, smooth landing at Meeks Field, touching down nine hours and forty minutes after lifting off from Goose Bay.

Because of unfavorable weather reports from Scotland, we spent two nights in Iceland. In the afternoon of the day after our arrival, along with members of Lieutenant Ernie Kiessling's Crew No. 29, Lieutenant Ernie Warsaw, navigator on Captain Bob Knox's Crew No. 36, and John Brady and his Crew No. 32, we arranged for transportation in a two-and-a-half-ton truck that took us into Reykjavik. The road into the city was flat and even but unpaved, its surface covered by volcanic cinder. Along the way, we passed several fields that

1. The actual site of Vinland is unknown, but scholars believe it the site of present-day Nova Scotia.

reeked of the smell of decaying fish that was so strong it was almost sickening. We were later told that this horribly foul odor came from a form of fish compost used as fertilizer.

We also overtook two columns of U.S. Army infantry troops in full battle dress walking in open, single file down each side of the roadway. Because of its importance as a submarine and air base, in July 1941, after the conquest of Denmark by the Germans, American and British forces occupied Iceland with the full assent of the Icelandic government.

That evening, we sought out the town hot spot, which turned out to be the old-world, dark, wood-paneled, dimly lit lounge of the Hotel Borg. Both the beer and the attractive young ladies, who were blond descendants of the ancient Norse and Celtic settlers of Iceland, were first-rate. However, both we and the lovely young ladies were greatly outnumbered by young Icelandic men and British and American servicemen who were stationed in Iceland. This left us no choice but to enjoy only the beer, which we did. When we returned to Meeks Field we had to close the blinds and cover our heads with sheets to sleep, because at more than sixty-four degrees north latitude, it was still daylight at midnight.

I don't recall the details of our six-hour flight to Prestwick, Scotland, on June 2, 1943, except for the monotonous thrumming of our four Wright Cyclone engines, an unending blue-gray overcast that hid the sun throughout, and the cold, heavy, dark waters of the North Atlantic. On our approach to Prestwick, we caught occasional glimpses of the hilly, emerald-green and charcoal-gray islands of the Outer and Inner Hebrides. We could see them through a broken 5/10 scattering of gray-white, puffy cumulus clouds. Our sense of relief that our long Atlantic crossing was finally over was short-lived. Within minutes of our arrival, we were told that we would be in Prestwick only long enough to refuel. We were told to prepare for an immediate departure to RAF Station 109, Podington, Bedfordshire, which would involve another two hours of flying time.

Even before we took off for our flight to Podington, I was greatly impressed by the aeronautical maps supplied to us by the RAF. Their maps revealed winding roads, serpentine railroads, rivers, streams, and remarkably exact green patterns for all the distinguishable forests and woodlands—all in incredible detail. Yet the detail of the maps could not do justice to my first aerial view of the beauty of the English rural scenery. During this flight, I was struck by its greenness, from the verdant forests and tended, groomed hills and fields of the North Country south into the Midlands; the fullness of the cultivation of the countryside, its peaceful, settled look of character and permanency; and its almost, but not quite, "planned" arrangement of tiny villages consisting of tightly packed cottages clustered around a green or old market square or ancient parish church.

Station 109 was a temporary home for the 100th BG. Although it had been built for RAF Bomber Command several years earlier and had been occupied by USAAF units for a short while in 1942, it was not an operational air base in June 1943. The 100th BG would be at Podington for one week while our permanent base at Thorpe Abbotts in Norfolk was being readied for our arrival.

That same day, the 100th BG had yet another change of command and reassignment of two of its senior officers. Colonel Howard Turner completed his task of taking the 100th to the United Kingdom and was replaced by Colonel Harold Huglin, whom none of us knew. In addition, Major Robert Flesher, the 418th's squadron commander, was appointed group operations officer, and Major John Egan, our group operations officer, was appointed squadron commander. In effect, Majors Flesher and Egan simply exchanged places; however, this change was of no significance to me. I never had a one-on-one meeting with Major Flesher, who communicated with his aircrews through their pilots. I doubted that he even knew my name. John "Bucky" Egan, one of three Buckys in the 100th, turned out to be another story.

Bucky Egan was thirtyish, spidery thin, and slightly hatchet-faced. He had a suave, slightly comical, pencil-thin mustache, dark hair, and black eyes. His trademarks were a soiled, crushed "fifty mission" hat and a white fleece-lined flying jacket. And, although he was from Wisconsin, he was captivated by the idiomatic speech of the characters in New York columnist Damon Runyon's popular stories of the tough "guys and dolls" that were popular in New York City before the war. He punctuated his speech with phrases such as, "I'm Mrs. Egan's bad boy, John." He was prewar Air Corps and seemed to feel that he had to live up to Hollywood's image of a dashing pilot—but unlike his standoffish predecessor, he was jovial and friendly. I liked Bucky Egan.

On June 3, 1943, the ground crews, armorers, military police, intelligence officers, medics, clerks, cooks, drivers, and the other technicians required to keep us flying and operating the base began arriving at Station 109 by train. They came to England after a rough eight-day crossing on the crowded *Queen Elizabeth*. My memory of our brief stay at Podington is of dreary weather and damp, cold buildings with blackout shutters. Blackout rules were strictly enforced in Britain during the Second World War. Since even a sliver of light could become an aiming point for German bombers, blackouts were a serious matter. At home in the United States, we never talked about the war, but now for the first time, we talked of our imminent involvement. Although I remember sensations of apprehension and excitement, I do not remember being afraid. On the night of June 4, 1943, many of us spent the evening in the bar of the officers' club exchanging signatures on each other's new British "short-snorter" bills. They were banknotes that everyone would sign and tape end to end as new bills were added to the collection. I still have my ten-shilling Bank of England note dated "Podington, England, June 4, 1943," signed by fellow combat air crewmen from the 100th, all of whom survived combat but are now deceased.[2] I recall the two dignified, bespectacled gentlemen from Barclays Bank dressed in dark suits, starched collars, ties, and all, who sat at a table in the club that night exchanging British pounds sterling for American dollars.

I was on what was probably the very first B-17 aircraft from the 100th BG to land at RAF Station 139, Thorpe Abbotts, which became the permanent home of the 100th BG in England until the end of the war. On June 7, 1943, Colonel Huglin, Lieutenant Colonel George Dauncey, our ground exec, and Major Flesher flew to Station 153, Framlingham, a new bomber station also under construction, and to our new base at Thorpe Abbotts to review preparations for arrival of the 100th BG two days hence. I was sent as navigator on the flight crew. At Framlingham, our officers conferred with officials of John Laing & Son Ltd., the British company responsible for construction of both Station 139 and Station 153. We then flew to Thorpe Abbotts where the senior RAF administrative officer on site immediately invited us to a sit-down meal in the officers' club. I do not recall the courses they prepared, only that it was expertly served by four or five young RAF airmen who were the equal of any professional waiters I have ever seen. I could not imagine

2. The bill was signed by Paul Englert, who failed to return over Stuttgart on September 6, 1943, flying *The Poontang* (230402); Bernard DeMarco, who failed to return over Bremen on October 8, 1943, flying *Our Baby* (23233); Charlie Via, who was seriously wounded over Bremen on October 8, 1943, flying *Just-A-Snappin* (23393); and John Hoerr, who failed to return over Münster on October 10, 1943, flying *M'lle Zig Zig* (230830).

such a formal-style luncheon at an American air base, but no people play themselves as effortlessly as the British.

We spent the night at Thorpe Abbotts on June 7, 1943, so early that evening I went to the officers' club, which was open to resident RAF and Laing company staff. The only other person at the bar when I arrived was a slender, bookish-looking RAF officer with a long, reddening nose, thick tortoiseshell glasses, slightly rheumy eyes, and dark hair. From his easy, gravelly voiced conversation with the bartender, it was evident that he was a regular. As we sipped our drinks, we introduced ourselves. He said he was Flight Lieutenant Williams and that he was clerk of the works on the RAF oversight staff at the base. He pronounced *lieutenant* as "leftenant" and *clerk* as "clark." I commented that, despite the ongoing work of hundreds of civilian laborers at Thorpe Abbotts, the 100th expected to move in two days later. In a resigned and long-suffering voice, he referred to the laborers as "Irish workers" in much the same fashion one would have spoken of Chinese coolies. Flight Lieutenant Williams opined that he was doing the best he could with what he had. I had no idea who the laborers at Thorpe Abbotts were or where they came from, but I considered it the better part of good judgment not to remind him that my name was Murphy.[3] For several more weeks until the base was released to the 100th BG, Flight Lieutenant Williams remained a nightly fixture at the Thorpe Abbotts officers' club bar.

---

3. Much later, I learned that the "leftenant's" remarks were not necessarily based on the historical tension between the English and Irish as much as it was an expression of frustration about the type of worker available. As most men who would have been available to work on building the many airfields across East Anglia were off to war, the construction companies were able to entice workers from Ireland with relatively handsome wages. Many of these laborers were "rough farm boys" who were more interested in getting into the pubs than building airfields. After all, it was not their war. I also much later learned that there were more Irish in England during the war than there were in the whole of Ireland.

All 100th BG aircrews flew from Podington to Thorpe Abbotts on June 9 as scheduled. As at Podington, the airfield at Thorpe Abbotts was altogether different from our air bases in the United States, which were wholly self-contained and completely isolated from the civilian world outside. At Thorpe Abbotts, the runways, hardstands, hangars, living quarters, and support buildings had all been squeezed in among quaint cottages, flat green fields, small forests, winding lanes, streams, and tiny crossroads that had clearly been in place for eons. It was indeed an ancient land; Thorpe Abbotts was one of eleven sites in the Norfolk area where round-towered stone churches had been erected by the Saxons almost a thousand years before the U.S. VIII BC arrived.

Little more than a mile west of Thorpe Abbotts is Pulham St. Mary, where we saw an old airship hangar left over from the First World War, still wearing its original, but peeling, camouflaged paint.[4] It immediately became a landmark for pilots and navigators in the unpredictable English weather and a welcome sight for all 100th air crewmen returning from air operations over Europe.

Our living quarters at Thorpe Abbotts were standard Nissen huts: olive-drab, half-round, corrugated steel buildings that were almost always damp and musty-smelling. They were grouped in scattered clusters in the countryside beyond the perimeter of the airfield. Each hut was sixteen feet wide, eight feet high at the center, and twenty-four to thirty feet long with four windows on each side. Their floors were concrete, and heat was provided by a small coal stove in the center of the hut that had a metal flue extending

---

4. During the First World War, there were two hangars built on this site. During the 1930s, one was dismantled and rebuilt at RAF Cardington, Bedforshire. The hangar we were so familiar with was torn down after the war.

straight up through the roof. There were several low-wattage lights in the ceiling.

Six to eight steel cots, depending on the length of the hut, lined the two long walls. There was a small table between each two beds and a footlocker at the foot of each cot. A long, wooden storage shelf with a rod for hanging uniforms on hangers was affixed to the wall. Each hut accommodated the four officers from each of three or four crews, depending on the length of the hut. Members of the same squadrons lived together. The officers of the Brady and Cruikshank crews shared a Nissen hut at Site 5 together—namely, John Brady, John Hoerr, Harry Crosby, Howard "Hambone" Hamilton, as well as Cruikshank, Graham, Gaspar, and myself. When Crosby was moved to Ev Blakely's crew, his bunk was filled by Dave Solomon.

There was no plumbing in the huts. Each squadron living area had separate "ablution" buildings with latrines and washbasins adjacent to the huts, but to do anything else, from going to eat to taking a bath, meant riding a bicycle to a communal area. We could *fly* to Germany, but we had to depend on *bicycles* for getting around the base.

THORPE ABBOTTS STATION 139

See map on page 4 of photo insert 1

Station 139 was located one mile northwest of Thorpe Abbotts village, Norfolk, four and a half miles east of Diss, and was 165 feet above sea level. It was allocated to the Eighth Air Force as a bomber base on June 4, 1942, but was occupied by the Eighth in June 1943. The station was officially transferred to the Eighth on July 20, 1943, and was transferred to the RAF December 20, 1945. John Laing & Son was the main contractor. The runways were concrete 6,300 feet; 4,200 feet; and 4,200 feet. Aircraft hardstands and thirty-six pans with fifteen loops were added late in construction. The hangars were two dispersed T2s. The base could accommodate 421 officers and 2,473 enlisted for a total of 2,894 personnel. My quarters were in

Site 5, which is located just above the map title "Sta. 139." I cannot recall the exact location of *Bastard's Bungalow*'s hardstand—it was either Number 45 or 46. To find these hardstands, locate the "Sick qtrs," which is above and slightly to the right of "Site 5," then look just above and to the right. Hardstand 45 is to the south of the perimeter track, and Hardstand 46 is to the north.

The 100th BG was one of five B-17 bomb groups sent to England in the spring of 1943 to form the new 4th Bomb Wing[5] under the command of stocky, dark-haired, cigar-chewing Colonel Curtis E. "Iron Ass" LeMay, who had been in England since 1942 as the commander of the 305th BG at Station 105, Chelveston. He had a reputation for uncompromising toughness and was indisputably a brilliant tactician. He ultimately became a four-star general and commander of the Strategic Air Command during the Cold War. Colonel LeMay officially assumed command of the 4th Bomb Wing on June 15, 1943.

Although the American combat crews joining the VIII BC in the spring of 1943 were unaware of it, at the Casablanca Conference in Morocco in January 1943, it was agreed by the assembled heads of state and military leaders, despite the misgivings of Prime Minister Winston Churchill, who preferred only night bombing operations, that a range of strategic German targets would be attacked by the British RAF by night and the USAAF by day. Mr. Churchill actually wanted American aircraft factories to abandon the B-17 in favor of the British Lancaster bomber and to forgo daylight precision bombing in favor of area bombing at night. It was only the impassioned arguments of General Eaker to both President Roosevelt and the prime minister that led Churchill to withdraw his requests and give his support to around-the-clock bombing.

However, by May 1943, it had become obvious that if the

---

5. From this point forward, I will use the abbreviation **BW** for *Bomb Wing*.

Combined Bomber Offensive, as the Casablanca plan was known, was to be successful, the German Luftwaffe had to be defeated. After Casablanca, the Eighth had commenced attacking Germany proper, rather than France and the Low Countries, as it had done earlier. And, of course, our battle losses had risen sharply. The RAF, although it delivered spectacular bomb tonnage on several Ruhr targets, did not fare much better. In forty-three major attacks on targets in Germany from March through June 1943, the RAF flew 18,506 sorties, from which 872 aircraft (a 4.71 percent loss ratio) failed to return. Another 2,126 aircraft were damaged, some so badly they never flew again. To accomplish this new objective of defeating the Luftwaffe, the Casablanca Directive, dated January 21, 1943, was amended by a new directive known as Pointblank, issued on June 10, 1943—the day after the 100th BG settled in at Thorpe Abbotts! The new directive stated:

> The increasing scale of destruction which is being inflicted by our night bomber forces and the development of the day bomber offensive by the Eighth Air Force have forced the enemy to deploy day and night fighters in increasing numbers on the Western Front. Unless this increase in fighter strength is checked we may find our bomber forces unable to fulfil the tasks allotted to them by the Combined Chiefs of Staff.
>
> In these circumstances it has become essential to check the growth and to reduce the strength of the day and night fighter forces which the enemy can concentrate against us in this theatre. To this end the Combined Chiefs of Staff have decided that first priority in the operation of British and American bombers based in the United Kingdom shall be accorded to the attack of German fighter forces and the industry upon which they depend.[6]

---

6. Dudley Saward, *"Bomber" Harris* (London: Cassell, Buchan & Enright, 1984), 206.

The VIII BC interpreted its part of this directive to require precision bombing of selected factories, despite the anticipation of strong opposition from German fighters. Operational commanders also recognized that U.S. bomber formations without fighter escort on deep penetration missions were vulnerable to heavy losses. Although Eighth Fighter Command and RAF Fighter Command would provide all the protection they could, the long-range fighter aircraft that were needed to escort the bombers simply did not exist. The aircrews of VIII BC had to go deep into Germany without fighter cover. The dangers faced by American bomber crews operating from England in mid-1943 were also due in large measure to our heavy bombers being spread thinner than a coat of paint all over the world. This meant that we could not be deployed in massed strength anywhere. Any flaws in the strategic bomber doctrine only added to the problem.

In the days before our first combat alert, pilots and crews spent hours and days practicing flying the box formation that was the hallmark of the Eighth AF. It was made clear to us in VIII BC that if there was a principal key to our survival, it was maintaining tight formations in combat so as to enable our gunners to bring maximum firepower to bear on enemy aircraft attacking from any direction. And, as we gained proficiency in our formation flying, it was self-evident that this was true.

All of us went to ground school on operational procedures, gunnery, and aircraft recognition using charts and models. Morale was high. This was the time for anyone with no stomach for aerial combat to reveal himself, but no one did. The 100th BG's first call to action came on June 22, 1943. The group was to fly a diversionary feint toward the North Sea to draw attention away from the main bomber force going to Antwerp, Belgium, and Hüls, Germany. The 100th put up twenty-one aircraft, which flew the diversion plan without incident. Throughout the war, the VIII BC operated diversion missions and attacked multiple targets on schedules designed to discourage German air defenses from concentrating on a single bomber stream and to put maximum strain on the limited range of the Luftwaffe's fighter aircraft.[7]

Two days later, on June 24, 1943, Crew No. 31 was dispatched on a seven-hour simulated combat mission. We proceeded north off the east coast of Scotland almost to the Orkney Islands; west across northern Scotland and the Minch; and on to a landing at a remote RAF station at Stornoway on the Isle of Lewis in the North Atlantic. The Stornoway station was on a lonely, windswept stretch of land and had no concrete runways—it could have passed for the last outpost. As soon as we landed, however, a boxlike truck with the letters *NAAFI* painted on the side drove out to our airplane, and several young ladies in RAF blue uniforms served us hot tea and cold biscuits. We were told the letters *NAAFI* represented the Navy, Army, Air Force Institute, the British equivalent of the American Red Cross.

We returned to Thorpe Abbotts the following morning, June 25, and discovered that the 100th BG was then out on its first actual combat mission to Bremen, Germany, with the 4th BW and the rest of VIII BC. The 418th BS was standing down; the mission was being flown by crews from the 349th, 350th, and 351st BS of the group. The 100th BG launched nineteen aircraft that day; three of them failed to return.

---

7. Readers interested in a good overview of the B-17 and the Eighth Air Force should read Roger A. Freeman's *B-17 Fortress at War* and his Eighth Air Force trilogy *The Mighty Eighth, Mighty Eighth War Dairy,* and the *Mighty Eighth War Manual.* Also of interest is a book produced by the Arizona Wing of the Confederate Air Force entitled *Sentimental Journey,* which contains excellent photographs of the restoration of a B-17G as well as the interior crew positions.

Lieutenant Alonzo P. Adams III, *Angel Tit* (23260)
9 died in action, 1 taken prisoner
Lieutenant Paul J. Schmalenbach, *Bar Fly* (230038)
6 died in action, 4 taken prisoner
Captain Oran E. Petrich, *Blue Bird K* (229986)
10 died in action

The loss of Captain Petrich's crew struck a particularly close chord with me. At the last minute that morning, Lieutenant Stanley Morrison of Lieutenant Kiessling's crew of the 418th, whose Nissen hut was next to ours, had been urgently called to serve as replacement bombardier on the crew of Captain Oran Petrich of the 349th BS.

8

COMBAT

The loss of three aircraft and thirty men on its first operational mission dampened any sense of adventure the remaining crews of the 100th may have felt about entering combat. Had we known that twenty-five of the thirty missing men had perished, the impact of that first mission would have been even more sobering. The sudden loss of these men also gave us our first exposure to the cold and dispassionate way the military managed casualties, procedures we would come to know all too well in the coming weeks and months. In less than twenty-four hours after their failure to return, all traces of our missing crews were gone. Apart from official records, they simply disappeared forever. As cold as it seemed at the time, I realize now that, realistically, there is no other way to handle casualties. Early in the morning following the loss of the aircrews, the 349th BS's adjutant and his staff stripped the MIAs' beds and boxed their personal belongings for shipment to the Army Effects Bureau at the Kansas City Quartermaster Depot.

Eventually, it was apparent that we would seldom have any idea as to the fate of the men who went down in combat unless an airplane was seen to explode or disintegrate, or the crew was seen abandoning a disabled airplane. Counting the number of men in parachutes was usually as much as we would ever know.

While that was happening, ground crews and aircrews of the 100th were preparing for another mission later in the afternoon.

The 418th had been placed on alert, setting into motion a series of actions that would also become familiar to us. At about 11:00 a.m., dressed in our flying clothing and carrying our gear, we climbed into trucks that took us to headquarters. A vigilant MP wearing a white helmet and a white armband checked us in. We filed into the briefing room and took our seats elbow to elbow on narrow wooden benches like playgoers at an oversold stage production. Curtains hid the wall behind the rostrum. A lectern stood on the left side of the dais, and to our right, we saw an easel covered by a large cloth, obviously to prevent us from getting a premature look. In the front of the room, a small table held a gadget for projecting photos and flimsies on a screen. It was a dramatic setting. I could not suppress a suspicion that this scenario, along with many of our other operational procedures, had been borrowed from the RAF. It just seemed like something they would do.

At the cry of "Ten-hut!" that signaled the start of every group military meeting I ever attended, we shuffled to our feet. A team of senior officers strode briskly down the center aisle and took their places along the front row. One of them was Major Minor Shaw, a veteran of the First World War, who was chief of S-2 (intelligence). He immediately stepped to the lectern, barked, "At ease," and motioned for the curtains to be opened. As they were swept aside, we saw a huge color map of the British Isles and western Europe almost completely covering the wall behind the stage. On the face of the map, a string of red yarn fastened with pins traced a line from an assembly point near Thorpe Abbotts to a departure point on the south coast of England, then stretched south across the channel to a point in France. It finally came back to England, showing us our return route.

Referring to the map with a pointer, Major Shaw solemnly intoned, "Gentlemen, your target for today is the Gnome and Rhône engine works at Le Mans, France." Silence. We were still a new group. Cries of horror, groans, and catcalls greeting the identification of our target would come later, but today, there was only silence. There was a lengthy explanation of operations at the French factory and a detailed listing of the German flak and fighter resistance we might encounter. We would soon find that all intelligence officers had a penchant for telling us the exact number of antiaircraft guns and the precise number and type of fighter aircraft we could expect to see.

As the lights were lowered, gray-and-white high-altitude blowups of the target were projected on a screen. Landmarks that would aid us in locating and identifying the target, such as tall smokestacks on key buildings, were described. We were told we would fly with three other groups of the 4th BW. The cover on the easel was then removed to reveal our formation plan. Each aircraft was represented by a *T* with the pilot's name written across the top. There was a weather briefing and, finally, the synchronizing of our watches: "Five, four, three, two, one, hack!" I have no specific recollection of it happening, but I am sure that at the conclusion of the briefing one of our senior officers said something like "Good luck and good hunting, gentlemen."

After this general briefing, the pilots attended a specialized briefing, the bombardiers met separately to pick up their target and ordnance data, and the navigators met to review the navigation specifics prepared by the group navigator. After the conclusion of these series of briefings, we were driven to the hardstand where *Bastard's Bungalow* (230062) was parked to begin the preflight procedures. As I disembarked the vehicle, I stood in the same awe of the B-17 as I did the first time I saw its powerful yet graceful outline.[1] As I

---

1. On the ground or in the air, a B-17 was then and remains quite a sight. The attachment I have to this aircraft is not unusual. Talk with military pilots today about the aircraft they are

usually did, I approached the left side of the nose area of the B-17 and threw my flight jacket, personal gear, clip-on parachute chest pack, and navigator's briefcase into the airplane through the small forward entrance door just below the flight deck. Then, grasping the inside edge of the opening with both hands above my head in a kind of chin-up maneuver, I swung my legs up into the opening, grunting and puffing, pulling myself up into the airplane through this same door. However, I often wondered about having to use this door to bail out of the aircraft since this placement of the door was just inches behind the arc created by a whirling left inboard Hamilton Standard propeller and only a few feet forward of the bomb bay doors, which, if open, could also prove hazardous.

Once inside the B-17, I had to crouch, for as sleek and overwhelming in size as the B-17 was from the outside, on the inside, all crew stations were very cramped. At five feet nine inches, I am not a tall person. Moreover, while sitting on my knees on the floorboard beside the escape hatch, I still had to be hunched over; otherwise, I would hit my head against the underside of the flight deck. Looking forward through the opening in the number 3 bulkhead into the bombardier/navigator compartment, I could see my small swivel chair with its adjustable seat and back permanently attached to the floor. Just beyond my chair was Augie's chair perched in front of the Plexiglas nose cone, right behind his Norden bombsight, still cloaked by its canvas cover. A straight-ahead .50-caliber machine gun was mounted in the Plexiglas nose of the airplane. Turning slightly to my right and looking over my shoulder, I could see through the open trapdoor to the flight deck and the interior mechanism for the top

---

assigned to fly, and they will offer nothing but glowing comments about their aircraft. In a similar vein, even today, decades after the war, surviving crew members of the Boeing-built B-17 and the Consolidated-built B-24 carry on a robust "discussion" as to which aircraft is the "best."

turret. During preflight procedures, Crankshaft was on the flight deck sitting in the left seat, Glenn was in the right seat, and, usually, Leonard Weeks straddled the passageway, assisting the pilots.

After I crawled through the relatively small entrance in the number 3 bulkhead into the nose compartment, immediately to my left and attached to the fuselage was my shelflike navigator's table that was approximately three feet long and eighteen inches wide. At the back of the table was a repeater set of basic flight instruments, such as an altimeter, airspeed indicator, and air-temperature indicator. To my right at the end of the table was my aperiodic compass. Before sitting in my chair, I usually placed my parachute under the table to the left and my briefcase on the table. Later, when I carried a steel helmet or flak vest, or both, for protection in combat, I generally put them under the table with my parachute. I put on my headset over my officer's hat, strapped on the throat microphone, put on my A-10 oxygen mask, and connected them to the appropriate jack boxes and fittings located on the left side of the bulkhead.[2] Once everything was connected, I functionally tested the equipment to make sure everything worked properly. Above my worktable was one small window where I could see the entire leading edge of the left wing. Above this window was an ammunition box for the flexible .50-caliber machine gun that was mounted in the left cheek window just forward of the small window. If I turned my chair to the right and leaned over slightly, I would see out another set of windows on the right side of the fuselage the entire leading edge of the right wing. A third flexible .50-caliber machine gun was installed in the right cheek of the aircraft midway in the nose compartment. Above me and toward the center of the nose area was the Plexiglas astrodome

2. For reasons I do not know, I was never issued a leather flight helmet with the built-in headset. These were issued to fighter pilots and the gunners of the crew but not to the officers.

for taking celestial observations but where I could also stand up at any time and have a 360-degree view, which included observing Crankshaft and Glenn in the cockpit.

As we prepared to take off, I had mixed feelings: anticipation, because we were about to see and experience what we had only read about; excitement, because the prospect of deadly combat quickens the pulse; apprehension, because we knew we were flying into harm's way; and a profound sense of worry because we did not know whether we would measure up. We knew what we were doing, but we didn't know what we were getting into.

The 100th BG dispatched twenty-three aircraft to Le Mans on June 26, 1943. The first bomber lifted off at approximately 4:00 p.m. with the rest of us following at thirty-second intervals. The group assembly and rendezvous with the other 4th BW groups, consisting of the 94th, 95th, and 96th BGs, was uneventful, as was our channel crossing. However, I will never forget the sense of vulnerability and anxiety that crept over me as I looked down on German-occupied France for the first time. I called it my "sitting duck syndrome," and it never left me while I was over enemy territory.

We were only a short distance into France when threads of ice-laced, feather-like cirrus clouds began to develop above us while the ground below became less distinct under a thickening layer of dull gray, fibrous altostratus clouds. By the time we reached our initial point (IP),[3] the ground was completely obscured. The 4th BW leader decided to abort the mission and turned the entire task

---

3. The *Initial Point* was a prominent landmark, which was used by the lead formation to make its final turn to the target area. This turn was no more and often less than forty-five degrees and was executed in a way that allowed the entire formation to stay together as an integral fighting unit. This was the beginning of the bomb run and the point in the mission that we were the most vulnerable. Once on the bomb run, we could not take evasive action because the bombardier, using the automatic flight control system (AFCS), was actually controlling the B-17 or was giving the pilot precise instructions through the electrical links

force back to England, taking our bombs home with us. I do not remember any Luftwaffe opposition that day, but I do remember a group of Spitfires coming out over the channel to cover our withdrawal. They were obviously circumspect when approaching our formation. While they were still well outside the range of our .50-caliber guns, they performed wingovers to give us a good look at their big elliptical wings with the distinctive RAF insignia painted on their undersides. They took no chance that we would mistake them for Germans. It was nearly 8:00 p.m. when we arrived back at Thorpe Abbotts. I was neither happy nor disappointed over the aborted mission. I *was* relieved that we had escaped danger, and I was gratified that we had actually flown over enemy territory, which I noticed didn't look any different from the air than friendly terrain. The bottom line was that we did not meet the enemy, we were not tested, nothing significant happened, and I walked away from the experience with no particular feelings that were noteworthy.

On Monday, June 28, 1943, along with seventeen other 100th BG aircraft, and three other 4th BW groups equipped with Tokyo tanks, Crew No. 31 set out to attack the German submarine pens at Saint-Nazaire, France. Because of the large number of antiaircraft guns ringing the port, it was known as "Flak City." Out of respect for this formidable array of defensive weaponry, our bombing altitude would be twenty-eight thousand feet, the highest bombing altitude of our combat tour. With our long-range fuel tanks, it was not necessary for us to fly over France; instead, we departed the English coast at Land's End at the southwestern tip of England, flew entirely over water around the Brest Peninsula, and made our bomb run from the sea over the Bay of Biscay. It was a beautiful sunny

---

from the bombsight to the pilot's directional indicator (PDI), a dial needle that showed flight attitudes with which the pilot complied.

day, but as we turned to our bomb run at the IP, I saw antiaircraft fire for the first time. It horrified me. The flak was easy for me to see since my navigator's table was immediately behind the bombardier, whose position was in the Plexiglas cone that formed the nose of the bomber. I could easily see past the bombardier and, of course, I had windows of my own, so getting an eyeful of flak bursts was unavoidable. When we entered the flak, it was an almost uninterrupted cloud of swirling black smoke filled with angry red explosions. Plainly, any one of those exploding shells could obliterate an aircraft and its crew without warning. When the group ahead of us entered this inferno, they all but disappeared. My heart felt as if it would stop. It did not appear possible that anyone or anything could fly into that hell and come out alive on the other side. But somehow, despite being buffeted by thunderous explosions and the incessant clinking, clanging, and pinging of shell fragments striking our airplane, we made it through.

I quickly learned to hate flak—it frightened the life out of me. We could not see it coming, nor could we fight back as we could with enemy fighters. The German gun-laying radar was incredibly accurate. The standard German antiaircraft gun, the 88 mm flak cannon, was capable of hurling an eighteen-pound shell to a maximum slant range of nine thousand yards. It took the shell twenty-five seconds to cover this distance, and during this time, its target would move almost two miles. Yet we seldom knew we were under fire until the antiaircraft shells began exploding in proximity to us, usually in simultaneous bursts of four black puffs from a single battery if it was light, or in thick concentrations of random explosions if several batteries were zeroed in on us. We couldn't take evasive action until we were already in the middle of it, and on a bomb run, we took no evasive action regardless of how intense the flak was. We had to fly straight and level so the bombardier could drop the bombs on target. The din inside the airplane was horrific—the continuous roaring of our four Wright Cyclone engines was almost deafening. Still, we could easily hear the muffled explosions of nearby flak bursts, and if they were really close, they made loud, cracking sounds like near-miss lightning strikes or breaking tree limbs. If German fighters attacked us, the airplane shook and vibrated violently from the operation of our flexible machine guns and power turrets, sounding much like someone thumping on washtubs with sticks. Dust and threads of insulation flew about the airplane, and shrapnel from flak, which varied in size from as big as baseballs to as small as gravel, rained on and often penetrated the thin skin of the airplane. Inside the Plexiglas nose of the airplane, it was as if we were in a fishbowl in a shooting gallery five miles up in the sky in an already-unforgiving environment. It is difficult to describe how exposed and unprotected we felt.

We generally knew the flak zones from our briefings. We encountered absolutely frightening, paralyzing flak at the most heavily defended targets, where the Germans had located 250 or more 88 mm and 105 mm guns: Saint-Nazaire, La Pallice, and Lorient on the Atlantic; and over the ports of Wilhelmshaven, Bremen, Hamburg, and Kiel on the North Sea. It was no consolation knowing that if we were lucky, we would be out of the range of the flak in a few minutes, because then we had to worry about being attacked by German fighters or being damaged by falling aircraft. It was a lot like going from one frying pan to another, and there was little to sustain us other than the thought of getting back to Thorpe Abbotts, where hot chocolate, SPAM sandwiches, and warm, soft beds awaited us.

Despite the trauma of combat that left us quaking, rubber-legged, and with the sensation that someone poured ice down the backs of our shirts, most of us felt that the only way we could go home with honor was to pull our necks in like turtles and endure it.

It *was* very important to us to go home with honor. Even though we were all civilians at heart, we knew that orders were orders, and we knew what was expected of us. If a man attempted to avoid combat altogether, he was held in complete contempt because the rest of us had to go. If a man who had been in combat said he wanted to go but admitted his guts were gone, we felt sorry for him. We might say that he was a chicken, but we never said he was a coward. Every one of us had been too close to that very failing ourselves. "We were *all* cowards. If you weren't a coward, you weren't human." Finally, we had to worry about more than just our own airplane. If one of the bombers above us was hit, it could be knocked out of formation and crash into another airplane flying below. I think I would rather have been in a submarine under the ocean than in a bomber under a flak attack. I believe most of the nonlethal battle damage suffered by our bombers was from flak. Even after all these years, at times I can still hear the din of battle and smell the cordite and fear; and I often wonder why Providence allowed me to survive when so many others did not.

We welcomed any lull in combat operations, regardless of the reason. Some would read, others played poker all night, and a few drank too much. Yet others looked forward to trips to London, where the gin-soaked whores in Piccadilly would provide a small measure of human, sensual comfort in an otherwise crazy and disorienting world. We all knew that it wouldn't be long before the weather cleared and, as the evening shadows lengthened into the fading night, the telexes in group operations would start clicking out the ominous message: "Stand by . . . Stand by." Then, like the old fire horse that tensed at the sound of the bell, we would try to steel ourselves to go out and do it again.

Miraculously, none of the crew was injured on our June 28 mission to Saint-Nazaire. All aircraft of the 100th returned safely to Thorpe Abbotts. However, our airplane, *Bastard's Bungalow* (230062), had flak holes and major structural damage to its right wing. It would be out of service until we flew it again for the July 24, 1943, mission to Trondheim, Norway. Although the Saint-Nazaire mission had been a frightening baptism by fire, we had little time to reflect on it. As soon as we landed at Thorpe Abbotts, we were informed that group operations had received another alert notice. The club bar was closed to the combat crews, who were not given the option of pondering their immediate future with the help of alcohol. The following day, June 29, 1943, we went back to Le Mans aboard an unnamed B-17F (25854) to attack the Gnome and Rhône aircraft engine overhaul depot. Once again, despite the lack of German opposition, the mission was a failure. The lead group missed the IP, and the following groups ended up scattered all over the countryside. The target remained untouched.

On July 2, 1943, the 100th BG had another change of command. Colonel Harold Huglin was replaced by Colonel Neil B. "Chick" Harding, an old B-17 pilot. He was one of the six B-17 pilots who flew the famous "goodwill tour" around South America in February 1938. He had also played quarterback for West Point on one of the greatest teams in Army history in the 1920s (All-American Army legend Chris Cagle was on the same team). Chick Harding had impeccable credentials.

The next mission for both the 100th and Crew No. 31 was an attack on the submarine pens at La Pallice, France, on July 4, 1943, flying aboard *"Muggs"* (230184). It was virtually an exact repeat of our mission to Saint-Nazaire a week earlier. Once again, we flew completely around the Brest Peninsula, made our bomb run from the sea, and had to endure the horrific, unnerving flak and air turbulence the explosions created over the target. However, this time, we also came under a savage attack by German fighters. On our bomb run, thirty-two-year-old Lieutenant Bob Pearson of the 351st BS pulled away from the formation and jettisoned his bombs even though all his engines appeared to be turning. He was under heavy attack by several Me 109 fighters as the crew began to bail out; one evaded capture, and nine were taken prisoner.[4] We learned later from the crew member who evaded capture that two of their engines failed simultaneously on the bomb run and a third was knocked out by one of the German fighters. Pearson had joined the Royal Canadian Air Force before America entered the war. After the Japanese attack on Pearl Harbor, he transferred to the U.S. Army Air Corps. We were to meet again three months later when I arrived in the South Compound at Stalag Luft III. He was one of the first individuals I saw when I moved into my room in Building 130, but more about that later.

The attacks by the VIII BC on the German U-boat shelters on the Atlantic coast of France during the summer of 1943 were of dubious value. Although each of our aircraft dropped two two-thousand-pound bombs, our heaviest ordnance, it was doubtful they had any effect. Every month since January 1941, British photographic reconnaissance planes monitored the Germans' progress in bombproofing these shelters with thick concrete. By January 1942, eighteen months before the attacks by the 4th BW, they knew it was unlikely that aerial bombing would interfere with the German operations. In December 1942, the British war cabinet admitted that Bomber Command's repeated night attacks

---

4. In recent years, considerable discussion has surfaced regarding the correct and accurate nomenclature for the single- and twin-engine fighters designed by Willy Messerschmitt; the 109 and the 110, respectively. As compelling as the recent literature is to have the **Bf** prefix attached to the 109 and 110 designs, we have found no references in VIII Bomber Command documentation that demonstrates the American use of the **Bf** designation. Accordingly, all references made in this book to Messerschmitt's designs will carry the **Me** prefix.

on Lorient and Saint-Nazaire had "destroyed almost everything but the pens." Only the continuing seriousness of the U-boat peril can explain why, notwithstanding the war cabinet's finding, RAF Bomber Command and our VIII BC were ordered to continue attacking these heavily defended targets.

Three days after our unnerving experience at La Pallice, and nine days after the hellish Saint-Nazaire raid, I wrote a letter to my mother commenting briefly on the operations in which I had been involved:

July 7, 1943

Dear Mom—
I don't expect you to get this letter for quite awhile so won't say anything much up to the minute, but things are moving. I have the feeling that I might get back home before Christmas, unless of course something big happens.

I can't tell you much about what I am doing but will give you a little. I believe I was most scared on my first mission, not that I still don't have a funny feeling when I know we are going. As a rule, we are told the night before that we are going (and I am surprised that I've always managed to sleep by just keeping my mind off the subject), but we don't know when or where we'll go. We are awakened by an orderly in time for a briefing on our target and takeoff time, which is usually from four to six in the morning. From then on we are busy checking our equipment and other items.

In flight everything is as it always has been until we cross into enemy territory where we are constantly on the lookout for "Jerry." It is the strangest feeling to fly over beautiful country where the people below are out to harm you. The return trip to

England is about the same as the one out in reverse order, but we're sure happy to see England and home again. At the dinner table there is always a lively discussion, just like after a big football game at home.

War is sad but I believe the people at home can be proud of the American Eighth Air Force here in England. Please keep writing and all of you take care of yourselves. I hope to see you soon and tell you about all the places I've been in the war.

All my love,
Frank

The 100th was alerted to a mission on July 9, 1943, but the mission was scrubbed when we awoke that morning to a blowing, window-rattling rain and zero visibility. However, the ever-persistent VIII BC put us back on alert the same evening. The next morning, Saturday, July 10, 1943, the 100th launched twenty-six aircraft for an attack on the Le Bourget airfield in Paris. When they were only ten minutes from the target, the bombers once again encountered 10/10 cloud cover and were forced to abandon the mission. As the 100th formation was withdrawing over the French coast near Dieppe, they were jumped by a swarm of Fw 190 German fighters, presumably from the elite Jagdgeschwader 26 based at Lille-Nord. In the ensuing melee, *Judy E.* (230050), flown by Lieutenant Charles "Scotty" Duncan of the 350th BS, was knocked out of formation and was seen going down with two engines burning and its crew bailing out; two evaded capture, and eight were taken prisoner. Scotty Duncan was a classmate of Crankshaft and John Brady in the advanced flying school at Spence Field, Moultrie, Georgia. Crew No. 31 did not fly this mission. The 418th BS was standing down, and Crankshaft, Augie, and I were in London on a two-day pass.

My recollection of this visit to London is now only a series of cameo flashbacks—the small Victorian train station at Diss; the flat, shaggy meadows of East Anglia; dingy, wartime-neglected structures alongside the railway approaches at Ipswich, Colchester, and Chelmsford; and our arrival at bustling, crowded Liverpool Street Station. It looked to me as if we arrived at the same time as all the British military and half of the American personnel in the United Kingdom. In London, we tried to find the life for which we were homesick. We looked for it in hotels, bars, restaurants, and theaters. During our visit, we saw the musical film *Stormy Weather,* starring Lena Horne and Cab Calloway and his band. We enjoyed a superb dinner of roast duck in the elegant dining room of the prestigious Dorchester Hotel on Park Lane across from Hyde Park. We sat on creaking, rickety stools in dark, noisy pubs, having a pint and watching pairs of decorous, elderly English ladies smoking cigarettes and sipping "gin and orange," a sight we certainly would not have seen in America in 1943. I remember an underground club in Knightsbridge, where a rotund entertainer named Reggie, who wore a rumpled tuxedo, played away on a battered old piano. The top of his piano was a mass of circular water stains imprinted from years of supporting wet glasses. When I spoke with him, he asked, "Where are you from?" As soon as I told him I was from Georgia, he began pounding out "(I'm a) Ramblin' Wreck from Georgia Tech," the Georgia Tech football song. I bought him a drink, which was added to the dozen or so already lined up on top of the piano. I was convinced that if I had told him I was from Timbuktu, Reggie would have immediately banged out an appropriate melody. Our trip to London was an interesting and pleasant experience for three young men who were a long way from home and whose fate at the time was far from clear. As I enjoyed the sights, sounds, and smells of London, I did not know that three months later, I would be wounded in action and a prisoner of the Germans.

Back at Thorpe Abbotts, I wrote my mother on July 14, 1943: "London is a lot like New York; that is, a big town with much going on. It's a good place to relax after a little flying, best food since I left the States. What a break our chairborne troops there get!"

There was one observation on which airmen of the Eighth, without exception, agreed: "They oughta cut the cables on them barrage balloons and let the island sink." They were speaking of the treacherous and changeable English weather. We were learning the hard way that weather governed the air operations of the VIII BC. Indeed, it controlled our every move. In the end, weather conditions decided when we would fly, where we would fly and, most importantly, whether we could strike our intended target. As I recall, in July 1943, northwest Europe was never completely free from cloud cover. Our procedure for taking off and assembling over England was almost as unnerving as combat itself. The weather over the target determined if a mission would be dispatched, so we often took off in poor visibility. It was not unusual for a group in the process of forming an assembly in the air to emerge from a corridor between narrowly separated deep clouds only to see another group at approximately the same altitude crossing in front of them while also circling and maneuvering into formation. The false starts and en route mission recalls we endured through the first half of July 1943 were exceedingly frustrating. We all felt that we were risking life and limb to no purpose when layers of clouds formed a protective shield over our primary targets and forced us to look for impromptu "targets of opportunity" or to bring our bombs home. Our next mission was a perfect example.

At about 3:00 on the cold, early morning of July 17, 1943, the CQ—charge of quarters—came into our hut switching on lights and yelling for us to wake up. Although I had slept soundly, I yawned through our usual motions of dressing, gathering our gear, and going to breakfast. Breakfast, however, was a treat. Hoarded and carefully doled-out fresh eggs were served to combat crews like the last meal of the condemned; we only got them when we flew a combat mission. Then, on to the briefing room for the tension-charged drawing of the curtains that would reveal our target for the day. This day's mission was a deep penetration foray to bomb an aeroengine plant in Hamburg. By this time, we were no longer the new boys of the VIII BC. There were cries of "Jeeee-sus Keee-rist!" "I quit," and "Where's the doctor? I need an operation." It wasn't really funny, but many laughed anyway. There were also a variety of whistles and more than a few honest gasps of dismay.

Over the North Sea, we donned our oxygen masks, climbed to our bombing altitude of twenty-four thousand feet, test-fired our machine guns, and "sweated out Jerry." When we made a right turn south of Helgoland into the Elbe estuary near Cuxhaven, the weather immediately worsened. Convection currents of warm, moist air rising from the ground condensed in the cold North Sea air to form large, billowy cumulus clouds. Apparently, we were about to make another futile run. At 9:55 a.m., the task force was recalled, but as we turned to withdraw, we were assaulted by swarms of German fighters and rocket-firing Ju 88s. As we were fighting our way back to the open sea, our airplane for this mission, *"Muggs"* (230184), rocked violently from a loud explosion and began a steep wingover to the right. I was instantly paralyzed. I saw through the Plexiglas nose window that we were plunging straight down into the sea from over twenty thousand feet. In Charlie Cruikshank's words: "We went out of formation very quickly, and I remember

Graham and I standing on everything. We lost six thousand to seven thousand feet. After we got her under control, I started looking for another group so we could stick our nose in somewhere. Finally, I saw another group two thousand or three thousand feet above us and burned out all four engines climbing, chasing after them and sliding into their formation. Once we got there, she flew well." I later estimated that we flew approximately forty-five miles alone, battling German fighters all the way. As soon as we were settled into the formation of the other group, our gunners reported that the trailing edge of our right wing was badly damaged.

Upon landing at Thorpe Abbotts, we saw that the 20 mm round that had almost taken us away had blown a gaping hole in the trailing edge of the right wing at its inboard hinge point with the right aileron. This displaced and jammed the aileron out of position, causing Crankshaft and Graham to temporarily lose control of the airplane. Master Sergeant Miller, our crew chief, visualizing the repair work he and his team had ahead of them, simply said, "My God." Though Sergeant Miller and the rest of his ground crew were almost finished with the repairs to our original aircraft, *Bastard's Bungalow,* a closer inspection of the damage to *"Muggs"* determined that the aircraft was beyond repair and, accordingly, was salvaged.[5] And, again, it was all for nothing.

Three days later, however, the VIII BC was on the verge of receiving the break in weather that we had needed for weeks. High-flying Mosquito aircraft of the RAF Weather Service and VIII BC weather reconnaissance B-17 aircraft reported clearing weather conditions far out over the North Atlantic, the breeding ground for

5. For additional insight about the ground crews, see Cindy Goodman and Jan Riddling's *The Forgotten Man—The Mechanic: The Kenneth A. Lemmons Story* (Little Rock, AR: CinJan Productions, 1999).

virtually all weather fronts carried into Britain and northern Europe on prevailing westerlies. The meteorologists at VIII BC, responsible for predicting winds, temperatures, humidity, dew points and cloud conditions, visibility, icing, and other precursors of northern European weather, tracked these reports. They drew and redrew their weather maps, crisscrossed with isobars, and concluded that it was finally going to happen. The coming weekend would bring a spell of good weather over Britain and northwest Europe that would be favorable for bombing operations.

On Saturday, July 24, 1943, General Eaker sent three task forces to attack Norwegian targets. Nine groups of the 1st BW[6] were dispatched to strike nitrate factories in Herøya. Four 4th BW groups[7] were sent to bomb port facilities at Bergen but encountered 10/10 cloud cover over the target and took their bombs home. The 95th and 100th BGs were sent to blast the port of Trondheim where, as I recall, there were rumors that the German battleship *Tirpitz* was in dry dock. Our long crossing of the North Sea was uneventful, as was our unopposed and successful bomb run against light, sporadic, and ineffective flak. Our elapsed flying time for this tedious mission was twelve hours, our longest of the war. However, it earned us another check mark against our "missions to go" list.

The 418th BS was again standing down the following day when twenty-five aircraft of the 100th, with other groups of the 4th BW, set out to attack the Heinkel aircraft works at Warnemünde and found the primary target under cloud cover. They flew to Kiel, where they were met with intensive flak. The 350th BS aircraft *Duration + Six* (25862), flown that day by Captain Dick Carey, operations officer of the 350th, who had taken the place of Bill DeSanders, the regular

6. Consisting of the 91st, 92nd, 303rd, 305th, 306th, 351st, 379th, 381st, and 384th BGs.

7. Consisting of the 94th, 95th, 96th, 100th, 385th, and 388th BGs.

pilot, was severely damaged and forced to ditch in the North Sea. Four members of the crew, including Dick Carey, survived and became prisoners of war.

The next day, July 26, 1943, Crew No. 31 participated in an assault on the Continental Gummi Werke, a rubber factory, at Hanover. However, our old nemesis, heavy overcast shrouding the target, was back, and we were recalled. But, as we were grinding home in clear weather over the North Sea, we spied a convoy of freighters sailing snuggled up to the coast of the Frisian Islands and made a bomb run on them. Although most of our bombs fell harmlessly into the sea, I saw several direct hits on ships.

Two days later, on July 28, 1943, the Eighth launched another "maximum effort," which included twenty-one aircraft from the 100th, to attack an aircraft assembly plant at Oschersleben. The bombing results were excellent. Crew No. 31 did not fly this mission but was put on alert to fly the following day.

On July 29, 1943, for the fifth day in less than a week, the 4th BW was out in force when eighty-one of its aircraft were sent to attack the Heinkel factory at Warnemünde, the same target that had been obscured by heavy cloud cover four days earlier. This time, we were successful and garnered another check mark by our name on our "missions to go" list. On our return, we were greeted by still another alert for a mission at dawn the next morning. We were chalking them up fast.

The following day involved what, to me, was one of the great mysteries of my wartime experience: why we were not blown out of the sky by leaking gasoline. I did not fly the mission on July 30, 1943, with Charlie Cruikshank and my regular crew against the Gerhard Fieseler Werke at Kassel, which manufactured under license the Focke-Wulf Fw 190A. Instead, I was assigned to fly aboard *Paddlefoot's Proxy* (25863) with Lieutenant John Brady and Crew No. 32, who lived in the same Nissen hut with us. John's regular navigator, Lieutenant Harry Crosby, had recently been transferred to Lieutenant Ev Blakely's Crew No. 35, and John had not yet received a replacement.

Wake-up, briefing, takeoff, assembly, and our climb out over the water to Europe were normal until we crossed the Belgian coast south of Antwerp, where we were immediately enveloped by intense, accurate flak. Suddenly, amid the usual deafening noise and my praying and hanging on for dear life, I heard a crackling sound like gravel being thrown against a tin roof. The airplane lurched violently, wobbled a bit, and appeared to founder. With that, we peeled off sharply to the left, away from the formation, and began a steep descent toward the sea. Lieutenant Howard "Hambone" Hamilton, the bombardier, and I just stared at each other. As we steadied up, John called me and said grimly, "We're going home, Murph. Which way?" While I frantically fussed and fumbled with my maps, charts, plotters, and E6B computer trying to work out a course home, I heard voices from the rear of the airplane reporting that we were streaming fluids. John commented that he detected the strong odor of aviation gasoline and wondered whether fuel or fuel fumes were seeping into the fuselage and cockpit area from somewhere. I can now envision both he and copilot John Hoerr scanning dials and flipping fuel cutoff switches while troubleshooting the system to determine if we had a damaged fuel feed or transfer line that had to be isolated. Gasoline fumes in the cockpit meant that we had a major fire and explosion hazard inside the airplane, which was still fully loaded with bombs. Our one thought was to get home to England and not have to abandon our airplane over occupied Europe. I have no doubt others in the crew were on pins and needles, but I clearly recall having a great deal of confidence in John Brady to get us home. I gave him a direct heading to Thorpe Abbotts. We flew all the way home just above the water and treetops.

When we arrived at Thorpe Abbotts, John ignored all normal landing procedures and took us straight in for a landing on our main east-west runway. We bumped down and rolled out. The airplane had scarcely stopped moving when John was on the intercom shouting, "Out! Everybody out!" Even as fire trucks and emergency vehicles were racing across the field toward us, we were scrambling, crawling, and jumping out of every opening in the airplane we could find and, as John said later, "running like hell into the woods like the brave and courageous fellows we were." I still don't know why the aviation gasoline didn't explode, taking the entire crew with it. I guess it just wasn't our time.

The Kassel mission ended the VIII BC's campaign during the last week of July, a period that later came to be known as "Blitz Week." We paid dearly for both our successes and our failures. Eighty-eight American bombers failed to return from a total of 1,047 effective sorties, a loss ratio of more than 8 percent per mission. Overall, the aircraft and crew strength of VIII BC was reduced by over 40 percent in this seven-day period. More than five hundred aircraft were damaged, eighteen of them beyond repair. The aircrews of the 100th BG, mostly its original crews who, in the postwar Bloody Hundredth folklore of the VIII BC, have often been portrayed as brash, undisciplined, and occasionally even incompetent, flew seventy-nine effective sorties with the loss of one aircraft, that of intelligent, steady, and dependable Captain Dick Carey from Long Beach, California. Dick would later be my roommate for almost a year as a prisoner of war. He was one of the finest men I have ever known. The performance of the 100th BG during this difficult period was gallant and dedicated. I know—I was there.

During this same week, the RAF carried out its "Battle of Hamburg," attacking the city four times in ten days, not counting two daylight raids by the Eighth 1st BW on July 25 and 26, 1943. The RAF however, lost only eighty-six bombers while flying over 3,000 sorties during this campaign, largely because of the introduction of Window, bundles of short metal strips, that were dropped and effectively confused German gun-laying radar. For the Germans, the appalling firestorms created by these attacks destroyed over 60 percent of the city and killed thousands of people. The devastation wrought on that proud Hanseatic city was fearsome beyond description and gruesomer than anything Dante could describe in his *Inferno*.

By the end of July 1943, Crew No. 31 was officially credited with nine missions against the total of twenty-five we needed to complete our combat tour. By VIII BC standards, we were a veteran crew. We had been involved in many air-to-air battles with determined and courageous Luftwaffe fighters but had not overcome the fear we felt each time we were engaged against them. The German fighters usually attacked from between eleven o'clock[8] and one o'clock level, the muzzle flashes of the guns in the leading edges of their wings twinkling like Fourth of July sparklers, gray-white puffs from exploding time-fused 20 mm cannon shells dancing into and through our formation. The German pilots were highly determined, skilled, and courageous; their fighters seemed to slip and slide through

8. Both the British and Americans employed a system of verbal shorthand for a crew member to alert the rest of the crew as to where and at what level a fighter attack was being directed at the aircraft. To understand this system, imagine a twelve-hour clock face superimposed over the bomber's silhouette, where the number **12** is adjacent to the nose and the number **6** adjacent to the tail. Thus **twelve o'clock high** indicates that a fighter was attacking the nose of the bomber from above, **six o'clock low** indicates that the fighter is attacking from behind and below the bomber, and **nine o'clock level** indicates the fighter is at the same altitude as the bomber with the attack coming toward the left side.

openings and cracks in the sky between our aircraft, or half rolling and snapping into a power dive straight down just before a head-on collision. We had also survived several repeats of the heavy flak we experienced at Saint-Nazaire. Twice, I had been in aircraft knocked out of formation by lethal enemy fire.

We had become accustomed to the thin, bitterly cold, subzero air and the crystalline ice that regularly formed on our windows at the high altitudes at which we flew. We were also accustomed to the layers of cumbersome clothing we wore: long johns, a wool uniform, a heavy flying jacket, thick gloves, boots, an oxygen mask, the Mae West life jacket, and, finally, our parachute harness. The mixed feelings of anticipation, excitement, and foreboding that I experienced upon arriving in England before we went into combat had long since vanished and had been replaced by a recurring sense of deep anxiety. If the 100th BG flew a mission and my crew was not scheduled to fly, I felt a great sense of relief. When we were on a mission and encountered flak or fighter aircraft, I always had an uncontrollable, fluttery feeling that never went away until I was out of danger. I was not alone. Most 100th BG airmen I knew readily admitted that, in the words of their most descriptive expression, they were "scared shitless" in combat and, after a tough air battle, were still shaky after landing back at Thorpe Abbotts.

VIII BC losses averaged more than 4 percent per mission in late July 1943 during Blitz Week. This meant that a crew member's chance of completing his combat tour was statistically zero. We were well aware of this, but I do not recall us talking about our situation in those terms. Clearly, the stresses and strains of continuous combat left us all with frayed nerves, but we usually settled down after a few days' rest. If a problem developed, it was normally indicated in personality changes—silence and withdrawal by an otherwise outgoing person, inexcusable irritability, and annoyance over trivialities one would normally ignore. The typical response to this behavior was for the rest of us to say half-jokingly to our disturbed colleague something subtle such as, "You're cracking up. You're going round the bend. Give us a break, pull yourself together." Most often, this was the end of it, except in the rare case of those who truly believed they were going to die. Then the crew was given a replacement. A subtler problem was air crewmen who developed chronic health problems or pilots who were plagued by persistent equipment malfunctions preventing takeoff on a combat mission, or who built a pattern of mission aborts. These things did not go unnoticed.

Throughout the war, my mother wrote me daily, except when she had no mailing address. She never failed to tell me she was following the progress of the war, that she was thinking of me and praying for my safe return. The news coverage of the activities of the Eighth during Blitz Week was devastating to her. On August 14, 1943, I wrote her:

Dear Mom,
You seem so worried about me. I realize that you are, perhaps even more than I am about myself. I wish I could comfort you but don't know how except to say that I'm as happy as I can be about the situation and wouldn't be with another squadron in the Army Air Forces. We don't live like dogs. In fact, we have worked out a pretty good set-up. We have warm barracks, a radio, and, in general, as good as we had it at home. Of course, fighting is the difference but keep praying. I think I will be home in just a few months.

All my love,
Frank

As I read this letter today, it does not seem very convincing. If I had it to do all over again, however, I really don't know what else I could have said that would have eased her anguish. In truth, the war was fought in many places, including in the hearts of countless mothers, fathers, wives, and other relatives. At least those of us who were in the combat theaters knew what was happening to us. Those at home did not and had to live with their own fears. We could not help them.

For the first two weeks in August 1943, VIII BC marked time to permit its exhausted aircrews to recover from the grueling ordeal of Blitz Week, to give our hard-pressed ground crews time to inspect and repair damaged aircraft, and to receive replacement crews and aircraft for those that had been lost. During July 1943, Crew No. 31 logged forty-seven hours of combat flying time and over twenty-six hours of local training time. From August 1 to August 14, 1943, we had less than eleven hours flying time, all local.

On August 12, 1943, the VIII BC launched 330 B-17 bombers of the 1st and 4th BWs to attack several German targets. But, as so often had been the case, the entire task force ran afoul of bad weather over their targets, and only two of the sixteen groups participating in the mission were able to bomb their briefed targets. And, once again, the bombers encountered fierce, determined opposition from the Luftwaffe. Of the 243 aircraft considered to have flown effective sorties, 25 failed to return, for a loss rate of more than 10 percent. The first mission for our crew in August 1943 was on the fifteenth when the VIII BC put up 280 aircraft from the 1st and 4th BWs to attack several Luftwaffe airfields in northern France. The 100th bombed the airfield at Merville-Lille. In VIII BC jargon of the day, this mission was a "piece of cake," or a "milk run." It was an easy mission. Nevertheless, four more American bombers were lost on that mission. Easy or not, none of our missions was cost-free, and the cost was never cheap.

In the early evening hours of the following day, on August 16, 1943, all crews of the 100th were placed on alert with a curious set of instructions. In addition to our flying gear, we were told to pack a blanket, a summer uniform, and sufficient underwear and toilet articles to last us several days. We were also told to expect to receive an early wake-up call the next morning. Something very unusual was afoot.

THIRD BOMBARDMENT DIVISION
Group Defensive Formation
Fall 1943
See diagram on page 11 of photo insert 1

The key building block for the group formation was the three-aircraft V element. For each V element, the B-17 to the right of the lead bomber was approximately fifty feet above and the B-17 to the left of the lead bomber was approximately fifty feet below. Two V elements constitute one squadron, and three squadrons constitute a group. The lowest B-17 in the high squadron was slightly above in altitude to the highest B-17 of the Lead Squadron. For the low squadron, the highest B-17 was slightly below in altitude to the lowest B-17 of the lead squadron. This provided an eighteen-bomber group formation with an effective overlapping defensive firepower. A review of 100th BG records indicates that this formation was modified by assigning the high squadron with nine instead of six B-17s. The group's formation charts also indicate a "trail" squadron, the function of which is not clearly defined but probably was reserved for aircraft that were scheduled spares or those that formed a composite group with aircraft from other groups. The overall size of this formation was approximately 900 feet high, 1,138 feet wide, and 640 feet deep.

THIRD BOMBARDMENT DIVISION
Combat Wing Defensive Formation Fall 1943
See diagram on page 12 of photo insert 1

The key building block for the combat wing formation constituted three group formations, each containing eighteen B-17s. The profile shows that the second, or low, group formation was below the lead group formation, and the third, or high, group was above the lead group. As with the group formation, the highest B-17 in the low group was slightly below the altitude of the lowest B-17 in the lead group, and the lowest B-17 in the high group was slightly above the altitude of the highest B-17 in the lead group. In keeping with the V element discussed in the group formation, the low group was to the right of the lead group while the high group was positioned to the left. The overall size of this formation was approximately 2,700 feet high, 2,845 feet wide, and 1,280 feet deep.

9

DANGEROUS DAYS, DESPERATE HOURS

On August 1, 1943, an armada of 177 B-24 bombers from five bomb groups of the Ninth AF in the Mediterranean, including three that were detached from the VIII BC, made a low-altitude attack on the oil fields and refineries near Ploiești, Romania (Operation Tidalwave). It was a very difficult raid that suffered from a series of misfortunes, including navigation errors. Fifty-four of the bombers, over 30 percent of the total attacking force, were lost. Adding insult to injury, although the targets were seriously damaged, they were not destroyed. Twelve days later, on August 13, 1943, the same five B-24 groups mustered enough strength to strike the Messerschmitt aircraft factory at Wiener Neustadt near Vienna, Austria, with much better results—inflicting heavy damage while losing only two aircraft.

The B-17 aircrews of the VIII BC in England were well-aware of these dramatic missions. They learned about them by way of *Stars and Stripes,* British newspapers, and the Eighth grapevine. It was a sign of the times that, while we could empathize with the aircrews involved, we saw no connection with us; we had our own hands full. Tragically, we did not find the loss of fifty-four aircraft and 540 men hundreds of miles away nearly as distressing and painful as the deaths of the men who flew alongside us. We did not need anything to remind us that the overarching threat to our continued existence was the Luftwaffe. However, to our commanders, the shocking losses at Ploieşti made it all the more clear that, unless the menace of German fighter aircraft could be sharply reduced, the future of American daylight bombing in Europe was in grave doubt.

In reality, the Ninth AF operations were all part of a comprehensive strategic plan. Early in July 1943, VIII BC and Ninth AF planners selected priority targets in four European towns and configured a joint mission intended to be carried out on the same day.[1] The targets were located in Schweinfurt and Regensburg, Germany; Ploieşti, Romania; and Wiener Neustadt, Austria. The goal of our raids was to cripple the German Luftwaffe. The Eighth would attack Schweinfurt and Regensburg; the Ninth would strike Ploieşti and Wiener Neustadt. Because of uncooperative weather, no mutually acceptable date for this joint operation could be set, so General Carl "Tooey" Spaatz, commander of Northwest African Air Forces, decided to proceed with his part of the plan alone, and did.

The initial plan for the Eighth was for both the 1st and 4th BWs to attack Schweinfurt. The 1st BW would then return to England while the 4th BW would fly to North Africa. In strict secrecy, each group was told to select a "lead crew" and send them to their respective bomb wing headquarters to prepare for the mission. The crew chosen by the 100th BG was Captain Ev Blakely's of the 418th

---

1. Strategic targets for the Eighth Air Force were identified by the American Committee of Operations Analysts (COA) in Washington, who designated German industries that, if destroyed at the earliest possible date, would seriously damage the German war effort. Suggested priority lists of key targets were sent by the COA to its counterpart organization in England, the British Ministry of Economic Warfare, who reviewed them with the Eighth Air Force and British Air Staff for priority and inclusion in the RAF/USAAF Combined Bombing Offensive (CBO) program. In the summer of 1943, German aircraft and ball bearing industries were at the top of the list.

BS. The remaining crews, who were totally unaware of this plan, were to follow their normal routine. The bombardiers of the lead crews—in our case, Lieutenant Jim Douglass—were shown models and photographs of the Schweinfurt targets but were not told the name of the town or its location. The lead crews were detached from regular operations to undertake practice-bombing missions. I later understood that when the Regensburg operation was added, many of the 4th BW bombardiers learned they would be bombing a completely different factory from the one they had studied so long and were given only a few hours to study the new target. In retrospect, it is difficult to see how a crew, perhaps apart from the bombardier, could effectively prepare to attack a target that was so secret even its identity and location could not be revealed to them until the very last minute.

By early August 1943, the detailed plan for the Eighth's assaults on Schweinfurt and Regensburg was ready. The vital target was Schweinfurt, where over 40 percent of Germany's ball bearings were manufactured in three factories. Regensburg was almost a diversion, even though it was the home of Messerschmitt AG's largest Me 109 factory that was turning out upward of 270 new Me 109 G-6 fighter aircraft each month.

A force of 146 long-range bombers from the 4th BW under Colonel Curtis LeMay would leave England first, attack Regensburg, and then fly on to North Africa. A fleet of 230 Forts from the 1st BW would enter German airspace ten minutes after the Regensburg force, strike Schweinfurt, and return to England. If all went as planned, the Regensburg force would fight its way in and the Schweinfurt force would fight its way out. Some 400 fighters would provide partial support for the bombers. These raids would take place on August 17, 1943, the anniversary of the first VIII BC B-17 raid of the Second World War. Coincidence or not, the August 17 "double strike" mission to Regensburg and Schweinfurt, as it was designed, would severely tax the capability and determination of the Eighth's men and machines.[2]

The aircrews of the 100th were awakened by their squadron CQs—charge of quarters—at 1:30 a.m. on August 17, 1943. Mission briefing was at 3:00 a.m. and taxi time at 5:30 a.m. It was evident from the start that something big was up: Thorpe Abbotts was a beehive of activity. The sounds of war were not limited to the rattle of gunfire and exploding shells. When we arose, the distinct buzz of human activity could be heard coming from the direction of the aircraft hardstands attached to the perimeter track encircling the airfield. Bomb trailers were hauling their deadly cargo to be hoisted into bomb bays by electrical power provided by noisy putt-putt gasoline-powered generators, armorers were loading boxes of .50-caliber ammunition into aircraft, and crew chiefs and mechanics were "pulling the props through" and firing up engines.

The early-morning air was calm, cool, and damp. With a towel around my neck and toilet kit in hand, I made my way to the ablution hut to shave and wash up. There was little conversation as we dressed and prepared for what we knew was going to be a long day. We gathered our flying gear, the blankets, changes of uniforms, and toilet articles we had been instructed to pack and quietly climbed into the trucks that had been sent to transport us to the crew mess for our "combat special" breakfast of fresh eggs.

After breakfast, we were taken to headquarters where our usual

---

2. The August 17, 1942, mission involved eighteen B-17Es of the 97th Bomb Group, six flying a diversionary sortie and the other twelve bombing the marshalling yards at Rouen, France. The pilots of the lead aircraft were Colonel Frank A. Armstrong and Major Paul W. Tibbets.

briefing agenda would be set in motion—target, routes, bomb loads, formation positions, assembly procedures, weather, timing, communications channels, call signs, enemy defenses, and the bidding of Godspeed. After stiffening to attention at the witching hour, we took our seats. An expectant hush settled over the briefing theater. The curtains parted. There was no raucous laughter and no whistles. There were no feigned expressions of pain. The red string pinned across the face of the map was unbelievable. It traced a route that was surely a suicide mission. The 4th BW would leave England at Lowestoft, cross the English Channel to Holland, turn south into Belgium, proceed southeast to Mannheim and across Germany at its widest part, where no Eighth bombers had ever been before, and then fly east to Regensburg, deep in Bavaria on the Danube River. After dropping our bombs on an Me 109 factory at Regensburg, we would fly south over the Austrian Alps into northern Italy. At Lake Garda, we would make a full circle to assimilate stragglers. After re-forming, we would proceed out into the Ligurian Sea near Genoa and fly down past Corsica and Sardinia to Algeria, where we would land at a base in the Algerian Desert.

I impulsively turned my head slowly from side to side, quietly rolling my eyes from right to left, searching the faces of the men around me to see if they would betray the fear born of realizing the dangers that lay ahead of us. I saw signs of nervousness on everyone, strain on many, a certain grayness in those who were usually the pinkest, anxiety in those who had not slept, and an overall look of acceptance and resignation. But I saw no signs of fear. That would come later.

The 4th BW would be led by Colonel LeMay himself, who would fly with the 96th BG in a formation with the 388th and 390th BGs. They would be followed by a box consisting of the 94th and 385th

BGs. The third and last box would include the 95th BG high and the 100th BG at the tail end in the "coffin corner."[3]

As with every combat mission, all engines on our B-17 had been run up to full power by the ground crew and flight engineer, Leonard Weeks, and were warmed up and ready when the rest of the crew arrived at the hardstand. Crankshaft then conferred with the crew chief and Weeks about the condition of the airplane and reviewed any relevant paperwork. Our usual engine starting sequence was first number 2 followed by 3, 4, and 1 because the inboard engines powered the electric-motor pumps in the hydraulic system that operated the brakes and cowl flaps.

Our taxi time was scheduled for 5:30 a.m. However, when we arrived at our airplanes at about 4:45 a.m., a dense morning mist was still clinging to the woods, fields, and hollows of East Anglia. We were told that our takeoff time had been delayed an hour, and we were instructed to stand by our airplanes until a decision was made whether the mission would proceed or be scrubbed. There are few tensions contrived by man that can equal the strain of waiting to see whether a delay would turn into a scrub, especially on a tough mission. All the weaknesses in man's struggle for survival widened as the pressure grew. The mist persisted. The suspense continued.

---

3. The terms *coffin corner* and *Purple Heart corner* describe the lowest and rearmost place in a bomber formation, whether it was a basic group formation of twenty-one aircraft or a larger formation of three bomb groups. The defensive strength of a bomber formation rested with staggered positions afforded by the lead, high, and low elements and the resulting overlapping gunfire from their .50-caliber machine guns.

However, those flying in the low squadron were usually the last aircraft in the V formation of three B-17s. They could not expect as much protection from the rest of the formation as the bombers flying in front of them. Thus, fewer guns could be directed at German fighters that attacked the formation from the rear, leaving those bombers much more vulnerable. Finally, a German fighter attacking from the rear had more time to focus on specific targets than fighters attacking from the front. Fighters making a frontal assault also had to avoid colliding with the bombers, and the rate of closure between the fighters and bombers was much quicker flying head-on to the front than catching up to the rear.

An hour passed, and our takeoff time was postponed for another half hour. Even though I heaved a sigh of relief with each delay, deep inside, I wanted to get this mission behind me in spite of the fact that we were flying in the Purple Heart corner. Men waited beneath their airplanes, bracing themselves for the drama that was about to unfold.

At approximately 6:45 a.m., a jeep raced to the hardstand and its officer-driver told us the mission was on and takeoff would be in thirty minutes. We were already loaded down with our gear, so we laced up, zipped up, buckled up, and about ten minutes before "Engine Start" time, we began climbing into our airplanes. As I usually did, instead of going around and entering the airplane through the main crew door, I approached the forward entrance door on the left-hand side of the nose area, flung my equipment and navigator's brief case up through the door, and did my chin-up into the aircraft. We began checking our vital systems, especially oxygen and the intercom. We would be on oxygen at least six hours, four of those hours inside German territory. Power turret operators checked motors and switches. Orlando Vincenti plugged in his radios and began twisting knobs. From the flight deck just above me, the voices of Crankshaft, Graham, and Weeks could be heard running through the mandatory USAAF verbal challenge/response checklist:

"Oka-a-ay. Preflight?"

"Complete."

"Form IA, weight and balance?"

"Checked."

"Controls and seats?"

"Checked."

"Fuel transfer valves and switch?"

"Off."

"Intercoolers?"
"Cold."
"Gyros?"
"Uncaged."

Then all of us waited those last few minutes until "Start engine!"

"All right, let's fire number two."
Pause.
"Energize."
Pause.
"Mesh."

As much as I loved the B-17, I recall no sound less reassuring and more tentative than the hesitant, straining, coughing noise of a Wright Cyclone engine, belching a huge cloud of white-gray smoke from its exhaust as it struggled to start up. Within minutes, however, aircraft engines were firing, coughing, sputtering, and coming to life all over Thorpe Abbotts. Now ready to taxi, Crankshaft and Graham signaled the ground crew to remove the wheel chocks. Fully loaded aircraft began moving awkwardly on to the taxi perimeter and converging in long lines at the east end of the main east-west runway. Because of our heavy bomb and fuel load, our gunners bunched up in the radio room to keep our weight forward for takeoff. On the perimeter track, Crankshaft ran up his engines. The rumbling sound rose and fell. The ship quivered and shook. We followed John Brady onto the main runway as the warmth of the rising sun was melting the morning mist.

100th Bomb Group Order of Battle August 17, 1943 Takeoff Order

Time	Serial	Squadron	Name	Pilot
0721	23393	418 Y	*Just-A-Snappin*	Everett E. Blakely John B. Kidd
	Returned on August 24, 1943			
0722	230061	418 Q	*Wolff Pack*	Robert H. Wolff
0723	23237	418 R	*Stymie*	John D. Brady
0723	230066	418 U	*Mugwump*	Charles B. Cruikshank John C. Egan
0724	230063	418 S	*Picklepuss*	Robert M. Knox
0725	25860	418 P	*Escape Kit*	Curtis R. Biddick
0726	230170	349 G	*Torchy 2*	Samuel L. Barr William W. Veal
0727	25861	349 J	*Laden Maiden*	Owen Roane
	Returned on August 24, 1943			
0727	230611	349 D	*Horny*	Henry A. Henington
0728	230042	349 L	*Oh Nausea!*	Glen S. Van Noy William L. Kennedy
0729	23229	349 A	*Pasadena Nena*	John K. Justice
	Returned on August 24, 1943			
0730	230002	349 F	*The WAAC Hunter*	Henry P. Shotland
0730	25864	351 A	*Piccadilly Lily*	Thomas E. Murphy Beirne Lay Jr.
	Returned on August 24, 1943			
0731	230059	351 G	*Barker's Burden*	Charles W. Floyd Jr.
	Returned early—engine failure			
0732	230080	351 F	*High Life*	Donald K. Oakes
0733	230358	350 X	*Phartzac*	Norman H. Scott Gale W. Cleven
0734	23232	350 V	*Flak Happy*	Ronald W. Hollenbeck
0734	230335	350 U	*Sans Finis*	Bernard A. DeMarco
	Returned on August 24, 1943			
0735	25867	350 O	*Alice from Dallas*	Roy F. Claytor
0736	230311	350 T	*Maybe*	Thomas D. Hummell
0737	230070	350 S	*Tweedle-O-Twill*	Ronald W. Braley
0738	230086	351 B	*Black Jack*	Victor E. Fienup

0739	230088	349 E	*Squawkin Hawk*	Sumner H. Reeder
	Returned early—spare aircraft			
0740	230152	418 X	*Messie Bessie*	Walter U. Moreno
	Returned early—spare aircraft			

When John began his takeoff run, Crankshaft and Graham eased our airplane on to the extreme east end of the main runway, set the brakes, locked the tail wheel, and ran the engines up to full power. As John was lifting off the ground at the far end of the field and beginning a shallow climb, Crankshaft released his brakes. We moved first laboriously and then swiftly down the center of the runway and were soon airborne. After our long delay, we had finally reached our point of no return. I was already experiencing the familiar, recurrent oversize knot in my throat, the cold shivers, and the gnawing, empty feeling in the pit of my stomach. However, as navigator, I felt I was lucky; I had my maps, charts, and log to keep my mind and hands busy. Augie and the guys in the back of the airplane could only sit, wait, and think. It really was going to be a long day.

The 100th crossed the Dutch coast at seventeen thousand feet shortly after 10:00 a.m. The 418th was the lead squadron for the group. The group operations officer, Major John B. "Jack" Kidd, was in the lead airplane with Captain Ev Blakely, bombardier Jim Douglass, and navigator Harry Crosby. John Brady was on Blakely's left wing, and Lieutenant Bob Wolff was on his right. Crew No. 31 was in the deputy lead position, leading the second element of the lead squadron. Our squadron commander, Major Bucky Egan, was in our airplane. Big, burly, gregarious Lieutenant Curtis Biddick from California was flying on our left wing, and Captain Robert "Bob" Knox was on our right. Leading the low squadron was my old Sebring crewmate Norman Hugh Scott, with his 350th Squadron

Commander, Major Gale "Bucky" Cleven. The high squadron was led by Major William Veal, commander of the 349th BS, who was flying with Lieutenant Sam "Little Sammy" Barr. Leading the third element of the high squadron was dark-haired, square-jawed Lieutenant Tom Murphy of the 351st BS. Flying with Thomas "Tom" Murphy in *Piccadilly Lily* (25864) was Lieutenant Colonel Beirne Lay Jr., one of seven officers who had gone to England in early 1942 with General Eaker to form the VIII BC. Beirne Lay was famous. Before the war, he had written a book, *I Wanted Wings,* that had been made into a popular film starring Veronica Lake and Ray Milland. After the war, Beirne Lay would write *Twelve O'Clock High* with Sy Bartlett, which was then made into an epic motion picture about the wartime VIII BC.[4]

Our fighter support was nowhere in sight as we approached the German border and saw the first German fighter aircraft climbing to intercept us. Within minutes, we were viciously attacked. Much has been written about the horrendous air battle at Regensburg, but Beirne Lay perhaps said it best: "The sight was fantastic and surpassed fiction. Emergency hatches, exit doors, prematurely opened parachutes, bodies, and assorted fragments of B-17s, and Hun fighters breezed past us in the slipstream. On we flew through the strewn wake of a desperate air battle, where disintegrating aircraft were commonplace and 60 parachutes in the air at one time were hardly worth a second look."[5]

South of Cologne, Charles Clark and James Johnson reported that Captain Bob Knox, flying in *Picklepuss* (230063) on our right

---

4. For additional information on Tom Murphy's crew and aircraft, see Paul M. Andrews, *We're Poor Little Lambs: The Last Mission of Crew 22 and Piccadilly Lily* (Springfield, VA: Foxfall Press, 1995).

5. Beirne Lay, *Personal Report on the Regensburg Mission, 17 August 1943,* Air Force Historical Research Agency Microfilm B0203, GP-100-SU-RE.

wing, was under attack from the rear, that pieces of his airplane were breaking off, and he was falling out of formation. He peeled off to the right and turned back toward England, but was immediately jumped by swarms of Messerschmitt and Focke-Wulf fighters and was shot down. Only four of the crew, including our talented artist Ernie Warsaw, survived.[6]

The only instance in all my combat missions in which I knew positively that my bullets were hitting home was during this battle. An elegant, mottled-gray Me 109 fighter had made a pass at us from the rear and foolishly flew straight through our formation instead of rolling over and diving. He was traveling only slightly faster than we were and was making a slow climbing left turn about one hundred yards to our left when he came into view. He gave me an easy deflection shot, and I poured it on with my left nose gun. I could see my tracers ricocheting from the bottom of his aircraft as he disappeared behind us. I have no idea what happened to him, but I have often wondered. Although I did my best to kill him, I now hope he survived the war and, like me, became a father and a grandfather. So many experiences in battle leave a lack of closure that feeds morbid curiosity.

The 100th BG proved to be particularly vulnerable at Regensburg. We were the last group in a task force of eight bomb groups

---

6. The most well-known and fascinating anecdote in the folklore of the 100th BG, which gained currency within the Eighth Air Force even during the war and has since become a legend, involved the downing of the Bob Knox crew on the Regensburg mission of August 17, 1943. According to the story, Captain Knox, while still over Germany, lowered the wheels of his disabled aircraft as a sign of surrender, but when German fighter aircraft closed in to "escort" him down to a nearby airfield, the gunners on the Knox crew shot down some of the escorts. The legend says that thereafter German fighter units regularly sought out the B-17 group with the square *D* identification of the 100th BG on their tails and inflicted heavy casualties on them in later raids. This story has been discredited by a number of Eighth Air Force historians who carefully examined all facts. I have been told by German fighter pilots who fought against us at the time that they were unaware of this story, that their ground control would never have permitted German fighter units to seek out one B-17 group, and that the markings on our aircraft meant absolutely nothing to them.

that stretched over a distance of at least ten miles. We were also the low group and had no fire support except for the 95th BG ahead and one thousand feet above us. As a result, we were met by wave after wave of frontal attacks as well as massed attacks from the rear. The Luftwaffe pilots flying the Me 109 and Fw 190 fighters were brave, determined, and skillful. On top of these fighter attacks, rockets fired from tubes beneath the wings of twin-engine Me 110 aircraft operating beyond the range of our .50-caliber machine guns were lobbed into our formation from all directions.[7]

Lieutenant Colonel Lay later wrote that from his position on *Piccadilly Lily* (25864), he observed a raging oxygen fire in the cockpit of Curtis Biddick's *Escape Kit* (25860), which was flying on our left wing. He saw copilot Richard Snyder crawl out of his window, hold on with one hand, reach back for his chute, buckle it on, and let go. He was instantly whisked back into the horizontal stabilizer and killed. His chute never opened. The airplane, with Curtis trapped inside, rolled over and spun to the ground. The battle continued in furious intensity. Biddick's body was located some three months later hanging in his chute harness from a tree branch.

Ten minutes of this kind of combat is measured as a lifetime; when it lasts for more than an hour, it is an eternity. During most of this time, Bucky Egan stayed in the horribly cramped nose compartment, firing the right nose .50-caliber machine gun, while I fired the left nose gun and Augie Gaspar handled the straight-ahead gun. Soon the nose of the airplane was ankle-deep in spent .50-caliber shell casings, and the cold air was thick with the smell of cordite. At one point, we ran low on ammunition. I detached my oxygen mask,

---

7. You may have seen those eerie green film clips during the 1991 Persian Gulf war that showed the night sky over Baghdad filled with ordnance. Although time and technology have changed, the experience remains the same, and I know what that feels like from the perspective of one who had to fly through it.

crawled back under the flight deck, and up through the floorboard door to the area behind the pilots' seats and where top turret gunner and flight engineer Leonard Weeks was positioned. This was a difficult undertaking because of my cumbersome flying clothing. I then edged my way back over the narrow catwalk through the bomb bay into the radio room and dragged a heavy box of .50-caliber ammo back over the same route to the nose with no oxygen. Adrenaline will work miracles!

When the 100th reached Regensburg, we had already lost six of our aircraft.

Lieutenant Roy F. Claytor, *Alice from Dallas* (25867)
5 evaded capture, 2 died in action, 3 taken prisoner
Captain Robert M. Knox, *Picklepuss* (230063)
6 died in action, 4 taken prisoner
Lieutenant Thomas D. Hummel, *Maybe* (230311)
2 died in action, 8 taken prisoner
Lieutenant Henry P. Shotland, *The WAAC Hunter* (230002)
1 died in action, 9 taken prisoner
Lieutenant Curtis R. Biddick, *Escape Kit* (25860)
4 died in action, 6 taken prisoner
Lieutenant Ronald W. Braley, *Tweedle-O-Twill* (230070)
1 died in action, 9 taken prisoner

We could see the target easily at a bend in the Danube River and made our bomb run with no opposition. Clearly, the Germans had not been expecting us to bomb a target so distant from England. The results looked great. We turned south. After a short while, we saw several Luftwaffe fighter aircraft off in the distance. They stayed around and shadowed us well outside our firing range but made no hostile moves toward us.

The Regensburg Messerschmitt plant had its own small *staffel* of six Me 109 Gs that came up to engage the American force and claimed four B-17s downed. I did not see them and suspect they had left the scene by the time the 100th BG reached the target area. The VIII BC raid stopped production at Regensburg for three weeks. A German casualty count on September 7, 1943, listed 392 dead, who were buried in a mass grave in the Upper Catholic Cemetery at Regensburg. Significantly, the August 17, 1943, raid by VIII BC stimulated the decentralization of aircraft production from Regensburg to other facilities as aircraft production was dispersed.

We crossed the Alps and entered Italian airspace over the Brenner Pass. As planned, we made a full circle above Lake Garda, the largest and easternmost of the glittering lakes in Lombardy's lake country, to permit straggling B-17s to rejoin the formation. We left mainland Italy near Genoa and began descending as we passed west of Corsica and Sardinia.

The 100th lost three more airplanes after leaving the target at Regensburg. Lieutenant Donald Oakes of the 351st BS took his battle-damaged *High Life* (230080) to Switzerland and belly-landed at the Dübendorf airfield near Zürich. Lieutenant Ron Hollenbeck's *Flak Happy* (23232) was seriously damaged before we reached the target, fell out of formation, and crashed in Italy, where two evaded capture and eight were taken prisoner. Lieutenant Glen Van Noy ran out of fuel and ditched *Oh Nausea!* (230042) in the Mediterranean. Ironically, his crew was rescued by a German flying boat. In the airplane with Lieutenant Van Noy was Colonel William L. Kennedy, commander of a gunnery school in the United States, who had come to England to study combat gunnery. When he heard that Regensburg was a deep penetration mission, he persuaded Colonel Harding to let him go along.

Shortly after 6:15 p.m., "with red lights showing on our fuel tanks" as Lieutenant Colonel Lay later wrote, the surviving seven aircraft of the 100th BG approached a remote air base in the desert near Telergma, Algeria, about sixty miles inland from Tunis, and "landed in the dust." The place appeared deserted and its facilities totally inadequate. There were only a few dilapidated, broken-down buildings surrounding a tower and operations center. The American and British forces that had been in North Africa were rapidly moving on to invade Sicily.

The inside of *Mugwump* (230066) looked the same as any B-17 did after every other long mission: hundreds of empty shells in the nose and waist of the fuselage clanked underfoot, where they mingled with discarded chewing gum wrappers, crumpled chocolate bar wrappers, crusts of sandwiches, and empty waxed boxes of emergency D rations. The noise from the mission we had just completed was still ringing in our ears. I could still hear our .50-caliber machine guns, smell the cordite, and see the seemingly never-ending attacks by the German fighters, the tracers crisscrossing the sky, and those time-fused 20 mm cannon shells exploding all around us. Even though we had landed safely, I still could not easily get over the sickening feeling of gnawing desperation that the German fighters would never stop coming and there was nothing anyone could do about it. I will never forget the feel of cold perspiration inside my heavy flight gear and the personification of fear and frustration in the eyes of Augie Gaspar and John Egan. Within hours after landing, we learned from the engineering officer in North Africa that *Mugwump* suffered severe damage to one of the main spars in the wings and would be grounded for repairs.[8]

---

8. *Mugwump* (230066) never returned to Thorpe Abbotts while I was there. Eventually, 230066 became an Aphrodite aircraft—a project involving radio controlled B-17s becoming flying bombs—and was destroyed on an October 30, 1944, sortie to Helgoland.

We spent our first night in Africa eating the small cans of cheese, dry crackers, and chocolate bars from boxes of K rations, drinking water from canteens brought from England, rehashing the day, and sleeping in and under our airplanes. Sometime during the night, I was awakened by a tugging at my blanket. Through the shadows, I could see that several ragtag local inhabitants of the area had brazenly entered our airplane and were snatching up everything not bolted down. For the first and only time in my life, I drew my .45-caliber pistol with the idea of protecting myself when I heard someone near me shout, "Get the hell out of here!" Our looters leaped out of the airplane and scurried away. The last we saw of these robed intruders, they were fleeing into the night, carrying off everything they had managed to steal from us.

The next morning, a jeep carrying several engineering and maintenance officers from the Twelfth AF drove out to our airplanes. They were followed by trucks loaded with handsome, healthy, tanned young men in khaki shirts and shorts, who were brought out to service the airplanes. These men were Italian prisoners of war. I have never seen happier, cheerfuller POWs. The 4th BW left eleven heavily damaged aircraft in North Africa after this raid, including *Mugwump* (230066), flown by Crew No. 31. Major John Egan and our crew, along with Bob Wolff and his crew from the 100th and several other crews from the 4th BW, would have to be airlifted back to England by ATC (Air Transport Command).

On August 20, 1943, we were picked up by an ATC C-47 aircraft and flown from Telergma to Marrakech, Morocco, where we were billeted in cottages on the grounds of the luxurious La Mamounia hotel, with its acres of rose and hibiscus gardens, and olive and orange trees. Each morning, a hotel employee pushed an empty wheelbarrow out to the orange groves and would return a bit later with a full load of newly picked oranges.

We took full advantage of our brief stopover in Marrakech. We hailed rickety horse-drawn calèches and clip-clopped to the ancient walled city. Its stone streets, with a hint of piquant spices in the air, were little more than paths through a bewildering maze of narrow zigzag canyons between tall, tottering buildings that appeared to have been designed by an architect who couldn't draw a straight line and built by laborers who couldn't describe a right angle. The Leaning Tower of Pisa would have been at home in Marrakech. We visited crowded souks and went to the great sprawling square of Jemaa el-Fna, where snake charmers, jugglers, and other entertainers pitched to the crowds for gratuities. We haggled desperately in humiliating negotiations with unconscionable street hawkers. We sipped coffee under umbrellas at sidewalk cafés and imbibed more potent potions sitting in the rattan-furnished hotel bar, where overhead fans, their motors softly humming, turned slowly and shafts of pale sun made their way through parqueted shutters. Over drinks at an outdoor bistro, we swapped our overseas caps with a group of passing Senegalese soldiers for their red fezzes with black tassels.

On Sunday morning, August 22, 1943, we were flown to Casablanca. That night, the ATC ferried us around Portugal and France and back to England. When we landed at Prestwick, we were met by Colonel Harding, who accompanied us to Thorpe Abbotts, where we were greeted by a group of news service reporters and photographers. Pictures and stories written that day about our return to England wearing our red fezzes appeared in the August 24, 1943, edition of *Stars and Stripes* and numerous American newspapers. My picture was printed in *The Atlanta Journal*. When asked how he managed to survive the Regensburg mission, John Egan gave a typical Egan response: "I carried two rosaries, two good luck medals, and a $2 bill off of which I had chewed a corner for each of my missions. I also wore my sweater backwards and my good luck jacket."

Immediately after meeting with the war correspondents, we went to a delayed post-mission interrogation by 100th BG intelligence officers. Normally, this debriefing would have taken place as soon as we landed from a mission. Combat crews were seated with elbows on long tables filled with forms and writing pads, drinking white mugs of strong coffee ladled from a five-gallon aluminum tub by a GI cook wearing a baseball-style khaki cap. More than a few airmen and their interrogators were puffing away, smoke curling in the air over dented Planters peanut cans filled with cigarette stubs. Over dry SPAM sandwiches and java, this was the time when the crews were asked, "What happened to you?" and "What happened to Pete, Bob, or John? Did you see any chutes open?" Demonstrating with their hands, the crews explained where and how we were attacked, by what kind of aircraft, and when and where we received flak and its intensity. But, as always, the most critical item was the fate of the crews that did not return: Where did they go down, what did we see, were there any chutes, and how many? We could always hear some of what was being told to our S-2 (intelligence) by other crews, and I sometimes wondered if we were all in the same battle, particularly when it came to claims of enemy aircraft shot down. I thought some of the claims were pretty doubtful. My suspicion that some claims might be exaggerated were confirmed when actual German losses were published after the war. Unless an enemy aircraft was seen to explode or the pilot bail out, it was difficult for me to verify a kill. I was never sure how much credence our S-2 gave to the claims of crew members.

Bucky Elton, our squadron operations officer, who usually sat in on these debriefings, once told me that writing letters to the families of men missing in action was his most difficult job. "We try to make the folks at home hope like we do that he bailed out and is okay. But sometimes it's extra hard."

The 4th BW was not alone. The 1st BW of VIII BC had an equally devastating experience on August 17, 1943. The same mist that delayed takeoff of the 4th BW for Regensburg for ninety minutes kept the 1st BW grounded for more than four hours before General Fred Anderson, commander of VIII BC, decided to launch the Schweinfurt component of the mission. The result was that the German fighter forces in northwest Europe that had savaged the Regensburg force earlier in the day had time to land, refuel, and rearm in preparation for our return trip to England. When informed of the Regensburg ruse, but that another American task force was about to enter German airspace, the Luftwaffe was ready and waiting for the Schweinfurt raiders. Before the day was over, thirty-six B-17 aircraft of the 1st BW would fail to return to their English bases.

The day after our return to England, I rode with John Egan and Charlie Cruikshank to Colonel LeMay's Regensburg mission critique at his elegant headquarters at Elveden Hall, Thetford. Colonel LeMay's natural expression always seemed to include a bit of a frown. However, for this meeting, he was calm, relaxed, and organized. The Eighth's appalling loss of sixty heavy bombers with their crews on August 17 was simply a notation on his post-mission review agenda. Even though every detail of the depressing events of that historic day was prominently displayed on the status board behind his desk, in a calm voice, LeMay questioned everyone—pilots, navigators, and bombardiers—in the style of an aggressive lawyer on cross-examination. I came away from that meeting with the impression, which I still have, that Colonel LeMay truly believed that if our air discipline had been better, our formation flying had been better, and if our gunnery had been better, the 4th BW might not have had such a bad day. There was no mention of the fact that the mission was not executed as planned. If Curtis LeMay had any doubts or misgivings about the Eighth's order of battle, operational procedures, or strategic goals, it was not apparent. The Schweinfurt/ Regensburg mission would have no effect on the prosecution of the war. Colonel LeMay knew it. We knew it. And we still had fourteen missions to go before we completed our combat tour.

In his lengthy, detailed, and graphic post-mission report to Colonel Harding, Lieutenant Colonel Lay recommended that every combat crew member of the 100th BG who participated in the Regensburg mission be awarded the Distinguished Flying Cross.[9] He also recommended that Major John Kidd be awarded the Distinguished Service Cross, and that Major Bucky Cleven receive the Medal of Honor. These recommendations were never implemented; however, Gale Cleven *was* awarded the Distinguished Service Cross.

Cleven was flying in the lead airplane of the low squadron with Norman Hugh Scott and his crew. They were severely mauled in the heavy fighting that took place before we reached the target. Their airplane received no fewer than six direct hits by 20 mm cannon shells. A 20 mm shell penetrated the right side of the airplane, damaging the electrical system and killing the radio operator, who had both legs blown off above the knees. Another 20 mm shell entered the left side of the nose, tore out a section of Plexiglas about two feet square, and ripped out the left gun installation, injuring the bombardier. A third shell penetrated the right wing, entered the fuselage, and shattered the hydraulic system, sending a flood of hydraulic fluid gushing into the cockpit. Yet another 20 mm shell hit the number 3 engine, destroying all engine controls. The engine

---

9. See appendix F for a true copy, with annotations, of Lieutenant Colonel Lay's personal report, which was written nine days after the mission.

caught fire, but the fire died out. A final 20 mm shell cut the control cables to one side of the rudder.

Lieutenant Colonel Lay's report stated that Scott and others on the crew wanted to bail out and that Scott panicked until Cleven told him bluntly, "You son of a bitch, you're going to sit there and fly this airplane." The airplane did make it to Africa, and because of the wide publicity given the Lay report at the time and since, this incident has been extensively covered in books and articles about the Eighth over the past half century, usually, unfortunately, portraying Scott and the crew in an unfavorable light.

Shortly after our return to England, I spoke to both Norman Hugh Scott and Don Strout, his modest, articulate crew navigator from Massachusetts who, as I recall, had attended Harvard University before the war. It was clear at the time that both were unsure of their futures. I was then, as I am now, convinced their uncertainty was related to the "panic" incident reported to Colonel Harding by Lieutenant Colonel Lay. Scott simply denied panicking or wanting to abandon the airplane. Don's situation was more complicated. He felt he might be facing a court-martial for cowardice in the face of the enemy. After returning to England, he had told his operations officer he refused to fly another combat mission. He told me the Regensburg mission left him completely unnerved, that by the time it was all over, he was paralyzed with fright and that he would never again be able to function in combat; he felt that he was extremely depressed and said he would be of no use to himself or his crew. He told me that if the brass wanted him dead for a lack of moral fiber, he would step up to the wall before a firing squad, but he would *not* fly in combat again. I told him I agreed with him. Someday, when he would be needed at his guns to stop a frontal attack, he could be frozen by fear, and his ship could go down and nine other men could die. He knew, however, that, at the very least, he had to go; he could no longer stay around after he had grounded himself. He would never have been punished, of course. However, this brief, passing episode illustrates the tensions and emotions at the time. A decent, honorable, intelligent man would be disconsolate over his inability to cope with mental and physical stresses no one should ever be asked to endure.

Years later, the bombardier, Lieutenant Norris Norman, said there was no panic on the crew at Regensburg, that no disciplinary action was taken against any member of the crew, and that all members of the crew, except Scott and Don Strout, were transferred to the 482nd BG, the specialized pathfinder group then being formed. Norman did not know the fate of Norman Hugh Scott and Don Strout. However, the late James R. Brown, navigator on Sam Barr's original Crew No. 4 and later 100th BG Association historian, wrote that Scott and Strout were transferred to a combat crew replacement center at Bovingdon Airfield to indoctrinate new crews. Whatever may be the truth, this was a tragic episode in the lives of two men I felt close to and still respect.

The Schweinfurt/Regensburg mission was a watershed for both the Eighth and the Luftwaffe. On August 18, 1943, *Generaloberst* Hans Jeschonnek, chief of staff of the Luftwaffe, put a gun to his head and killed himself over the inability of the Luftwaffe to turn back the Eighth the previous day and their failure to repel a heavy RAF attack on Peenemünde that same night. He concluded, correctly, that the German Air defenses would never prevent USAAF/RAF attacks on Germany proper.[10] As for VIII BC, the loss of sixty bombers over Europe represented the loss of 10 percent of its aircraft strength and 17 percent of its available aircrew strength—all in one day! This was clearly a loss rate that could not be sustained.

---

10. General Jeschonnek was no armchair warrior; he won the Knight's Cross of the Iron Cross on September 27, 1939, and served with great distinction during his career.

The need for a long-range fighter aircraft to escort the bombers on deep penetration missions into Germany was now indisputable. But how many of us would live to see the day?

Before Regensburg, our quarters at Thorpe Abbotts sometimes resembled a college campus back home. We had pictures on the walls of girls in bathing suits, photos of our families, a lot of litter, and a phonograph playing Glenn Miller's "Moonlight Serenade." We would talk about the guys missing in action the way we might have talked about the guys who graduated last year and wouldn't be around for football season this year. It changed after the Regensburg raid. Although it was my eleventh mission, and depressing losses were not new to me, I was profoundly affected by the African shuttle mission of August 17, 1943. Nine of our aircraft with their crews, more than half the attacking force from the 100th BG, were lost. Dozens of bright, talented men were gone. They were close friends with whom I had enjoyed so many hours of joy and so much camaraderie; and yes, occasional sorrow and anguish, both on and off duty. They were gone in one fell swoop. Why some of us survived while others did not was a complete mystery. Though some suggest otherwise, courage and skill played little part in an airman's likelihood of survival in the great air battles over Europe in the Second World War. One was just in the wrong place at the wrong time or he was not. A bullet had your name on it or it didn't. It was the luck of the draw. It was as simple as that.

Exactly one week after the Regensburg raid, I wrote my mother:

August 24, 1943

Dear Mom,
I'm sorry I haven't written quite so often, but haven't been in a position to do so for the past few days. I know you must be

terribly worried because the newspapers are always carrying on so about the war. So far, I'm still okay and healthy, but can't say how long it'll be this way; the war is getting to be a nightmare for me. Just keep up the letters and pray for me once in a while—I'll certainly need it.

I do not remember whether I felt I had said anything to worry my mother, but the next day I cabled her: "Dear Mom. Feeling fine. Still okay, will write immediately. Visiting the sights." It really did not matter. My mother was already praying for me night and day and making novena after novena for me at Sacred Heart Catholic Church in Atlanta.

There was no single reason why men who looked death in the face over Europe in 1943 went back into battle day after day. The airmen of the Eighth were amateurs, not professional soldiers. We had no idea whether we were good soldiers or not, but we had not collapsed in the face of a difficult enemy. Duty, honor, country played their part, certainly, but not because these precepts were drilled into us by the army. It was just the way we were. In my view, however, the single driving force that kept us going was the bond one felt with the men who stood steadfastly beside him when all their lives were at stake. When I saw my crew climb into the airplane, I had to go and help. After Regensburg, I felt what men repeatedly committed to combat have almost universally agreed upon. However much combat soldiers wish to escape the horror of war, honor and devotion to a special brotherhood shared by only those who have been in battle together keeps drawing them across unknown fields and skies to their rendezvous with destiny. At the end of the day, combat soldiers do not fight for love of country or because they hate the enemy. They fight for each other. If Crankshaft, Graham, Augie, Weeks, and the fellows in the back of our airplane had to go, I would never have stayed on the ground, regardless of the target.

I might add that it helped immensely to be young. I was twenty-one years old when we went to Regensburg, roughly the median age of an Eighth AF crewman in 1943. We knew the odds were against us. None of us considered it a lead-pipe cinch that he would complete his combat tour of twenty-five missions, but relatively few considered it preordained they would not survive. To me, it is beyond question that belief in one's immortality and survival is a quality in the young that diminishes with age. There is a haunting British verse dating from the First World War that imaginatively captures this sixth sense:[11]

> *The Bells of Hell go ting-a-ling-a-ling*
> *For you, but not for me.*
> *For me the angels sing-a-ling-a-ling*
> *They've got the goods for me.*
> *Oh, death, where is thy sting-a-ling-a-ling*
> *A grave Thy victory!*
> *The Bells of Hell go ting-a-ling-a-ling*
> *For you, but not for me.*

On August 27, the Eighth flew a short mission just across the English Channel to bomb an unusual construction area on the French coast. As it turned out, the target was a launching site for the V-weapons the Germans would use later in the war. Lieutenant Colonel Beirne Lay Jr., who had flown to Regensburg with Lieutenant Tom

---

11. This verse is loosely based on a well-known biblical passage on death, 1 Corinthians 15:55: "O death, where is thy sting. O grave, where *is* thy victory."

Murphy of the 351st BS, flew this mission with Crew No. 31. After climbing on board, he sat in the nose chatting with Augie and me. Lieutenant Colonel Lay struck me as being quiet but friendly and serious in nature but not withdrawn. When the time came for the firing of the green flare from the control tower, signaling start engines, nothing happened. After a few moments, Lieutenant Colonel Lay became visibly perturbed. He began looking anxiously at his watch and out all the windows as if trying to see if he could tell whether something had gone wrong. Finally, he seemed very frustrated and commented that we had rendezvous times with other groups to meet. Crouched in his bombardier's position in the Plexiglas nose of the airplane, both elbows resting on his knees, Augie Gaspar had been quietly taking it all in. "Don't worry," he said. "You'll get there soon enough."

In the last few days of August and most of September 1943, VIII BC essentially concentrated its attention on airfields and other Luftwaffe support installations in France, in part due to poor weather conditions over Germany, and in part to enable the bomb groups that had suffered substantial losses at Regensburg to receive replacement crews and reorganize. Our last mission in August came on the thirty-first, when, as one of nineteen aircraft from the 100th and other 4th BW aircraft, we were dispatched to bomb aircraft repair shops and a depot at Meulan–Les Mureaux, near Paris. History continued to repeat itself. Once again, heavy clouds obscured the area, and we brought our five-hundred-pound bombs home.

Although the Cruikshank crew stood down the first week in September 1943, except for local training flights from Thorpe Abbotts on September 3 and 4, the air war continued unabated. On Friday, September 3, 1943, seventeen crews from the 100th attacked the airfield at Beaumont-le-Roger, sixty miles from Paris. Five air-craft and four crews were lost, one crew having been saved after ditching in the channel.

Lieutenant Charles Winkleman, *Torchy* (230035)
7 evaded capture, 1 died in action, 2 taken prisoner
Second Lieutenant Charles W. Floyd Jr., *Barker's Burden* (230059)
8 died in action, 2 taken prisoner
Lieutenant Richard C. King, *Sunny* (230089)
1 evaded capture, 5 died in action, 4 taken prisoner
Captain Henry Henington, *Horny* (230611)
10 returned to duty
Lieutenant Victor E. Fienup, *Janie* (25865)
3 evaded capture, 2 died in action, 5 taken prisoner

Another original crew of the 100th, that of Vic Fienup of the 351st BS, was among the missing.

The magnitude and severity of the recurring weather problems that obstructed daylight precision bombing by the Eighth in the summer of 1943 was tested three days later. On September 6, 1943, a series of manufacturing plants at Stuttgart, Germany, were the tar-get for the VIII BC. It was obvious as the task force neared the target that their objectives were completely obscured by clouds and enemy smoke screens. However, the task force leader, ignoring VIII BC survival rule number one, made the decision to make a 360-degree turn for another run over the target: something you did not do. When the 100th formation finally turned away from Stuttgart to look for targets of opportunity, they were ferociously attacked by a swarm of German fighters. In a matter of minutes, three more of Thorpe Abbotts' aircraft went down.

Captain Sam R. Turner, *Raunchy* (230057)

1 died in action, 9 interned

Lieutenant Walter J. Grenier, *Sans Finis* (230335)

1 died in action, 9 taken prisoner

Captain Edgar F. Woodward Jr., *The Poontang* (230402)

1 interned, 9 taken prisoner

One of the 100th crews lost at Stuttgart was Crew No. 33, another original crew of the 418th BS that had been with us since Boise. The pilot was tall, sandy-haired Lieutenant Edgar "Woody" Woodward, who, at six feet two, loomed over the rest of us. He lost an engine and was unable to feather the prop. With *The Poontang*'s (230402) prop windmilling, they headed for Switzerland and bailed out. Unfortunately, except for Woody, all members of the crew landed in Germany and became POWs. Woody came down in Switzerland and was interned there for the rest of the war. The navigator on the Woodward crew was Lieutenant Emanuel "Cass" Cassimatis, from St. Louis, the best poker player in the 100th BG. From Boise to Wendover to England, Cass was the pride of his fellow junior officer fliers because he regularly cleaned the clocks of the colonels and generals, including General Robert Travis, his task force leader at Stuttgart. Cass was also the squadron bankroller. If someone needed a stipend to tide him over, Cass covered him, no questions asked.

On this mission, Lieutenant Sumner Reeder, the pilot, Lieutenant Harry Edeburn, the copilot, and Lieutenant Russ Engel, navigator, of Crew No. 9 of the 349th BS were all awarded the Distinguished Service Cross.[12] On a bomb run at an airfield in France, their brand-new unnamed aircraft (25957), later named *Horny II,* was riddled by 20 mm shells. Harry Edeburn was killed instantly. Both Reeder and

---

12. Edeburn's Distinguished Service Cross was awarded posthumously.

Engel were seriously wounded. Russ Engel had one eye torn out, but after helping remove Edeburn's body, he climbed into the copilot's seat to assist Reeder in any way he could. Despite continuing fighter attacks, Reeder managed to reach southern England by ducking from cloud to cloud and landed on the grass at an RAF fighter base. I remember having a hair-raising discussion of this incident with Russ Engel, who was wearing a patch over his missing eye, about a week after this mission.

Coming only three weeks after the intense, expensive Schwein-furt/Regensburg missions of August 17, 1943, this poorly executed Stuttgart mission could have been undertaken for only two reasons. First, to show the Germans that even after the loss of sixty bombers and six hundred men less than three weeks earlier, the Eighth could dispatch a force of over four hundred bombers on a deep penetration mission into Germany. Second, to demonstrate to the people back home that we still had plenty of fight left in us. It is possible, I suppose, that, after the costly August 17 episode, it was also intended to vindicate America's pioneer advocate of an independent air force, General Billy Mitchell, who, as a consequence of his experiences as commander of all United States Army Air Service forces in France in the First World War, passionately believed that the next war would be won in the air by airmen, who would destroy the enemy's industrial base and will to resist.[13] As a target, the factories

---

13. Mitchell was court-martialed in 1925 and chose to resign from the army. However, in the next year, 1926, fifteen years before the Japanese attack on Pearl Harbor, one of Mitchell's faithful young disciples, Major Henry "Hap" Arnold, later commander of all United States Army Air Forces in the Second World War, astonishingly prophesied:

"The next war between first-class powers probably will start with a host of aircraft arriving unheralded over strategic points. Antiaircraft guns will bark a response from the ground and aircraft will rise from the ground to give battle and drive the invaders from the skies. Incendiary, gas, and demolition bombs will destroy, or cause the evacuation of concentration centers and munitions factories; but following precedent, the largest and best equipped Air Force will be victorious, thus leaving the vanquished at a serious disadvantage."

at Stuttgart, which were almost as deep in Germany as Regensburg, were not that important. Largely because of the ill-advised decision to circle the target, the atrocious weather, and the lack of Tokyo tanks in 1st BW aircraft, a dozen B-17s ran out of gas and went into the drink in the English Channel that day. Overall, forty-five aircraft were lost on a mission that, as a strategic bombing mission, was a failure. Whether it achieved its intended psychological effect is another question.

The following day, September 7, 1943, Crew No. 31, in a formation of eighteen airplanes from the 100th, and with other 4th BW groups, went back to bomb the mysterious installation being constructed at Watten on the French coast just across the channel from England. We encountered no flak or enemy fighter opposition, but our bombing results were poor, once again owing to broken cloud cover over the target.

On September 13, 1943, as the cool, misty morning's pale sun and the subtle transformations of color in the hardwoods around Thorpe Abbotts to a darker green were announcing an impending change of seasons, a major reorganization of VIII BC occurred. Its purpose was to assimilate the new bomb groups and replacement crews arriving in Britain daily into more manageable groups. The 1st BW became the 1st Bomb Division.[14] A new 2nd BD was created composed entirely of B-24 aircraft. Colonel LeMay's old 4th BW became the 3rd BD, and he received his first star. Along with the 95th and 390th BGs, the 100th BG became a part of a newly created 13th Combat Wing within the 3rd BD.

Within the 100th, rounds of promotions were taking effect because of heavy aircrew losses and the continuing inflow of

---

14. From this point forward, I will use the abbreviation **CBW** for *Combat Wing* and the abbreviation **BD** for *Bombardment Division*.

replacement crews. Charlie Cruikshank, John Brady, and other pilots were promoted to captain, as they were the experienced men who would lead the individual flights, squadrons, and, occasionally, the group or combat wing on future missions. Four of the eight original crews of the 418th BS had been lost in combat, and two others had been reorganized. Major Egan appointed me squadron navigator. I wrote my mother, "I might be in England longer than I thought. Next week I'm leaving the boys and going away to school in London for awhile. I am now squadron navigator and it may be I'll get promoted to captain." I was promoted but was never sent for additional training. There are at least two valid reasons for this: first, the Eighth was flying combat missions at every opportunity and had few veteran crews available; second, I was well over halfway through my combat tour.

Before September 1943, it was clear that cloud cover over the target, and not the formidable German air defense system, was the single greatest limitation to the effectiveness of daylight bombing. During the summer of 1943, it was unusual if we had more than ten days a month where the skies were completely clear over a target. Since we had no electronic navigation or bombing aids, we could hit our targets only on those days when the skies were clear. In September 1943, the 100th BG had no fewer than seven missions scrubbed or abandoned with no effective results because of weather: one mission was scrubbed after an evening alert, three were scrubbed after the crews were briefed but before takeoff, and on three occasions, the group was recalled after being airborne.

The Eighth set about to address these weather uncertainties. In August 1943, it established a group of pathfinder aircraft as both the Germans and British had done earlier. Raiding formations would operate with a pathfinder aircraft in the lead; if the bombardier could see the target, he aimed the bombs visually; if not, they would be aimed using radar.

As a navigation tool on days when the ground was significantly obscured by cloud cover, the Eighth began installing the British GEE, or Grid, system of navigation in B-17 aircraft. The GEE system had been in use by the RAF for over a year and had been originally intended to improve bombing accuracy but had been subjected to such powerful jamming by the Germans that, as I have since understood it, by the time it was installed on American aircraft, it was essentially unusable over Germany and much of western Europe and was largely used as a navigation aid when the airplane was clear of German territory. GEE was the forerunner to the later postwar loran navigation system in that it employed three ground transmitters radiating a complex train of impulses in a set order. Inside the receiving airplane, the navigator had a special radar receiver that measured the time differences between receipt of the signals from the ground transmitters and displayed them as video pulses on a cathode ray tube. These time measurements enabled the navigator to read lines of position by reference to a special GEE map. It was supposed to be accurate up to about four hundred miles. I had only one local flight on a GEE-equipped airplane and minimal familiarization with the system, probably because we had no qualified instructors available. At the time, I saw GEE as a clumsy gadget that occupied half of my navigator's table and offered only blips on a screen that had to be interpreted on a multicolored map crisscrossed with grids resembling isobars on a weather map.

Our days, however, were not all work and no play. The War Department and USAAF were genuinely concerned for our individual and unit morale. USO shows, British entertainers, and famous film

personalities regularly visited Thorpe Abbotts to boost the spirits
of the troops. About this time, I spent several hours one evening in
the bar at the officers' club at Thorpe Abbotts, imbibing and chatting with Adolphe Menjou, a suave, stylish major Hollywood star
of both comedy and drama in the '30s and '40s. He was informal,
gracious, and generous in his kind words for us. And every VIII BC
base had a small Red Cross office staffed by a half dozen or so attractive young American women sent there to arrange off-duty recreational and social activities for the men at the base. These pretty
young ladies in their spiffy, neat blue-gray military-style uniforms
and caps were, naturally, popular and the center of attention for
American airmen wherever they went. It was pointless, however,
to think of dating them, particularly for enlisted men and junior
officers. Why? There were six of them and over two thousand of us!

Although I have little recollection of all their specific activities
because of our flying schedules, I do remember our Thorpe Abbotts
Red Cross girls operating a large, light gray vehicle resembling a
minibus with the words AMERICAN RED CROSS CLUBMOBILE lettered
on each side. These vehicles were converted single-decker British
Eastern Counties buses with several long window-like openings
on their right sides with push-up horizontal panels and fold-out
shelves, through which, when open, the girls, wearing stylish wrap-
around white smocks over their regular clothes, served hot brewed
coffee and fresh doughnuts to men working the flight line and aircrews returning from a mission. The Red Cross office also arranged
monthly dances at the base and sent out trucks to bring in local
English girls who had been invited. I recall, in particular, one conversation I had at one of these dances with a very pretty English girl
who defended the ritual and spectacle of what I thought was the
overwhelmingly one-sided British sport of foxhunting on grounds
that foxes are "nasty, cunning little creatures." She told me that she

enjoyed the parties at all the American air bases but preferred the dances at the fighter bases because she thought the food and the bands were better. However, in what I now suspect was a moment of pity for me, she said she also thought the names we American bomber crews gave our airplanes were "cute."

The Eighth had also leased several beautiful English country estates as Rest and Rehabilitation homes. They were designated as "army posts" and given official station numbers. However, their green lawns, colorful flowers, and lily ponds bore no resemblance to army posts. Fatigued fliers were sent to these homes by flight surgeons who thought they needed rest from the strain of many hours of combat flying. We heard that these estates retained all the furnishings of their former occupants: carpeted floors, windows richly draped, oil paintings, expensive table lamps, coats of arms of the estate, and libraries full of books. The fliers could wear civilian clothes, play badminton or tennis, or do nothing. These army posts were staffed by flight surgeons. The only thing a "guest," not a patient, could not do was talk about the war.

I never knew anyone who was sent to one of these "flak houses," as they were known to aircrews. However, I suspect this therapy would have really made it more, rather than less, difficult for me to return to the nerve-racking rigors of combat. I have read that after having been rehabilitated at one of these palatial estates, there were Eighth airmen who turned in their wings and asked to be grounded.

The fifteenth sortie for Crew No. 31 came in the early evening of September 15, 1943. Once again flying our regular aircraft, *Bastard's Bungalow* (230062), the 13th CBW attacked the Renault Works, just outside of Paris. At 6:55 p.m., from above broken clouds, eighteen aircraft from the 100th each released twelve five-hundred-pound bombs on the target. The rally point for the combat wing was directly over the city; beneath puffs of heavy, black flak, the red roofs far below glowed in the fading orange sunlight. Lieutenant Arthur Vetter's airplane (23452), with a 349th replacement crew on their fourth mission, was seen to just disappear in the clouds; seven evaded capture, one died in action, and two were taken prisoner. An 88 mm flak that burst under the front of Lieutenant Sam Barr's 349th airplane caused extensive damage to the cockpit and nose and seriously injured the navigator, James R. Brown.[15]

The following day, while the Cruikshank crew was standing down, seventeen aircraft of the 100th participated in a long flight around the Brest Peninsula by the 13th CBW to bomb the aircraft works at Bordeaux, France. Finding the primary target obscured beneath a heavy overcast, the combat wing went to its secondary target, the submarine pens at La Pallice. Lieutenant Bob Wolff and his crew, one of the first replacement crews in the 418th BS, failed to return from this mission.

On the days when our crew was standing down, especially if the group was out on a mission likely to be rough, at the hour when those flying were scheduled home, we rode our bikes out to the squadron hardstand area and perimeter track and joined with our ground crews to "sweat 'em in." The unforgettable clusters of three-airplane Vs that had formed into squadrons, groups, and combat wings earlier in the day and gone off to war like flocks of geese in perfect formation were returned as crippled planes with gaping holes in their structures. Airplanes with smoking and feathered engines were strung out behind the formation struggling to make it home. The leader always flew straight down the center of the main runway. Aircraft with wounded aboard fired red flares and peeled

---

15. From this injury, Jim never flew combat again. As noted, for several years after the war, Jim was the 100th Bomb Group Association's historian and archivist. Richard Le Strange and Jim coauthored *Century Bombers: The Story of the Bloody Hundredth.*

out of formation, as they were permitted to land first. In the course of all this, we were counting the returning aircraft, looking for gaps in the formation to see where aircraft were missing, and trying to remember each squadron's place in the formation. Ambulances met airplanes with wounded at the end of the runway. Fire trucks stood by for possible crash landings by damaged aircraft. When the last returning aircraft turned into its hardstand, we silently pedaled back to our quarters; tomorrow, it would be our turn to become the central characters in a repeat performance of this dramatic scene.

On September 20, the 100th flew an abortive mission to Paris from which all aircraft, including Crew No. 31, were recalled after having been airborne for half an hour. Sortie number sixteen for our crew took place on September 23, 1943. Flying our old warhorse, *Bastard's Bungalow* (230062), we led the second element of the high squadron on a milk run to the airfield at Vannes-Meucon, France. It was another dawn mission; we were wheels up at just after 5:30 a.m. and touched down back at Thorpe Abbotts a few minutes after 11:00 a.m. At 8:25 a.m. fifty-five B-17s from the 13th CBW dropped six hundred and sixty five-hundred-pound bombs on the barracks and flight line at Vannes airdrome.

Our seventeenth and final mission for September 1943 took place on the twenty-sixth. It was a late-afternoon-takeoff, early-evening-return operation. Twenty-two 100th aircraft, along with aircraft of the 95th and 390th BGs, were sent to destroy a truck assembly plant near Paris. The Cruikshank crew was flying a recently delivered Douglas Aircraft Company-built B-17G (the first G model at Thorpe Abbotts), serial number 42-3508, which would be eventually named *Bastard's Bungalow II,* and was flying as a "spare," or supernumerary. The purpose of a spare was that if any 100th aircraft aborted the effort before entering enemy territory, the spare was to take his place. Our turn came over the channel when Lieutenant

Bill Lakin, of the 350th BS, flying *Invadin' Maiden* (230823), peeled out of the high squadron with an engine oil leak and returned to Thorpe Abbotts. Frustratingly, we encountered 10/10 cloud cover over the target and were, seemingly for the umpteenth time, forced to abandon the mission and take our bombs home.

As we made our way toward the English coast south of London, the early-evening western horizon was slowly dissolving from deep blue to purple below streaks of gold piped with red. It was almost 7:00 p.m.; there was two-and-a-half- to four-mile visibility in haze, and four- to seven-mile-per-hour winds were coming from the north. I was poring over my charts and papers when Augie Gaspar suddenly and painfully grasped my right arm and pointed out the Plexiglas nose of our airplane at the formations straight ahead. As I turned, I glimpsed a giant orange fireball off in the distance fading into a hanging black cloud. Beneath this ill-omened cloud, a field of debris was spreading as bits and pieces of aircraft, some recognizable, some not, plummeted, spiraled, and fluttered to earth. Two aircraft from a group up ahead of us had been involved in a midair collision. I immediately experienced a sick feeling in the pit of my stomach. Twenty men here one instant, gone the next, on a mission that accomplished nothing.[16]

---

16. At the time, we did not know which group or who was involved in this incident, but in doing research for this memoir, we discovered what happened. The 385th Bomb Group, stationed at Great Ashfield, was also returning from the same mission. As they let down from altitude, the pilots reported that their windows were frosting over. Lieutenant Paul M. Yannello, who was piloting *The Dorsal Queen* (230264) with a crew of eleven, was flying to the left wing of Lieutenant John T. Keeley's *Raunchy Wolf* (23290) with a crew of ten, and Lieutenant Thomas Morgan was flying on Keeley's right wing in *Winnie the Pooh* (23422). While in a turn, *The Dorsal Queen* slid under *Raunchy Wolf* and encountered its prop wash. Morgan, in *Winnie the Pooh*, moved to the right to give Yannello room to regain control. After moving into the slot vacated by Morgan, Yannello then pulled up and to the left to regain his position. As John Adams (tail gunner aboard *The Dorsal Queen*) reported, "I raised my head to keep on the lookout for any enemy fighters that might have followed us from France. As I turned my head to the right, I saw the right wing of another Fortress coming at

The potential for a midair collision with another B-17 aircraft was ever present in the VIII BC in the Second World War and, tragically, happened all too often, both in combat and in training. To put these unnerving accidents in perspective, however, one might contrast the incredible congestion of military air traffic over England and western Europe during the war with present commercial air traffic and its tightly drawn rules of aircraft separation. Today, large aircraft under radar control, regardless of weather, must be no closer than three miles side by side, five miles ahead and behind, and separated by one thousand feet of altitude if traveling in opposite directions. An entire combat wing in tactical formation regularly operated in bad weather and under deadly air battle conditions in less space than that separating two aircraft under today's commercial rules.

The lull in air operations over Germany in September 1943 allowed the steady flow of new aircraft and crews from the United States to rebuild and increase the effective strength of the VIII BC. With the arrival of October, the high priests of American daylight precision bombing, General Hap Arnold in Washington, General Tooey Spaatz in Africa, and Generals Eaker and Anderson in England, redirected their attention to Germany. They undoubtedly felt political pressure. Despite the heavy losses over Germany in late July and on

---

our aircraft. I reached for my microphone switch and just as I was about to shout a warning, the other aircraft had hit us." Yannello's maneuver resulted in the leading edge of *The Dorsal Queen's* vertical stabilizer striking the trailing edge of *Raunchy Wolf's* right wing between the wingtip and the number 4 engine. As a result, *Raunchy Wolf's* wingtip was cut off, and *The Dorsal Queen's* tail section separated near the tail wheel position, sending *Raunchy Wolf* into an immediate dive. It crashed in a field one hundred yards west of Thorndon Avenue in East Horndon, and *The Dorsal Queen* went into a vertical climb before eventually crashing on Tillingham Farm, Bulphan, four hundred yards southwest of the East Horndon railway station. Tail gunner Adams, the sole survivor, later reported: "I had my chute on so I pushed myself back to the severed section of the tail and bailed out." In all, twenty men died.

the "double strike" missions to Regensburg and Schweinfurt, they were being given the resources for which they had so persuasively argued. Behind the scene, Bomber Harris, commander of the RAF Bomber Command, who firmly believed that the Allies were on the verge of a showdown in the bombing war, after talking to Eaker and Anderson, made his strongest representations to his superiors and Prime Minister Churchill that American leaders in Washington were neglecting VIII BC by leaving it "far below planned strength" and its crews "hopelessly outnumbered," thus permitting the enemy to concentrate its defenses. American airmen had to prove what airpower could do.

In Germany, the fierce air battles over their homeland in July and August forced the Germans to recognize the seriousness of the American threat. Defense of the Reich became their first priority. The Luftwaffe began transferring both day and night fighter units from Russia and the Mediterranean to the west. From six hundred fighter aircraft in the west at the beginning of the summer, Luftwaffe fighter strength in Germany climbed to almost one thousand aircraft by early October. Further, the Luftwaffe tightened its rules of engagement. Insofar as possible, American bombers would not be attacked when escorted by supporting fighter aircraft. Luftwaffe fighters would concentrate on making massed head-on attacks against American bomber formations, while German twin-engine fighters carrying 21 cm rockets flying just outside the range of American .50-caliber machine guns would fire them into the bomber formations to break them up, making individual B-17 aircraft easy targets.

On October 7, 1943, Eighth AF meteorologists in England predicted the next few days would bring the most favorable flying weather the Eighth had seen in weeks; the weather was expected to be clear over both England and virtually all of western Europe. At his headquarters in a mansion amid manicured green lawns at High Wycombe, code-named Pinetree, Ira Eaker sprang into action. VIII BC would go all out, beginning immediately with assaults on several targets in Bremen and Vegesack, Germany, that were already in the works. All our bomb groups were told to prepare for a "maximum effort" mission the following morning.

Twenty-one crews of the 100th were awakened about 7:00 a.m. on October 8. This would be our twentieth mission. By this time, we mechanically accomplished our usual briefing and preflight procedures. The target for the 3rd BD was Bremen. The 100th would lead the 13th CBW with Major John Kidd in Captain Ev Blakely's lead airplane, *Just-A-Snappin* (23393). Crew No. 31, flying our originally assigned airplane, *Bastard's Bungalow* (230062), would lead the second element of the lead squadron with Lieutenant David Miner on our right wing and Lieutenant Walter "Big Chief" Moreno on our left wing. The first airplane off the ground, at 11:43 a.m., was *Our Baby* (23233), flown by Major Bucky Cleven and Captain Benny De-Marco, who would lead the high squadron. We took off at 11:50 a.m.

My recollection of this mission is indistinct, as we flew so many missions so close together during this period. However, official records show that over the North Sea, our numbers 2, 3, and 4 engine–driven generators failed and we aborted the mission at 2:16 p.m. and returned to Thorpe Abbotts. We could count ourselves among the lucky ones. The combat wing was savagely attacked by German fighters as they approached the target. On the bomb run, John Kidd and Ev Blakely's airplane was severely crippled by a near-miss burst of flak. After dropping their bombs, they fell out of formation, went into a spin, and had a harrowing experience that ended when, thanks to the skills of Kidd and Blakely, they managed to crash-land in a field near Ludham, England. The 100th lost seven aircraft at Bremen on October 8, 1943. Among the missing were

Major Bucky Cleven and Captain Benny DeMarco and their original crews, and Captain Tom Murphy, who had taken Beirne Lay to Regensburg, and his 351st squadron operations officer, Captain Alvin Barker. However, before night fell on Thorpe Abbotts that evening, the Bremen mission was, as had been so many others in the brief history of the 100th, relegated to the past, but the crews failing to return to Thorpe Abbotts would not be so easily forgotten.

Captain Bernard A. DeMarco, *Our Baby* (23233)
11 taken prisoner
Second Lieutenant Raymond J. Gormley, *Marie Helena* (23386)
10 died in action
Captain Thomas E. Murphy, *Piccadilly Lily* (25864)
6 died in action, 5 taken prisoner
Second Lieutenant Arthur H. Becktoft, *War Eagle* (230154)
1 died in action, 9 taken prisoner
Lieutenant Frank H. Meadows, *Phartzac* (230358)
8 died in action, 2 taken prisoner
Captain William H. McDonald, *Salvo Sal* (230818)
1 evaded capture, 1 died in action, 8 taken prisoner
Second Lieutenant Herbert G. Nash Jr., unnamed (230840)
5 died in action, 5 taken prisoner

By 6:00 p.m., the teletype machines in groups operations were clattering away as another alert and standby for a new field order were being prepared for a 7:30 takeoff the next morning. That meant being pulled out of bed at 3:00 a.m.

The operations scheduled for October 9, 1943, were truly deep penetration missions. The 1st BD would attack Anklam, while the 3rd BD aircraft, equipped with long-range Tokyo tanks, would strike targets east of Denmark. The bombing objective for the 13th CBW, plus the 385th and 94th BGs, was a large Fw 190 aircraft assembly plant in Marienburg in old East Prussia, over two hundred miles east of Berlin. Because of the distance we would fly and the reported absence of heavy air defenses, we would make our bomb run at the unprecedented low altitude of twelve thousand feet.

As a result of the costly Bremen mission the previous day, during which seven aircraft were missing in action, a further six sustained significant battle damage, and one later had to be salvaged, the 100th could assemble only seventeen serviceable aircraft for the Marienburg operation. We would be the high group in the combat wing behind the 390th BG, who would follow the 385th and 94th BGs. Crew No. 31 would lead the 100th BG, with Colonel Chick Harding flying in our airplane, which for this mission was *M'lle Zig Zig* (230830).

With a string of airplanes on the perimeter track behind us, Chick Harding and Charlie Cruikshank eased onto the runway. Because of our heavy fuel and bomb load, they set the brakes and advanced their engine throttles to full power. The airplane shuddered. At the green light from the control van, they released the brakes. We didn't leap forward, we crept. We didn't race down the runway, we lumbered. Near the end of the runway, we staggered off the ground. With the tops of trees flashing by a few feet below us, we began to climb. It was exactly 7:30 a.m.

Our route took us across the North Sea above the Frisian Islands, across Denmark immediately south of Copenhagen, and into the Baltic Sea. We passed just south of the island of Bornholm off the south coast of Sweden, made our landfall near Gdynia, and at 12:45 p.m. began our bomb run on Marienburg at our prescribed altitude of twelve thousand feet.

On the ground, Corporal James "Chipper" McLoughlin, from

Broughty Ferry, Dundee, Scotland, whipped off his shirt and waved and yelled as bombs from the 13th CBW, United States VIII BC, came tumbling down in a tight pattern on the assembly plant for Focke-Wulf fighter planes at Marienburg. McLoughlin had been a salesman in an importing business in Dundee before the war and had become a soldier, stretcher-bearer, and gravedigger when he went to France with the British Expeditionary Force in early 1940. He was captured by the Germans at Saint-Valery as the British made a last stand on the edge of the channel in the spring of 1940 and had been a prisoner of war for more than three years. On October 9, 1943, Chipper was a medical orderly at a hospital just outside of Marienburg, East Prussia, and along with other prisoners of war had been taken to the assembly plant at Marienburg to see Hermann Göring dedicate a new runway to test new Fw 190 aircraft before they went into battle against the Eighth. At seven minutes to noon, a formation of Forts came over Marienburg like a swarm of bees and put on a show for the men at the Marienburg prison camp. He was called to clear away the wreckage of the plant and take away dead Germans. He said, "It was as bloody good fun as opening Christmas parcels."

Bombing results at Marienburg are now generally recognized to have been among the Eighth's most accurate and effective of the entire war. Augie and the other bombardiers had done a magnificent job at Marienburg. And apart from being a long mission at eleven hours and forty-five minutes of flying time for us, it was not stressful; we had no fighter opposition either going to or returning from the target. Not so for the rest of the Eighth. Ira Eaker lost thirty bombers due to enemy action on October 9, 1943. However, even as we were relentlessly grinding our way across the gray, glassy North Sea back to England, field orders were being prepared for another maximum effort the next day. We touched down on the main east-west runway at Thorpe Abbotts at 6:16 p.m. As soon as he alighted from our airplane, Colonel Harding was informed that the group was on standby for another maximum effort the next morning, Sunday, October 10, 1943. There was no rest for the weary.

In a letter of commendation to his commanding generals of Eighth Bomber, Fighter, and Air Support Commands on October 12, 1943, General Eaker wrote:

> Last Sunday, October 10th, after seeing the pictures of the effort of the preceding Saturday and particularly the destructive effects on the German fighter factories at Anklam and Marienburg, I sent a cable to General Arnold, from which the following is a quotation:
>
> Marienburg undoubtedly destroyed. It will be a better example of pinpoint bombing, better concentration even than Regensburg. It looks like a perfect job. Believe you will find October 9th a day to remember in the air war. The Prime Minister is sending message to crews.
>
> Subsequent examination of photographs supports this estimate.
>
> Convey to all your officers and men my unbounded admiration for the courage and boldness with which they pushed their attacks into enemy territory and the accuracy and skill with which they disposed of their targets. They have, by their effort, won the respect and admiration of the air leaders of Britain and that great band of fighting men, the Royal Air Force. They have outfought a tough, experienced and battle-tried enemy. Their success has altered the course of the war and hastened its favorable conclusion.
>
> IRA C. EAKER
>
> Lieut. General, U.S.A. Commanding

To the combat personnel of VIII BC, General Eaker added this note:

It is my privilege to be the instrument of bringing directly to you as individuals the comments and commendations from these distinguished sources. Such expressions of appreciation of your efforts are extremely gratifying.

An even one hundred combat crewmen of the 100th BG who crewed on ten of the group's aircraft that participated in the Marienburg mission only three days earlier would never receive this message. By the time it was written, thirty-four of them were dead, having been killed in action, sixty-five were prisoners of war, and one was hiding out on the ground in Holland attempting to avoid capture.

Missions of Frank D. Murphy, Crew No. 31
June 22, 1943–October 9, 1943

June 22	230062	*Bastard's Bungalow*	Diversion
June 26	230062	*Bastard's Bungalow*	Le Mans, France
June 28	230062	*Bastard's Bungalow*	Saint-Nazaire, France
June 29	25854	unnamed	Le Mans, France
July 4	230184	*"Muggs"*	La Pallice, France
July 10	230184	*"Muggs"*	Le Bourget, France
July 14	230184	*"Muggs"*	Le Bourget, France (Returned Early)
July 17	230184	*"Muggs" (Salvaged)*	Hamburg, Germany (Salvaged)
July 24	230062	*Bastard's Bungalow*	Trondheim, Norway
July 25	230063	*Picklepuss*	Kiel, Germany
July 26	230062	*Bastard's Bungalow*	Hanover, Germany
July 28	230062	*Bastard's Bungalow*	Oschersleben, Germany
July 29	230062	*Bastard's Bungalow*	Warnemünde, Germany
July 30	230061	*Wolff Pack*	Kassel, Germany
August 12	230062	*Bastard's Bungalow*	Bonn, Germany
August 15	230062	*Bastard's Bungalow*	Merville-Lille, France
August 17	230066	*Mugwump*	Regensburg, Germany

August 27	unknown		Watten, France
August 31	unknown		Lile Meulan, France
September 7	unknown		Watten, France
September 15	230062	*Bastard's Bungalow*	Paris, France
September 23	230062	*Bastard's Bungalow*	Vannes, France
September 26	23508	*Bastard's Bungalow II*	Paris, France
October 2	23508	*Bastard's Bungalow II*	Emden, Germany
October 4	23508	*Bastard's Bungalow II*	Hanau, Germany
October 8	230062	*Bastard's Bungalow*	Bremen, Germany
October 9	230830	*M'lle Zig Zig*	Marienburg, Germany

Note: There is evidence that 230062 flew on the June 22, 1943, diversion mission, but it has yet to be determined which crew flew the aircraft.

DOUBLE QUEUE

See diagrams on pages 15–16 of photo insert 1, in order as described

TACTICS DESCRIPTION

On either side of the squadron and at approximately two thousand yards, the single-engine fighters queue up for attacks in trains. They are about five hundred yards above the level of the lead squadron, flying a parallel course. These formations vary, but at points X and Y, the fighters are in trains of two or three to the side, ready for alternating dives, with from five- to ten-second intervals between. In other words, two or three e/a (enemy aircraft), in train, dive from point X, then two or three e/a, in train, from point Y. The procedure is repeated until all planes (sometimes eighteen or more) have taken their turns in diving. Fighters diving from point X pass under the lead squadron, while the e/a from point Y do a shallow dive, a slow roll, then a belly-up dive (split S) when within five hundred yards (or less) of the lead element of the squadron. *The low squadron can be attacked in the same manner. The same tactics are employed in dives through the formation, (i.e., between the lead and low squadrons or between the lead and high squadrons).*

TACTICS LESSON

If these attacks are not properly coordinated, it is a gamble to take evasive action against either of them; if they are coordinated, the nose attack with no deflection is most dangerous. Don't give the fighters a no-deflection shot.

Because of decoys, this maneuver, probably more than any other, tends to draw fire from Fortress gunners. The group or squadron showing the poorest combat formation is usually the one to come under attack.

THE SCISSORS MOVEMENT

See diagrams on pages 15–16 of photo insert 1, in order as described

TACTICS DESCRIPTION

This maneuver is conventional and designed to break up the Fortress formation. The trailing e/a (on the top) pulls up at about five hundred yards' range and does a fast climb over the squadron. The leading e/a (on the bottom) comes in closer (usually to four hundred yards) and, with a wing up, dives away to the right. Other single-engine e/a can often be observed lining up for similar attacks from other clock positions, sometimes from high; sometimes from level, the attack is often suicidal for a fighter that tries to pull up and climb over the squadron. The scissors movement can be commenced from clock positions ranging from ten to two. It could be used against the lead squadron, with the leading a/c (aircraft) diving away to the left.

TACTICS LESSON

Avoid giving fighters a no-deflection shot. Make a slight turn into the attack. Wing a/c must hold the formation on this attack and not take individual evasive action to avoid fire. Gunners must be alert to targets in their respective sectors. One of these fighters will be available to the top turret gunners, while the other will be available to the ball turret gunners.

THE SINGLE-ENGINE TAIL-PECKER

See diagrams on pages 15–16 of photo insert 1, in order as described

TACTICS DESCRIPTION

A fighter flies on level (three hundred yards below the horizontal plane of Fortress No. 4), but at points 1, 2, and 3 lifts the nose and fires a few bursts of shot. The peel-off is to the right or the left at point X ,which is approximately eight hundred yards behind Fortress No. 4.

This typical tail-pecking attack is sometimes made against Fortress No. 5 or Fortress No. 6.

TACTICS LESSON

Although quite common, this type of attack is not too dangerous. The ball turret gunners can have a lot of fun with the tail-pecker, which comes in from below, but should avoid long shots.

THE SISTERS ACT

See diagrams on pages 15–6 of photo insert 1, in order as described

TACTICS DESCRIPTION

The Me 110 and Ju 88 attack simultaneously, as indicated in the diagram. At point Y, the Ju 88 breaks away to the right, wing up, while the Me 110 does a slow roll and a breakaway to the left in a rather steep dive.

Sometimes this maneuver is performed by a pair of Me 110s.

TACTICS LESSON

Each gunner must cover his sector. Coordinated attacks are common. The tail gunner in Fortress No. 5 must be alert to this type of attack. Top turret gunners in the rear of the Fortress formation should watch for e/a attacking from high, astern.

THE ROCKETEERS

See diagrams on pages 15–16 of photo insert 1, in order as described

TACTICS DESCRIPTION

This attack was first employed on the Schweinfurt mission,

October 14. In a line abreast, the single-engine e/a approach on level or slightly higher position. Aircraft A, B, C, and D, after firing their rocket projectiles, peel off as indicated in the diagram. Aircraft E and F, which are not equipped with rocket armaments, close in to attack any Fortress that may have been crippled by the rocket projectiles or that, for any other reason, seem to straggle. How close aircraft E and F press home their attacks depends upon the prospect of a "kill." This same line-abreast formation is used by twin-engine e/a when firing rocket projectiles. After the projectiles are fired, the twin-engine e/a often close in for a cannon attack.

TACTICS LESSON

It's a two-to-one bet that the e/a that will close in for attack is or are located in the center of the formation. The straggler's number is up. Keep in formation at all cost after the explosion of rocket projectiles.

The tail gunner (officer) in Fortress No. 1 must be alert to this attack and warn the formation leader when e/a are jockeying into position.

Don't be led away from the main attack by e/a peeling off.

Don't waste ammunition on long shots. The best defense against rocket attacks from the rear is slight weaving of the formation. Due to the high trajectory and low velocity of rockets, slight weaving will carry the formation out of the effective range of the bursts.

THE TRIPLE THREAT

See diagrams on pages 15–16 of photo insert 1, in order as described

TACTICS DESCRIPTION

This maneuver, as practically all other head-on attacks, is performed by single-engine aircraft. The fighters, flying parallel to the Fortresses as indicated in the diagram, pull ahead into positions at eleven, twelve, and one o'clock for commencement of their respective dives. At this time, they are approximately two thousand or twenty-five hundred yards ahead and five hundred yards above the level of the squadron to be attacked. They appear to be converging as they come head-on.

Breakaways are made as follows:

C does a wing-up breakaway to the left at eight hundred yards.

B does a slow roll and a belly-up dive (the split S) at five hundred yards, pulling out to the left when well below.

A does a wing-up breakaway to the left at three hundred yards and dives until out of range.

Sometimes dives are extended as indicated by the black lines in the diagram, with slow rolls and belly-up dives (split S) underneath the squadron. The same diving attacks are often made from the rear of the Fortress formations. Fw 190s and Me 109s can and do make these angular attacks, singly and head-on or from astern. Such attacks can be made from any clock position from ten to two, or four to eight.

TACTICS LESSON

A slight turn will make all these attacks a deflection shot. A *slight* dive or climb will uncover more turrets.

IO

MÜNSTER

Once more unto the breach, dear friends, once more.
—WILLIAM SHAKESPEARE, *HENRY V*, ACT 3, SCENE 1

I n the grim seven days that would be referred to later as Black
Week (October 8–14, 1943), the VIII BC's strategic air campaign
endured its ultimate ordeal, a staccato succession of trials by fire
on a scale unprecedented in aerial warfare. In the air over northwestern
Europe, push now came to shove in a wave of ferocious and relentless
slugfests in which no holds were barred and no quarter given or asked.
For days, the stratosphere became, as the French say, a titanic *moudre
des bataillons,* a meat grinder into which both sides mercilessly threw
legions of aircrew and machines without respite and without any
surety of outcome. This madness was not without reason. Enormous
stakes teetered in the balance. Most obviously, for the USAAF, this
first half of October was a mortal struggle to wipe out plump targets
thought critical to the Reich's war potential. But we now know the
days of October were more—much more. For the Allies, it was a
matter of air superiority over northwestern Europe. On air superiority rested the fate of strategic bombing as a means of shortening the
war. Down the road, winning air superiority meant the possibility of
invading the continent, for no invasion could be contemplated without control of the air. And yes, it is also true—the reputations and

professional careers of Generals Arnold, Eaker, Spaatz, Doolittle, and others hung in the balance. It was up to them to prove their ideas would work, and they intended to do so. For the Luftwaffe, the first days of October 1943 also chalked fearful handwriting on the wall. It and it alone stood between the *Viermonts*[1] and death-blows to the Fatherland, destruction of which would prostrate the German economy and sooner or later end the war in defeat. Until October, Hitler's air defense—flak and fighters—had demonstrated a capability to inflict horrific losses, as they did on August 17, 1943. Yet these successes were not consistent enough to bring the VIII BC operations to a halt. This inconsistency set the stage for the October 7, 1943, meeting at Obersalzberg, Hitler's Alpine retreat, where *Reichsmarschall* Hermann Göring said:

> This is final, however; the *Jagdwaffe* [day fighters] is going to give battle to the last man. Those are my orders and I shall see them carried out regardless. If it does not, it can go and join the infantry. The German people doesn't [*sic*] give a damn about *Jagd-waffe's* losses.[2]

Göring's declaration coupled with predictions of good flying weather for northwestern Europe brought in the grand question to the forefront: Which side would survive the bloodletting and dominate the German skies?

Not surprisingly, then, VIII BC's medium-depth raid against Münster became yet another quickstep through hell. The whirling,

---

1. Literally "four motors" or "four-engine ones," German shorthand for Allied heavy bomb-ers such as the American B-17, and B-24, as well as the British Lancasters and Halifaxes.

2. As cited in Johannes Steinhoff's *The Last Chance: The Pilots' Plot Against Göring 1944–1945* (London: Hutchinson, 1977), 35.

howling, gut-wrenching melee that ensued over the city in the midafternoon was brief. It only lasted twenty-five minutes. But in terms of the number and concentration of opposing aircraft locked in battle over a single city, the battle over Münster was one of the greatest air battles in history. In terms of its sheer violence and intensity—and casualties on both sides—it remains unmatched. Indeed, the air battle between the VIII BC's 13th CBW and the German Luftwaffe over Münster, Germany, at three o'clock in the afternoon of October 10, 1943, has been described as the Omaha Beach of the USAAF.[3] Whether it was or not, like so many other momentous battles in history, it all began so routinely.

On Sunday morning, October 10, 1943, day broke quietly at Thorpe Abbotts. On the ground, it was fresh and cool. All indications were that we would be flying in clear, dry, crisp weather under a weak autumn sun. At 7:30 a.m., the flight crews of the 100th BG, placed on alert the night before, grumbled as they tumbled out of bed, spouting streams of obscenities and epithets at the fast-retreating orderlies who had been sent to wake us up. Once again, we dressed reflexively and climbed into the trucks waiting to take us to breakfast and then to the mission briefing. It would be Crew No. 31's twenty-first combat mission. We complete this one and we would have had only four more to go.

At 9:00 a.m., following the usual preliminaries, the curtains covering the huge wall map behind the podium in the briefing theater were, as always, dramatically opened. I recall no spontaneous outcries of shock or dismay. Unlike our tiring twelve-hour trip to Marienburg the previous day, the mission displayed on the

---

3. Omaha Beach was the American landing at Normandy on June 6, 1944. To understand what that means, the reader is invited to see the opening scene from Steven Spielberg's 1998 film, *Saving Private Ryan*.

wall map this morning did not appear to be particularly rough or troublesome. True, the red string delineating our flight plan crossed the German border, but just barely. Major Minor Shaw, our S-2 (intelligence) briefing officer, stood up and announced that our target for the day would be the railroad marshalling yards in the built-up eastern section of the beautiful cathedral city of Münster, Germany.

Münster had been the capital of Westphalia since the time of Charlemagne and was where the treaty ending the Thirty Years' War had been signed in 1648. The main rail lines from Osnabrück, Amsterdam, Gronau, Emden, and Berlin formed a junction north of Münster; while rail lines from the Ruhr formed another junction to the south. Within the city were large freight yards and locomotive and rolling stock repair shops. Münster was the key rail center through which principal rail traffic to and from the Ruhr and northern Germany passed. Moreover, the Dortmund-Ems Canal, which carried iron ore and other strategic materials north and south from the port of Emden, passed through Münster. Reaching the city did not entail a deep penetration mission: Münster is only thirty-five miles from the Dutch border.

Major Shaw went on to explain that the 13th CBW would lead the entire VIII BC in this effort. The 95th BG would lead the combat wing. The 100th BG would come next as the low group. The 390th BG would follow the 100th as the high group. Engine start was at 10:30; taxi time at 10:45; and takeoff was set at 11:00 in the morning. Our bombing altitude would be twenty-three thousand feet, where we would drop clusters of M47A2 one-hundred-pound jellied incendiary bombs. The 418th BS would again be our lead squadron with our squadron commander, Major John Egan, flying with Captain John Brady as group leader. Our crew would fly deputy lead, heading the second element of the lead squadron. Our fighter cover consisted of 216 P-47 Thunderbolts from the 4th, 56th,

78th, 352nd, and 353rd Fighter Groups of VIII Fighter Command. Their operational range made it possible for them to provide escort and support for VIII BC almost all the way to the target—*almost* all the way.

Our route would take us over Holland just below Rotterdam, then eastward generally following the Waal River to its confluence with the Lower Rhine. Near Wesel, we would leave the river and continue eastward to our IP at Haltern at the top of the Ruhr Valley southwest of Münster. We would make our bomb run to the northeast, permitting our bombardiers to use Aa Lake, a large and clearly visible landmark, for target orientation.

At this point, it would be well to note that with the publication in 1984 of Ian Hawkins's extensive research on the Münster mission, a controversy began to bubble over exactly what the VIII BC was supposed to bomb on October 10, 1943. The differences of opinion revolve around what the designated target or targets were, and whether Münster cathedral was an aiming point. Captain Ellis Scripture, lead navigator for the 95th BG, who led the Eighth that day, has stated that the briefing officer at the 95th base at Horham asserted that the purpose of the Münster mission was to hit the center of the city and disrupt the lives and morale of its working population. He said the aiming point for the lead bombardier of the 95th was the front steps of Münster Cathedral. Captain Scripture also said that, at the time, he and several other airmen of the 95th expressed misgivings about such a mission to their group commander who reminded the captain that "this was war . . . spelled W-A-R."[4] Years after the war, Major John Egan, flight commander of the 100th BG, also said that the aiming point for the 100th BG

---

4. Ian L. Hawkins, *The Münster Raid: Before and After* (Trumbull, CT: FNP Military Division, 1999), 72–75.

on October 10 was the center of the city. He, along with others at the 100th BG briefing, said he found himself on his feet cheering that he would have a chance to "avenge" the loss of his friend Major Bucky Cleven over Bremen, Germany, two days earlier. *However,* Major Egan added that the mission was essentially intended to disrupt rail transport in the Ruhr Valley.[5] Captain Marshall Shore, lead navigator for the 390th BG at Framlingham, the third and last group in the 13th CBW, has said that the aiming point for the 390th was the train station.[6]

Augie Gaspar and I, independently of each other, recall that the aiming point for the 100th BG on October 10 was the railroad marshalling yards at Münster, which were in the heavily built-up eastern part of the city. Neither Charlie Cruikshank, Augie, nor I remember any cheering at the 100th BG briefing. We agree, however, that *had* there been any demonstrations of joy or pleasure, it was unlikely we would have joined the chorus, because we were far too apprehensive about any foray into Germany to have engaged in war whoops or battle cries. Moreover, I have long felt it unlikely that the leaders of VIII BC would have committed their limited assets and hard-pressed aircrews to any mission of doubtful or marginal strategic military value. Further, the bombing of the German civilian population as a primary mission objective would appear to have been inconsistent with the Eighth's directives from above as well as its target selection process at the time. Third, the weather over Münster on October 10 was excellent. Except for an insignificant ground haze, the city was clearly visible from twenty-five thousand feet, and except for enemy opposition, our bombardiers would have had no problem identifying and hitting specific targets. *At the same*

5. Ibid., 76.

6. Marshall Shore, personal papers, memo, April 1985.

time, as Roger Freeman has pointed out, our Eighth AF leaders had no qualms whatsoever about bombing strategic targets located in large cities or other highly populated areas.[7] Collateral damage to nonstrategic targets as well as death and injury to civilians could not be avoided.

Major General Thomas S. Jeffrey, commander of the 100th BG from May 9, 1944, to February 1, 1945, was air executive at the 390th BG on October 10, 1943. General Jeffrey says the primary target for the 390th that day was the center of the city and there were no protests or complaints from the 390th aircrews over the fact that their target was the civilian population of the city of Münster. I would add here that no misgivings as to the purpose of the mission were expressed at the 100th BG briefing.

In April 1985, Marshall Shore, the lead navigator for the 390th BG on the October 10 mission, discussed the mission to Münster target by the VIII BC with the then commander of the 3rd BD, General Curtis LeMay, at the latter's home in Newport Beach, California. Their mutual conclusion was that the records and documents necessary to resolve the specific identity of these targets once and for all probably no longer exist. As it turned out, additional operational documents have been discovered.

In recent years, I have seen a series of strike photos of the bombing of Münster on October 10, 1943, that were taken by a camera mounted in an unidentified B-17 aircraft attacking the target. These photographs show bombs falling and exploding in the city. The bombs of this particular group fell mainly into the center of the city south of the cathedral.

I have also examined a high-altitude photograph of Münster taken by a reconnaissance aircraft from 541 Squadron, RAF Medmenham,

7. Personal correspondence with the author.

at 1630 hours on October 11, 1943, and RAF Photo Interpretation Report No. K 1778 dated October 12, 1943, which sets forth an assessment of the damage resulting from the USAAF attack on the city on October 10. This report states, "The weight of the attack has fallen in the center and eastern parts of the town. In addition to public buildings, railway facilities, and army depots, there is some damage to business and residential property." The report also states that one spire of the cathedral was damaged and the roof destroyed by fire. The RAF reconnaissance photograph shows that the heaviest concentration of bombs was in the center of the city south of the cathedral. The next heaviest concentration of bombs was at the railway facilities.

Then there is the testimony of other eyewitnesses. In the summer of 1987, I visited Heinz Hessling at his home in Beckum, Germany. In 1943, Heinz was an eighteen-year-old *Luftwaffenhelfer* (youth auxiliary force with the Luftwaffe) defending Münster. His gun position on October 10 was on the Dortmund-Ems Canal, just north of the city. He witnessed the air battle over Münster and recollects much of what happened that day. Heinz arranged for a small aircraft for us to use. In retracing the path the VIII BC took in our attack on Münster some forty-four years before, we flew from our IP at Haltern northeast to Münster and approached Aa Lake, the city center, Münster Cathedral, and the railroad yards, in that order. Since it was not unusual for Eighth planners to assign different aiming points to different bomb groups during the same operation, with only minor deviations in course, any one, or all, of these landmarks could have been targets for the VIII BC on October 10.[8]

---

8. A recent review of the tactical mission folders held at the National Archives, College Park, Maryland, has shed some light on this issue. Field Order Number 113 issued to all 3rd Bomb Division Groups lists the target as "GH 472." The "Target" listed on each group's J Form, which recorded aircraft takeoff and landing times, was also "GH 472." A review of each

No matter what the aiming points at Münster were, the VIII BC and the 100th BG were toeing the threshold of exhaustion in trying to attack them. Even before Crew No. 31 set out, our group had been terribly maimed by the incessant unescorted operations and the Luftwaffe's no-quarter defense of past weeks. On the evening of October 7, the 100th BG had thirty of its thirty-seven crews available for operations. Two days later, by the evening of October 9, just nineteen of thirty crews (63 percent) were flight-ready. These nineteen were not even enough to fill the standard twenty-one aircraft formation of six B-17s in the lead and low squadrons and nine in the high squadron.

The same pitiful anemia could be seen on the hardstands at Thorpe Abbotts. Forty-eight hours before Münster, the 100th BG had possessed forty-three aircraft. Of these, ten were in various stages of undergoing repairs or modifications and as such were not operational, reducing the number available for combat to thirty-three. As a result of the October 8 mission to Bremen, seven aircraft failed to return, and an eighth crash-landed in Britain and was declared beyond repair. An additional nine aircraft suffered such serious battle damage that they could not be repaired within a week's time. Therefore, for the arduous twelve-hour Marienburg mission

---

Group's "Combat Bombing Flight Record" lists the objective as "Münster," the Aiming Point as "Center of Town" or "Center of City," and the initial point as "Haltern." The lack of specificity appears in all of the Groups' records except for the 94th Bomb Group, where the aiming point was "Built up section of North East tip of Marshalling Yards." A review of the records at the Air Force Historical Research Agency, Maxwell Air Force Base, reveals that "GH 472" is the Target Folder Operation Number. The "Survey Information Sheet" lists "GH 472" as "Münster," the category as "Transportation," and the subcategory as "Railway Junctions." Nowhere in the target folder is there even a mention of the cathedral. Clearly, if a group briefing stated that the target was to bomb anything but the railway junctions, that particular unit was not in concert with VIII BC Headquarters' intentions. Equally clear, the cathedral would stand to be affected by collateral damage from stray bombs—a situation compounded by the fact that the mission was to take place on a Sunday.

on Saturday, October 9, the 100th BG could count just nineteen combat-ready Flying Fortresses. And although the 100th Group lost no aircraft on the Marienburg operation, this mission may have exacted a price of its own, as we shall see.

100th Bombardment Group Operational Readiness (as of 8:00 p.m.)

	Effective	Aircrews		B-17s					
Date	Strength	Assign	Avail	Assign	OH	Op	1	7	7+
Oct 7	30	37	30	43	43	33	7+	2	0
Oct 8	19	30	20	36	36	19	0	12	5
Oct 9	18	30	19	35	34	18	5	11	0
Oct 10	9	18	9	22	25	7	2	9	7

For each date, information is provided about the effective strength, number of aircrew assigned (Assign) and available (Avail) for combat as well as number of B-17s assigned (Assign), on hand (OH), operational (Op), operational within twenty-four hours (1), operational within a week (7), operational sometime after one week (7+).

NOTE: The fact that the 100th BG had three additional B-17s on hand than were assigned is a result of B-17s from other groups landing at Thorpe Abbotts.

Though only eighteen B-17s were considered operational and only nineteen aircrews were available for combat, the hardworking ground crews of the 100th BG did what they could for the Münster mission and managed to prepare, fuel, and arm twenty aircraft. Two of these aircraft were eliminated from taking part almost at once. *Nine Little Yanks and a Jerk* (23271) of the 351st BS had engine problems and was unable to take off. *Hard Luck!* (23413) of the 350th BS was to be ferried to Station 153 at Framlingham to pick up a 390th crew but did not depart Thorpe Abbotts until 10:44 a.m. It arrived at Framlingham too late to pick up its crew and returned to Thorpe Abbotts, landing at 12:14 p.m. A third 100th aircraft, *Little Mike* (23234), had taken off for Framlingham at 10:40 a.m. to fly as a "spare" with the 390th BG. It participated in the mission with the 390th crew of Lieutenant Robert Schneider. The 100th BG formation on October 10, therefore, was an emaciated and already battered lot of seventeen aircraft when it lifted off from Thorpe Abbotts.

For Münster, Crew No. 31 was assigned to fly a relatively new B-17F, serial number 42-30725, which belonged to the 350th BS, and which had arrived at Thorpe Abbotts on September 3. The aircraft had flown a few missions in early September before being sent to the air depot at Honington to receive the latest combat modifications, where it remained until sometime before September 26, when it participated on the mission to Paris. The aircraft had been given the unusual name *Aw-R-Go,* the basis for which has been a mystery to me ever since. Our crew was trucked to the 350th flight line to permit us to put our gear on board and take the airplane back to the 418th parking area so that we could assume our proper place in the taxi order. As we moved out, the hardworking 350th crew chief who gave us his airplane walked us out of the hardstand on to the taxiway, waved, and saluted. We all saluted back.

At exactly 10:30 a.m., the silence in the morning air of the peaceful, pastoral countryside surrounding Thorpe Abbotts once again gave way to the reverberation and roar of aircraft starting their engines. Minutes later, the familiar processions of aircraft crept along the perimeter strip to the ends of runways, where each would await his turn to take off. We were fourth in line, behind Lieutenant Robert "Rosie" Rosenthal and, I believe, Lieutenant John Flanigan, Major John Egan's wingmen. At 11:11 a.m., Egan swept down the field and took to the air for Münster. Two minutes later, at 11:13 a.m., Crew No. 31 made its final takeoff from Thorpe Abbotts.

The 13th CBW assembled over Great Yarmouth, then flew southwest to radio beacon Splasher Seven near Braintree to permit two other combat wings of the 3rd BD to form a column behind us. This combined armada then turned east. We departed the English coast at Felixstowe at 1:48 p.m. The 100th BG was flying at twenty-three thousand feet.

Misfortune struck the ill-fated 100th almost immediately. Within thirty minutes after we passed over the English coast, four of the seventeen aircraft in the 100th formation peeled off over the English Channel and returned to Thorpe Abbotts with mechanical or equipment problems. Three of these aircraft, plus the aircraft that had failed to take off at Thorpe Abbotts that morning because of engine problems, had flown the grueling twelve-hour mission to Marienburg the previous day, but had been put back into the air on a combat mission less than twenty-four hours later. Was the Marienburg operation taking its toll? We will never know; however, when we made our landfall in Holland south of Rotterdam, the 100th formation was down to thirteen aircraft.

100th Bomb Group Order of Battle
October 10, 1943 Takeoff Order

Time	Serial	Squadron	Name	Pilot
FTO	23271	351 L	*Nine Little Yanks and a Jerk*	Robert L. Hughes Failed to take off—engine trouble
1020	23234	351 E	*Little Mike*	Robert Schneider Flew with 390th BG
1044	23413	350 V	*Hard Luck!*	Unknown Arrived at Framlingham too late to pick up crew
1111	230830	418 U	*M'lle Zig Zig*	John D. Brady/John Egan
1112	26087	418 Z	*Royal Flush*	Robert Rosenthal

1112	26094	418 Q	unnamed	John Flanigan Returned early—#2 low oil pressure
1113	230725	350 Z	*Aw-R-Go*	Charles B. Cruikshank
1114	230047	350 Q	*Sweater Girl*	Richard B. Atchison Jr.
1115	23237	418 R	*Stymie*	John F. Stephens
1115	23307	351 N	*Skipper*	Unknown Returned early—engine ran out of oil
1116	230723	351 D	*Sexy Suzy Mother of Ten*	William M. Beddow
1116	230734	351 G	*Slightly Dangerous*	Charles H. Thompson
1117	23534	349 N	*Ol' Dad*	Unknown Returned early—could not keep up with formation
1118	23229	349 A	*Pasadena Nena*	John K. Justice
1119	23433	350 W	*Leona*	Robert P. Kramer
1119	230087	351 M	*Shack Rat*	Maurice E. Beatty
1120	230823	350 Y	*Invadin' Maiden*	Charles D. Walts
1121	230090	349 B	*El P'sstofo*	Winton L. MacCarter
1140	230023	349 M	*Forever Yours II*	Edward G. Stork
1237	230061	418 T	*Wolff Pack*	Unknown Returned early—could not test-fire guns

Without one burst of flak or one German fighter attack, our standard twenty-one-plane formation had been reduced by 38 percent. Worse yet, we had lost the use of ninety-six .50-caliber machine guns, vital to the formation's defensive protection from Luftwaffe fighter tactics.

The Germans were aware of an impending large-scale attack by the Eighth for the third day in a row long before we departed England. A defense "wall," the Kammhuber Line—a chain of radar stations stretching from Norway across northern Germany, Holland, Belgium, and northern France—was equipped with Mammut and Wassermann early-warning radar sets, improved versions of Germany's famous 1936 GEMA Freya radar, that could detect aircraft up to 200 miles away and give accurate information on the height, range, and bearing of aircraft up to 150 miles away. By October 1943, the Germans were regularly watching the Eighth as we formed up over England. A full half hour before we set out for Münster, Luftwaffe controllers were alerting German day and night fighter units as far away as Jever in northern Germany and the elite Fw 190 Jagdgeschwader 26 at Lille, France, to prepare for combat.

The strategically located sector operations rooms for Luftwaffe fighter control were housed deep underground in concrete shelters. After the early-warning radars gave advance warnings of the approach of our bombers, the tracks of both the bombers and intercepting Luftwaffe fighters were monitored and plotted on a sophisticated grid table known as a *Seeburg Tisch*.[9] The radar positions of both bombers and fighters were displayed on a huge map of Holland on a translucent glass plate as moving spots of light: red spots for enemy bombers and green spots for Luftwaffe fighters. The plotting was done by young female Luftwaffe auxiliaries, known in slang as *Blitzmädels*,[10] who sat at batteries of microphones and headphones. The girls would get information on the range, bearing, and height of incoming bombers via telephone with coastal stations operating high-definition Würzburg tracking radar. Three girls were allocated to track the plots of each giant Würzburg. Using the data they obtained, the young women would project lights on the table map to maintain a continuous plot of aircraft positions. As the red light

---

9. German for "Seeburg table."

10. Literally, German for "lightning girls." However, *Blitzmädel/Blitzmädchen* was military jargon for *Nachrichtenhelferin* (a Signal Corps) and more likely meant "signal girl." The insignia they wore on the sleeves of their uniforms was a lightning bolt, representing electronic communications. The German word *blitz* means "lightning."

for the bombers moved over the table, their track was traced on the glass. A Luftwaffe officer sitting on a dais overlooking the table would direct fighter intercepts by radio link.[11]

The heavy concentration of over two hundred Luftwaffe fighter and rocket-firing aircraft that intercepted the 13th CBW as we spearheaded the Eighth AF generated subsequent speculation that the Germans, in some fashion, knew in advance that our target on October 10, 1943, was Münster. This, however, is now considered most unlikely, as the German intelligence network in England was exceedingly poor and their command and control net on the continent could only guess at the Eighth's target on a given day, as we could, with a few degrees change in course, attack any number of strategic targets in northwestern Germany.

In war as in peace, rumors abound when situations are not fully understood by the participants. Such is the case with the VIII BC bomber crews and our understanding of the Luftwaffe's prowess. We were not aware of the many factors used by VIII BC mission planners to plot our route to and from the selected target for the day. For example, we were not aware the total time a German fighter such as the Me 109 or the Fw 190 could spend in the air from take-off to landing was no more than one hour and twenty minutes. We were not aware that the diversionary feints used by the VIII BC or those minor midcourse changes to our route compounded the command and control problems the Luftwaffe had in vectoring its airborne fighters to intercept us. We were not aware of the problems facing the Luftwaffe in concentrating its fighters in sufficient numbers at the "right place" and at the "right time" to provide an

---

11. In addition, the Germans may have been watching us from the air. After the mission, at least one 390th BG crew reported having seen a Me 110 aircraft high in the sky over Framlingham, and it appeared to be able to observe as the group took off and assembled over their base.

effective air defense. We understood all too well the impact on us when the Luftwaffe did show up in force as they did on our August 17 mission to Regensburg. And when they did, the always-present rumors ran rampant of an extensive German spy network in England, observing our activities and detailing to Berlin what was the target for today. Even the elderly lady whose farmhouse was near the end of one of Thorpe Abbotts runways was rumored by some to be a German operative. These rumors about this lady were not true, and the effectiveness of the German spy network was highly overinflated.

When we as the aircrew were flying and the Luftwaffe fighters could be seen in the distance, our collective heart rates accelerated, our breathing quickened, and our anxiety increased. When we saw that black dot in the distance stop moving, we did not care, even if we knew, that the Me 109 or Fw 190 had only a limited amount of time in the air for combat. We did not care if there were serious difficulties facing the Luftwaffe's command and control of its fighter forces. When that black dot in the distance stopped, it meant that the German fighter pilot had focused his attention on to our aircraft. At that moment, global issues involving the grand strategy of war and why we were fighting took a back seat because the war for us became a very personal test of will, skill, and luck between our crew and that German fighter pilot.

As noted, there were thirteen aircraft in the 100th BG formation when we crossed the Dutch coast below Rotterdam at approximately 2:30 p.m. Except for light, inaccurate flak thrown up by the southern defenses of Rotterdam well off to our left, we encountered no enemy opposition as we overflew the peaceful patchwork of pastel green, brown, and tan fields beneath us. We arrived at the German border about 2:45 p.m. Five minutes later we reached our IP at Haltern. The

95th BG made a forty-five-degree turn to the left and commenced its bombing run.

The 100th BG continued its original course for about one minute, then turned left to follow the 95th over the target. We began our bomb run at our prescribed altitude of twenty-three thousand feet. I remember looking back through my navigator's astrodome to see if we had any American fighter support. Far behind us, I saw several flights of P-47 aircraft turning back for England. They had missed their rendezvous with us, but it made little difference. Their fuel was low, they had run out of range, and were at the end of their string; they had no choice but to go home. It was the first time that day that I had seen any of our scheduled fighter support. At almost the same time, I heard a voice on the intercom calling, "Fighters, fighters, nine o'clock low, two o'clock low, three o'clock low."

The sky quickly filled with airplanes. At varying altitudes, below us and on all sides, German single-engine fighters were almost hanging on their props, climbing steeply to intercept us. I stopped counting at more than sixty German fighter aircraft rising to resist us before turning to charge my guns in preparation for firing. The depleted, undermanned 100th formation, comprised of only thirteen airplanes, the low group now widely spaced from its two companion groups in the 13th CBW and flying straight and level toward Münster, presented an inviting target for the courageous and skilled German fighter pilots.

On the ground at his headquarters on Manfred-von-Richthofen-Straße in Münster, Dr. Bernhard Fischer, commander of the Warn-kommando (warning unit) of the Luftgaukommando (district air defense unit), had been monitoring reports on the approaching American bombers. Around noon, his deputy, Alois Rauch, telephoned him at home and informed him that German radar units had detected large formations of bombers above the eastern coast of

England. This usually meant that it would take the Americans from two to two and a half hours to reach Germany. Later, as the American formations appeared to be heading south of Münsterland, Dr. Fischer breathed a sigh of relief. Nevertheless, he gave orders for an air raid alert as soon as the bombers reached the Rhine River.

At 2:44 p.m., when the head of the American bomber formation reached Kevelaer, an air raid alert was sounded. Six minutes later, when the American formation changed course at Haltern, and the Germans recognized that Münster was the bomber's target, an all-out alarm was sounded. At that point, General Schmidt, commander of Luftgaukommando VI, who apparently did not possess the latest information on the incoming bombers, telephoned Dr. Fischer and complained that the alarm had been sounded prematurely.

On the streets of the city, the citizens and visitors to Münster on October 10, 1943, are also said to have been surprised when the air raid alert sounded at 2:44 p.m., almost immediately followed by the all-out alarm at 2:50 p.m., even as the bells of St. Paul's Cathedral were ringing for afternoon vespers services. Inexplicably, it is reported that nobody could really believe an air raid would happen on this clear, warm, autumn Sunday afternoon and, even after the all-out alert, people were standing in the streets, searching the skies with their eyes, and only a few sought protection in shelters.

The waiting, previously deployed, Luftwaffe aircraft struck the 100th BG full force at 2:53 p.m. The fighters came after us in steady waves, climbing and racing out ahead of us in trail, winging over and swarming to the attack with all guns blazing and, at the last second, flying directly through our formation, veering away, or rolling over and making a split-S just yards in front of us to drop away toward the ground. As one element broke away, another turned to the attack far ahead of us. They came, and came, and came, often passing so close we could distinctly see the German pilots in their cockpits. I have a recollection of someone, possibly Glenn Graham, crying out, "Here they come! Fire! Fire now! Fire! Fire! Fire!" More than once, I stopped shooting, turned my head away, held my breath, and closed my eyes as I trembled and shook, expecting head-on collisions that miraculously did not happen. Every fifth bullet in our ammunition belts was a tracer. I could see from the intersecting streams of our tracers that we were showering our attackers with heavy machine-gun fire, but they seemed to have no effect. The fighters came on with complete disregard for our guns. Inside the airplane, it was as if we had a half dozen jackhammers all going at once. As we approached the city, the fighter attacks ceased, and we ran into heavy, accurate flak. Unknown to our intelligence, two days earlier, on October 8, the Germans had placed two batteries of 105 mm heavy "railroad" flak two and a half miles west of Münster, directly in the path of our bombing run. Flak in the target area was intense.

Having passed our IP, we were now midway through our bomb run; John Egan and John Brady's *M'lle Zig Zig* (230830) was still about one hundred feet directly in front and about fifty feet above us. With the bomb bay doors open and just a few minutes before bombs away, a horrendous fiery explosion erupted about twenty-five to thirty feet directly under *M'lle Zig Zig*. In our previous twenty missions, we experienced a few close hits from flak. The concussion from an 88 mm or 105 mm shell exploding was one thing; the concussion from this explosion was two, maybe even three times more intense, and it struck us so violently that it felt as though we had stopped in midair for a moment or two, as if having hit a brick wall. At the time, I thought it was a flak burst. Brady's aircraft began to sink, trailing black smoke and fluids. Charlie Cruikshank followed it down for a few moments, but recognizing that Egan and Brady were going down, he pulled up and we continued our bomb run.

I believe that at this point, our small, incomplete, undermanned formation, already in mortal danger, may have lost its unit compactness and cohesion.[12]

We completed our bomb run, dropped our bombs, and began a long, gradual left turn to our rally point with the 95th and 390th BGs. I looked out my left window and saw a B-17 about five hundred to six hundred feet below us falling away steeply with its left wing enveloped in sheets of red and yellow flames. A large white square was painted on both sides of the vertical stabilizer's upper portion and on the right upper wingtip area. Inside the square, the capital letter "D," the identification for the 100th BG, was painted in insignia blue. As we turned away from the city, the Luftwaffe

---

12. I am now convinced that the explosion just beneath Brady's aircraft was not from flak but from a WGr.21 (Wurfgranate 21, "21 cm mortar shell"; or Werfergranate 21, "mortar projector or launcher 21"), launched from a Me 110 that was standing off outside the range of our defensive .50-caliber machine guns. Each Me 110 carried two of these air-to-air rockets under each wing, each rocket weighing approximately 240 pounds with an 88-pound warhead, with a timed fuse set to detonate four seconds after launch. This was slightly less than three times the size of an 88 mm flak shell. The tactic is similar to that described in "The Rocketeers." Karl Boehm-Tettelbach, on October 10, 1943, was an *Oberstleutnant* (German for "lieutenant colonel") commanding III Gruppe / Zerstörergeschwader 26 (III/ZG 26—heavy fighter destroyer squadron). The tactic was straightforward—use the 21 cm rockets against "closed" bomber formations from beyond the range of our defensive machine guns with the intention of breaking up the bomber formation. This would then defuse the defensive power so that individual bombers could be attacked. Boehm-Tettlebach stated, "In the early afternoon of 10 October 1943, elements of the ZG 26 were deployed from Wünsdorf to Hanover by the German air defense command for arming and refueling to intercept known incoming Eighth bomber formations." Boehm-Tettlebach was leading a flight of four Me 110s in a "finger four" formation. He was the first to fire his four rockets into the formation. The German pilot also noted that this tactic was not feasible when there were American escort fighters because the underwing stores made the Me 110 very vulnerable. Based on what I saw and this description, it is quite likely that it was one of these rockets or rockets from other III/ZG 26 Me 110s that forced John Brady out of formation. It is also quite possible that other rockets found their mark. The result was that our formation, undersized as it was from the beginning, was scattered, giving other German fighters the opportunity to attack individual B-17s. In reviewing this incident, I shudder to think what would have happened to John Brady and his crew if the Me 110 pilot was flying a slightly higher altitude, and I am equally aware of the consequences to our B-17 and its crew if the pilot was flying a slightly lower altitude and had launched the missile a fraction of a second earlier.

fighters returned with a vengeance. We seemed to be all alone. Moments later, as I was firing the left nose gun at the attacking German fighters, a violent explosion just behind me and to my left sent me crashing to the floor. I immediately felt a burning sensation in my left arm and shoulder as they began to ache and go numb. I knew I had been hit. As I struggled to stand up, slipping and sliding on expended shell casings, Augie Gaspar turned and vigorously motioned with the palm of his right hand down for me not to get up.

Out of the corner of my eye, I saw someone coming down through the floorboard door from the pilots' compartment. It was Glenn Graham. He had taken off his oxygen mask. He motioned with his right arm that I was to follow him, pulled the emergency release handle on the forward crew door, kicked it away, and bailed out. I was aghast as I watched him rapidly drop away and disappear behind the airplane. I had not heard the alarm bell under the navigator's table go off and saw that my intercom controls were shot away. But I knew. It was all over. We were going down. I clipped on my parachute chest pack, crawled to the door, and dangled my feet in the opening. The countryside twenty-thousand feet below me was a vast, multicolored checkerboard of dark strips of forest and rich, green fields neatly and meticulously laid out. But it looked a hundred miles away. I eased out the door with my hands at my sides. The earth was spinning around me. I realized I was tumbling. I shut my eyes and waited until I felt sure I had cleared the airplane—undoubtedly no more than a matter of seconds. I jerked the "D" ring of the rip cord on my parachute so hard I have no idea what happened to it. A mass of material flashed in front of my face. Almost simultaneously, I heard a loud *thwack* sound and felt a sharp jerk as my fall was broken. Mercifully, my parachute had opened. I remember looking at my watch; it was 3:10 in the afternoon.

Suddenly, it seemed deathly quiet. There was no more battle

noise, no guns firing, no smell of cordite, no engines straining and groaning, no intercom chatter. I had removed my gloves to fire my machine guns, and now my hands were freezing. The first finger on my left hand had been split open by a splinter from the cannon shell that had exploded behind me in the airplane. I thought of my mother, who had worried so much about me. Moments later, while drifting earthward in my parachute, the 390th BG formation approached from the south and had commenced a long, sweeping left turn almost directly above me when there erupted a huge flak barrage from an 88 mm battery. The explosions made were loud, sharp, crackling, earsplitting sounds, like thunder accompanying nearby bolts of lightning coming in rapid succession—it was quite terrifying. Not since I was a little boy petrified with fright by that first intense lightning and thunder of a rainstorm that brewed from one of those hot, humid summer afternoons in Atlanta had I been so terrified of light and sound.

Since March 1942, when I first sat at my navigator's table aboard a B-17, I had flown over 612 hours in training and over 126 hours in combat. In that time, I had grown accustomed—as much as anyone could—to the deafening racket made by those four Wright Cyclone engines turning 2,300–2,500 rpm and pulling forty-five to forty-six inches of mercury with everything to the firewall in combat. Above this din, if a flak burst had come close to our aircraft—which it did several times—I heard a deep thump. Other times, I only heard the tinkling of shrapnel raining on the aluminum skin of the B-17, making a noise similar to that of a handful of pebbles striking a metal bucket. Not until I bailed out into that cold and quiet air at twenty thousand feet did I truly realize how noisy it was inside the B-17. I also experienced for the first time the incredible force and intensity of the flak that we constantly saw exploding all around us from inside the airplane. From the outside, it was incredible. Off in the distance, a lone Me 109 was making a wide arc around me. He abruptly winged over and flew straight at me. I froze. I prayed. I shut my eyes and squeezed them. I held my breath. I scrunched up as best I could with my deadweight hanging in a parachute. Was he going to open fire? He did not. He did, however, pass so close above me as he flew away that I began to swing wildly in the violently turbulent air created by his prop wash. Once more, I was totally panic-stricken, certain my parachute was going to completely collapse, throwing me into a free fall to the earth from eighteen thousand feet. I almost wished the Me 109 pilot had shot me. After a few moments, to my intense relief, my parachute again blossomed open above me, and all was quiet. I continued my fall into I knew not what.

Just over four miles north of Münster, on the main road to Greven, a narrow east-west bridge spans the Dortmund-Ems Canal. In October 1943, a regular Luftwaffe antiaircraft artillery unit was positioned on the north side of the road at the east end of this bridge. In addition to its two batteries of 88 mm flak artillery, this unit had four wooden towers equipped with 20 mm "light" flak guns to protect them against low-flying enemy aircraft. It was 88 mm flak from this position that I saw bursting around the 390th BG a few moments after I bailed out of our aircraft.

The 20 mm flak guns at this site were manned that day by a six-man team of young Luftwaffe auxiliary personnel known as *Luftwaffenhelfers*—schoolboys, actually—who were "helpers" on weekend duty with the active forces. One of them, Heinz Hessling, age eighteen, watched the air battle over Münster on the afternoon of October 10, 1943, through a pair of binoculars. Sometime after 3:00 p.m., he saw a single B-17, its right wing trailing fire and dense, black smoke, flying in a northeasterly direction away from Münster.

It was receiving fire from its rear from two German fighter aircraft and appeared incapable of defending itself.[13] This was B-17F, serial number 42-30725, flown by Crew No. 31 of the 100th BG. As he watched, Hessling saw the crew begin to abandon the burning airplane.

In October 1943, the tiny farm community of Holzhausen, situated in the flat, low-lying country seventeen miles northeast of Münster near the tiny village of Kattenvenne, was little more than a crossroads providing access to a half dozen single-family farms. The small farm on the southwest corner of this crossroads, devoid of improvements except for a characteristic Westphalian brick-and-wooden-beam cottage, has been owned by the locally prominent Haarlammert family for more than a century. During the Second World War, the Haarlammerts leased the farm to Wilhelm Rawe, a German army veteran of the First World War who was then fifty-one years of age. He lived on the farm with his wife, Frieda. In October 1943, the Rawes had two teenage daughters living with them. They also had one son, who, at the age of nineteen, had been killed in action while serving with the Wehrmacht on the Russian front. Frieda Rawe, then forty-seven years old, would never recover from the grief of losing her son and died shortly after the war. The Rawe family operated a small post office on the side in 1943, which was managed by their eldest daughter.

On the lovely Sunday afternoon of October 10, 1943, the Rawe family was entertaining numerous visitors: Frau Rawe's sister and brother-in-law, Fedor Yackel, and their son, Fedor Yackel II, from

---

13. Research has yet to reveal and may never reveal the identities of those two fighter pilots, but it is also possible that one of those two was also involved in the incident described above as I parachuted earthward.

On top of 100th BG control tower are Col. Neil "Chick" Harding and Maj. John "Jack" Kidd, 100th BG senior officers "sweating 'em in." On lower level are Maj. Sam Barr (back to camera), Maj. Robert Flesher, Capt. Sumner Reeder, Capt. Cosgrove, and Maj. Marvin Bowman (S-2 Intelligence Officer).
Courtesy of the 100th Bomb Group Foundation

War correspondents talk with Lt. Cruikshank and Lt. Wolff's crews after the August 17, 1943 Regensburg mission. Frank is in top right corner, wearing a red fez, and to his right are unknown officer, Lt. Charles Cruikshank, Lt. Glenn Graham, and Lt. Augie Gaspar.
Courtesy of the 100th Bomb Group Foundation

Capt. Heinz Knoke, ME 109 pilot with Jagdeschwader II (Fighter Wing II), was a Luftwaffe "Ace" (forty-two air victories) who survived the war.
Hans Hoehler

Lt. Robert Rosenthal's crew, the only 100th BG crew which returned to Thorpe Abbotts on October 10, 1943. Kneeling, left to right: Lt. Ronald Bailey, Lt. Robert Rosenthal, Lt. Clifford Milborn, and Lt. W.T. Lewis. Standing: S/Sgt. Loren Darling, T/Sgt. Michael Bocuzzi, S/Sgt. James Mack, T/Sgt. Clarence Hall, S/Sgt William DeBlasio, and S/Sgt. Ray Robinson. Rosenthal completed fifty-two missions with the 100th Bomb Group.
Courtesy of the 100th Bomb Group Foundation

Photo taken after crash of *Aw-R-Go* (230725), Berdelmann Farm, Lienen, Germany.
The Berdelmann farmhouse is in the background.
Murphy Collection

Another postcrash photo of *Aw-R-Go* (230725) showing remnants of tail section.
Murphy Collection

Capt Richard A. Carey, 350th
Operations Officer, shot down
July 25, 1943. Dick Carey was
Frank's roommate at Stalag
Luft III for almost a year.
Courtesy of the Carey Family &
100th Bomb Group Foundation

Interior view of Room 3, Block 133, South Compound, Stalag Luft III (circa 1944).
Courtesy of the Friends of the U.S. Air Force Academy Library

Stalag Luft III. The barracks, known as blocks, are in the background. The goon (guard) tower is on the left. The warning wire, in the lower portion of the photo, is located thirty feet from the barbed wire.
Courtesy of the Friends of the U.S. Air Force Academy Library

Frank is front row, fourth from left, in this photo of the Luftbandsters.
Courtesy of the Friends of the U.S. Air Force Academy Library

An aerial view of Stalag Luft III. From left to right are the West Compound that flanks the North and South Compounds, that are separated by an open space. Next is the German Lager, followed to the right by Center and East Compounds.
Courtesy of the Friends of the U.S. Air Force Academy Library

Germans trying to match identification cards with prisoners—a hopeless task.
Courtesy of the Friends of the U.S. Air Force Academy Library

Crowded conditions inside the tents at Stalag VIIA.
Courtesy of the Friends of the U.S. Air Force Academy Library

A view of the barracks a Stalag VIIA shortly after liberation.
Courtesy of the Friends of the U.S. Air Force Academy Library

General George S. Patton, Jr., Commander of the Third Army, visits
American POWs at Stalag VIIA on May 1, 1945.
Courtesy of the Friends of the U.S. Air Force Academy Library

Harry Crosby, Robert Rosenthal, and Everett Blakely, 1979 100th BG Reunion, San Antonio, Texas.
100th Bomb Group Memorial Museum

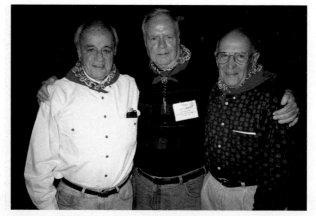

1993: 100th BG Reunion, Little Rock, Arkansas. Fifty years after being shot down on 10 Oct. 1943, three survivors from B-17 *Aw-R-Go* meet again, left to right, Charles Cruikshank (pilot), Frank Murphy (navigator), and Gus Gaspar (bombardier).
Murphy Collection

Ann and Frank on their wedding day, September 9, 1949, also Frank's twenty-eighth birthday.
Murphy Collection

In a September 1987 visit to Beckum, Germany, Frank met with Heinz Hessling and was introduced to former members of the Luftwaffe. From left to right: Hubert Kosters, a radio operator and gunner on a German bomber; Heinz Hessling; Heinz Knoke, an ME-109 fighter ace with fifty-eight victories; and Frank.
Murphy Collection

Frank D. Murphy,
August 1945.
Murphy Collection

Frank's brother
John H. Murphy,
an 18-year-old
pharmacist's mate,
U.S. Navy, 1945.
Murphy Collection

Frank's brother Michael V.
Murphy, Jr., a senior medical
student at Emory University
School of Medicine, Atlanta,
Georgia, 1944.
Murphy Collection

Dortmund, and an eight-year-old girl from Aachen who lived with the Rawe family during the war. Also at the house was a neighbor, Frau Elisabeth Woldmann, a frumpish lady of about forty years of age. She had a cherubic face and rented a house across the road. Frau Woldmann had moved into the neighborhood in 1942. Her husband owned a coal business with their son in Münster. He visited her occasionally, mostly on weekends. She had worked for a shipping company in Hamburg before the war and spoke fluent English. The two Rawe daughters were out riding on their bicycles.

As the Rawes and their guests were enjoying a warm, sunny Sunday afternoon, they heard distant explosions. They went outside to see what was happening, and high in the sky above them, they saw several men in parachutes falling into Holzhausen. As they watched, one of the parachutists came down just over a line of trees running west from the farmhouse and landed heavily in an open field about one hundred yards from the house.

An VIII BC airman using a standard chest-pack parachute in the Second World War descended at a rate of approximately one thousand feet per minute. It was not, however, until I was several hundred feet above the ground that I actually realized how fast I was falling, almost seventeen feet per second. And, although the aircrews in England had often discussed the need to relax just before striking the ground, and even though I knew better, I instinctively stiffened slightly just before I landed. It was like jumping from the second floor of a building. Upon impact, I turned my left ankle very badly and immediately crumpled over. My left arm and shoulder were in shock and without feeling as a result of numerous small shrapnel wounds. Several shrouds from my parachute were strung on top of me crosswise. I felt weak and exhausted and was having much difficulty trying to unbuckle my parachute harness using only my right arm. As I struggled to extricate myself from this tangled web, two men and a boy cautiously approached me. The older of the two men, a short, compact man in a white shirt and dark trousers, and wearing a pea cap, edged closer to me. In height, build, and facial features, he reminded me of my German grandfather. Behind him, Fedor Yackel and his son, Fedor II, then age eleven, carefully looked on. All were completely unarmed. In an inquiring voice, Wilhelm Rawe asked, "*Deutsche?*" I knew he was asking if I was German.

"*Nein,*" I answered. "American."

The three Germans took a quick step back. I am sure they were concerned that I may have been armed. I was not. I very rarely carried a sidearm on a combat mission. My goal, if I was shot down, was to evade capture, not to get involved in a confrontation and shoot-out with the Germans. The idea of jumping up and running away was out of the question. Not only was I physically and mentally drained, I was no match for the three healthy people standing over me. Moreover, it was one thing to fall into France or one of the Low Countries, where a sympathetic local native might assist an Allied airman to avoid capture, but it was another thing altogether to parachute into Germany, where it was highly unlikely that anyone would assist an enemy airman to escape.

Moments later, when I was finally able to stand, the men indicated that I should follow them. I had started to walk, hobbling very badly when they stopped me and insisted that I go back and retrieve my parachute, which I had left on the ground where I landed. With a bit of a struggle, I gathered my parachute in my arms, and we began walking down a small dirt wagon path through some trees. We had gone only a short distance when I saw two or three women standing alongside the path just ahead of us. As we drew near these ladies, Frau Elisabeth Woldmann said, in perfect English, the words that would be the first that hundreds of American airmen would report hearing upon being captured: "For you, the war is over."[14] These same words were spoken so often to newly captured Americans that I assume they had somehow become a common German wartime expression. I have, however, never known whether they were used with Germans, under appropriate circumstances, as well as Americans, or whether they were intended as words of sympathy or condemnation. They could have been used either way.

I must have presented a dismal sight: tired, disheveled, bloody, and hopping along on one foot with my used parachute gathered in my arms. Frau Woldmann then commented, "You are hurt," and motioned for me to follow her to the Rawe farmhouse about one hundred yards farther on. When we reached the house, Frau Rawe and Frau Woldmann took me inside to the kitchen. Curiously, after some discussion among the entire group, the men went outside and closed the door. The two women drew water into an enameled washbasin from an old-fashioned pump just inside the front door and placed it on a small table. I took off my shirt and began trying to cleanse the blood from my left arm and shoulder. As I was doing this, Frau Rawe brought me a plate of bread. About this time, a young neighbor girl, Gerda Berdelmann, entered the kitchen. She had been close by and saw us bail out of our airplane. She watched me come down and ran to the Rawe house to see what was going on. Several minutes later, the two Rawe daughters returned home from riding their bicycles; word was rapidly spreading throughout the community that men were falling in parachutes all over the area. In

14. Reportedly, this phrase was part of a German psychological warfare tactic. The German press carried stories encouraging civilians to say in English, "For you, the war is over," if they happened to meet a captured combatant. I do not recall that hearing this phrase had any particular impact on me at the time or while I was a prisoner of war, though it must be noted that nearly every prisoner that I have ever spoken to during the war or after was also told the same phrase.

fact, six B-17s and thirteen American airmen fell in the immediate vicinity of the tightly clustered villages of Kattenvenne, Holzhausen, and Lienen. I was later told that for years after the war, the Germans in this tiny locality often spoke of the dramatic air battle over Münster on October 10, 1943, and its consequences on them, and that they frequently wondered whatever became of all the Americans who landed there on what was to be that most eventful day.

Although the war in Europe was entering its fourth year in October 1943, most of the people in this small rural area northeast of Münster had, until the tenth day of that month, been spared the violence of the war. This was a traditionally quiet, peaceful farm area with country towns and wide places in the road not significantly different from similar places in the United States. Neither from the air, nor as we were driven through the region afterward, did we see any evidence of the devastation of war.

I had been inside the Rawe house for approximately twenty minutes when Wilhelm Rawe opened the front door and came in together with a small, thin, dried-up stick of a man with a Hitler-like mustache, wearing a black uniform and holding a small automatic pistol in his hand. The uniformed man immediately pointed his pistol at me. He was Walter Bakke, a local policeman in Kattenvenne and Holzhausen. While I was being attended to by the ladies, Wilhelm Rawe had managed to get word to Officer Bakke that I was at his home. When I saw the gun pointed at me, I instinctively began to raise my arms above my head. However, waving his pistol toward the front door, the policeman motioned for me to go outside. I hurriedly took off my wristwatch and offered it to the two ladies. They wisely refused to accept it.

Outside, a crowd of perhaps two dozen people, including several children, had gathered in front of the house. Mr. Bakke talked to them, telling them to keep cool. They were, in fact, cold, but made no unfriendly moves toward me. I had a package of Juicy Fruit chewing gum in my left hand shirt pocket, which I offered to Fedor Yackel II. He refused to take it. While I was inside, my bloodstained parachute had been spread out on the ground in front of the house. Walter Bakke, Wilhelm Rawe, and Fedor Yackel again directed me to pick it up. A hostile-appearing man in the crowd made a contemptuous comment to me in German that I did not understand. I have, however, since been told that his words were, "Here, you carry your own cross." Regrettably, I later learned that the Rawe family received severe criticism from a number of people in the community for the remainder of the war. It turned out that taking a prisoner into their home was unacceptable.

Accompanied by Officer Bakke; Fedor Yackel and his son; Elf-riede Rawe, the youngest of the Rawe daughters; and Gerda Berdel-mann, and with my parachute in my arms, I began limping down the main road in front of the house. They were taking me in a southerly direction to the small village of Kattenvenne, just over a mile away.

We had walked no more than a half mile when a long, highly polished, rich green, open Mercedes-Benz touring car with enor-mous waist-high wooden-spoked wheels and deep running boards passed us. In the elegant leather front seat of the car were two older men wearing green uniforms and old-style Prussian spiked helmets, members of the Volkssturm, the Home Guard. In the back seat of the car was Charlie Cruikshank screaming, "Murph!" and pound-ing the back of one of the men and pointing to me. Although the two men were furious, they stopped and picked me up. My spirits immediately went up 1,000 percent at the sight of Charlie Cruik-shank and the knowledge that he was unhurt.

Charlie Cruikshank told me that after staying with John Egan's disabled aircraft for a few moments as it began its mortal descent, he realized they were going down. He pulled up and assumed the lead of the 100th BG, as there was no one ahead of us and he did not know how many, if any, 100th aircraft there were behind us. We proceeded to make our bomb run on the target. At bombs away, and as he was making a long left turn, he became aware of a dangerous fire behind the firewall of our number 4 engine. Neither feathering the prop nor pulling the CO_2 charge were of any avail; the fire was out of control. We were also under heavy attack from the rear by German fighters. He felt his flight controls go "mushy." It was, he said, like trying to fly "a plate of spaghetti." The airplane had an out-of-control engine fire and was sinking, and there was nothing he could do about it. We were finished. He rang the alarm bell and told Glenn to go. Glenn wasted no time leaving. Augie Gaspar came on the interphone and said, "Crank, you don't mean to jump, do you?" Crankshaft retorted, "You'd better get outta my way. I'm coming." With that, he snapped on his parachute and climbed out of his seat. He looked at the clock on the instrument panel: it read 3:00 p.m. He saw that Leonard Weeks was gone and that there was a major fire in the radio room, but he did not see Orlando Vincenti. He went down to the nose hatch and looked into the nose compartment. Both Augie and I were gone. He bailed out.

Although Charlie Cruikshank never actually saw our airplane after bailing out, he "sensed" that it exploded moments later. He landed in a field approximately one-half mile west of the Rawe farm, where he was roughed up by a group of civilian men until a young *Luftwaffenhelfer* came up and took over. He was taken to a police station for a brief time, then turned over to the two men of the Home Guard driving the open touring car that picked me up a few minutes later.

Five miles northeast of Holzhausen, on the southern slopes of the Teutoburger Wald, which is a series of low hills rolling like ocean swells, lies the farm community of Lienen. One of the larger farms in Lienen has been operated by the Berdelmann family for 150 years. The main house faces generally south, meaning that Münster is off to the right about fifteen miles away. The entrance road to the farm runs directly north and south. The view in the direction of Münster from the front of the Berdelmann house is completely unobstructed.

Between 3:20 and 3:30 p.m. on the clear, calm, cool afternoon of Sunday, October 10, 1943, two small boys of the Berdelmann family, relatives of Gerda Berdelmann, Helmut, age twelve, and Fried-helm, age three, were playing and amusing themselves in front of the graceful, elegant old family farmhouse when they heard explosions coming from the southwest. They began looking in that direction. A few minutes later, their grandfather came out of the house and, after sternly reprimanding them, ordered them to go to the cellar of the house at once. When they pretended not to hear him, their grandfather grabbed the youngest, Friedhelm, and dragged him bodily inside the house.

Helmut continued to look to the southwest. In the distance, beyond the small village of Lienen, he saw a single Flying Fortress high in the air closely pursued by two German fighters. The B-17 seemed to be in trouble and was under attack by the fighter, which appeared to be scoring hits. Heavy smoke was pouring from the right wing of the bigger aircraft. Helmut saw eight parachutes come from the disabled B-17, the first six in fairly quick succession and, after a short pause, two more.

As the doomed airplane drew nearer, he saw that it would come directly over the Berdelmann farm. When the aircraft reached the southern edge of the farm, it was burning fiercely. Suddenly, it rolled over, flew briefly in an inverted position, then broke into several large sections. Debris fell everywhere—ammunition, ammunition boxes, a pair of flying boots, and other items littered the ground. A .50-caliber machine gun fell near the farmhouse. The center section of the aircraft fell onto a gently sloping shaggy meadow about a hundred yards from one of the farm outbuildings. The tail section sailed a short distance farther on and plopped right side up near a fruit tree some thirty yards in front of the main house. An aircraft engine fell to the ground about three hundred yards north of the wreckage of the fuselage.

B-17F, serial number 42-30725, built by the Boeing Company in Wichita, Kansas, delivered to the Air Corps on July 17, 1943, and arrived in the United Kingdom on September 2, 1943, assigned to Thorpe Abbotts shortly after that, enigmatically named *Aw-R-Go,* and operated by Crew No. 31 of the 100th BG on the October 10, 1943, mission to Münster, had reached its final resting place.

When members of the Berdelmann family were finally able to recover their composure from the shock of having a large aircraft unexpectedly crash on their farm, they approached and examined the wreckage. Inside the severed tail section, they found the body of Sergeant Charles Clark of Highland Park, Illinois, in his rear gun position. He had a self-applied cloth bandage wrapped around his head; otherwise, he appeared to be asleep. Approximately 150 yards away, inside the center section of the aircraft, they found the badly burned body of Technical Sergeant Orlando Vincenti from Carbondale, Pennsylvania. The bodies of both men were removed to a large farm outbuilding a short distance from the main house. The following day, Mr. Berdelmann, the grandfather, made wooden boxes for the bodies of the two men who were then buried in the Roman Catholic churchyard at Lienen (Vincenti in plot P-9-208 and Clark in plot P-9-203). After the war, their bodies were removed to the American Military Cemetery at Neuville-en-Condroz, Liège, Belgium. In 1949, at the request of their families, the remains of both men were repatriated to their hometowns in the United States.

The first place the Home Guard in their old-style green uniforms and spiked helmets took us was to the police station in Katten-venne, about one mile away. There we were asked to produce our identification. Then questions were put to us by Frau Luise Brink-mann, a local schoolteacher then in her midthirties, who spoke ex-cellent English. It was then that I found out for the first time that I had committed the most serious blunder a combat serviceman could possibly make: I left my dog tags on my bedside table when I dressed that morning. I could only tell them my name, rank, and serial number. I could not prove who I was.

From Kattenvenne, we were driven directly south for about seven miles through several villages to the city hall in the small city of Ostbevern. The Ostbevern city hall was a white building that looked more like a residence than a public building. It had obvi-ously been designated as a collection point for American airmen being picked up in the area. For the next hour, newly captured American airmen in ones and twos were led into the building, sometimes by civilians, sometimes by soldiers or by the police. Off and on, well-dressed civilian men came and went. On the wall near the front door hung a large black-and-white framed photograph of Adolf Hitler. As each man entered and left, he would mechanically proclaim, "Heil Hitler!" just as we had seen in films.

About dusk, a half dozen or more small passenger automobiles driven by civilian men pulled up in front of the building to take us away. We later understood that the drivers of these cars were mem-bers of the Nazi Party, as only party members were allowed to own private automobiles during the war.

When I entered the car that I was to ride in, I saw Bob Bixler, ball turret gunner on our crew, slumped in the back seat. His face was ashen, and although he had his flight jacket clutched tightly around him, it was clear that he had suffered a severe chest wound. He was having extreme difficulty breathing. I was sure he had a punctured lung and immediately told the driver that Bob urgently needed to be taken to a hospital. The driver made no response as he drove away and assumed his place in a caravan of vehicles.

Our destination was Münster-Handorf Airfield, a Luftwaffe night-fighter base (Ju 88 and Me 110 aircraft) situated only three to four miles northeast of Münster. Darkness was falling over the area when we arrived at the air base. We were placed in a building with jailhouse bars on the windows that had been designed as a brig or detention center. Approximately thirty American prisoners, among them Augie Gaspar, were already in the building when we arrived. Roughly one hour later, I was called to be taken to the base hospital by a watchful, nervous-appearing young airman wearing the familiar coal scuttle and blue-gray German helmet and carrying a rifle with a bayonet attached. As we walked to the hospital in the semi-darkness, my escort kept the point of his bayonet pressed firmly, and uncomfortably, in the center of my back. I was still hobbling and fearful of falling. I dared not stumble for, if I made a misstep, I was sure my jumpy guard would either shoot me or drive his bayonet through my heart. Approaching the hospital, I saw a long line of civilians out front, undoubtedly victims of our bombing, waiting to be treated for injuries. Fortunately, my guard took me through a rear door and put me in a small, private examining room. I was seen by a Luftwaffe doctor, who cleaned and bandaged my wounds and released me. My walk back to the detention building was a repeat of our earlier trip. That evening, two or three German pilots came to our building. One of them spoke quite good English. We discussed the battle, and they were very complimentary of us; we likewise acknowledged their skill and courage. This was an informal and private discussion among fellow airmen who had faced each other in battle, and our mutual respect was genuine. One of them asked if we had been given anything to eat, and when we told him we had not, they took us to their dining hall, where I had the best bowl of soup I would ever get as a prisoner of war.

Augie Gaspar said that he also opened his parachute almost immediately after leaving our doomed airplane and that he found himself in the middle of the terrifying flak barrage directed at the 390th BG as they passed over him. When he hit the ground, he was near a group of German soldiers, who immediately took him into custody. As he was being walked away, a young German woman carrying an infant in her arms came over to him and, in heavily accented English, repeated the familiar words, "For you, the war is over."

Also in our group of new prisoners that evening was Lieutenant Dick Atchison, a 418th BS pilot who flew the 350th BS airplane *Sweater Girl* (230047) on our right wing that day. With him was his bombardier, Lieutenant Sol Goldstein, who was a bit apprehensive as to what treatment he could expect, as he was Jewish. To the best of my recollection, we all received the same treatment. Interestingly, another American prisoner at Münster-Handorf Airfield that evening was Lieutenant John Winant Jr., pilot of the 390th BG airplane *Tech Supply* (230262), who had been shot down on his thirteenth mission. He was the son of the then United States ambassador to Great Britain, John Winant Sr., and would eventually be sent to a facility for "special" prisoners.

On that first night of our captivity, our conversation got around to speculation as to how long we might be held as prisoners of war, and our prospects were gloomy. The German army was still deep in Russia, the American army had just secured a small beachhead in southern Italy, and all of Europe except for Sweden, Switzerland, Spain, and Portugal was occupied by the Germans. While we still believed that in the long run America would win the war, we were not sure that at the moment the VIII BC was winning the air war. The Luftwaffe was a brave, disciplined, formidable fighting force. Estimates that evening of the time we might spend as POWs ranged from one to ten years. I remember being horrified, "My God, ten years! I'll be an old man before I get home."

The following morning, we were taken to the Münster train station, marched through a hostile crowd, and put aboard half of a third-class passenger car with four guards, isolated from other passengers. It did not escape our attention that the trains were operating; we had apparently not seriously damaged the railroad yards the previous day. From Münster, we traveled south to the Ruhr and along the Upper Rhine, which, even in wartime, was a beautiful sight: ancient castles, battlements, and ramparts on citadels high on hills overlooking the river, latticed vineyards on steep mountainsides, and low-slung barges plying up and down the river snaking its way through the Rhine Gorge. At Düsseldorf and Cologne, we saw acres of devastation from RAF night bombing, but, at every train station from Münster to Frankfurt, at Düsseldorf, Cologne, Bonn, Koblenz, and Wiesbaden, we saw signs that read, *Wir rollen für den Seig.*[15]

As we neared Cologne, the train stopped, and we were taken off to have a meal with a unit of the Wehrmacht positioned nearby. Our meal turned out to be a single bowl of soup ladled from a large container the size of an oil drum. As the German soldier poured the soup into my bowl, I thought I saw a piece of exposed bone in the

---

15. German for "We Are Rolling for Victory."

soup container that resembled the skull of a small animal. I recall hoping that the Germans had not become so desperate that they had taken to eating dogs and cats. I later concluded that I may well have seen the skull of a rabbit in the soup, as the Germans did raise large numbers of rabbits for food purposes during the war.

We pulled into the main railroad station at Frankfurt late in the afternoon of October 11, 1943, and were led single file through the grimy, run-down wartime lobby of its main railway station between groups of glaring, angry, gesturing, but fortunately disciplined, crowds. As we left the station, I saw a group of men with the Star of David on the back of their shirts working on piles of rubble, presumably from a recent bombing raid. We were hungry, unshaven, and disheveled. We had been unable to bathe or wash up. We were still in the clothes and flying suits we had on when we were captured. While flying, I was wearing long johns, a GI olive-drab wool shirt and wool pants, heavy wool socks, a heavy fleece-lined B-6 shearling jacket, heavy gloves, my yellow Mae West life preserver, chest-pack parachute harness, my zippered sheepskin A-6 flying boots over regular low-heel oxford shoes, and an overseas cap. However, I had removed my gloves to fire my machine guns and pulled off and discarded my cap, oxygen mask, and radio headset before bailing out of the airplane. I jumped from the airplane bareheaded and with no gloves (my face and hands felt frozen when I hit the ground).

Next, we were put on a streetcar for the twenty-minute ride to the Luftwaffe interrogation center, known as Dulag Luft. At a sort of reception office in the center, what flying clothes we had left (jackets, boots, and gloves) and what personal belongings we still had (combs, cigarettes, matches, money, etc.) were confiscated. We were fingerprinted and photographed. I was given an oversize American GI overcoat. We were taken into a reasonably decent mess hall operated by British POWs and given a bowl of bland soup.

From the mess hall, we went directly into solitary confinement.
Each man was placed in a dirty cell ten and a half feet long, five
and a half feet wide, and eight feet high. There was a single window
high on the outside wall that had frosted glass or had been painted
over and was closed and locked. The only furnishings in the room
were an iron cot with a straw mattress, a stool, two blankets, and a
slop jar. There were no sheets or pillows. I do not recall an electric
light of any kind, and while I do not know whether the cell walls
were insulated, the only sounds I remember hearing came from the
hallway outside my door. We were required to place our shoes on
the hall floor outside the door each time we entered our cell. Twice
a day, we were taken out of the room to use a smelly latrine. In the
morning and evening, we were given one slice of sour, black bread
with a thin coating of *ersatz*[16] jam and a cup of ghastly *ersatz* tea
made from a variety of non-tea leaves or *ersatz* coffee made from
grain. Our noon meal was a bowl of soup, usually made with potatoes, or occasionally cabbage, but never any meat.

Midmorning on Wednesday, October 13, 1943, I was taken from
my cell to an interrogation room. My interrogator was an initially
affable German major about fifteen years older than I was who
spoke flawless American English. I gave him my name, rank, and
serial number, the traditional POW statement. However, he immediately reminded me that I had been captured without dog tags and
could be a spy or saboteur with any name I liked and that spies and
saboteurs could not claim the protection of the Geneva Convention. He said I could be shot. Even though my heart was pounding,
I told him that if I was a spy or saboteur, I would have picked a
subtler way to enter Germany. He then said that if I was a navigator,
what did I know about the British GEE navigation system? I told

---

16. German for "artificial."

him, essentially truthfully, "Nothing." Although I wasn't aware of it, the Germans knew everything about GEE. By June 1942, they had recovered twenty operational GEE sets from downed RAF bombers and were aggressively jamming British GEE signals. I now surmise that most likely, the German major was interested in learning the effectiveness of their jamming. I could not have otherwise helped him even if he put me on the rack, and I am quite sure he knew it.

This sort of harangue went on for several sessions over my six-day stay in solitary confinement. The major finally told me that he knew all about me and the 100th and began reciting in incredible detail things about the group, my squadron, our crews, and its missions that even I didn't know. The Luftwaffe knew far more about the Eighth's order of battle than I did. I believe the Germans knew all along that I was who I said I was and finally, and most important, that I had no information of value for them. Their threats were never seriously pursued. The German intelligence network in the Second World War was astonishing. They studied every Allied newspaper, book, or magazine for information and every scrap of paper they could find on a prisoner or downed airplane. Every fragment of information they gathered from a prisoner or otherwise was carefully scrutinized and filed. One American mother regularly gave all her son's letters written from England to her local newspaper, which published them. When he was eventually shot down, his German interrogator at Dulag Luft told him they certainly enjoyed reading all his mail from home.

On Thursday, October 14, I was not called out of my cell and had been lying on my cot a few minutes after finishing my noon bowl of unpalatable soup when I began to hear the haunting, eerie wail of air raid sirens rising and falling from several locations, some nearby, others far distant. They seemed to come from all over Frankfurt. After about ten minutes, the sirens fell silent. Thirty minutes later, however, they resumed, and I began to hear a heavy, deep throbbing, which I recognized as the rising sound of hundreds of aircraft engines. I knew immediately it was the VIII BC. As the droning of engines reached its peak, I detected the thumping of heavy antiaircraft gunfire in the distance. The Eighth! I thought of my situation. How quickly my life had turned topsy-turvy. Soon, most of the men in those airplanes would be going home, back to England; I would still be a prisoner of war. I had hoped to be home by Christmas. I thought about my mom, my dad, Mike, and John. My mom had no idea what happened to me and would be utterly devastated when told that I had been shot down. I knew that my goal had to be to survive the war and get home, whatever it might take and whenever it might happen. Little did I know that in two days, we would have plenty of company at Dulag Luft. The raid that was taking place that day was the now historic second raid on Schweinfurt, which cost the Eighth another sixty bombers.

I recognize, especially as a former prisoner of war, that American military personnel must be expected to conduct themselves as loyal Americans in captivity. Cooperation with an enemy of the United States by any American serviceman, in my judgment, should be a capital offense. Yet for us flying missions over Europe in 1943, we had no training, either stateside or in England, as to what we should do if shot down and captured, except to give only our name, rank, and serial number. The average prisoner of war had no information of significant tactical or strategic value to a reasonably sophisticated enemy. Moreover, from my perspective and the perspective of other prisoners, German intelligence during the Second World War had complete files on all Eighth AF personnel. I said things other than my name, rank, and serial number during my lengthy interrogations by the Germans. At the same time, I tried to be as ambiguous and evasive as I felt I could get away with to avoid telling them anything of value. And although I did not, I tend to think that prisoners of war should be allowed to sign anything they want to sign and say anything they want to say if they fear mistreatment or torture, *but* let the entire world know that this is American policy. Then, whatever any prisoner might say will be of no value to the enemy. I am convinced that the best policy is to be sure that combat airmen have no secret information and, if they are shot down, they can say whatever they want to say.

I know of only one American POW who truly possessed information of value to the Germans. He was Brigadier General Arthur W. Vanaman, who served as assistant air attaché at the American embassy in Berlin from 1937 to 1941 and spoke fluent German. He was personally acquainted with Hermann Göring and other wartime leaders of the Luftwaffe. On May 26, 1944, General Vanaman became chief of intelligence for the Eighth AF, learning for the first time about ULTRA and the success the Allies had against reading coded German messages. To improve the relevance of the intelligence briefings given to the aircrews, General Vanaman thought that the briefers needed combat orientation. General Doolittle, commander of the Eighth, listened to General Vanaman's contention and reluctantly yielded to Vanaman's request by allowing the general to fly aboard a B-17 as an observer on Lieutenant Clarence E. Jamison's crew against military installations at Saint-Martin-l'Hortier in northern France. What was to have been a short orientation mission on June 27, 1944, became an intelligence nightmare for the Allies.[17]

---

17. This incident involved *Big Barn Smell* (232093) of the 379th Bomb Group, and though there was no MACR formally issued, a review of the unit records revealed a draft MACR. Lieutenant Jamison's description of the event states:

We were making our first run on the primary target. Flak started coming up and I heard it hit the ship. A few minutes after we got the flak the formation turned and we followed them.

Even though he went through the usual interrogation process at Dulag Luft, General Vanaman never disclosed his knowledge about ULTRA to the Germans. Following his capture, the Germans told him he would be sent to a special camp for VIP prisoners of war. However, General Vanaman insisted on being sent to Stalag Luft III, where he immediately became the senior American officer and the only man who could sign a parole and visit the three American compounds at Sagan. It was fairly widely suspected by the American "kriegies"[18] at Sagan that General Vanaman may have been sent to Germany to organize a rescue attempt or to look after the interests of American prisoners at Stalag Luft III. This was not true; his purpose in flying the mission was just what he said it was. He did become an important go-between with the Germans for the

---

Right after that I heard someone yell over the interphone that the #4 engine was on fire. I was still flying formation. I looked over at #4 and cound'nt [sic] see anything wrong with it. The copilot kept looking out the right window [sic] and then I looked again and could see flame comint [sic] out of the oil filler plate on the side of the nacelle so I have the order to prepare to bale [sic] out. This was at 1915 hours, right on the head. The copilot wasn't getting ready to bale [sic] out so I motioned him out and down. This was one minute after the warning. Then I called over the interphone, 'Bale [sic] Out'. I yelled that about three times.

Then I started out and got caught in the controls and could'nt [sic] get out. Just as I started out I put the ship on AFCE. The elevator control would'nt [sic] work and was in a full nose-high position. The nose of the ship pulled up sharply. I pulled it down again and tried to center the lights on the AFCE but could not do so, so I started out again. Just at this time I heard someone in the waist call over the interphone to say the fire was out. We were at about 24,000 feet and as the bomb bay doors were still open I dropped the bombs in an open field at this point. I looked out the window [sic] and couldn't see any more fire so I just kept flying the ship. It seemed as though the fire was really out so I turned and tried to follow the formation. I was too busy to follow them though as I only had three engines. I just headed straight for the nearest water, crossed the channel, found the base and landed.

The B-17 returned to the base at Kimbolton without the copilot, navigator, bombardier, top turret gunner, and the observer, General Vanaman. Aside from the capture of General Vanaman, the rest of the missing crew evaded capture and eventually returned to base. The B-17 was sent for repairs on July 1, 1944, returned to the 379th on July 24, and would fail to return on August 9, 1944, from an operational sortie.

18. *Kriegie* is the slang word we used, which is a shortened version of the German word for "prisoner of war"—*Kriegsgefangenen*.

American POWs at Stalag Luft III and Stalag VIIA. By not learning of the existence of the ULTRA project from General Vanaman,
the Germans perhaps missed the biggest intelligence coup of the
Second World War.

On Sunday, October 17, along with several dozen other new
American prisoners, Charlie Cruikshank, Augie Gaspar, and I
were taken out of solitary confinement, permitted to shave, take a
one-minute shower, then put our dirty clothes back on, and board
40-and-8 boxcars taken from the French for the three-hundred-
mile trip to Stalag Luft III at Sagan.

From the appearance and smell of the boxcars, its most recent
passengers had four legs.[19]

The price exacted from the Eighth by German air defenses, primarily the loss of 148 four-engine bombers and almost 1,500 men
missing in action, during the six-day period, October 8 through 14,
1943, had a radiating effect extending far beyond the windswept
pastures, grain fields, and airfields of East Anglia. On October 7,
my mother wrote:

My dearest Frank,

Aunt Lillie [my father's sister] called me to say they heard from
Jimmie [my first cousin] and received his APO. It looks as if he is
heading in your direction. I'll let you know when I find out for sure.

I'll write another airmail tomorrow giving you all the news
about the different boys. In the meantime, I'm getting anxious to
hear from you again, so find time to write me a few lines, honey,

---

19. From the French *40 Hommes–8 Chevaux,* a boxcar designed to hold forty men or eight
horses. When they were used to transport prisoners of war, the Germans always put fifty or
more men in each car, which made them very crowded; one either stood up all the time or
sat on the floor with his knees drawn tightly up against the body.

even if it's only a V-mail. Things at home are just about the same. Take care of yourself and let me hear from you.

Always, Mom

Six days after we were shot down, on October 16, 1943, my mother again wrote me:

My dearest Frank,
There isn't anything new to say except that I have been hearing about all those raids last weekend and the one last Thursday, and of course you know how that kind of news makes me feel. I surely do wish, darling, that you could cable me after a raid like that. I sent you one last Sunday [October 10] asking for a reply, but I don't guess you got it or had any way or opportunity to answer.

After any raid like that that you are on and get a leave to go to London, maybe you could cable then. I got the one you sent after the shuttle-bombing raid in just a few days. Please keep writing, Frankie, for now I'm just waiting and waiting for some word from you since those raids. You are on my mind every minute and my prayers are being offered up every hour—day and night. Keep up your courage, even though I know it's hard. All my love always,

Mom

Two days later, on October 18, 1943, my mom wrote me again:

Frank, darling,
I couldn't write you my usual weekend letter because I cut my finger badly yesterday, but it will be okay in a few days. I wrote you on Thursday, though.

Honey, I have been reading and hearing of all those fierce raids the past ten days and can hardly wait to hear from you. I wish I could get a cable in answer to the one I sent you. I am still praying hard for the safety of you and the boys, and that keeps me going. I'll be so happy when I hear that you are through with those missions. I know they are the very toughest in any part of the world today, but God can bring you through. Keep up your faith, dear, and write me. My love and prayers always.

Mom

Of course, I did not receive any of these letters. Weeks later, they were returned to my mother from Thorpe Abbotts, with *Missing in Action* handwritten by Captain Tom Toomey, 418th squadron adjutant, who also signed and dated his notation.

Late Friday afternoon, October 22, my mother, my father, and my brother Mike were sitting, chatting in the glassed-in sun room on the front of our house in Atlanta, overlooking our street, Pasadena Avenue. It was the beginning of the weekend, and Mike had just come in from his classes at Emory Medical School. As they talked, my mother noticed a Western Union delivery boy on his bicycle pedaling slowly up the street. When he reached our house, he turned in to our driveway, parked his bicycle, and began climbing the steps to our front door. My mother's heart sank. She knew. In her quiet voice, she said to my brother, "Mickey [his nickname at home], please answer the door." My brother answered the door, signed for the telegram, opened the envelope, and read:

Washington DC Oct. 22

Mrs. Mary S. Murphy:
The Secretary of War desires me to express his regret that your son, Captain Frank D. Murphy, has been reported missing in

action since ten October in European Area. If further details or
other information are received you will be promptly notified.

Ulio, The Adjutant General.

Two days later, on October 24, up in Chickamauga, Georgia,
Mrs. Dallie Wofford, mother of Lieutenant Drewry F. Wofford,[20]
an VIII BC B-17 pilot shot down on the August 17, 1943, "double
strike" shuttle mission to Schweinfurt and Regensburg, read in *The
Atlanta Journal* that I was missing in action. She immediately sat
down and wrote my mom:

Dear Mrs. Murphy,
It is with a heavy heart and lack of words that I write. I realize
there is nothing anyone can say at such a time that will give you
peace and comfort. To say that as long as there is the least ray of
light, there is hope, does not remove the heavy burden from one's
heart. But, it can give one courage to look forward, always hoping
and praying and keeping in mind that there is a Divine Being who
said that all things work together for good for them that love Him.

When such things happen, it seems that life should end right
then, that it is more than one can stand; but, time goes on and
life goes on; people look to you for comfort and strength, they
depend on you to give them the tender care that only a mother
can give; they lean on you until they are able to make their own
ways and still they look to you for advice. These are only a small
part of the things a mother is called upon to bear, but they make
up a great part of what our boys are trying to preserve.

---

20. Drewry F. Wofford Jr. was assigned to the 384th Bomb Group, 545th Bomb Squadron. On
the day his plane was shot down, he was flying *Mary Kathleen* (23230), which also may have
been named *Yankee Powerhouse II*. All crew members became prisoners of war, MACR 293.

When I received my message that my son was missing
in action I thought my world had ended. However, God was
merciful and stood beside me in my sadness and sorrow. He will
do the same for you. Our prayers are with you and for Frank that
he may be safe from harm.

On the thirteenth of September I received a message that my
son was a prisoner of the German government. And on the third
of October I received a letter from my son. I feel almost confident
your son has been captured by the Germans. If he had been killed,
surely one of the boys would have survived and brought the plane
in. I truly believe God has taken your boy in His hands and guided
him. You know, Mrs. Murphy, I feel much more contented with
D.F. in a prison than I would feel if he was still in England going
out on raids. I feel you will soon hear the best news. This war has
left none of us untouched but it can't last always, and it is my hope
and prayer that it will come to an end soon, and that our boys will
be home again. There is nothing we can do but hope and pray for
the best, and have faith and courage.

With a heart full of love,
Dallie Wofford

The patriotism of the mothers of America's fighting men in the
Second World War, their veiled anguish as they sent their children
off to war, their love and support of us, and the strength with which
they covered the desolation in their hearts over seemingly endless
reports of their sons being killed, wounded, or missing in action, is
a story that has never been, and now never will be, fully told.

In a transatlantic radio broadcast to the American people on the
night of October 10, 1943, only hours after the Münster raid,

Lieutenant General Ira Eaker, commander of the VIII BC, stated that four thousand men had been involved in each of the Bremen and Marienburg missions on October 8 and 9, and that the Eighth had dropped more than 4,400 tons of bombs on Germany and shot down 450 German fighters thus far in the month of October 1943. He also said, "We are just past the fifth inning. It is the task of the VIII BC and the RAF to destroy the factories and transport and weapons of the Germans so that our invasion casualties will be cut down. That is our stern assignment this winter. We shall not shirk it." Understandably, he did not mention that on the morning of October 8, he had 652 heavy bombers and 507 combat crews but, by the time of his Sunday evening transatlantic broadcast on October 10, those numbers had dropped to 335 and 440, respectively. In this three-day period, 88 bombers with their crews failed to return.

The front-page headline in *The New York Times* for October 11, 1943, the day after the Münster raid, read, U.S. FLIERS DOWN 102 NAZI PLANES IN BLOW AT MÜNSTER RAIL HUB. The final flight of Crew No. 31 of the 100th BG, and twenty-four other American crews of the 13th CBW of the United States VIII BC, was reported in the subheadline that followed. It said simply, WE LOSE 32 CRAFT.

11

STALAG LUFT III

Mercifully, our miserable overnight train ride from Dulag Luft in Frankfurt ended in the early afternoon of October 22, 1943, on a rail siding near Sagan, Germany. We were dog-tired, grainy-eyed, grungy, stiff, and sore from lying all night on the hard boxcar floors. Many of us were more than a little queasy, since our bowels had not functioned normally for several days. After being ordered off the train, we were led about a half mile down a dirt road through a forest of scraggly pine trees that opened into a vast cleared area. In the center of this area, we saw a large complex of huts, buildings, and sheds entirely surrounded by a pair of barbed wire fences. They were about ten feet high and five feet apart. The place looked like a concentration camp. Between the fences were heavy coils of concertina wire. At one-hundred-yard intervals around the perimeter of the enclosure, wooden guard towers were manned by Germans with rifles, machine guns, and searchlights. The main entrance to the camp was a heavy wood-frame structure that supported two large, hinged doors with an opening big enough to accommodate a two-and-a-half-ton truck. On one side of the gate was a small personnel door.

Stalag Luft III[1] was located about half a mile south of Sagan, Germany, a town of twenty-five thousand in 1943. Sagan, some

---

1. The abbreviation for German Stammlager Luft III.

ninety miles southeast of Berlin, is approximately halfway between Berlin and Breslau. It is situated on the Bóbr River near the old German-Polish border. The Germans had specifically selected this site to be a prisoner of war camp because they believed its soft, sandy soil would hamper tunneling efforts by the prisoners and because, at the time it was built, it was far from all combat zones. The camp opened in the spring of 1943 to accommodate the transfer of several hundred RAF officers and NCOs from Barth and other Luftwaffe prison camps in Germany. At that time, there were only two prison compounds at Stalag Luft III—one for officers and another one for NCOs.

However, because of the increase in both British and American officer prisoners because of increasing Allied bombing activity in 1943, Stalag Luft III was designated an Allied flying officers prison camp and expanded to accommodate additional prisoners. The original RAF officers' compound became the East Compound. The British NCOs were transferred to another location, and their compound became the Center Compound, which was set aside for American officer prisoners. A new compound for RAF officers, the North Compound, was opened on March 29, 1943, and a new South Compound for American officer prisoners was opened on September 8, 1943, only one month before we were shot down. Crankshaft, Augie, and I went into the South Compound.

After filing into the *Vorlager,* the administrative and supply center of the camp, we were lined up and searched. We were then photographed and fingerprinted for the index card kept on file for each prisoner in the camp's administrative office. We were then issued bedding: two thin blankets, one sheet, one mattress cover that also served as a bottom sheet, a pillow filled with straw, and one towel. We were also given eating supplies: one large German military-issue crockery bowl, a cup, eating utensils, and toilet articles, which included a toothbrush, razor, and comb. Finally, we were issued metal German "dog tags" with our prisoner of war numbers stamped on them. My German POW number was 3090. Then we walked the short distance to the entrance to the South Compound.

The South Compound was several hundred yards square and was also enclosed behind two parallel barbed wire fences about five feet apart with rolls of concertina wire between them. Thirty feet inside the perimeter fence, and parallel to it, a "warning wire" made out of thin strips of wood about thirty inches high ran completely around the compound. The zone between the perimeter fence and the warning wire was a no-man's-land, and any prisoner entering this forbidden zone could be shot without warning. At each corner, and at about one-hundred-yard intervals along the perimeter fence, were guard towers identical to those seen in the *Vorlager*. Outside the fence, the scraggly pines surrounding the compound had been cleared back to a distance of about thirty yards. Inside the compound were three rows of five single-story, drab, gray buildings, fourteen of which were barracks. The fifteenth was a theater then under construction by the kriegies.[2] There was also a cookhouse, a fire pool filled with water, and several other smaller buildings.

A large crowd of prisoners had gathered inside the compound near the gate when we arrived. They were a seedy lot, dressed in all manner of frayed, mixed, and mismatching odds and ends of American, British, and French military uniforms. Many had long hair, beards, or luxurious handlebar moustaches. The arrival of a new "purge,"[3] a group of new prisoners, was a big event at Stalag Luft III. Newly captured prisoners brought information and insights from

---

2. As noted, prisoner slang for *Kriegsgefangenen,* meaning "prisoner of war."

3. This term was picked up from the British. In forensic pathology, "purge" refers to the fluid that drains from corpses. Perhaps it represented our passing from being operationally alive.

the outside world, which for many of those on the inside was a long-ago memory. They also brought the latest news from home, perspectives on the progress of the war, or perhaps even the situation at one's old unit if one of the new prisoners was from that fighter or bomb group. It was almost certain there would be catcalls and gales of laughter from friends previously captured: "Crankshaft, Murph, Gaspar, where have you been? What took you so long? We've been waiting for you!" And from somewhere in a purge of new kriegies, there was usually a voice saying, "So, this is where we are going to spend the best years of our wives." We could have had no better reminder that, despite being prisoners of war behind barbed wire in a German prison camp, Americans were always Americans.

We were no different. We were met by a number of our old 100th BG comrades when we arrived: Nick Demchak,[4] who was shot down on the very first mission of the 100th on June 25, 1943; Scotty Duncan, Ollie Chiesl, and Bill Forbes,[5] who disappeared over the channel coast of France on the Paris–Le Bourget mission of July 10, 1943; Bob Pearson,[6] last seen going down at La Pallice on July 4, 1943, provided wise counsel on survival as a POW; the gentlemanly Dick Carey;[7] Pinky Helstrom, Harold Curtice;[8] and

---

4. Navigator aboard *Angel's Tit* (23260), failed to return on June 25, 1943; nine died in action, and one was taken prisoner (MACR 271).

5. Charles "Scotty" Duncan was the pilot, Oliver "Ollie" Chiesl, and William "Bill" Forbes were aboard *Judy E.* (230050) when it failed to return on July 10, 1943; two evaded capture, and eight were taken prisoner (MACR 268).

6. Pilot aboard *Nevada Wildcat* (230051), failed to return July 4, 1943; one evaded capture, and nine were taken prisoner (MACR 272).

7. Pilot aboard *Duration + Six* (25862), failed to return on July 25, 1943; six died in action, and four were taken prisoner (MACR 117).

8. Harold "Pinky" Helstrom was the pilot and Harold Curtice was the navigator aboard *Badger Beauty V* (230604) when it failed to return on October 4, 1943; four evaded capture, and six were taken prisoner (MACR 843).

Russian-speaking Charles Sarabun,[9] who was shot down two days before we were. And others, such as Hank Keller, my navigation classmate at Turner Field, who was captured in Tunisia in early January 1943. Five days after our arrival at Sagan, John Egan[10] would be among the prisoners in another new purge entering the South Compound. After bailing out over Münster, he managed to avoid capture for four days before being picked up by the local police about fifty miles from where his parachute landed. He spent ten days at Dulag Luft and arrived in Sagan with frozen feet and 20 mm shell fragments in his face.

It was evident from the exchanges of paperwork at the gate between the Germans and the senior American officer prisoners that individual room assignments in the barracks, known as "blocks," were made by the Americans. Crankshaft, Augie, and I were all assigned to Block 130, but in different rooms. Once inside the compound, we took stock of our new surroundings. The buildings were constructed of prefabricated wood panels. Each had an indoor latrine with one urinal and two commodes, all of which were used mainly at night after the ten o'clock lockup; a washroom with a concrete floor and six washbasins with cold-water faucets; and a kitchen with a two-burner coal-fired cookstove. The kriegies lived in fourteen rooms of varying sizes in each block, all of which were entered from a central corridor that ran the length of the building with doors at each end. When originally built, the rooms were intended to house from 2 to 10 men according to their size. Each block was supposed to hold 84 men, and the entire compound was

9. Navigator aboard *Piccadilly Lily* (25864), failed to return on October 8, 1943; six died in action, and five were taken prisoner (MACR 948).

10. Mission pilot aboard *M'lle Zig Zig* (230830), failed to return on October 10, 1943; one died in action, and ten taken prisoner (MACR 1029).

designed to hold 1,175 prisoners without overcrowding. In time, these numbers would be greatly exceeded. The wooden beds were all double-deckers, four posts with planks screwed along the sides and ends. Each bunk had about six flat bed boards laid across the side planks. Mattresses of a woven paper material filled with wood shavings were laid across the bed boards. Furnishings were austere and consisted of a simple wood table, benches, wooden stools, and a coal stove in each room. During the day, even in extremely cold weather, we used the *aborts,* large pit latrine outhouses with twenty seats and accumulation pits that emitted nauseatingly foul odors when not emptied on schedule. When a "honey wagon" would finally make its appearance and begin pumping an *abort* out, the stench was so overpowering, vile, and malodorous that every kriegie within hundreds of feet fled the area seeking fresh air.

All barracks buildings were constructed several feet above the ground to prevent the prisoners from digging tunnels under them. German guards wearing blue overalls and referred to as "ferrets" patrolled the inside of the compound and were constantly crawling under the buildings to eavesdrop on conversations or to discover any signs of prisoner tunneling efforts. Small crawl spaces built into the attics of the barracks were also used by the ferrets to eavesdrop on kriegie conversations.

The Germans had built a shower hut in the compound but never furnished the necessary operating equipment. To take showers, the prisoners jerry-rigged hoses with one end attached to one of the cold-water faucets in a washbasin and the other secured to a tin can with holes punched in its bottom. I do not remember having a hot bath or hot shower during my entire time at Stalag Luft III.

We could, however, take sponge baths, which we did far more frequently than we took cold showers, especially in the winter. The best time for a kriegie to take a warm sponge bath was at night after the evening meal. He would heat a *Kein*[11] of water on the kitchen stove and take it next door to the washroom. Every room had a blue crockery pitcher used to carry hot water from the cookhouse to the room.

Within one or two days of his arrival, each new kriegie was carefully questioned by two or more old prisoners about his civilian and military background, the schools he attended, his military unit, and whether he knew any of the other prisoners in the camp. The interrogators often brought in a kriegie from the hometown of the new prisoner to question him about his background. All of this was to confirm the identity of every new kriegie and to unmask any German "plants." Also, unknown to all but a few senior officers, Lieutenant Ewell McCright,[12] from Benton, Arkansas, was secretly and at great personal risk meticulously compiling a detailed personal record on every prisoner who would pass through the South Compound at Stalag Luft III from 1943 to 1945. Incredibly, McCright successfully concealed this activity from the Germans despite numerous and regular thorough searches of all our buildings. His original ledgers containing this monumental record, the only one of its kind systematically codified in any prison camp, anywhere, anytime, are now preserved at the United States Air Force Academy.

While the Germans exercised firm overall control of Stalag Luft III, behind the wire, the South Compound was run by a smooth, coordinated, efficient prisoner military organization headed by Colonel Charles G. Goodrich, who was the senior American officer.

---

11. Each room had a metal pitcher labeled *Kein trinkwasser,* meaning "not for drinking water." The kriegies dropped the *trinkwasser* and called the pitchers *Keins.* The word was also used in other situations such as "*kein* mail" for "no mail." A frequent rallying cry in the South Compound was, "*Kein trinkwasser uber alles.*"

12. Bombardier aboard *Beats Me* (124567), 303rd Bomb Group, failed to return on January 23, 1943; seven died in action, and three were taken prisoner (MACR 15571).

He was a 1925 graduate of West Point and had been shot down and seriously wounded in Africa on September 19, 1942. Reporting to Colonel Goodrich were four American lieutenant colonels who operated counterpart organizations of the U.S. military: personnel, supply, operations, and intelligence. Personnel assigned rooms, kept daily roster reports, and ran a tally with the Germans on our daily *Appells*.[13] Supply concerned itself with food, clothing, mail, parcels from home, and the like. Personnel and supply worked directly with the Germans. Operations and intelligence were clandestine undercover activities. From Colonel Goodrich down, there was a clearly understood chain of command. The senior officer in each block was the block commander, and the senior officer in each room was the "room führer."

At 9:00 a.m. and 5:00 p.m. every day, all prisoners were required to form up by blocks in rows, five men deep, on the parade ground for *Appell*. We usually stood relaxed until the German *Lageroffizier*, *Hauptman*[14] Galathovics, approached, at which time the block commander standing in front of his formation would call the group to attention. As he came to a halt, *Hauptman* Galathovics would salute the formation and address us, "Good morning [or afternoon], gentlemen." The block commander would return the salute and the greeting and, if relations between the Germans and the kriegies were going well, the prisoners in the ranks might also shout a response, "Good morning [or afternoon], *Herr Hauptman*." With the German *Hauptman* and Lieutenant Colonel McNickle,[15] the American administrative officer in front, and a German sergeant, *Oberfeldwebel*

---

13. German for "head counts."

14. German for "captain."

15. This is Melvin F. McNickle, pilot of P-47 27961, 78th Fighter Group; failed to return on July 30, 1943 (MACR 135B). Lieutenant Colonel McNickle arrived in Stalag Luft III on August 24, 1943.

Hohendahl, behind, they would count each row of five to obtain a total, which they tallied with Colonel McNickle. If there was no discrepancy in their numbers, the Germans moved on to the next block. If, however, there was a discrepancy in their numbers and a prisoner appeared to be missing, the Germans would scurry all over the place looking for him. We occasionally had *Appells* that lasted for up to two hours while the Germans searched all the buildings trying to reconcile their numbers. If a kriegie overslept or missed *Appell* with no excuse, he could expect to hear from Colonel Goodrich in the strongest terms. In rainy weather, when the athletic field was transformed into an impossible quagmire, or when the air temperature was freezing and the ground covered by deep snow, *Appells* were held in the hallway of each block.

Theoretically, we were to receive the same food rations as German depot troops. However, we were actually allotted the same rations as the nonworking German civilian population, the lowest food ration in Germany and insufficient for a healthy existence. However, because of regular arrival of Red Cross food parcels during my first year of captivity, we actually ate better than the German camp staff at Stalag Luft III, who, curiously, were receiving the same food rations as their prisoners. To their credit, the German staff at Stalag Luft III never commandeered or diverted the prisoners' Red Cross food parcels for their own use.

There was no central mess hall in the compound, and the cookhouse was capable of little more than boiling water and making the unappetizing soup we were served several times each week. Consequently, all food that went into each room, whether in the form of German rations or Red Cross parcels, was pooled and prepared as communal meals. Our food staple was the heavy, soggy, sour, five-pound loaf of dark black bread, delivered unwrapped, stacked on large wagons, several times a week and distributed at roughly one loaf per person per week. Breakfast was usually one or two thin slices of German bread with a light spread of *ersatz* margarine or jam and a cup of *ersatz* coffee. Three times a week, lunch was a bowl of thin soup prepared in the cookhouse, usually mostly potatoes, but occasionally other vegetables, and one slice of bread. The soup was sometimes ghastly, containing small amounts of ground horse-meat or a bit of sausage, generally blood sausage made of congealed blood mixed with meal, and a bit of onion. I could not stomach the blood sausage and never touched it. It reminded me of having once read that, during the American Civil War, Confederate troops had long periods during which they subsisted solely on a distasteful concoction of salt pork and meal, which they derisively named "son of a bitch."

Supper was our main and best meal of the day because of the American Red Cross food parcels, each of which contained a can of SPAM, corned beef, salmon, cheese, Nescafé coffee, a can of Klim (milk spelled backward) powdered milk, jam, prunes or raisins, sugar, chocolate, soap, and cigarettes, which supplemented our German rations. Occasionally, we would experience the best of all worlds when we received a mixture of American and British Red Cross parcels during the same week. The British parcels contained condensed milk, oatmeal, dry eggs, and tea. When I entered Stalag Luft III, Red Cross food parcels were being issued at the rate of one parcel per man per week.

Each prisoner was allowed to send three one-page letters and four postcards a month, on printed forms provided by the Germans, to anyone he wished. A team of English-speaking German women in the *Vorlager,* however, censored all outgoing POW mail to ensure that no negative comments, particularly about Germans or Germany, went out. On October 28, 1943, I sent my first letter, to my mother:

Dear Mom,

I hope you know before this letter arrives that I am a prisoner
of war. We had a little bad luck and had to bail out of our ship. I
was slightly wounded but am okay. If you can arrange it, I would
like to have a package sent to me. I need socks, underwear, and
handkerchiefs. Also, chocolate if it is available. The Red Cross
will give you all of the information as to how to send the package.
Please write my commanding officer and tell him I am a prisoner.
I am in reasonably good health so please don't worry about me.
Tell everyone hello for me and that I will see you all again some
day. And, give my love to Dad and the family.

    Frank

Three days later, I sent my mother a postcard:

Dear Mom,

Hope you received my letter telling you that I am a prisoner of
war. Also, please check with the Red Cross about what you can
send me. I especially need socks, underwear, and chocolate. Give
the family my love.

    Frank

Thankfully, my mother knew I was a prisoner of war long before
she received these messages. My card and letter were both delivered
to her at our home in Atlanta on December 13, 1943. However,
on November 3, only three weeks after being informed that I was
missing in action, my mother received a second Western Union
telegram from the War Department:

Report received through the International Red Cross states that
your son, Captain Frank D. Murphy, is a prisoner of the German

government. Letter of information follows from Provost Marshal General.

Ulio the Adjutant General.

The long months that followed were repetitious except for the comings and goings of seasons and weather changes. They crept by torturously, and the letters from home became more and more the focal point of my humdrum existence. This was especially so during the cold, bleak European winter and rainy spring, where weeks passed without a sign of the sun breaking through. There was no limit on the number of letters a prisoner could receive. However, there were long periods during which we got no mail and others when it arrived in batches. Invariably, our mail was two to three months old when it was delivered. This was frustrating because I knew that my mother, as long as she had an address for me, wrote me every day. But I wasn't alone. Every kriegie in the South Compound knew that Captain Carmichael,[16] the compound mail officer, posted a small card in the window of his room daily stating how many letters were received. After the nine o'clock morning *Appell,* there was usually a crowd around his window checking on the mail.

On November 24, 1943, I wrote my mother asking that she send all her letters by airmail. On January 31, 1944, I wrote her telling her that I had received no mail but that I felt "sure that you have known for some time where I am now and that mail is on the way. Also, if you can send a package of any kind soon, please include a pair of pants, socks, tooth powder, razor blades, and shaving cream." On March 18, 1944, I sent a card informing my mother and father that I

---

16. Most likely this is Edwin Carmichael, navigator aboard *Invasion 2* (25070), 91st Bomb Group, failed to return on April 17, 1943; ten were taken prisoner (MACR 15571).

had just received my first letter from home: five months after having been captured.

There was, however, a particular kind of letter that was given the most satirical and entertaining treatment we could contrive. Unfortunately, we received more than our share of "Dear John" letters from former sweethearts, and occasionally wives, who were unhappy with the addressee's capture or who had simply decided not to await his return. Also, kriegies occasionally received letters that displayed ignorance and insensitivity to our living conditions and surroundings. When these letters became known to us, we treated them as philosophically and cynically as possible for the sake of the recipients—who usually burned them. The more egregious ones were published in *The Circuit*, the camp newspaper put out three times a week, and posted on the cookhouse wall. One wife wrote, "I still love you even though you are a coward." Another wrote, "You were missing for a month, so I got married." And, "Darling, I married your father. Love, Mother." Or, "I am enclosing a calendar. It should come in handy as it has several years on it."

On the wall next to his bunk in Block 133, Lieutenant Ed Baxley[17] created a "rogue's gallery," row upon row of color and black-and-white formal portraits and snapshots of exes, blondes, brunettes, including one in her bridal dress, and redheads whose ardor had waned while sweating out their kriegies' return from the war. All his photos had been given to him by jilted kriegies. Ed started his collection of "impatient maidens" when his roommate and fellow Texan, Lieutenant C. W. Cook, received a letter from his father telling him that his fiancée had married another. Each

---

17. Formally known as Edwin, pilot aboard *Spirit of Alcohol* (124483), 91st Bomb Group, failed to return on May 19, 1943; six died in action, and four were taken prisoner (MACR 15632).

month's mail brought more "Dear John" letters and still more photos
for Ed's collection.

No clothing of German origin or manufacture was ever issued to
us, probably to preclude it from being used in support of an escape
attempt. For weeks after my capture, the only clothes I had were
those I was wearing when I was shot down, plus the overcoat given
to me at Dulag Luft. All our flying jackets and boots had been confiscated in Frankfurt. When France fell and the British evacuated
Dunkerque in 1940, the Germans acquired large stocks of French
uniforms and a quantity of British military uniforms that were subsequently doled out to prisoners of war. By the time I reached Stalag
Luft III in October 1943, little of it was left. I received my first parcel
from home with a pair of pants sent by my mother on June 1, 1944.
I was a POW for another month before I was issued a pair of GI
suntan cotton pants and a shirt. In September 1944, I received a
pair of enlisted men's GI olive-drab wool pants and a shirt. This gave
me, finally, three pairs of trousers, three shirts, an overcoat, a wool
cap, and, thanks to my mother, a sweater and changes of underwear
and socks.

While all this was going on, I remained totally ignorant of my
mother's plight. As a kriegie, I did not know that, although there was
no limit on the number of letters that could be sent to an American
prisoner of war in 1944, this was not true with respect to parcels
containing food or clothing or tobacco products. Parcels containing these items required that the POW's next of kin obtain a parcel
or tobacco label from the Prisoner of War Division of the Army
Service Forces in Washington and paste it on the outside of each
package before mailing. Moreover, the army would not issue parcel
and tobacco labels unless the prisoner had been officially reported
as interned and his permanent address known, and then only one
parcel and two tobacco labels were issued in any label-issue period,

which in 1944 was every sixty days. Next of kin were required to strictly adhere to a list of permissible items that could be included in POW parcels, which could not exceed eleven pounds in weight or forty-two inches in combined length and weight. The contents of the parcel had to be listed on a post office customs form, and no victory slogans, such as "Buy War Bonds," could appear anywhere in or on the parcel.

There were no dry-cleaning facilities at Stalag Luft III. Everything, even woolen items, had to be hand-washed. We had a washhouse with drainboards on the sinks on which kriegies could lay out and scrub their clothes, and we had several rinsing tubs. We also had ample soap from Red Cross parcels but no hot water. We heated our own water individually. We hung our wet clothes in our rooms to dry—which, in cold, damp weather, took forever. One kriegie from Appalachia in the room next to us constantly complained that he was "sick and tired" of having to constantly "wrench out" all his clothes. In a letter written on July 30, 1944, I told my mother:

> For some reason you seem to be worrying, and I wish you wouldn't for there is no reason to. I know that from your standpoint it is hard not to worry, but please take my word for it and don't. You have done wonderfully well; everything I could expect from you has been included in my parcels. I am just where I want to be insofar as clothes are concerned. I'm sure you can imagine why I only want a few clothes when you realize that I have to wash them all myself—including my overcoat.

In my view, it is no exaggeration to say that in Luftwaffe prison camps in Germany during the Second World War, the British prisoners set the example for the Americans on how to be prisoners of war. When the first USAAF POWs began arriving in Sagan in the latter half of 1942, they were installed in the East Compound, which, at the time, was occupied by over five hundred British RAF officers and a handful of Americans who had joined the British and Canadian air forces and had been shot down and captured. Many of the British prisoners had been, in their words, "in the bag" for more than two years, some for almost three. By 1943, they had evolved from a disorganized, discontented group of unhappy men during their first year of captivity into a well-structured, up-and-running operation based on military customs and traditions. Although I only knew of him by reputation, this transition was largely due to the wisdom and efforts of the first senior RAF officer, Wing Commander Harry Melville Arbuthnot Day, known to all as "Wings" Day. He was shot down in October 1939, only five weeks after the start of the war. It was Wings Day who decided that the British should conduct themselves as military officers and first brought his little group to attention during the daily head count. It was Wings Day who organized the RAF kriegies and decided that all food and Red Cross parcels should be pooled.

However, Wings Day's most valuable contribution to all the kriegies at Stalag Luft III was his development of a massive escape organization. He knew that the majority of the prisoners, perhaps 90 percent, would make no escape attempt. They were not afraid; they simply did not believe they could make it from Sagan through a hostile Germany to a neutral country. But he correctly concluded that those who did not wish to make an escape attempt would do everything asked of them to assist the 10 percent of men who would accept any risk given an opportunity to escape. Wings created an "X" organization headed by Squadron Leader Roger Bushell, a South African fighter pilot, to develop and approve all escape plans. He also believed, prophetically, that such an effort would give all who participated the feeling that for them the war was not over and a sense of pride that they were still contributing to the war effort.

The first American airman captured by the Germans who would spend his entire captivity at Stalag Luft III was Lieutenant (j.g.) John E. Dunn, a U.S. Navy pilot who became lost on patrol and ditched at sea off Norway on April 14, 1942. However, the first senior American officer to fall into the hands of the Germans was Lieutenant Colonel Albert P. "Bub" Clark Jr.,[18] West Point class of 1936. While flying a familiarization fighter sweep with an RAF Spitfire squadron over France on July 26, 1942, he was shot down when an Fw 190 damaged his engine, causing it to lose power. He was sent to Stalag Luft III and installed in the East Compound with RAF officer prisoners. By December 1942, over sixty USAAF officers, including Colonel Charles Goodrich, who immediately became the senior American officer, were in the East Compound at Sagan. All were readily accepted by the British and integrated into the RAF prisoner of war system, including all British clandestine activities. When these American officers were eventually transferred to the new all-American South Compound in September 1943, they brought the tried and proven fundamentals of the British system with them. They immediately set up a cloak-and-dagger organization with Colonel Clark as "Big X." Major David "Tokyo" Jones, so nicknamed because of his participation in the Doolittle B-25 raid on Tokyo in April 1942,[19] was appointed "Little X."

Because of these old kriegies, all the Americans in the South

18. Spitfire pilot with 31st Fighter Group, but he was listed as failed to return on July 19, 1942. After the war, Lieutenant General A. P. "Bub" Clark would eventually become superintendent of the United States Air Force Academy.

19. Jones was later shot down in December 1942 while flying a B-26 medium bomber in an attack on Biserta, Tunisia.

Compound adopted RAF slang in referring to the Germans and camp facilities. Every German, whether he was an officer or a soldier, was a "goon," a name taken from a Neanderthal comic strip character. The guard towers were "goon boxes." I have already mentioned the Abwehr soldiers who constantly patrolled inside the compound during the day in their blue overalls. They were responsible for security and antiescape duties and walked in and out of our rooms unannounced, crawled under and over our barracks to eavesdrop on conversations, carried out searches, and performed all manner of other duties. They were known as "ferrets" and given such nicknames as "Keen Type," "Blue Boy," "Phil," and "Schnozz." When one of them entered one of our barracks, the first kriegie to spot him shouted, "Tallyho!" or "Goon in the block!" to alert everyone to watch what he was saying or doing.

The German *Kommandant* at Stalag Luft III in October 1943 was *Oberst*[20] Friedrich Wilhelm von Lindeiner-Wildau, an aristocratic Luftwaffe officer who was sixty-two years old. Colonel Lindeiner had joined the German army in 1908 and had been severely wounded in the First World War. I had no contact with him but clearly remember observing him striding through the compound on several occasions. He was an impressive officer who was said by those who communicated with him to be absolutely loyal to his country. He was unwaveringly strict but scrupulously fair in his handling of prisoner affairs. The Germans generally fell far short of their obligations under the Geneva Convention of 1929 governing the treatment of prisoners of war. During the Second World War, this was particularly so regarding food, clothing, and sanitation and hygiene facilities. However, our senior Allied officers felt that Colonel Lindeiner was an honorable man who did the best he could with the limited resources

---

20. German for "Colonel."

he had. They held him in high respect as a thoroughly professional soldier. He was, as were most Germans, strong on military customs and courtesy. When saluted by a scruffy kriegie while walking through the compound, Colonel Lindeiner never failed to render a smart military salute in return.

I now know from their respective postwar memoirs that Colonel Lindeiner persistently tried to persuade Colonel Goodrich, Colonel Delmar Spivey,[21] the ASO in the Center Compound, and RAF group captain H. M. Massey, British senior officer in the North Compound, to prevent prisoner escape attempts from Stalag Luft III on the grounds that he was doing everything he could to protect the safety, health, and welfare of the prisoners under his control there, but that he would be unable to protect them in the event of a major escape incident. He did not reveal to them that he had been given a decree that all escaping officers would not be returned to their POW camps but would be handed over to the Gestapo. Lindeiner feared that he himself might be directed to liquidate captured escaped prisoners as a retaliatory measure and made it clear to his officers that he would never carry out such an order. However, the American and British senior officers at Stalag Luft III could not, and did not, agree to squelch or suppress prisoner escape attempts in any way.

The senior German officers under Lindeiner were competent. Below them, however, the German staff was inadequate and consisted mostly of men who were very young, very old, or not fit for combat duty. They gave us considerable leeway in managing our own internal affairs and taking on duties and responsibilities that would foster our own interests. We quickly took advantage of the

---

21. Observer aboard USS *Aliquippa* (230081), 92nd Bomb Group, failed to return on August 12, 1943; eleven were taken prisoner (MACR 655).

situation. Inside the compound, senior American officers exercised virtually complete control over all prisoner activities.

The grinding, repetitive daily life of a Stalag Luft III kriegie, whether on a cold, dreary winter's day, during our unceasing, morale-sapping spring rains, or on a bright, sunny summer's morning, began the moment the Germans lifted the heavy wooden latch bars that had been placed there the night before to secure our barracks. During the night, while searchlights in the goon boxes swept back and forth over the compound, German soldiers, known to us as *Hundführers,* with Dobermans or German Alsatian hounds on leashes, prowled the open areas between our barracks to sniff out, apprehend, or perhaps even attack any kriegie found outside his building after lockup.

The first men up and about in the barracks were the "room stooges," the "gophers" for the day. The kriegies in most rooms took turns cooking and stooging. Since some men enjoyed cooking and others did not, individual cooking arrangements were possible. Normally, turns at cooking were for a week at a time. Stooging, however, was another matter; it was an all-day drudgery job that lasted from sunrise until lights out and was rotated daily. A room roster listing the stooging schedule was a serious order of business in most rooms.

In cold weather, the first job of the stooge was to clean the ashes out of the room stove and then build a fire. He then fetched the room's blue-and-white crockery water pitcher and headed for the cookhouse to obtain hot water for morning coffee. At the cookhouse, he usually had to wait in line for fifteen to twenty minutes for the water, which was dispensed by one of the American sergeants through an open window. Upon returning to his room, the stooge carefully measured Nescafé coffee powder into cups and made the coffee. He then picked up a couple of loaves of black bread and took them to the nearest block that had a hand-turned bread slicer, where he cut the correct number of slices for his room, doing so as evenly as possible. Back in the room, the stooge spread each slice of bread with the same amount of margarine or jam. If there was a fire in the stove, the stooge might place the bread on top of the stove to toast it.

By this time, the other men in the room were dressing, preparing for the morning *Appell,* and crowding around the stove if the weather was cold. After breakfast, we streamed from all blocks and headed for the *Appell* field. The only enforceable obligation we had at Sagan was our twice-a-day attendance at *Appell.* Because of our status as officers, we were not required to work, under the Geneva Convention governing the treatment of prisoners of war. The Germans never challenged this rule.

After *Appell,* we were free to pass the rest of the day as we wished, except for the stooges, who returned to the cookhouse to get more hot water so they could wash the breakfast dishes. Other men took their clothes to the washhouse. It was estimated that in reasonable weather approximately two hundred men used the wash facilities daily. Other men took Klim cans of water heated on the room or block stove to the barracks washroom to undertake the difficult process of shaving, which few did every day. Apart from the fact that razor blades were at a premium and most were used well beyond their intended life, we had to stand in line watching our can of hot water turn cold as we awaited our turn at one of the washbasins. Once there, we hurriedly lathered up and began shaving, quickly sloshing the razor in a tin of fast-cooling water. Meanwhile, the stooges were taking turns sweeping their rooms with the block broom and, if it was a "soup day," setting out soup bowls.

After the morning *Appell,* those of us who were not stooging or working as volunteers on such camp activities as mail handling or parcel distribution had a variety of options. Many passed by Captain Carmichael's room to check on the amount of daily mail to be distributed. In any passable weather, large numbers of men, individually and in groups, walked circuits on the track that ran entirely around the perimeter of the compound just inside the warning wire. A routine activity for virtually all of us at some time every day was a visit to the newsroom, which had daily updated maps of all the battlefronts, both eastern and western, on its walls. The lines depicting the fronts strictly followed the daily communiqués of the OKW[22] and those shown in the *Völkischer Beobachter* and other German newspapers. Positions of the opposing armies were marked with arrows. Alongside the maps, English translations of articles from German newspapers were tacked to the walls. Many kriegies made and kept maps of the changing war situation in their rooms.

In their newspaper reports of Allied air attacks on Germany, the German press always referred to American and British airmen as *Terrorfliegers* or *Luftgangsters*.[23] In their cartoons, we were depicted as thugs and gorillas in flying suits. Unfortunately, in 1944, an American bomber crew flying an airplane they had named *Murder Incorporated* was shot down over Germany. On the back of his leather flight jacket, one of the crew members who was captured had hand-lettered the words *Murder, Inc.*[24] His photograph, together with

---

22. OKW stands for *Oberkommando der Wehrmacht*, which is German for the German High Command.

23. German for "terror fliers" and "air gangsters," respectively.

24. Generally, command often turned a blind eye in these unofficial decorations to aircraft and flying apparel such as flight jackets, and it was the group commander who usually set the standards. This incident involved a 351st Bomb Group bombardier, Lt. Kenneth D. Williams, who was not flying his regular aircraft, *Murder Incorporated* (229858), on November 26, 1943, but in *Aristocrap* (237817). Once captured, Lieutenant Williams's decorative flight jacket became an immediate propaganda tool for the Germans. While the high command's

pictures of the words painted on his jacket, were published in German newspapers nationwide, which also carried long articles about the barbaric and criminal intentions of the Allied air forces. It was our later understanding from newly arriving prisoners that, because of this incident, the USAAF ordered that all names given to American airplanes by their crews be approved by the group commanding officer.

On the wall of the cookhouse, beneath a loudspeaker that carried German radio broadcasts, a typed English translation of the previous day's official communiqué from the OKW was posted. Next to the communiqué was a copy of the regularly published South Compound newspaper, *The Circuit,* that carried news of interest in the camp and from the home front in the USA. A highlight of almost every day was the reading of the "soup," a handwritten summary of war news as reported in BBC newscasts of the night before and heard on the camp "canary," the undercover radio whose location was known only to the kriegies who had custody of the receiver and listened to the broadcasts. While several kriegies maintained a lookout for the German ferrets, a runner visited each block and read the news to the prisoners who were gathered together in a single large room. The reader would then move on to the next block.

After catching up on the war news, the world situation, and camp news as best he could, a kriegie could visit the camp library. It was well stocked with both fiction and reference books received from home and routinely donated by all kriegies. Individual books could be checked out overnight. He could also attend the Kriegie

---

directive has not been located, it was clear the VIII BC could not afford another incident. The name of 229858 was changed to *Censored.* Another B-17 assigned to the 385th Bomb Group, also named *Murder Incorporated,* had its name changed to *Grim Reaper* (230179), but this change took place well before the November 26 incident. It is not clear which, if any, other aircraft had their names changed because of this incident.

Kollege, which offered classes in foreign languages, economics, various fine arts, and technical subjects, except those considered by the Germans to be escape-related. It was taught by kriegies who had taught school back home.

The principal pastime at Sagan was visiting the rooms of friends from our old units, flying schools, hometowns, and elsewhere. We talked about food (we were always hungry) and sex (mostly lies). We also exchanged gossip and rumors about home, the war, the Germans, happenings in the camp, and almost everything except a "There I was" story. The rule among the old kriegies was that a new kriegie was permitted to tell the story of his capture one time, to get it off his chest. Thereafter, he was forbidden to ever speak of it again, for we all had such a story to tell. The man who broke this rule quickly found himself talking to an empty room.

As night fell, especially in the chill of a winter sunset after evening *Appell,* there were always kriegies who took solitary turns around the perimeter circuit for exercise and fresh air to be sure, but also for personal flights of fantasy. We had so few opportunities to escape from tiring, boring conversations, the sameness of one day after another, our lack of privacy, our inescapable dreary and often squalid surroundings, our obscure future, but, most of all, the inexorable fading of our memories of the outside world.

Evening meals were both a preparation and scheduling problem. The single kitchen stove in each block had only three square feet of heating surface and a small oven. Since every room in the block had to use this stove, each room chef had only about thirty minutes to cook his meal. This was especially difficult for the chefs in the larger rooms with ten or more men, because two rooms shared the stove at one time. As a consequence, main meal times varied from as early as 2:30 p.m. until after dark. The Germans provided no cooking equipment for individual rooms. Expert kriegie tinsmiths fashioned all manner of cooking utensils, baking pans, pots, grinders, and other items by using rolled-out metal from salvaged Red Cross food tins. Their ability to make leakproof cooking pots was nothing short of astounding.

The room stooge was responsible for washing, peeling, and cutting up the potatoes, kohlrabies, or turnips for the evening meal. The chef and stooge opened and carefully divided the meat or fish for the meal. We had SPAM, corned beef, tuna, or salmon, all separated into equal portions. Since we had no refrigeration, we had to be particularly watchful for spoilage because the Germans, before distributing Red Cross parcels to the compounds, punched holes in the tops of all canned foods to prevent food hoarding by the prisoners. The chef, with the help of the stooge, carefully doled out the vegetables, meats, or fish to the individual kriegies in equal amounts. With coffee, the better chefs served cake leavened with German tooth powder, which worked effectively as baking powder, or a pie with a crushed cracker crumb crust and filling of condensed milk with lemon powder or melted chocolate D-bars. To ensure that all slices of pie were equal, the man who cut the pie got the last piece.

After dark, all blackout shutters in the blocks had to be closed. Kriegies could visit friends in other blocks by walking on the main inner camp roads. But to walk between buildings or near the warning wire meant taking the risk of being shot without warning. Everyone had to be in his assigned block by ten o'clock when the doors were barred and the *Hundführers* with their guard dogs entered the compound to begin their nightly patrols. Inside the buildings, men turned out their single, dim 40-watt light and climbed into their bunks for the night. We wore sweaters, long underwear, sweatshirts, balaclavas, and, occasionally, pajamas sent from home. There were four hand-crank phonographs with recordings supplied by the

YMCA War Prisoners' Aid organization that were rotated around the South Compound. If one of these phonographs happened to be in the room, one of the men in a lower bunk would play a record or two while the dedicated smokers enjoyed their last cigarette of the day. Home was always on our minds. Everyone went to sleep dreaming of home and better times.

I had been in the South Compound only two or three weeks before learning from conversations with my fellow kriegies that the compound had a fifteen-piece big band, the *Luftbandsters*, styled after the popular "name" bands back home, that periodically gave jazz concerts for the rest of the prisoners.[25] The band practiced in a back room of the theater then under construction next to Block 139 in the southwest corner of the compound. I immediately made it a point to find out about the band and their schedule so I could try to attend their next rehearsal, which I did about mid-November.

The director of the band was Major Hal Diamond, then thirty-eight years old, from Van Nuys, California, who had been a professional musician for years before the Second World War and who was a virtuoso performer on clarinet and saxophone. He had played with the Philadelphia Philharmonic, and when the 1939 war broke out, he was a Hollywood studio musician recording soundtracks for motion pictures. Hal Diamond was also a private pilot who joined the British RAF before the attack on Pearl Harbor. When America entered the war, he, along with other Americans in the RAF, transferred to the USAAF and was shot down on July 17, 1943, while flying a B-26 medium bomber in an attack on the railroad yards at Naples, Italy. He bailed out of his aircraft and landed on Mount

25. The name of the band was a wordplay on *Luft III*.

Vesuvius. He was immediately captured by the Italians, who turned him over to the Germans.

I told Major Diamond of my band background in college and asked for a chance to audition with the band if an opening for a saxophone and clarinet player came to pass. He lent me a clarinet to practice on for a few days and then let me sit in with the full band. I was taken on to play clarinet and tenor saxophone with the band, which was then rehearsing for a Christmas show that Major Diamond hoped would take place in the new theater.

It would probably come as a surprise to most Americans today but, in addition to Major Diamond, there were other gifted musicians in the band: Lieutenant Bill "Dusty" Runner,[26] from New Jersey, who had been shot down at Schweinfurt on October 14, 1943, had been a trumpeter with the Woody Herman band in New York. Lieutenant Dick Jones,[27] another trumpet player and B-17 pilot from Chicago, had played with the Isham Jones band. Captain Alexander Simpson,[28] a trombonist and B-24 pilot from Palo Alto, California, had also been a professional musician before the war. Lieutenant Lee Forsblad,[29] a B-17 pilot from Kingsburg, California, was a brilliant arranger who orchestrated most of the music for the *Luftbandsters*. After the war, he would go on to become a composer-arranger of music for radio, television, and films and a professor of music at Fresno State University in California. In customary musician

26. Bombardier aboard 25714, 91st Bomb Group, failed to return on October 14, 1943; one evaded capture, one died in action, and eight were taken prisoner (MACR 899).

27. Probably this was the pilot aboard *Bad News* (229653), 379th Bomb Group, failed to return on October 14, 1943; four died in action, and six were taken prisoner (MACR 956).

28. Pilot aboard *Bathtub Bessie* or *Big Eagle* (123678), 93rd Bomb Group, failed to return on October 9, 1942; no other details.

29. Formally known as Leland, pilot aboard *Stric Nine* (229475) 91st Bomb Group, failed to return on July 10, 1943; eight died in action, and two were taken prisoner (MACR 34).

fashion, because I was from Atlanta, Dusty Runner immediately gave me the nickname "Peachtree."

The South Compound Theater would become the center of entertainment for the entire camp and an outlet for all kriegies who wanted to participate in any phase of its activities. Kriegies with engineering, bricklaying, or carpentry backgrounds were assiduously sought out and recruited. Construction began in October 1943. Although the floors, walls, and roof were composed of large, prefabricated sections of wood supplied by the Germans, the building was erected entirely by the American prisoners who laid the foundation, put up the walls, and installed the ceiling and roof. Four hundred seats, designed from Canadian Red Cross shipping boxes, were mass-built with reclining seats and backs. The seats were installed in rows on an inclined floor and jogged so as to permit an unobstructed view of the stage from any seat. Seat rows were lettered and numbered in professional theater style. Tickets with reserved seat numbers were printed and issued for all performances. Although it could not be raised or lowered, an orchestra pit was built in front of the stage, and footlights and spotlights were fashioned from large British biscuit tins. Choice seats were reserved for senior American and German officers when relations with the prisoners were not strained, and who regularly attended musical and dramatic performances in the theater.

In early December 1943, Colonel Lindeiner, at the request of senior American officers, agreed to permit a limited change of compounds for American prisoners in the Center and South Compounds who wished to be transferred to the other compound to be with friends. We knew from conversations with former kriegies in the Center Compound who had been relocated to the South Compound when it opened in September that several of our old 418th BS colleagues were in the Center Compound. We heard that John

Brady, John Hoerr, Dave Solomon,[30] John Dennis,[31] navigator on the Curtis Biddick crew, Ernie Warsaw,[32] Bucky Cleven,[33] and others were in the Center Compound. Crankshaft, Augie Gaspar, John Egan, and I put our names on the list to be reassigned from the South to the Center Compound.

German authorization for the move came two weeks later, which was much quicker than we'd expected. This meant that I had to immediately tell the band that I would be leaving the South Compound right away. The reaction of my fellow band members to this surprise announcement was unexpected, particularly on the part of Dusty Runner. All of us had worked very hard on the Christmas show, and I felt I was letting the band down and that the Germans would probably approve similar moves later. I went to Lieutenant Colonel McNickle, the South Compound adjutant, and requested that my name be taken off the move list.

A few days before Christmas 1943, I walked to the East Gate of the South Compound with Crankshaft, Augie, and John Egan to tell them goodbye and that I would join them as soon as I could. It was the last time I would see any of them until after the war: the Germans would never again authorize kriegie changes of compounds. My separation from my fellow members of Crew No. 31 of the 100th

---

30. John Brady was the pilot, John Hoerr the copilot, and Dave Solomon the navigator aboard *M'lle Zig Zig* (230830), when it failed to return on October 10, 1943; one died in action, and ten were taken prisoner (MACR 1029).

31. Navigator aboard *Escape Kit* (25860), failed to return on August 17, 1943; four died in action, six taken prisoner (MACR 675).

32. Navigator aboard *Picklepuss* (230063), failed to return on August 17, 1943; six died in action, four taken prisoner (MACR 677).

33. Mission pilot aboard *Our Baby* (23233), failed to return on October 8, 1943; ten taken prisoner (MACR 950).

BG was now complete. The departure of Crankshaft and Augie had a depressing effect on me. On Christmas Eve, I joined several members of the band and a small group of carolers from the chorus going from block to block playing and singing traditional Christmas music, and on Christmas Day, we had extra rations sent in by the Red Cross. By night, however, my memories of Christmases past, both in and out of the USAAF, and the reality of my situation caught up with me. I was dispirited, melancholy, and desperately homesick. How my world had changed! Only three months earlier, I had fully expected to be home for Christmas with my mom and dad, Mike, and John.

My mother dearly loved Christmas. She loved the penetrating dampness of a gloomy day or the bright stars on a clear, cold December night in Atlanta. She loved shopping among fussy, jostling crowds in Rich's brightly decorated, red-ribboned, and green-wreathed department store. She loved the echoing music of the brass quartets and bell-ringing lassies of the Salvation Army, with their black bonnets and kettles on downtown street corners. She loved the continuous playing of Christmas music on WSB Radio as she busily wrapped and tied bows on gifts or helped my father string colored lights on our tree. She loved Midnight Mass at Sacred Heart Church with its banks of flickering, glowing candelabra, altar boys in their red cassocks and white surpluses, priests in their white-and-gold vestments on the marble, poinsettia-covered altar exchanging haunting medieval Latin chants with the choir. Finally, she loved preparing her marvelous traditional Christmas dinner. But my mother always ruefully said that Christmas *night* was her loneliest night of the year: the floor around the Christmas tree was bare, the tree itself was dying and its needles quietly but steadily dropping to the floor. There was no more Christmas music: it was all over until next year. And here I was, a prisoner of war thousands of miles from home in an uncertain world, adding to my mother's heavyhearted sadness on this, her loneliest night of the year. Thankfully, most people do not know how it feels to be so lonely, so far away from everything they know and love, and so unhappy in what should be a joyous season.

The first German violation of the Geneva Convention that led to serious friction between the Germans and the Americans in the South Compound occurred about 10:00 p.m. on December 29, 1943, when a German guard patrolling the outside of the perimeter fence fired several rifle shots into Block 133 during an air raid blackout. He claimed that he saw "figures" moving outside the building. One bullet passed through a window and through both of Lieutenant Colonel John D. Stevenson's[34] legs above the knee, breaking the bone in his left leg. Colonel Stevenson would spend six months in the hospital, and the wound left him partially crippled. Although the senior American officers strongly protested this incident to the Swiss Protective Power, it was of no avail. Unfortunately, this was not the last such incident.

On January 13, 1944, I wrote home:

Dear Mom and Dad,
I hope you celebrated New Year's Eve for me as well as for yourselves. Have managed to get a clarinet but need practice so badly am afraid I'll drive the people around me mad; it doesn't help to lay off as long as I have. The winter isn't as rough as I expected. It gets quite a bit colder here than at home but up to now I have been able to weather it without a lot of discomfort. I hope all is well at home and that you are over what must have been an initial shock. Please give my love to all.
Frank

34. Lieutenant Colonel Stevenson, assigned to 91st Bomb Group (L), was flying an A-36, serial number 284101, when shot down on June 8, 1943 (MACR 357).

Opening night at the new South Compound Theater took place on February 15, 1944. The first production was a musical variety show, *Strickly from Hunger*. The pencil beams of light from the searchlights on the goon boxes sweeping back and forth over the crowd outside the theater gave it a real Hollywood atmosphere. Kriegies with first-night tickets filed into the theater and were shown to their seats by ushers. As the houselights dimmed and the footlights came up, the curtains opened and the *Luftbandsters* in the orchestra pit struck up our first tune. Acts that night included a vaudeville song-and-dance team, a chorus of fifty voices, and as a finale, a small group of us from the band climbed on to the stage and played "Summertime," "The Sheikh of Araby," and Dixieland jazz improvisations on the traditional twelve-bar blues chord progression.

All the stage sets and props were designed, built, and painted by kriegie craftsmen and artists. Bandstands for band shows had the letters *LB*, which stood for *Luftbandsters*, painted on their fronts. The theater was in constant use—whether featuring sparsely attended German movies showing German military victories or well-attended band shows, dramas, and concerts by our excellent chorus. In one of our later productions with a Latin theme, Lieutenant Al Batich,[35] from Cleveland, Ohio, who had been shot down at Hamburg on July 25, 1943, brought the house down shimmying and shaking in a tight-fitting costume, complete with a huge spray of fake fruits and vegetables on his head, with his mean imitation of Carmen Miranda. Behind him, the band played a lively mambo.

Costumes were either handmade or rented from Berlin at extravagant prices. The general policy was for the prisoners to offer some form of entertainment in the theater every night. Theoretically,

---

35. Formally known as Albert, navigator aboard 25917, 379th Bomb Group, failed to return on July 25, 1943; four died in action, six taken prisoner (MACR 1767).

officer prisoners of war were to receive pay at the same rate as members of equivalent rank in the military of the detaining government. However, none of the kriegies at Stalag Luft III ever saw a payday because all payroll transactions at Sagan were bookkeeping entries only. Fifty percent of the payroll funds were automatically set aside to pay for letter and postcard forms, postage, entertainment, and a small canteen that carried a few items, such as tooth powder and matches, that were not generally available to the prisoners. Some funds were transmitted to NCO camps, as they received no pay; however, none of the remaining funds was ever paid to individual officers.

A report prepared by War Department Military Intelligence on Stalag Luft III in November 1945 stated in part: "The *Luftbandsters,* playing on YMCA instruments, could hold its own with any name band in the U.S.A. according to those who heard them give various performances." This generous overstatement illustrates the value of the theater in the everyday lives of my fellow POWs at Sagan. In his last letter to me, dated January 7, 1990, my outstanding kriegie roommate and comrade in arms, the late Pinky Helstrom, wrote that he clearly recalled the faraway, wistful, nostalgic faces of the kriegies filing out of the theater into the snow following our last band concert in late 1944 while, on the stage, the band played chorus after chorus of the Woody Herman band's famous "Woodchopper's Ball." No performers anywhere could have had more appreciative audiences than the South Compound audiences at Stalag Luft III.

On the night of March 24–25, 1944, seventy-six RAF prisoners in the North Compound at Stalag Luft III, separated from us only by a perimeter wire fence just behind my Block 130, and led by Roger Bushell, escaped through a tunnel named "Harry" before the Germans discovered the hole in the ground outside the wire.

The Germans immediately launched the most extensive and far-reaching manhunt for escaped prisoners of the Second World War. All German police, military personnel, and civilians were warned by radio to be on the lookout for the escaped prisoners. We knew right away that something significant and consequential had taken place in the North Compound during the night. On the morning of March 25, all the RAF kriegies in the North Compound seemed to be outside in the open, and we could see heavy German armed activity all around the barracks and buildings.

Unknown to the prisoner population, high-level Luftwaffe and Gestapo officials descended on Sagan from all over Germany. At first, the Germans had no idea how many RAF prisoners had escaped through Harry, only that the number was high. On March 26, Colonel Lindeiner was relieved of his post as *Kommandant*, placed under house arrest, and told that he was going to be court-martialed.[36] He was temporarily replaced by *Oberstleutnant*[37] Cordes, who had been a POW during the First World War. Shortly thereafter, Cordes was replaced by *Oberst* Braune, who would re-

---

36. Colonel Lindeiner was a man of great integrity and courage. In 1944, he attended a meeting at which he was informed that all prisoners of war, except for Americans and British, who escaped and were recaptured would be shot without trial. When he returned to Stalag Luft III, he told his staff that he would rather be hanged than carry out such a barbaric order. After the Great Escape from Stalag Luft III on March 24, 1944, all seventy-six escapees were recaptured, and on Hitler's order, fifty were executed. However, Colonel Lindeiner's objections to how the escapees were treated resulted in his being relieved of his command on March 26, 1944, and his being court-martialed on October 5, 1944. He was sentenced to a year in prison, but the sentence was never carried out. On February 12, 1945, Colonel Lindeiner was wounded in action and captured the following day by Americans. After the war, eighteen members of the Gestapo and the chief of criminal police for Breslau were put on trial for the murder of the escapees. Fifteen were sentenced to death (but one had his sentence commuted to life in prison). Colonel Lindeiner survived the war and died on May 22, 1963, at the age of eighty-two.

37. German for "lieutenant colonel."

main as *Kommandant* of the Sagan complex until it was evacuated in January 1945.

Most of the seventy-six men who successfully escaped through Harry were picked up in a few days. They were not, however, immediately returned to Sagan. Many were taken to a Gestapo prison at Görlitz, forty miles from Sagan, and returned to the North Compound a few at a time. On April 6, 1944, Group Captain Massey was called to the office of the *Kommandant* and stiffly told that forty-one of the recaptured prisoners had been shot. That same day, orders were read to Colonel Goodrich stating that the Luftwaffe could no longer be responsible for officers found outside the wire. The following day, April 7, 1944, a memorial service for the RAF airmen who had been shot was held on the *Appell* field in the South Compound. In the days that followed, the Germans raised the total of murdered British officers to fifty. Later, the cremated bodies of the dead were brought to Sagan in urns, which were placed in a memorial vault.

Reprisals against all the kriegies at Stalag Luft III for the Great Escape were not long in coming. On March 25, 1944, the Germans retaliated in the South Compound by ordering six to seven extra *Appells* each day. We were continuously moving in and out of our rooms and buildings. At all hours of the night, the Germans would suddenly enter our blocks screaming, "*Raus, raus!*"[38] and send us outside to stand in the cold, snow, or rain for one or two hours while they methodically searched the buildings for evidence of escape activities. Finally, Colonel Goodrich had enough. On March 27, he authorized a disorderly *Appell*. As the Germans approached each block to begin their count, the kriegies milled about and refused to form ranks. We were angrily dismissed and ordered back to our barracks. An hour later, the Germans returned with a convoy of

---

38. German for "out."

armored vehicles with heavy weapons and armed soldiers. With the guns of this small army trained on us, we lined up and gave them a count. However, our protest paid off—the harassment stopped.

The story of this heroic, extraordinary escape, though essentially tragic, has been told and retold extensively in countless books, magazine articles, television documentaries, and in a remarkably accurate major motion picture film in 1963. I can only add my deep admiration for the resourcefulness, ingenuity, dedication, patience, perseverance, and courage of the men who participated in this incredible undertaking. The boldness of the ambitious Roger Bushell escape plan and the magnitude of the effort required to carry it out is mind-boggling to one who was a prisoner of war at Stalag Luft III at the time. To have seriously advanced the idea of a mass escape of up to 20 percent of the prisoners in a German prison camp at the height of the Second World War could, justifiably, have been considered evidence of madness. But they pulled it off. These magnificent men, they pulled it off!

Unknown to the Germans, thanks to a carefully devised security system, over five hundred men worked on this massive effort for almost a year. Trapdoors were made to camouflage tunnel openings, which were started in kitchens, washrooms, under toilet seats, behind sinks, under stoves, or any other place not readily reachable by ferrets crawling under buildings. Three tunnels, designated Tom, Dick, and Harry, were dug simultaneously by individuals sprawled full-length on homemade trolleys strong enough to carry two sandboxes or one man, in dimly lit passages thirty feet underground, working alternately in stifling heat or freezing cold and suffering from perpetual cold symptoms while passing back damp earth and shoring up their narrow openings with bed boards as they went. Trolley tracks were made from barracks moldings. Fresh air was delivered into the tunnels through pipes fashioned from Red Cross milk cans by pumpers operating a homemade bellows.

Forgers created paybooks, identity cards, passports, and other documents indistinguishable from original copies of papers loaned by guards compromised by bribes from smooth-talking kriegie linguists. Typewritten text was perfectly re-created by hand, including strikeovers, imperfect letters, and faulty shifts. German stamps were diligently carved from the rubber heels of shoes. Tailors made civilian clothes and close copies of Luftwaffe uniforms from RAF uniforms, blankets, sheets, towels, and sweaters. Tea and coffee and coloring from boiled bookbindings were used as dyes.

An Australian and an American officer made dozens of compasses. They magnetized old sewing needles or razor blades by stroking them in one direction on a "liberated" German magnet for hours at a time. Razor blades were sliced into needles using a metal window hinge. The needles were set in plastic from pieces of old phonograph records that had been gently heated, formed, and overlaid with a hand-drawn compass rose. They were then enclosed in tiny tin containers topped with circles of glass cut from broken barracks windows. Every compass was stamped: MADE IN STALAG LUFT III.

Mapmakers painstakingly traced a variety of maps of Germany and the local area around Sagan, acquired from guards willing to bargain. Local train schedules obtained from the same sources were carefully copied and updated as necessary. While work was in progress, dozens of stooges kept watch on the ferrets. Other kriegies assigned as "penguins" helped dispose of sand from the tunnels.

Although no Americans were among the escapees in the Great Escape, dozens of Americans, notably Lieutenant Colonel Clark, as head of security, and David "Tokyo" Jones, in tunneling operations, were deeply involved in the digging of tunnels Tom, Dick, and

Harry. All of them, however, had been transferred to the new American South Compound when it was opened in September 1943. Had it been within their power, Roger Bushell, Group Captain Massey, and Wings Day would have expedited the completion of Harry so as to permit their American colleagues to participate in the escape, an experience that in view of the subsequent murder of fifty British officers, they were providentially spared. Nevertheless, the Americans took their North Compound expertise with them to the South Compound. During my entire confinement in the South Compound, I was aware of ongoing clandestine tunneling efforts and briefly participated as a stooge keeping watch on the ferrets and as a penguin disposing of sand from a tunnel. I shall never forget my first look down into a dimly lit thirty-foot shaft where other kriegies were hard at work. American tunneling efforts would never be as successful as those of the British, largely due to increased German security after the Great Escape and the eventual course of the war.

Less than three weeks after the spectacular British mass escape, on Easter Sunday, April 9, 1944, we experienced another instance of a German guard inexcusably firing directly into the compound, which further increased the friction between the German camp staff and the prisoners. About 11:30 a.m., air raid sirens began to sound from the direction of Sagan and, according to standing German orders, all kriegies immediately went inside their buildings.

About noon, a group of American NCOs were working in the cookhouse. One of them, Corporal Cline C. Miles, an infantryman from Cameron, Missouri, who had been captured by Arabs at Kasserine Pass in North Africa and turned over to the Germans, was leaning against one of the doorways to the cookhouse, talking to other prisoners, when a German guard just outside the perimeter fence took aim and fired a shot that killed him. The Germans later contended that Corporal Miles was properly shot without warning because he was not entirely inside the building. According to several eyewitnesses to the incident, however, Corporal Miles was inside the doorway and had done nothing provocative when he was shot. Corporal Miles was buried in the prison cemetery at Stalag Luft III in a service officiated by Captain "Padre" Murdo Ewen Mac-Donald, a paratrooper with a British airborne division who was also an ordained Church of Scotland minister. Padre MacDonald was an eloquent speaker with a rich Scottish accent but was never recognized as a clergyman by the Germans because he was captured "out of the cloth." He was the only resident chaplain in the South Compound and was immensely popular with Americans.

Two days later, on April 11, we saw the first formation of Forts to be sighted by the prisoners at Stalag Luft III. A B-17 Combat Wing of the 1st Air Division[39] of the Eighth AF was attacking targets no more than thirty miles to the west of us. I clearly remember the target-marking smoke bomb from the pathfinder lead aircraft tracing a wavy white thread against the blue sky as it snaked down. It was a memorable and uplifting sight, but it was also a nostalgic experience for the American kriegies.

As spring came and the number of new kriegies coming into the South Compound kept growing, the Germans increased the number of men assigned to each block by approximately 25 percent. Both German and kriegie carpenters began triple-decking the double-decker bunks. A six-man room became an eight-man room; a twelve-man room became a fifteen-man room. In their two-man room 6 in Block 139, Captains Dick Carey and Pinky Helstrom of the 100th BG were told that a third man would be added to their two-man room. The end rooms in each block were assigned only

---

39. By this time, *Bombardment Divisions* had been renamed to *Air Divisions*.

to kriegies with the rank of captain or above. Dick and Pinky invited me to move in with them, and I promptly accepted. Moreover, Block 139 was next door to the theater, where the band practiced.

This was a fortunate move for me. The 100th BG had lost one of its most promising leaders early on when the quiet, unassuming, intelligent, sensible Dick Carey, operations officer of the 350th BS, went down in July 1943. He and the steady, outgoing, eventempered Pinky Helstrom were quintessential roommates; they always carried more than their share of the load and never complained. Besides, Pinky Helstrom volunteered to do the cooking and was, in my judgment, the best chef in the South Compound.

In late March 1944, the original commander of the 100th BG, Colonel Darr Alkire,[40] passed briefly through the South Compound before going over to open the new West Compound as senior American officer, a position he held until Stalag Luft III was evacuated in 1945. Only a few weeks after having been relieved of his command of the 100th BG almost a year earlier, Colonel Alkire was appointed commander of the 449th BG, a B-24 group that, after training in the U.S., was sent to an air base in Italy. Colonel Alkire flew eleven missions in quick succession and was shot down on his twelfth on January 31, 1944, near Aviano, Italy. He bailed out of his disabled aircraft, landed on a German air base, and was immediately captured by Luftwaffe personnel. In Italy and at Stalag Luft III, Colonel Alkire proved to be a personally courageous officer with demonstrated leadership qualities.

While I was reasonably settled into my routine of reading and playing in the band, by the middle of April 1944, I must have been quite dejected about my mail situation. On April 18, 1944, I sent my parents an indefensible postcard message that I would later regret:

---

40. Pilot aboard *Lurchin Urchin* (129223), 15th Air Force, 449th Bomb Group, failed to return on January 31, 1944; three died in action, eight were taken prisoner (MACR 2403).

Dear Mother and Dad,
I can't understand why I'm not getting any mail unless you are
not writing me too often. You can write every day but don't make
the letters too long. My health is all right, I weigh 135 pounds
now. I'm gaining. Love to all,
    Frank

The cruel mention of my weight was a veiled reference to the fact
that I had lost about thirty-five pounds since having been captured.
Although I had been a POW for only eight months when June 1944
arrived, and none of us doubted that the Americans, British, and
Russians would eventually be victorious in the war, we could see no
timetable as to when that might occur or any light at the end of the
tunnel. I was trying to adjust to the possibility that I could be a POW
for several years. There were, after all, British kriegies in the North
and East Compounds at Sagan who were approaching their sixth
year as prisoners of war. On June 4, 1944, two days before the D-day
invasion of France, I sent another letter to my mother about mail:

Dear Mom,
Your letter written last Christmas Day just came and by the time
you get this another Christmas will be rolling around. I hope
things there at home haven't changed so much that I'll feel like
a stranger because I have been away so long. I'm glad to see
summer come; we keep reasonably warm in winter but it is so
much better to get outside. Please give Dad my best wishes for his
birthday (August 1) and celebrate mine for me. Love,
    Frank

The invasion of France by American and British forces two days
later, on June 6, 1944, had an electrifying effect on the American

and British prisoners of war at Stalag Luft III. The news was first heard about midmorning on German radio through a loudspeaker mounted on an outside wall of the cookhouse. The afternoon edition of the *Völkischer Beobachter* proclaimed, "*Die invasion hat begonnen.*" Jubilant kriegies with homemade maps in hand immediately converged on the newsroom in the theater and crowded around our German-speaking kriegie translators beneath the outdoor speaker on the cookhouse. All initial reports released by the OKW spoke, of course, of the carnage and terrible losses inflicted on the Allies at Utah, Omaha, Gold, and Juno Beaches. All German communiqués issued during the first days after the invasion expressed confidence that the invasion would be repelled and the Americans and British driven back into the sea. It was apparent, however, that this was not true. As maps of the area published in German newspapers continued to show the locations of the Allied beachheads and identify the places where the fighting was taking place, it was clear that the invasion was successful. Moreover, we were getting the other side of the story regularly from our kriegies tuned to BBC radio on the camp canary.

Obviously, my spirits perked up. On June 10, 1944, I wrote my mother:

Dear Mom,
In the past several days a few of your March letters arrived.
Evidently the trans-oceanic stamps made the difference. Your
March parcel sounds great—I'll be happy to get it. The news from
home is fine. I'm glad everyone is doing well.
    Frank

The kriegies of the South Compound went all out in their celebration of the Fourth of July 1944. In the afternoon, water polo games and a swimming meet were held in the fire pool, which had been emptied, cleaned, and refilled with fresh chlorinated water. For the evening *Appell*, the entire compound, all with military haircuts and wearing GI suntan cotton uniforms, marched to the parade ground to the music of the band. I have few memories of events that impressed me more than the sight of 1,600 thinning American prisoners of war in their worn, wrinkled, hand-washed uniforms marching erectly on to the parade ground of the South Compound at Stalag Luft III, Germany, on July 4, 1944, exactly two years to the day after I graduated from the navigation school at Turner Field, Georgia.

That night, the kriegies in almost every block had bashes. Many of the parties included the imbibing of "kriegie brew," an alcoholic drink concocted by fermenting a mixture of carefully measured amounts of sugar, dried prunes or raisins from Red Cross parcels, and yeast procured from one of the guards in exchange for American cigarettes. Our old kriegies had brought the British recipes for kriegie brew with them from the North Compound; the Brits, who had a tradition of home brewing, were serious producers of kriegie brew. The "must"—the combination of ingredients in the liquid— was fermented in earthen crocks for several weeks before being considered ready for consumption. As I recall, the master brewers used balloons to capture the gases bubbling out of the solution and prevent unclean air or contaminants from gaining access to the "must." I never tried kriegie brew, but from observing those who did, I can attest to its exhilarating effects, as well as the appalling headaches, vomiting, and miserable illnesses it also produced.

On July 20, another event occurred that significantly boosted our morale and lifted our hopes for an early end to the war. A group of senior German military officers, frustrated by Adolf Hitler's repeated failures as a military strategist, made an assassination attempt on his life during a meeting at his secret headquarters retreat in Rastenburg. Just before the start of the conference, a bomb inside a briefcase placed under the conference table near Hitler by Colonel Count Claus Schenk Graf von Stauffenberg exploded, killing two conferees and injuring several others. Amazingly, Hitler was only slightly wounded and shaken. The uprising had failed. Shortly thereafter, Count Stauffenberg and several of his coconspirators were summarily executed. The incident was given widespread publicity on German radio with condemnation of the conspirators, martial music, and expressions of gratitude that Hitler had survived this cowardly attack on his life. To the kriegies at Stalag Luft III, however, this incident was clear proof of serious dissension at high levels within the German government.

One fine afternoon in September, we got the shock of our lives. As the kriegies of the South Compound were leisurely passing time with their usual pursuits—reading, writing letters, pounding the walking track inside the perimeter fence, playing volleyball, or snoozing—we heard a pulsating, thunderous, roaring sound, accompanied by a high-pitched whistling noise, coming from somewhere far off in the sky. I was sitting in our room in Block 139 with the window open. There had been no air raid warning. Suddenly, I heard a kriegie cry out, "What in the name of God is that?" I went outside. Several kriegies were pointing to a black speck streaking across the sky southwest of the compound. Coming into view and making a wide circle was a twin-engine airplane traveling at an absolutely unbelievable speed—at least five hundred miles per hour. As we watched, the pilot of the airplane, obviously aware that we were a Luftwaffe prison camp for Allied flying officers, swooped down low over our barracks and made a slow roll to the right as he climbed out. It was a breathtaking sight. The kriegies were speechless.

The airplane we had seen was, of course, the Messerschmitt Me 262, a twin-engine jet fighter with a cruising speed of five hundred miles per hour and a service ceiling of more than thirty-seven thousand feet, the first operational jet aircraft in the history of aviation—the aircraft that would eventually bring an end to propeller-driven piston-engine military aircraft. It had no equal in any Allied aircraft inventory at the time.[41] However, fortunately for the Allies, this remarkable and unprecedented weapon would never realize its potential. Although built to be a fighter, Adolf Hitler, who had no knowledge of the subject, obstinately insisted that the Me 262 be used as a bomber and ordered all weapons removed from the plane so that it could carry bombs, even though its maximum bomb load would be little more than one thousand pounds. Arguments against this decision by his experts only brought Hitler's anger down on their heads. Finally, late in 1944, Hitler issued an order flatly forbidding all further discussion of the subject.

Even though we were all flying officers, there was a valid basis for our surprise and astonishment at our first glimpse of the Me 262. In 1941, the United States government ordered the American aircraft industry to concentrate on the development of aircraft designs that already existed, not the development of new airplanes and engines; it was believed the war would not last long enough for new designs to enter service. And increasing the power of engines was believed to be the quickest route to higher aircraft performance.

41. Although both the British and Americans were well into the development of jet fighter aircraft in 1943–44, the British Gloster Meteor Mk III was the only Allied jet aircraft to become operational during the war. Both British and American engines were superior to the Junkers Jumo engines on the Me 262, principally because shortages of nickel in Germany forced German engine designers to use material that could not withstand the high operating temperatures of the nickel-based alloys used for turbines in the United States and Great Britain. Thus the German engines had shorter operating lives, were less reliable, and suffered more frequent premature engine failures, requiring engine changes.

The Rolls-Royce Merlin engine that powered the 1944 American P-51 had double the power of the Merlin engine fitted to the original British Spitfire. This explains why more scientific research and technical advances in aircraft design were achieved in Germany than by Britain or America during the Second World War. Despite the general antiscientific philosophy of the Nazi regime, the German Air Ministry, which handled aeronautical research, provided German scientists with the freedom and security they needed to advance the state of the art. The result was that swept-back wings to overcome drag at high subsonic speeds, higher wing loadings to achieve better aerodynamics, twin engines mounted in wing pods instead of a single engine in the fuselage, delta wings, variable sweep-back wings, and the introduction of leading edge flaps because conventional trailing-edge flaps are less effective on a swept-back wing than on a straight wing—all came from the Germans.

If the Germans had not been militarily defeated in the Second World War, it is likely that their aircraft industry would have been as dominant as the American aircraft industry in the last half of the twentieth century. In addition to their revolutionary aircraft designs, the Germans developed the world's first mass-produced guided missile, the German V-1, and the first ballistic missile, the V-2. By the end of the war, the Germans had a rocket missile that homed on an enemy plane by tracking the heat from its engines, a ground-to-air missile, and a complete proposal for their giant A-11 three-stage booster rocket that could place a winged V-2 into orbit—or be programmed to hit New York.

At the same time, for all their sophistication and future promise, the German "V" weapons achieved practically nothing militarily in 1944–45 and probably did Germany more harm than good. These missiles were notoriously inaccurate and could only be used as terror weapons against large, populated areas. The subsonic V-1 pilotless airplane was relatively easy to shoot down, and many were destroyed in flight by British antiaircraft guns and fighter aircraft. In their seven-month V-2 campaign against London, for which the British had no defense, 517 V-2s fell on the city, killing 2,700 people and seriously injuring 6,500. By contrast, in only fourteen hours, the German city of Dresden was devastated and estimates range between 35,000 and 150,000 people killed or missing because of combined RAF/USAAF raids on the city on February 14–15, 1945. The cost to deliver the approximate one-ton warhead on both "V" weapons was not justified in terms of the immense effort of skilled men and the scarce materials and fuels that were consumed on these programs. In the end, the American decision to fight the war with overwhelming numbers of then current state-of-the-art weapons was the correct one.

Once the American and British forces broke out of their Normandy beachheads in France in the summer of 1944, the war was obviously going to end with an Allied victory. But for the kriegies at Stalag Luft III, life was going to get much worse before it got better. On September 11, the Germans put all compounds at Stalag Luft III on half Red Cross parcels. Instead of one parcel per man per week, we would receive half a parcel per man per week. There was no shortage of Red Cross food parcels. The pipeline was full. Red Cross food packaging plants in Philadelphia, Chicago, and New York were all in high gear. And the packages were moving on approved safe-conduct routes from U.S. ports in Red Cross–owned and –chartered ships directly to Marseille, France, and Genoa, Italy. The sides of the ships, which traveled fully lighted at night, were painted with a large Red Cross. From Genoa and Marseille, the boxes were shipped to Geneva, Switzerland, by rail and stored in huge warehouses. The problem in the fall of 1944 was that all German transportation facilities, roads, bridges, and rail lines in southern Germany were being systematically destroyed by Allied air attacks.

We quickly came to know perpetual hunger on our reduced rations and spoke continually of the great restaurants we intended to visit after the war and the fantastic dishes our mothers and wives were going to prepare for us. I particularly remember the kriegies from the East, especially from the New York and Boston areas, talking about "pizza pie." I had no idea what they were talking about. Coming from Georgia, I had never heard of pizza pie.

Moreover, the goons seemed determined to find ways to annoy us. On October 6, the German camp administration ordered that an empty Red Cross box with all empty food cans be turned in before a new parcel was issued. This caused an uproar among the kriegies, especially our tinsmiths, as the only metal we had to make cooking utensils and escape implements was salvaged food cans from Red Cross parcels; the Germans provided no cooking pots or other kitchen tools to the prisoners. On October 12, we had a knife, fork, spoon, cup, bowl, and towel *Appell*. We all had to march to *Appell* with these articles to be checked by the Germans. Later, in November, the German camp *Kommandant* notified General Vanaman that only one day's ration for each POW would be allowed in the compound. Out of fear that it would be confiscated, we bashed the food we had saved. And, on November 22, we had a picture *Appell*. We all filed past Germans while they checked our identification from the picture on the index card kept on file in the camp administration office.

Also in October, because of the ever-increasing number of new prisoners, the Germans once again upped the number of prisoners assigned to each block. Dick Carey, Pinky Helstrom, and I were required to take a fourth man into our room. I managed to get Dusty

Runner to move in with us. The total number of prisoners in the South Compound, which had been built to accommodate fewer than 1,200 men, was now approaching 2,000.

Although I have no recollection of my feelings at the time, I clearly felt a sense of guilt about some of my letters to my parents, which obviously upset them. On October 10, the first anniversary of the day I was shot down, I wrote them:

Dear Mom and Dad,
In several of your recent letters you mention things I have said that make me ashamed of myself. I now realize how easy it was for you to misunderstand what I meant to say in my April mail. Neither of you have hurt my feelings in any way—heaven knows, far from it. I wanted merely to remark that various would-be helpful and informed people aren't portraying our situation here exactly accurately. To date I have a hundred or so of your letters and three swell parcels. I am a little off on weight, but if you remember, I can stand that. I know you are writing and sending everything you can, but can't wait to eat some of your cooking. My health is good so, please, let's have no more worry. All my love,
    Frank

With the good war news, the theater was busier than ever. In late September, a half dozen kriegies who had been in radio back home set up a simulated radio station, Station KRGY, in a back room of the theater, broadcasting over a loudspeaker furnished by the YMCA. Programs included weather reports, a compound news commentary, English translations of communiqués from the OKW, and both popular and classical music from recordings received by kriegies from home. All text and announcements were read by kriegies who possessed the precise pronunciation and voice inflections of experienced radio broadcasters back home. They always signed off with, "KRGY, an overseas division of the American Broadcasting System." The last week in October, the band, then led by Dusty Runner, as Major Diamond had gone on to other duties, put on a six-day *Concert in Jazz*. The camp newspaper for November 4, 1944, reported: "The stomping, shouting, *sudlagerites*[42] would not leave until Dusty and the boys encored with *The Sheikh*."

That same week, the oldest American kriegie in Sagan, Bill "Kriegie" Hall, an original member of RAF 71 Eagle Squadron, who was shot down on July 2, 1941, and had been a POW for more than three years, built his own barber chair and opened a barbershop in the east end of the unusable shower building. He was open for business from ten until noon and one to four o'clock each afternoon. In payment, Kriegie Hall would accept cigarettes or anything else he could trade for clothing, food, or other items.

My second Thanksgiving as a prisoner of war came and went quietly as we prepared ourselves mentally for a cold winter. It would not be long before we would see our first snow and again experience the freezing temperatures so characteristic of the season. The coal ration provided by the Germans had been substantially reduced, and we expected to spend a lot of time with no heat in our buildings. Moreover, the coke briquettes supplied by the Germans were of poor quality and provided very little heat. These one-pound bricks were fabricated from what was left over after coal-conversion plants in Germany had extracted all the energy ingredients from the original coal to manufacture synthetic oil, margarine, and anything else that could be refined from them.

---

42. A combination of German and English, referring to the prisoners in the South Compound.

In the last three months of 1944, the British RAF dropped a total of 163,000 tons of bombs, most of them their one-thousand-pound medium-capacity bomb, on major targets in Germany, including Berlin. The POWs at Stalag Luft III were well aware of this activity. Late in the evening or in the early morning hours of dark, cold nights, kriegies bundled up in their bunks inside barracks with open or broken windows would regularly see the searchlights in the goon boxes sweeping the compound go out, indicating that an air raid by the RAF was imminent. Minutes later, through the thin, cold air came the distant *thump, thump, thump* of heavy bombs falling on Berlin ninety miles to the northwest. We did not know the ordnance being dropped on Berlin by the RAF in the winter of 1944 were four-thousand-pound bombs known as "cookies." We could tell, however, that they were very heavy bombs that in those days we called "blockbusters." We sensed that soon the war would be over. In the midst of these raids, there was always a kriegie saying from his bed, "Great! Give it to them."

I was in far better spirits at Christmas 1944 than I had been a year earlier. Although the news of the German offensive and fighting then raging in the Ardennes Forest in Belgium—now known as the Battle of the Bulge—was the major topic of optimistic German radio propaganda, its disturbing effect was limited because we knew the battle was not going to affect the outcome of the war. And the eyes of the kriegies at Stalag Luft III were not looking west: they were turned to the east, where "Uncle Joe" Stalin and the "Russkies" were poised for a major offensive into Germany. This meant that the Russians, not the Allies, would probably be our liberators.

As we had the previous year, in the days before Christmas, members of the band and a group of carolers went from block to block playing and singing Christmas music. On Christmas Eve 1944, three shows were presented in the theater—the chorus singing the *Messiah,* a KRGY Radio Show, and a jazz concert by the *Luftbandsters.* On December 28, I sent my mother a postcard:

Dear Mom,
I received about ten of your letters on Christmas Eve and am
glad to hear that you finally have my clothes. We had a little
turkey on Christmas. It was almost too good to eat. I do a little
of everything, help cook, wash dishes and what have you. I'm all
right. Love to all,
    Frank

On New Year's Eve 1944, a group of kriegies in Block 136 gave a minor bash to welcome in 1945. There were few refreshments, as we had barely enough food for our next meal. However, Dusty Runner took his trumpet, I grabbed my clarinet, Lieutenant Ted Grezlak[43] from Indiana, shot down in July 1943 at Hanover, brought his guitar, and Lieutenant Bob S. Sederberg,[44] a P-40 pilot shot down in a fighter sweep over Sardinia in July 1943, lugged his string bass to the party. We played some up-tempo tunes like Fats Waller's "Honeysuckle Rose," but also great old ballads such as "I'm Confessin' That I Love You," and "I'll Be with You in Apple Blossom Time." Our fellow prisoners loved live music, and as we played we could see in their eyes that they were thinking of home. Some of them had been kriegies for a long time, and this was my second time to

---

43. Navigator aboard 230156, 306th Bomb Group, failed to return on July 26, 1943; three died in action, and seven were taken prisoner (MACR 127).

44. Lieutenant Sederberg of the 325th Fighter Group, piloted a P-40, serial number 210898, when shot down on July 30, 1943.

welcome a new year as a POW. But New Year's Eve 1944 was a bit different. We all believed that 1945 was the year in which we would be going home.

On January 1, 1945, the Russian front was only slightly more than one hundred miles east of Sagan. More than 3 million Russian troops in 6 armies consisting of 155 infantry divisions and 15 tank corps were waiting for Marshal Stalin's order to unleash the Red Army's winter offensive along a frozen eight-hundred-mile front that ran from the Baltic to the Balkans. In November 1943, the Russians had rolled to a stop on a line running roughly north and south from Warsaw. At that time, they paused to regroup for what Stalin promised was to be the Red Army's "final mission." Whereas the British and Americans were struggling against 75–80 German divisions in the Ardennes and the west, the Russians were facing up to 200 Axis divisions, 180 of them German, in the east.

The POWs at Stalag Luft III were well aware of these developments, not only through German news reports and the camp canary but also from disillusioned goon guards who kept muttering, "*Alles kaput.*" In anticipation of the Russian advance and the likely German evacuation of Stalag Luft III, everyone began preparing to leave. Most simply selected the clothing and what rations they would take with them, while others used their excess clothing to make wool face guards for further protection against the cold, and knapsacks out of blankets and extra trousers. Still others made sleds from bed boards. Rumors were flying daily about what the Germans, or the Russians, might do if Stalag Luft III was overrun in the fighting. Finally, General Vanaman sent a message to all compound SAOs urging that all rumors be stopped and that all prisoners be prepared for a forced march.

I wrote my last letter as a prisoner of war on January 15, 1945:

Dear Mother,

I've said it once but will repeat myself just to make sure you know. Your parcel came, I'm not sure which month it was sent, but it contained cake flour, baking powder, and spices that I asked for so many times. I had almost given up hope of ever receiving it, so you can imagine how happy I am. The only thing that shook me was the absence of saccharine. You don't realize how small I feel always asking for things and, God knows, I wish I didn't have to. I have actually wondered from time to time whether you have come to think of me as the perennial beggar. Explanations are terribly hard at times and this is such a time. When I get home I promise I won't be so greedy. My love to you and Dad.

    Frank

At dawn on Friday, January 12, on the rolling, snow-covered plains of Poland, the Red Army exploded out of its fixed positions following one of the most intensive artillery barrages ever seen. Russian troops and armor began moving west. In two days, using their "Katyusha" rockets, heavy guns, and flamethrowers, they had advanced forty miles through German mines and pillboxes and were establishing pincers north and south of Sagan. On Saturday, January 20, Russian troops of the First White Army of Marshal Zhukov crossed the German border into Silesia. Now the fighting was growing closer to us, and we began to hear the distant rumble of heavy artillery day and night. As best we could, the kriegies at Stalag Luft III intensified our preparations for our probable departure from Sagan.

At four o'clock in the afternoon of Saturday, January 27, Adolf Hitler held a conference in an anteroom of the Reich Chancellery in Berlin. The room was filled with high-ranking military officers, including *Generaloberst*[45] Heinz Guderian, army chief of staff and commander of the eastern front; chief of operations *Generaloberst* Alfred Jodl; *Generalfeldmarschall*[46] Wilhelm Keitel, chief of the OKW, Hermann Göring, and other military and civilian officers. High-ranking officials sat around the table in heavy leather chairs while aides and lesser attendees stood or found straight chairs. Only thirteen months earlier, in November 1943, Hitler's empire, larger than the Holy Roman Empire, spread from deep in Russia west to the Brest Peninsula in France, and from the North Cape in Norway south through almost the whole land mass of Europe, and across North Africa from Egypt to Morocco. But his forces had not won a major battle since and were now isolated and facing enemy armies standing along German borders to the east, south, and west. Guards poised with machine pistols and sidearms ringed the room. Hitler had aged greatly in the past year and distrusted almost everyone because of the attempt on his life in July 1944 by so many of his high-ranking officers.

The conference opened with General Guderian reporting accurately and honestly on the impending disaster in the east. As he was talking, Hitler interrupted him to order that all necessary measures be taken to evacuate all prisoners of war at Sagan before the Russians could liberate us. An adjutant immediately left the room to carry out the order. Although the meeting would last until after six o'clock that evening, our fate had been settled by Hitler's first decision of the day.

By January 27, however, we were essentially ready. For several days, we had expected a change in our situation. The distant rumble of artillery had grown steadily louder. Through our guards, we

---

45. German for "Colonel General."

46. German for "Field Marshal."

learned that a Russian spearhead had reached the river at Steinau about eighteen miles from us. Our pathetic kits and packs were stacked in our rooms. It was biting cold and snowed heavily and continuously all day. All we could do, however, was wait. What was happening beyond the barbed wire fence and snow-laden pine trees was unknown to us. The snow kept piling up.

That evening at about 9:30 p.m., while four hundred men were in the theater watching a kriegie production, the Kaufman and Hart play *You Can't Take It with You,* Colonel Goodrich entered the theater, climbed on the stage, and said, "The goons have just come in and given us thirty minutes to be at the front gate. Get your stuff together and line up." Meanwhile, Lieutenant Colonel McNickle was making the rounds of the blocks, passing the word to the block commanders.

In Room 6 of Block 139, Dick Carey, Pinky Helstrom, Dusty Runner, and I were huddled around our small stove trying to keep warm, the paltry coal supply we were getting only permitted a fire for a couple of hours each night, when Colonel McNickle banged loudly on the entrance door to the building just outside our room and rushed in shouting for the block commander. We went out into the corridor with other kriegies who also heard the commotion and were coming out of their rooms. Colonel McNickle told us that Colonel Goodrich had been informed that the prisoners in the South Compound were to be ready to vacate within the hour. It was no surprise; there was no talk or comment. We immediately began to quietly put on extra clothes. I put on at least three pairs of socks, two pairs of trousers (one of cotton and one of wool), two shirts, a wool cap, gloves, and an overcoat. I rolled up a blanket, threw it over my shoulder, and placed my double-edged razor, razor blades, and a bar of soap in an overcoat pocket. I carried nothing else. We hurriedly heated water on our stove to make our last cups of Nescafé at Sagan and bashed what little food we had left. About 10:00 p.m., we were told to assemble outside.

It was pitch dark and bitterly cold. The freezing air temperature was in the low tens and felt colder and more penetrating because of a strong, icy wind blowing in from the west. By nightfall, the snow that had been falling all day was six to eight inches deep. I pulled my wool cap as far down on my forehead as best I could and wrapped my scarf around my face so as to cover my nose and mouth. The kriegies in each block were forming lines in front of their buildings. We stood around stamping our feet in the snow for about a half hour before receiving the order to move out.

12

LIBERATION

The two thousand men of the South Compound were the first to leave Stalag Luft III. We passed out of the west gate of the South Compound at about 11:00 p.m. and marched up the narrow road between the West and North Compounds. As we streamed by, the kriegies behind the wire on either side of us shouted their goodbyes and wished us good luck. From outside the main gate of the *Vorlager,* we could hear the barking and yelping of the sentry dogs used by the *Hundführers.* German guards lined the sides of the road as we passed through the gate and took our last look at Stalag Luft III, where so many of us had spent months and years.

Within minutes, we were in open country, where there was no barbed wire. Most of us could scarcely remember such a feeling of freedom. Everyone was in good spirits. The more optimistic kriegies thought the Russians would overtake and free us before we walked too far. However, after no more than two hours of plodding through the snow, with only a five-minute rest stop each hour, there was no more conversation. The only sounds to be heard were the crunching of feet in the snow, the sighing of the wind, and creaking noises in the snow-laden pines all around us.

We had marched about five hours before our first long stop, which lasted approximately forty-five minutes. We stopped on top of an overpass above an empty, desolate autobahn covered with ice and swept by subzero winds. Already weary, most of us simply sank into the nearby snow to rest. Men made fires out of logbooks and newspapers they had brought with them as souvenirs to take home. To lighten their loads, tired kriegies began removing extra clothes, mementos, and other items from their overcoats and backpacks and casting them aside in the snow alongside the road. Rope-drawn sleds that had been so carefully constructed in anticipation of our evacuation were abandoned by kriegies who no longer had the strength to drag them through the snow. The Germans gave us our first food from the horse-drawn wagons hauling their supplies: thick slices of black bread and margarine.

Following this stop, we marched the rest of the morning before arriving at a small town called Grosselten around noon. We had covered eighteen kilometers since leaving Sagan. It was a dreary, depressing scene: a shabby, desolate, secluded village set in a frigid, colorless, all black-and-white landscape showing no signs of life. We had been in the open for fourteen hours struggling through deep snow in the bleak, painful, arctic weather. At Grosselten, chilling winds were still blowing, snow was falling, and the numbing temperature felt even colder than the night before. During the march, several men had already dropped by the side of the road from exhaustion and the effects of the cold. We could only beg and plead with them not to give up and implore them to keep walking with us. We told them we would carry their belongings. Long before we reached Grosselten, I had lost all sensation in my legs below the knees, even to the touch, as I could no longer feel my feet touching the ground. I had shivered so long I had given up trying to control my trembling and shaking or the chattering of my teeth. Recognizing that we were completely worn out from our march, the Germans permitted us to sleep in any one of three barns in which we could find room to lie down. Usually, two men would lie down together, try to wrap up in their blankets, and bury themselves in the straw. It became increasingly difficult to fight off despair. We had no idea where we were or where we were going.

Colonel Goodrich did not order that there be no escape attempts by South Compound kriegies during our march but did pass the word that he was strongly opposed to such attempts because of the atrocious weather conditions and the fact that we were in a war zone in an enemy country. It was dark, windy, paralyzingly cold, and again snowing hard when we left Grosselten about 6:00 p.m. that evening, after having been forced to stand outside for an hour before departing. Once more, we began trudging silently through the night with no idea where we were going. And once more, after our first hour of marching, still more men began dropping into the snow beside the road, their strength gone. Sometimes a man could be seen lying by himself, perhaps dead or because his friends had been unable to help him or persuade him not to give up. At other times, men would try to help their fallen fellow kriegie, who would usually respond by saying, "I've had it. I can't go on." Our German guards, most of whom were older than we were, were in as bad of shape as their prisoners; in fact, I recall an American sergeant carrying the rifle of one elderly guard who, though he had been rotated and had a chance to rest, was completely exhausted. Where they had space in their horse-drawn supply wagons, the Germans picked up kriegies who had collapsed in the snow; if a prisoner in a wagon later regained sufficient strength to start walking again, he would get out of the wagon to make room for the next fallen man.

From time to time, as we pushed on, we passed groups of wretched, despairing refugees who were fleeing by the thousands from their homes and farms in Poland. They traveled in slow-moving wagon trains on the same roads we were using, adding to the congestion and misery of everyone. While the hardy shuffled alongside, the young, the old, and the sick sat in horse- or cattle-drawn wagons on top of piles of pitiful personal belongings. Occasionally, a column of grim-faced, glum German infantry clanked and rattled by us on their way to the front. Although some men appeared fit, most of these soldiers were noticeably older and younger than usual first-line troops; many were boys no more than sixteen years of age. Many were marching toward certain death. It was clear that the German army was on its last legs. Much of their equipment was also carried in horse-drawn wagons or loaded in one motorized truck with a hitch pulling a similar truck for which they had no fuel.

We finally halted at the town of Muskau about 1:00 a.m. after having slogged another twenty-seven kilometers. It had stopped snowing, but it was turning much colder. We were forced to stand outside two large buildings for another hour while Colonel Goodrich negotiated our future with the goons. We were then led into one of the buildings. It was a pottery factory. Pinky Helstrom and I found a place along a wall where hot running water was passing through some large pipes. We staked out a place on the floor beside the pipes and warmed our blankets by laying them on the pipes. We also dried our wet socks by laying them on the pipes and, thoroughly exhausted, stretched out on the floor and tried to get some sleep. We had been awake and on the road for thirty-six hours with little or no sleep.

The next morning, the Germans gave us our second ration of goon bread and margarine and were ready to resume the march, but Colonel Goodrich flatly refused to move. After an ugly confrontation, the Germans agreed that we would spend the night in Muskau, which we did visiting with friends and taking turns shaving at the single sink in the building that had hot running water.

At eight o'clock the following morning, Tuesday, January 30, having finally had a decent rest, even though it included no food, we began marching again. The weather was still bleak and freezing cold. Along the way, as we passed through small German villages, some of the kriegies managed to swap soap and cigarettes with local towns-people for bread, apples, or other fruit. After persevering for eigh-teen more kilometers, we straggled into the small town of Graustein at about 6:00 p.m. Darkness flowing in from the east quickly envel-oped us, and we were once again quartered in cold, drafty, uncom-fortable barns and chicken houses.

We left Graustein early Wednesday morning and marched until noon, at which time we reached the town of Spremberg, where we were led on to the grounds of a large building and each given a bowl of watery, but hot, barley-and-potato soup. It was the first time the Germans had made a serious effort to feed us since we left Sagan. Afterward, we resumed our march and walked to the train station at Spremberg, two kilometers away. Our long march had ended. At the Spremberg train station, we were locked in 40-and-8 boxcars, fifty or more men in each car. The train left Spremberg at seven o'clock that evening.

Conditions inside the boxcars were unspeakably hideous. We could not lie down; we either stood or sat on blankets on the hard floor packed together with our knees drawn up tightly under our chins. Every few hours, we tried to stretch our legs and slept in shifts. Many men passed out from the cold and lack of food. Others were so ill they vomited or lost control of their bowels, and we had no way to clean ourselves. Some men were so miserable they cried. The stench inside the cars quickly became so sickening that it alone was enough to make anyone ill.

It was only after the train pulled into Chemnitz late the follow-ing afternoon that the boxcar doors were opened for the first time, almost twenty-four hours after our departure from Spremberg. Our stop lasted no more than a half hour. While some Germans were leisurely handing us up more goon bread and margarine, others locked the doors, and the train left the station, returning us to our appalling circumstances before many men had a chance to receive additional rations.

The train arrived at the station in Regensburg at approximately two o'clock the next afternoon. When the doors were opened, those with enough strength left to do so leaped from their boxcars to relieve themselves shamelessly beside the tracks, in ditches or in nearby fields. The locals were treated to the sight of dozens of men squatting in the snow with their coattails pulled up over their heads. We were then put back on the train and, six hours later, were shunted off on a siding in Moosburg, where we were left locked in our boxcars for a third night. All during the night, men hammered on the boxcar doors, pleading for water or to be let out of our indescribably filthy environment. These were the three most miserable nights of my entire life. Words alone simply cannot describe, nor will I ever forget them.

At eight o'clock the next morning, the doors were opened. Along with most of the other prisoners, I felt so dirty, so tired, and so weak, stiff, and sore that I had great difficulty trying to stand. Because we were slow in disembarking from the train, German guards climbed into our cars and began pushing and herding us off the train. One of them grabbed me roughly with both his hands and physically threw me from the train into the snow, but I was beyond caring. Upon entering our new camp, Stalag VIIA, we saw that we had been transferred to a prison camp far different from Stalag Luft III. Stalag VIIA was a run-down enlisted men's camp that was already crowded with POWs of all Allied nationalities—American, British, South Africans, Australians, and many Sikhs and Gurkhas from the British Fourth Indian Division who had been captured in Africa and Italy.

Stalag VIIA was in a flat area surrounded by hills in Upper

Bavaria, approximately twenty miles northeast of Munich and about one half mile from the city of Moosburg, a town of approximately 5,200 inhabitants. It had been constructed as a camp for POWs in the fall of 1939 and originally designed to hold 10,000 prisoners. The camp was divided into three main compounds, which were in turn subdivided into stockades. It had been a camp for USAAF NCOs until October 1943, when all 1,900 were transferred to Stalag XVII-B. Thereafter, it was a transit camp from which Allied officers and men captured in Africa and Italy were sent to permanent camps. In February 1945, however, it was principally a headquarters for working parties of Allied ground forces of private rank who were sent out to work on farms, or to cities to clean rubble from British and American bombings.

Upon entering Stalag VIIA, we were searched, deloused, and given a short, lukewarm shower. I was initially placed in a ramshackle pigsty of a building housing American army privates sleeping in flea-, bedbug-, and lice-infested triple-decker bunks, from which they were required to arise each morning at four o'clock to be sent on trains to Munich to clean up rubble from Allied bombings or to work on farms. They would not return to our squalid, vermin-ridden slum until 11:00 p.m. Officers and NCOs were not required to work; however, soldiers of private rank were sent out to work sixteen to eighteen hours a day. I have never felt so sorry for anyone as I did for these men—or as angry about their mistreatment. Shortly thereafter, I was moved to another building for officers that had a large open bay, again filled with dirty, triple-decker bunks also infested with parasites, and a kitchen with a large woodburning stove and a washroom. The building was permanently cold and damp with all its windows opened to the outside: there was no glass in any of them. To get warm, we took turns huddling around the kitchen stove.

In our early days at Stalag VIIA, we were issued random items of food from Red Cross parcels, but that soon ended. Thereafter, our food consisted mainly of the usual goon bread and daily bowls of thin, tasteless soups, called "Green Death" by the prisoners. It was made with dehydrated vegetables, margarine, and occasional bits of meat of unknown origin. Nothing was clean, including our cooking equipment and our eating utensils. Our only water for both washing and drinking came from a single tap in the kitchen. Dysentery was rampant. I had the "GIs" during my entire time at Stalag VIIA, an illness that is physically debilitating and psychologically eviscerating. There were long lines day and night, rain or shine, at our odious, foul-smelling, open slit latrines that were never treated with lime, chlorine, or any other chemicals.

On Valentine's Day, February 14, 1945, in response to an inquiry to his office in Atlanta by my father, U.S. senator Richard B. Russell, from Winder, Georgia, sent my mother the following Western Union telegram from his office in Washington:

> War Department advises that Stalag Luft Three is thought to have been moved westward into the central part of Germany and that the addresses of prisoners there will remain unchanged. Am making further investigations and will notify you upon receipt.
> Richard B. Russell

In late February, the Germans stopped supplying us with coal or wood for our stove. Our X Committee organized groups of men to go under the building and rip out the subflooring. I was in one such group and was working away on the damp ground one afternoon when there came a tap on the floor above and I heard a German voice speaking to the prisoners. My heart raced. Had I been discovered, it would have meant days in the "cooler," solitary confinement. Fortunately, the Germans went away without further incident.

Our harsh, debilitating, demoralizing living conditions at Moosburg would have been little more than the tip of the iceberg in our mental struggle to survive in February 1945 had we known that there was at least one serious high-level German proposal to execute all British and American airmen prisoners of war held in Germany. Immediately following the devastating British/American bombings of Dresden on February 14–15, Dr. Joseph Goebbels, Adolf Hitler's influential propaganda minister, argued that the provisions of Article 2 of the 1929 Geneva Convention, to which Germany was signatory, requiring that all prisoners of war be protected and reprisals against them prohibited, had lost all meaning when enemy pilots, using "terror tactics," could kill tens of thousands of civilians "in two hours." He further argued that Germany should consider this provision of the Geneva Convention invalid and prevent another Dresden by executing all British and American air force prisoners of war in Germany on the basis that they had "murdered civilians." When his press officer, Rudolf Semmler, warned that Germany could expect reprisals on German prisoners held by the Allies, Goebbels ordered Semmler to find out how many Allied airmen were in German hands and how many German airmen were in Allied hands. Goebbels took his case to Hitler, who agreed in principle but postponed a final decision. In the interim, Joachim von Ribbentrop, German foreign minister, dissuaded Hitler from further considering Goebbels's grotesque proposal.[1]

---

1. In fairness, it should be noted that a great many German civilians and noncombatants suffered terribly in Allied bombing raids. Their rage was very real, as was the tragedy their leadership had brought upon them.

My primary recollections of Moosburg are of ice and snow; rain and mud; perpetual cold from which there was no escape; my inability to keep clean in grimy, crowded, bedbug-infested and lice-ridden barracks; chronic nausea and diarrhea; a complete lack of sanitation facilities; and the total absence of any information or recreational outlets. At the same time, while at Moosburg, I witnessed one of the most inspiring events I have ever seen. One clear, sunny day in April, we observed an American air raid on Munich, a steady stream of a thousand bombers, cluster after cluster of Forts, thundering relentlessly through a cloudless blue sky toward their target with hundreds of fighters weaving back and forth above them.[2] The world will never again see a sight to equal that of the United States Eighth AF in full battle array moving majestically through the skies over Germany toward the end of the Second World War. It was every bit as inspiring to us as it was terrifying to the hapless Germans who suffered through the bombing.

With each day in April, more refugee prisoners arrived, telling horror stories of their prior camps, of having been bombed, and recounting rumors of the nearness of American ground forces. There were also rumors that the Germans would again move us farther south. On April 26 and 27, we heard artillery to the north. On the twenty-eighth, some kriegies thought they saw an American tank patrol reconnoitering the area appear at the top of a nearby hill, then turn around and leave. An American P-51 fighter swooped low over the camp and disappeared over the horizon. There were rumors that some of our senior American officers were nowhere to be found. That night, we heard trucks as most of our guards pulled out of Stalag VIIA, leaving only a skeleton force of Germans behind.

---

2. This is probably the April 9, 1945, mission to Munich-Riem airfield. On this day, the 3rd Air Division struck several targets throughout Germany with 1,252 B-17s and B-24s.

At six o'clock on Sunday morning, April 29, Combat Command A of the U.S. 14th Armored Division was at its command post at Puttenhausen, Germany. Eight miles to the southeast was the division's 47th Tank Battalion, involved in the attack on Landshut, but had now been instructed to turn its attention to the Moosburg prison camps. Three miles north of Puttenhausen was the division's 68th Armored Infantry Battalion; having encountered stiff resistance the preceding day, the battalion was halted at Mainburg to avoid a night ambush. One minute before 6:00 a.m., an unusual group of men walked into the headquarters of Combat Command A and requested a meeting with Brigadier General C. H. Karlstad, the combat commander. The group included a German major representing the commander of the Moosburg prisoner of war camp and two prisoners of war, Colonel Paul S. Goode of the U.S. Army and a senior British RAF officer. The German major brought a written proposal from his commander for the creation of a neutral zone surrounding Moosburg and a halt in the movement of Allied troops in the vicinity to permit representatives of the Allies and Germany to negotiate the disposition of Allied prisoners in Moosburg.

The German proposals were rejected. The German emissary was given until 9:00 a.m. to return to Moosburg and secure an unconditional offer of surrender to the American forces; otherwise, they could expect an American attack. In response, German SS troops moved outside Moosburg, set up a defense perimeter, and awaited the attack. At exactly 9:00 a.m., the 47th Tank Battalion and 94th Reconnaissance Squadron of the American 14th Armored Division launched an attack on the German defenders of Stalag VIIA. A fierce firefight took place just outside the north and west entrances to the camp. During the fighting, some of our braver kriegies tried to climb on buildings to see what was happening. Most, however, including me, flattened themselves on the ground and in ditches to avoid the bullets that were ricocheting all around us. Several kriegies were hit by stray bullets. The skirmish lasted about an hour, and when it was over, all the surviving Germans had disappeared. At approximately 11:00 a.m., an American Sherman tank crashed through the front gate of the camp to the cheers of the prisoners, who swarmed all over it.

The struggle for survival was the objective of every combat soldier, sailor, or airman during the war; however, men who became prisoners of war were immediately called to answer a different summons. Once captured, American airmen POWs were no longer subjected to the unrelenting violence, the fright, and the risks of injury or death still confronting their brother fliers who would later return from all their missions, complete their combat tours, and be reassigned to other duties related to the war effort. However, as the struggle continued, survival for prisoners of war meant maintaining the resolve to win each day and prevailing over the disheartening effects of their complete loss of freedom and continuous confinement under often hard conditions totally beyond their control and that, for most of us, would continue until the end of the war. The war itself became the common enemy of prisoners of war.

The German comment most often heard by newly captured American airmen prisoners of war in Germany that "for you, the war is over" was never true. Those of us who became prisoners of war were simply handed an entirely different set of mental challenges and physical hardships. Mental stress for prisoners of war was not our bare existence, or the tedium of captivity, or the cold, or the indignity of our lack of privacy, all of which were part of our POW experience. It was the uncertainty inherent in waking up each morning, day in and day out, week in and week out, year in and year out, in an enemy prison camp, never knowing when it all would end.

I feel very deeply about the men who were prisoners of war with me. All the men of the Mighty Eighth were my brothers, but in my heart, I have a special place for my fellow kriegies. A prisoner of war experiences real-time feelings of helplessness and you're-on-your-own that cannot be imagined unless you have been there. It is difficult to put into words the sense of powerlessness and vulnerability one experiences when standing completely defenseless before a formidable armed wartime enemy of your country, knowing that the entire might of the United States is of no benefit to you. I have often thought that when Thomas Paine said, "These are the times that try men's souls," he was talking about prisoners of war.

This all changed for me and other prisoners on April 29, 1945, at about 12:30 p.m. In the midst of our rejoicing, congratulating one another, handshaking, and backslapping, a strange hush began to settle over Stalag VIIA as several ex-prisoners were seen pointing to a flurry of activity taking place around two high church steeples off in the distance above Moosburg. As we watched, we experienced the most emotional moment any of us would ever know as prisoners of war. Tears flowed from 8,000 unashamed faces as Old Glory was hoisted atop one of the steeples and began snapping defiantly in the wind.

Official estimates of the total number of Allied prisoners of war freed at Moosburg were 110,000, including an estimated 38,000 from the Soviet Union and 8,000 USAAF combat officers—all of whom had been held in a prison camp originally designed to hold 10,000 men. Once the pitched battle at Moosburg was over, the 600-man 47th Tank Battalion of the U.S. 14th Armored Division took

2,000 German prisoners, and the 600-man 94th Reconnaissance Squadron took 2,000 more. The 14th Armored Division total for the day was set at 12,000.

On May 2, the colorful General George S. Patton Jr., commander of the U.S. Third Army, accompanied by Major General James A. Van Fleet, III Corps commander, and Major General Albert Cowper Smith, 14th Armored Division commander, visited Stalag VIIA with an entourage of staff officers and newspeople. General Patton was quite tall and dressed to the teeth in the uniform we had always seen him wearing in his photographs: GI steel helmet, battle jacket, wide black belt with a large silver buckle, an ivory-handled six-gun on each hip, long trousers, and combat boots. He walked swiftly down the street, stopping frequently to speak to groups of American prisoners. Many stories are attributed to General Patton's activities that day. For example, after catching sight of a German flag still flying, the general reportedly instructed one kriegie, "I want that son of a bitch cut down, and the man who cuts it down, I want him to wipe his ass with it." When a prisoner asked him, "When are we going home, General?" Patton was said to have replied, "You look healthy enough to me. You can leave now if you want to." When General Patton stopped in front of my group, he looked at our malnourished, ragtag gathering, shook his head, and said, "I'm going to kill these sons of bitches for this." With that, he turned around and strode briskly away.

For the first few days after our liberation, nothing changed. The U.S. forces that released us had continued their advance, and their support troops had not caught up with them. Several prisoners took off to explore nearby towns and villages and, perhaps, find food, for the only food given us by our liberating forces was GI white bread, which, though delicious, still left us ravenously hungry, causing some of the kriegies to cry, "Bring back the goons! At least they fed us once in a while." Two days before V-E (Victory in Europe) Day, May 8, 1945, an American medical unit came into Stalag VIIA, deloused us, gave us new clothes, collected our old clothing for disposal, and gave us some GI ten-in-one rations.[3]

On May 9, I was in a group of prisoners taken in GI trucks to a bombed-out, abandoned German airfield at Ingolstadt, loaded on a C-47 aircraft, and flown to Liège, Belgium. That night, I had my first long, hot shower in nineteen months. It was the first time I felt really clean since having been captured. Early the next morning, I was put on a train that carried a large group of former Stalag Luft III prisoners to Camp Lucky Strike, near Le Havre, France. Camp Lucky Strike was a collection point for RAMP (Recovered Allied Military Personnel). I was given a medical examination and immediately hospitalized. The army doctors said chest x-rays showed evidence of pneumonia. I was treated with penicillin, a new drug that was said by my doctors to work miracles, and kept in the hospital for two weeks.

On May 15, my mother received a telegram from the War Department in Washington:

> The Secretary of War desires me to inform you that your son Capt. Murphy Frank D returned to Military Control 29 Apr 45.
>
> Ulio the Adjutant General

One afternoon at lunch in the hospital tent mess hall, Dwight Eisenhower, General of the Army and Supreme Commander of the Allied Expeditionary Force, stepped in and spoke to several former

---

3. Ten-in-one rations were field rations for combat troops. They got their name from the fact that they came in a box with enough rations for ten men, as opposed to K-Rations, which was a boxed meal for a single person.

prisoners. He asked an ex-kriegie sitting across the table from me, "Is everything all right, son?" When the reply was, "Fine, sir," General Eisenhower said to all of us, "Thank all of you for what you have done. We are going to get you home as soon as possible."

On May 17, I wrote a one-page V-mail letter to my mother:

Dear Mother,
I've written you several times since my liberation and hope
that by now you have received at least one of my letters. I also
sent you a cablegram through the Red Cross. I have been in the
hospital here in France for a couple of days and that has slowed
me up some. But, I'm out now and on my way. Anything else I
have to say can wait until I get home, except that I send all my
love to you, Dad and the family.
    Frank

When discharged from the field hospital at Camp Lucky Strike, I was told that, for follow-up medical observation purposes only, I would be sent home on a hospital ship. I was permitted to send a message to my mother through U.S. Army Signal Corps channels that I would be leaving Le Havre and would arrive at Fort McPherson in Atlanta upon my return home. I was then taken directly to the old Moore-McCormack line cruise ship *Argentina* that had been fitted as a hospital ship. After a call at Southampton, England, to pick up more patients, we set sail for home. Because the Pacific war was still in progress, we traveled for thirteen days in a large convoy of slow-moving ships with a heavy U.S. Navy escort of destroyers and smaller destroyer escorts. I was ill a good part of the trip, owing to heavy weather across the North Atlantic. However, as we approached Boston, our U.S. destination, the ocean calmed, and the ship's public address speaker began carrying live music broadcasts from a Boston radio station. Perhaps it was because I was from Atlanta, the home of Coca-Cola, but I shall never forget hearing the Andrews Sisters singing "Rum and Coca-Cola" as we approached Boston. The *Argentina* docked at the Boston Fish Pier on June 12, 1945.

We were immediately transported by bus to Camp Myles Standish in Taunton, Massachusetts, and treated to a sumptuous steak dinner, which few of us could eat because of the lingering effects of our poor diet as prisoners of war. At Camp Myles Standish, we were given orders putting us on leave and assigning us transport home. For all intents and purposes, my active military career ended as it had begun: with a train ride. After a few days, I was taken to the train station and put aboard a troop train bound for Fort McPherson in Atlanta. Most of the men on the train were enlisted men, combat veterans of the European campaigns in Italy, France, and Germany. Because I was an officer, I was designated a car commander. My fellow passengers were mostly small-town and farm boys from Alabama, Georgia, Florida, South Carolina, and Tennessee. For the most part, they were combat infantry and tank veterans from the 2nd Armored Division—"Hell on Wheels"—who had also been overseas for two years and were also returning home.

The ancient coach-type train car to which we were assigned was dirty and in disreputable condition because of its long use on troop trains. The fabric on the seats was threadbare and torn. The seats themselves were agonizingly uncomfortable, and all the windows were stuck; none of them could be opened. Moreover, as a nonessential wartime train, we had no schedule priority, so every few hours, we were shunted off on a siding to permit a high-priority train carrying essential wartime cargo to go through. It was midsummer and stiflingly hot. The temperature inside the car was unbearable, and we spent hours baking and sweltering inside what felt like an oven. Late in the afternoon of our second day on the road, the men in my car asked if they could knock the glass out of a couple of the windows on each side of the coach so that we could get some fresh air. At first, I declined, and they obeyed, but as we entered our third day of snail's-pace travel under our oppressive conditions, I also had had enough and, in response to their repeated requests, told the men it was okay with me if they knocked out a couple of windows. They wasted no time doing so.

The train commander was a major from the Transportation Corps, who was unathletic-looking, fairly short, slightly over-weight, and had an accent that did not identify where from north of the Mason-Dixon Line was his hometown. Within an hour after we had knocked the glass out of several windows, he passed through our car and, first thing, noticed the open windows. He immediately demanded to know who the car commander was. I unenthusias-tically identified myself. The major then told me that he intended to recommend that charges be brought against me for damaging government property. With that, my 2nd Armored veterans, all of whom knew that I was a combat airman and former prisoner of war, immediately formed a tight circle around me. One of them turned to me and asked, "Captain, do you want us to kill this son of a bitch or just throw his ass off the train?" An awkward, tense silence en-sued. There could be no doubt that the question posed was a serious one and the men were equally serious to carry out the answer. I said nothing. The Major said nothing. We combat veterans had already paid a price far higher than the cost of a few broken windows. Yet this Transportation Corps Major probably did not and could not understand this. A Major in rank only, he could not and probably would never compare in stature, respect, or leadership qualities to those I had met and flew combat with during my four-month stay at Thorpe Abbotts and the 100th BG. He was no Jack Kidd, John

Egan, Sam Barr, Robert Flesher, William Veal, or Gale Cleven. Before my train trip drew to a close at Fort McPherson, the Major passed through our car at least ten more times, never again mentioning the broken windows. Given the mood of these 2nd Armored veterans in my car, he was lucky to still be on the train.

As soon as I got off the train at Fort McPherson, I telephoned my parents. My mother answered the phone. At the sound of my voice, she broke down. "Oh, Frankie," she said softly, "it's been so long." An hour later, I was standing on the street at the front gate at Fort McPherson when my mom and dad drove up in our black 1938 Pontiac. We hugged and cried again, but this time for joy. It had been more than two years since I had last seen my parents and more than eight months since I had any word from them.

After four weeks home on leave in June 1945, I reported to Kelly Field in San Antonio, Texas, for possible reassignment to the Pacific Theater of Operations, as the war against Japan was still in progress. However, after the bombings of Hiroshima and Nagasaki and the surrender of Japan, I took advantage of the fact that I had accumulated enough service points to be released from the military and requested that I be separated from the USAAF and returned to civilian life. I was sent to the Army Overseas Replacement Depot in Greensboro, North Carolina, a "repple depple" that had been converted into a separation center. I was relieved of active duty with the USAAF effective January 17, 1946, just two days short of the fourth anniversary of the day I raised my right hand, took the oath, and joined the Army.

EPILOGUE

Nearly twenty-five years elapsed after I left Thorpe Abbotts for the mission to Münster until I once again returned to England. As already mentioned in the prologue, memories of my wartime experiences began receding into the far corners of my mind almost immediately with the end of the war and my return to civilian life, but all these memories came rushing back that February day in 1968. Only then did I begin to realize the profound effect the war had on me.

Before I go into greater detail about what happened after my first meeting with Ian Hawkins in 1983, I have been encouraged to summarize some of the major events affecting my life since returning to the United States and being relieved of active duty with the USAAF effective January 17, 1946.

I was not the only member of my family to serve in the military during World War II. My older brother, Michael Vincent Murphy Jr., who was born on May 21, 1920, graduated from Emory University School of Medicine in 1944. He interned for a year at Kings County Hospital, Brooklyn, New York, after which he went into the navy. He was assigned as a medical officer on the heavy cruiser USS *Chester*. In August 1945, the ship was transiting the Pacific when two atomic bombs were dropped, ending the war. His ship returned to Philadelphia, where it was decommissioned. Dr. Murphy became a resident in internal medicine at Grady Hospital in Atlanta, Georgia, for two years and then entered private practice. In 1950, he was recalled to active duty as a lieutenant commander and was stationed at the Brooklyn Navy Yard for three years. He returned to his private practice in 1953 and was a visiting professor of diagnostic medicine at Emory Medical School until suffering a severe stroke in 1986. Following a series of debilitating illnesses, he passed away on December 16, 2000.

My younger brother, John Hope Murphy, was born on January 13, 1927, and graduated from high school in 1944. He immediately went into the navy and became a medical corpsman, but he did not see combat. He was discharged from the navy in 1946 and entered Georgia Tech. He graduated with a BS degree in mechanical engineering in 1951 and worked for the Sandia Corporation in Albuquerque, New Mexico, for a year before deciding to go back to school. He reentered Georgia Tech and eventually obtained MS and PhD degrees in mechanical engineering. He was a professor of engineering and research scientist at Georgia Tech until his retirement. He and his wife, Diane, split their time between houses in Atlanta and the mountains of North Carolina.

My English-born paternal grandfather, William Patrick Murphy, died on January 9, 1936, almost six years before the United States entered World War II. My paternal grandmother, Phoebe Parsons Murphy, died four years after her husband, on November 12, 1940, at the age of eighty. My maternal grandmother, Ida Nix Gidish, who was born in Cherokee County, Georgia, likewise did not live to see me enter the service. She died on August 18, 1940, at the age of seventy-one. However, my classically self-educated, German-born maternal grandfather, John L. Gidish, survived his wife and lived to see me fight the country where he was born. He died on May 9, 1954, at age eighty-eight. After living to see all her sons return safely from the war, Mary Sibyl Gidish Murphy passed away prematurely on December 8, 1957, at the age of fifty-eight. Following the death of his wife, my Virginia-born father, Michael Vincent Murphy, lost interest in life and died on May 4, 1960, at age sixty-five. My parents, all four of my grandparents, all my aunts and uncles, and several of my first cousins are all buried at Westview Cemetery in Atlanta, Georgia.

As already mentioned, I was released from active duty on January 17, 1946. In March 1946, I reentered Emory University in Atlanta. Before the war, I had taken some premedical courses at the urging of my older brother. However, I was more interested in playing in dance bands. When I returned to school, I had no particular career goals, so I pursued a combination of science and business courses. I received my BA degree from Emory University in 1948.

As soon as I graduated from college, a close friend in school—an ex-USAAF B-17 pilot who also graduated from Emory only three months ahead of me—persuaded me to interview with his company, Crawford & Company, Insurance Adjusters, which had been started by an army veteran and was almost entirely staffed by young World War II veterans such as myself. I liked the company and joined them. They sent me to Tallahassee, Florida, for a year. When I returned to Atlanta, I met my future wife, Ann Parks; we were married on September 9, 1949, my twenty-eighth birthday.

In 1951, I accepted a better position in the claims department of the Fireman's Fund Insurance Company in Atlanta. Soon thereafter, my supervisor, who was a lawyer, urged me to go to law school. I entered the night law program of the Atlanta Law School in 1951. It was not an easy decision, because by this time, our first child, Frank Jr., had been born. However, I graduated in 1954, passed the

Georgia bar exam in July, and was admitted to practice in October of the same year. Even though I have never actively practiced law, I have been a member of the State Bar of Georgia ever since.

In the fall of 1955, I found my niche in life. Marsh McLennan, insurance broker for the Lockheed Aircraft Corporation, recommended me for a position in the insurance department of the Georgia division of Lockheed in Marietta, Georgia. I was offered and immediately accepted the job. It would give me an opportunity to once again be associated with aviation and its people. Beginning in the early 1960s, I had several assignments with Lockheed, all of which had to do with aircraft sales. From 1966 on, I worked exclusively in Lockheed's international operations, handling aircraft sales and follow-on contacts with governments, air forces, and airlines in some twenty countries in South America, Asia, Europe, and the Middle East. I was the resident representative of the Lockheed-Georgia Company in Saudi Arabia and lived in Riyadh for ten years working with the Royal Saudi Air Force and Ministry of Defense. I retired in 1987 as vice president of Lockheed Georgia International Services.

Ann and I had four children. Frank Jr. was born on August 30, 1950, and served in the U.S. Army for six years, during which he was assigned to the 25th Infantry Division, Schofield Barracks, Hawaii, and later the Seventh Signal Command, Fort Ritchie, Maryland. He is a graduate of the University of Maryland and now lives in Virginia. He has spent twenty-three years with the Department of Defense and has worked for Defense Logistics Agency, Fort Belvoir, Virginia, since 1992. His children are Michael, Laura, and Natalie.

Ann Elizabeth Murphy Melas, born March 31, 1953, received her BA degree from Mercer University at Macon, Georgia, in 1974, where she majored in English literature. She also has earned an

MA degree in English literature from Northern Arizona University, Flagstaff, Arizona. She is a writer of children's stories and has been published in numerous children's magazines. She has also had two books published. She and her husband, George Melas, and their two children, Chloe and Stefan, live in Plano, Texas, where George is an architect.

Patricia Alice Murphy Rosser was born on March 4, 1955, and also graduated from Mercer University. She did graduate work at Emory University, where she obtained her teacher's certificate. Pat taught in her old high school for a year but was a bit disenchanted with the system and went to work for a private company. In September 1987, she was diagnosed with cancer, and after receiving treatment she seemed to improve; however, in 1989, her cancer metastasized. Following extensive diagnostic work at Memorial Sloan Kettering Cancer Center in New York, she received follow-on treatment at Emory University Hospital. Tragically, the war she fought with her own body was one she could not win; she died at Emory University Hospital on September 7, 1989, leaving her husband, Frank, and a five-year-old son, Benjamin. Benjamin is now sixteen and lives with his father in Atlanta.

Michael Kevin Murphy, the youngest, known to all of us as Kevin, was born on October 5, 1958, and graduated from Kennesaw State College, Kennesaw, Georgia, in 1992 with a degree in international studies. Prior to this, Kevin served in the U.S. Navy from 1983 to 1986, where he originally trained as an emergency medical technician (EMT) and worked in clinics and outpatient surgery at the Philadelphia Naval Hospital. Later, he trained in field medical service at Marine Corps Base Camp LeJeune and served as a field medic with the First Marine Division and Marine Forces medical team at Camp Pendleton, California. Kevin, with his wife, Alicia, who works for America West Airlines, live in Reno, Nevada. Kevin has his own business as a television cameraman, and he and Alicia have one son, Patrick.

After first meeting Ian Hawkins in 1983 and reading for the first of many times the Missing Air Crew Report 1028 (MACR 1028), I began what might be viewed as a personal quest—to learn more about what happened on that Sunday afternoon in the skies over Münster. In early June of the following year, 1984, I traveled to Düsseldorf, Germany, where I met the warm, generous Heinz Hessling. Heinz was the eighteen-year-old *Luftwaffenhelfer* with the flak battery on the Dortmund-Ems Canal just north of Münster on October 10, 1943. Heinz witnessed the air battle over Münster through a pair of binoculars and watched as Crew No. 31 was shot down. Heinz was a talented aviation artist and has several paintings in museums in Germany and England.

We drove out to the Rawe farm at Holzhausen, where I landed by parachute after bailing out of our airplane, and to the Berdel-mann farm near Lienen, where our aircraft crashed. I spoke with both Helmut and Friedhelm Berdelmann, who showed me four photographs of our demolished aircraft that were taken on October 11, 1943, the day after we were shot down. I explored the crash site with Helmut Berdelmann, then fifty-two years of age, the only eyewitness to the crash. He meticulously pointed out the exact locations where major sections and components of our aircraft fell on their farm.

Neither re-creating the sequence of events nor confirming the Berdelmanns' recollection of *Aw-R-Go*'s final moments is an easy task. My recollection is generally limited to what happened in the nose of the airplane. After leaving the formation, I heard Charles Clark come on the interphone reporting fighter attacks from the rear. It was undoubtedly during these attacks that Don Garrison,

Bob Bixler, James Johnson, and I were wounded. There were fires in the right wing and radio compartment. Glenn Graham went out the nose door first, I was next, followed by Augie Gaspar and Charlie Cruikshank. MACR 1028 provided additional information. Leonard Weeks bailed out through the open bomb bay doors, and Bixler, the most severely wounded among us, was probably assisted out the waist door. These were the six parachutes that Helmut saw initially. The two parachutes Helmut saw open "after a short pause" were unquestionably those of Johnson and Garrison, but here is where the sequence of events becomes muddied.

In MACR 1028, there are statements by Weeks, Garrison, and Johnson made sometime after the war regarding the fates of Clark and Vincenti. Johnson reported that he was "blown" out the aircraft when it "exploded" and that Garrison bailed out. Garrison reports that he too was "blown out" of the aircraft when it broke apart and he "fell out." Consequently, despite Helmut's recollection of two delayed parachutes, it seems apparent that the aircraft broke apart with Johnson and Garrison on board, and after being "blown out"—or more correctly, thrown out—of the aircraft, they were able to pull their parachute "D" rings. According to Weeks, Bixler saw Charles Clark, our tail gunner, attempting to open his escape door. It is apparent that Clark was never able to open the door and perished in the crash. According to Johnson, his parachute deployed at five thousand feet shortly after the aircraft broke apart. The enigma is what happened to Orlando Vincenti.

The conflicting reports regarding whether Vincenti was blown out of the airplane, or bailed out with his parachute on fire, or whether his parachute caught fire shortly after it blossomed are totally irreconcilable. We only know positively that Vincenti's body and dog tags were both badly burned. Whether he abandoned the airplane under his own power or was blown out, it seems difficult to believe that, even if he left the airplane with his parachute ablaze, his body would have been badly burned and his dog tags scorched as he fell. It would seem more likely that as his parachute vanished in flames, he would have simply fallen to the ground and been killed upon impact. The fact that he was last seen alive moving around inside the airplane by all eyewitnesses suggests that, for some unknown reason, he never left the airplane and could have been found inside as claimed by the Berdelmann family.

Because both James Johnson and Don Garrison stated that they fell from the airplane when it broke apart, it follows that their parachutes opened above the Berdelmann farm. Thus the sequence of events was that six parachutes blossomed immediately, followed by the aircraft breaking apart, and then two more parachutes blossoming. That Helmut Berdelmann recalls these events out of sequence is understandable considering that he was only twelve years old when he witnessed the terrifying crash of a heavy bomber on his parents' farm and was recollecting these events almost forty-one years after the fact. Added to this is the fact that the surviving crew members, who would later provide information about Clark and Vincenti, witnessed these rapidly unfolding events under monumentally stressful circumstances.

The remarkably clear German photographs, together with the firsthand accounts of the Berdelmann family of the events at their farm on October 10, 1943, and the postwar recollections of our surviving crew members suggest what may have happened to *Aw-R-Go* during the final moments of our doomed mission.

The obvious flight path of the aircraft from its known position when both pilots bailed out to the point where it crashed on the Berdelmann farm suggests that, within moments after its flight control system was lost, the aircraft pitched forward into about a forty-five-degree, nose-down attitude and commenced to dive. As it lost altitude, it gained airspeed but, incredibly, maintained a northeasterly heading; it never fell into a spin or plunged straight down to the ground. The ground distance traveled after both pilots bailed out indicates that the aircraft was airborne in a stable dive mode for perhaps as much as one full minute before it finally rolled over and broke apart.

Crew No. 31
(Based on information in MACR 1028)
Pilot, Captain Charles B. Cruikshank—POW
Fourth out of nose hatch.
Copilot, Lieutenant Glenn E. Graham—POW
First out of nose hatch.
Navigator, Captain Frank D. Murphy—WIA/POW
Second out of nose hatch, wounded in the shoulder.
Bombardier, Lieutenant August H. Gaspar—POW
Third out of nose hatch.
Top Turret Gunner, Technical Sergeant Leonard R. Weeks—POW
Bailed out of bomb bay.
Radio Operator, Technical Sergeant Orlando E. Vincenti—KIA
Weeks reports *Vincenti* told him over the interphone about fighting a fire in radio room.
Johnson reports *Vincenti* was "blown out" of aircraft.
Weeks told *Garrison* that *Vincenti's* chute was on fire when he bailed out.
Ball Turret Gunner, Staff Sergeant Robert L. Bixler—WIA/POW
Wounded by a "number of bullets," most likely the first to bail out of waist entrance with the assistance of *Johnson* and/or *Garrison*.

Left Waist Gunner, Staff Sergeant James M. Johnson—WIA/POW

Wounded with a "scalp injury," reports "blown out" of aircraft.

Right Waist Gunner, Staff Sergeant Donald B. Garrison—WIA/POW

Serious leg wound. Reports "blown out" of the aircraft.

Johnson says *Garrison* bailed out.

Tail Gunner, Sergeant Charles A. Clark—KIA

Bixler told *Weeks* that *Clark* was kneeling by the tail door, trying to open it.

Johnson told *Garrison* that *Clark* was kneeling by the tail door, trying to open it.

The jagged metal edges seen at the fuselage breakpoint in the German photographs suggest that the aft fuselage and tail assembly separated violently from the rest of the airplane at approximately fuselage station 6K, immediately aft of the waist gun ports. This is consistent with the statements of Garrison and Johnson, the two waist gunners, both of whom stated that they fell out of the airplane when it broke apart. The doped fabric covering on the rudder is completely shredded and in tatters; the underlying web-type metal structure is undamaged.

The largest single piece of the airplane, which included the center fuselage section, a portion of the right inner wing inboard of approximately wing station 7, and the left inner and left outer wing, struck the ground right side up in about a forty-five-degree nose-down attitude. In the photographs, the number 4 fuselage bulkhead, only slightly misshapen, with the entrance to the bomb bay clearly visible in its center, is still standing, stoutly holding the remains of the aircraft together. The inner wings with engine numbers 1, 2, and 3, their bent propellers still attached, are buried in the ground to the top of their nacelles but remain firmly joined to the fuselage. All wing leading edges and spar caps are gone. The rib trusses of the left inner wing are exposed. The right main landing gear and retractable struts can be seen crushed under the number 3 engine nacelle.

There are no photos of the number 4 engine or right outer wing. The Berdelmanns stated, however, that the number 4 engine was found approximately three hundred feet north of the main wreckage of the airplane. Neither are there any photographs indicating conclusively what happened to the forward fuselage, which contained the bombardier-navigator and pilots' compartments and top turret (i.e., everything forward of the number 4 fuselage bulkhead), which is shown in the pictures. There is much debris in the pictures, but it is impossible to identify its origin. Again, however, the Berdelmanns told me that, in the rubble, they found a U.S. officer's cap with captain's bars affixed; it would have belonged to either Charlie Cruikshank or me and would have been in the forward fuselage section. It is, therefore, clear that virtually all the remains of the aircraft fell into a circular area that was no more than one thousand feet in diameter.

What had happened to us was clear. We were shot down by devastating cannon fire from German fighter aircraft that disabled the aircraft's flight control system and ignited two major uncontrollable fires, one in the radio compartment and one in the right wing in the area of the number 4 engine. There is no indication of any damage from ground-based antiaircraft artillery, even though flak over the target was intense. There was no explosion; the aircraft was not destroyed instantly as a result of any external or internal violent force. On the other hand, it did not hit the ground intact; it broke apart in midair above the Berdelmann farm.

The altitude of the airplane when its flight control system was destroyed and its altitude at the time of its breakup are almost as much of a mystery as the fate of Orlando Vincenti. Estimates of our altitude when the aircraft became disabled range from twenty thousand, as believed by Charlie Cruikshank and me, to twenty-five thousand feet as estimated by Don Garrison. It was clearly not twenty-five thousand feet, as we made our bombing at approximately twenty-three thousand feet.

It is my belief that, in its last moments, the seriously fire-damaged right wing of the aircraft sheared off just outboard of the number 3 engine, causing the aircraft to roll violently to its right into an inverted flight position, at which time, the structurally weakened empennage was torn from the center fuselage between the waist gun ports and aft crew door. The forward half of the airplane, minus the sheared right wing and, possibly, part of the forward fuselage, then struck the ground at a steep angle. Upon impact, what may have been left of the forward fuselage was completely demolished, revealing sturdy bulkhead number 4, its mating point in the manufacturing process. The center fuselage then crumpled to the ground.

I made several trips to Germany to see Heinz. On my last visit in 1987, Heinz presented me with a painting of the shooting-down of Crew No. 31. On December 20, 1989, Heinz Hessling, who had been so generous and so helpful in finding out what happened to me and my crew, passed away.

The 100th BG lost twelve aircraft with their crews at Münster on October 10, 1943. When darkness fell on Europe that evening, the 100th had lost forty-five aircraft together with their crews in less than four months of combat operations. In a study made in 1983, the original 100th BG historian, James R. Brown, determined that, of the original thirty-five aircrews that went to England with the 100th BG in June 1943, twenty-seven crews were lost, and parts of eight crews completed twenty-five missions, but no original crew of ten finished a combat tour of twenty-five missions. Because of its heavy losses at Regensburg, Bremen, and Münster in August and October 1943, the 100th BG became known throughout the Eighth AF as "the Bloody Hundredth," a sobriquet it carries to this day. The truth, however, is that the overall combat loss record of the 100th BG in the Second World War was consistent with those of the other heavy bomb groups operating within the Eighth AF at the same time.

Further, despite the heavy loss of American aircraft and crews at Regensburg, Schweinfurt, Bremen, and Münster, the daylight air battles over Europe in the summer and fall of 1943 were not one-sided. Although claims by Eighth air gunners of enemy aircraft downed were often inflated by a factor of two to three, in part because it was difficult to resolve the multiple claims made by gunners when a German fighter was shot down, Luftwaffe records show that German fighter pilot losses in western Europe from July to October 1943 were, in fact, in the hundreds each month, and monthly aircraft losses consistently ran 15 percent or more of the aircraft available for duty at the beginning of each month. Moreover, many German fighter pilots were shot down several times, only to be returned to combat; if a German fighter pilot went down over France or Germany and survived, he was returned to duty as long as he was physically capable of being restored to flying status. When an American bomber with ten men aboard went down over Europe, even those crewmen who survived uninjured were permanently lost to the Eighth. Evaders who managed to avoid capture were transferred out of the Eighth. But when the long-range P-51 Mustang fighter first provided escort service in early December 1943, the die was cast. By June 1944, the American Eighth AF and British RAF owned the skies over Europe.

On our worst day, the German air defenses never repulsed or

drove off the United States Eighth AF. If the target could be seen, every aircraft that could reach it pressed home an attack. I saw many B-17 aircraft go down, but apart from disabled aircraft unable to stay with the formation, they all went down holding station. Every one.

In its December 14, 1992, issue, the *Air Force Times*, a newspaper in Washington, D.C., for active and retired members of the United States Air Force, published an article under the heading of THE "MIGHTY EIGHTH," commemorating the fiftieth anniversary of the establishment of VIII BC headquarters at High Wycombe, England, to conduct heavy bombing operations against strategic targets in Germany. At the top of the article was a picture of a B-17 crew in England in the summer of 1943. It was a photo of Crew No. 31 of the 100th BG!

Although a representative of the Department of Defense office that supplied the photo of our crew to the *Times* later told me that the picture was randomly selected, I like to think that, from among the countless pictures of the thousands of bomber crews that served with the Eighth AF during the Second World War, any one of which would have been completely appropriate, the unseen hand of the All-Knowing played a silent part in choosing a picture of Crew No. 31. It was only fitting, I think, that the crew picture accompanying the *Times* article be that of a crew that not only participated in air operations that brought fame and glory to the Eighth AF but was also representative of the thousands of young American airmen in England in 1943 who, day after day, climbed into their airplanes and went out to fight, but one day went out and did not come back. Crew No. 31 was such a crew.

During its tour of duty with the VIII BC, Crew No. 31 participated in twenty-one combat missions. Every member of the crew was present for every mission; the best information available to me indicates that Crew No. 31 flew more missions as an intact unit than any other original crew in the 100th BG. The crew participated in the longest bombing mission flown by VIII BC in 1943, to Trondheim, Norway, and the first shuttle mission from England to Africa for the bombing of Regensburg. We were the lead crew for the 100th BG on the long, demanding mission to attack the Focke-Wulf aircraft factory at Marienburg in East Prussia, where the bombing results were considered among the Eighth's best of the war. The next day, we were shot down over Münster, Germany. Five members of the crew—Leonard Weeks, James Johnson, Don Garrison, Bob Bixler, and Charles Clark—were officially credited with shooting down enemy aircraft. Two members of the crew were killed in action, four others were wounded in combat, and eight members of the crew were prisoners of war for almost nineteen months.

Since you are by now all too familiar with their names, here is what I know about those who survived with me on that October day in 1943 in the skies over Germany.

Charles Bean "Crankshaft" Cruikshank, our pilot, was liberated from Stalag VIIA and arrived home on June 10, 1945, and remained on active duty. After a two-month leave, he was briefly assigned to the Pentagon before being given a field assignment. Following a variety of assignments, he transitioned into jets. In 1961, he retired as a lieutenant colonel with twenty-three and a half years of service. Following his retirement from the air force, he worked for the FAA in their air traffic control system. He survived his spouse and one daughter and has one son and another daughter.

Glenn E. Graham, our copilot, was liberated from Stalag VIIA and stayed in the air force. In January 1959, while assigned to U.S. Military Assistance Advisory Group headquarters in Pakistan, Glenn was killed in the crash of a Pakistani air force transport aircraft while on an official trip from Rawalpindi to Karachi. Glenn and his wife, Frances, had four children.

Augie H. Gaspar, our bombardier, was also liberated from Stalag VIIA, on or about July 21, 1945, and returned to the bakery he worked for before the war. He remained in the reserves and was recalled during the Korean War, serving as a B-29 bombardier. He retired from the reserves in the grade of lieutenant colonel in 1977, and at age sixty, he also retired from the Bakers and Confectionery Union. He has been married to his wife, Mary, for many years, and has no children. They live in their waterfront property at Bethel Island, California. In 1989, the Gaspars bought a motor home and since then have spent most of their free time traveling.

Leonard R. Weeks, our flight engineer and top turret gunner, was held at Stalag Luft III and then moved to Stalag XIII-D. Weeks passed away in Sacramento, California, on February 25, 1999, and he is buried at Arlington National Cemetery.

Robert L. Bixler, our ball turret gunner, was liberated from Stalag XVII-B, but his processing back to civilian life was not completed until January 25, 1946. Bixler went on to work as a construction engineer and passed away in Wickenburg, Arizona, on February 29, 1996.

James M. Johnson, our left waist gunner, was held at Stalag Luft III and then moved to Stalag XIII-D. Johnson passed away in Camarillo, California, on December 9, 1983.

Donald B. Garrison, our right waist gunner, was repatriated back to the United States, probably through the International Red Cross on or about September 22, 1944. Don passed away on March 24, 1958, a few weeks before his thirty-fifth birthday.

If I could poll all the men of Crew No. 31, they would unanimously vote to define themselves as ordinary Americans but would take pride that a photograph of our crew appeared in the December 14, 1992, issue of *Air Force Times*. They would have laughed and rejected outright any suggestion of their being patriots or heroes. I know other veterans feel the same way. I remember some missions very vividly and others hardly at all, yet there is no question about the fact that my trepidation and anxiety about combat applied to all of them. The gut reactions I have described for Hamburg, Regensburg, and Münster ring true for all my missions. A great deal has been written about combat, but I am convinced that it is difficult to convey the full range of emotions to those who were not there or who have not been exposed to combat. Those absorbing the immense body of literature on war may have an intellectual understanding of what war is all about, but unless they were once in combat, they cannot know what it is to do the actual fighting.

As I draw my reflections on the air war during the Second World War to a conclusion, I confess without reservation that in close combat, I have said it all:

> *Please, God, help me! Please help me!*
> *Somebody! Anybody! Get me out of here!*

If you had the luck of the draw and made it back to base, life gradually returned to a semblance of normality before the next mission. A postmission shot of whiskey, a warm meal, writing a letter home, or a two-day pass to London could not wash away completely the surrealistic, if not nightmarish, images of aerial warfare. Life never returned to complete normality, because "normal" is a relative term. Completing a sortie etched another emotional scar into your soul. These scars could not be seen by anyone, but everyone knew they were there. As I found out during my February 1968 business trip to Europe, my own scars never completely went away. I do not remember when, but I quickly reached the point where I did not like to fly combat, yet I had to go until, for me, the "war was over." If you ask me, "Why?" I do not have a complete answer. Perhaps in part it was simply because someone had to go, and we all agreed to go, and we did. More likely it was a matter of pride. No matter what, we could not just quit. None of us were flag-wavers, but all of us *were* soldiers and for the most part would rather have died than be branded as cowards. In any event, when commanded to stand, we stood, and when commanded to go, we went.

If I could ask the men of Crew No. 31 to place their actions in the proper historical context, they would answer that they, along with their fellow airmen of the Eighth AF, were simply doing the right thing. I believe that a balanced history of the American contributions to the air war in Europe during the Second World War would conclude that we of Crew No. 31, the 100th BG, and the Mighty Eighth, did what was asked of us. Men of the Mighty Eighth acquitted themselves well between the first bombing mission on August 17, 1942, and the last mission on May 7, 1945, when the Eighth AF dropped 426 tons of food to the citizens of Holland.

Over fifty-five years have passed since war disrupted the tranquility of Thorpe Abbotts and altered forever the lives of visitors and inhabitants alike. The sights, sounds, and smells associated with men and machines assigned to the 100th BG left a permanent mark upon the landscape. A stroll through Thorpe Wood reveals the remains of Nissen huts overtaken by bramble bushes that dissuade those from getting too close to the past. Silence, once shattered regularly by B-17s and routine base activity, is now broken by pheasants and rabbits bolting from one clump of cover to another. Nightfall sends a chilling shiver up the spine. Like others dotting the East Anglia countryside, the abandoned field at Thorpe Abbotts is illuminated only by moonlight, but there is no question that locked within its innermost sanctum are the collective experiences of men at war. Crew No. 31 and *Bastard's Bungalow* are but one crew and one heavy bomber of the many that forged the United States Eighth AF during the Second World War. Paraphrasing a comment by a Union officer at the close of the American Civil War, my wish is that when Judgment Day comes, I want to be standing with the men of the Mighty Eighth.

APPENDICES

100th Bombardment Group
June 22, 1943–October 14, 1943
Data Compiled by Paul M. Andrews and Michael P. Faley
Updated March 31, 2022

The National Archives at College Park, Maryland, the Air Force Historical Research Agency at Maxwell Air Force Base, Alabama, and the Smithsonian Air and Space Museum in Washington, D.C., hold thousands of feet of documents relevant to the air war during the Second World War.

In theory, the records should make it possible to retrace an individual or an aircraft's history. Reality takes over because not all the documentation generated during the war can be located. Those unit records, which had to be accomplished in a timely manner and before there was Wite-Out or word processors, did contain errors—names were misspelled, serial numbers transposed, and "facts" misstated. Despite these limitations in quality, consistency, specificity, and availability, there is still a wealth of information available.

Compiled from official records, published sources, and ongoing research efforts, the following appendices provide a snapshot of the 100th Bombardment Group and place Frank Murphy's experiences into a larger historical context. The timeframe is from June 22, 1943, which is the date of the 100th Bomb Group's first mission, which was a diversionary feint, to October 14, 1943, the conclusion of the VIII Bomber Command's Black Week.

A. Operational Summary
B. Operational Losses, June 22, 1943–October 14, 1943
C. Aircraft Markings and 100th Bombardment Group Aircraft History
D. 418th Bomb Squadron Original Aircrews
E. Operational Matrix—1943
F. Personal Report on the Regensburg Mission, August 17, 1943

APPENDIX A.
OPERATIONAL SUMMARY

To the extent known, significant events affecting the 100th Bombardment Group are provided. From left to right is the field order number (FON), group sortie number (GSN), date (DATE), number of aircraft taking off (TO), number credited with a sortie (CS), number of aircraft that did not return (DNR), battle damaged (BD), and salvaged (SAL). Additionally, information is provided about the number of personnel who evaded capture (EVD), interned in a neutral country (INT), killed in action (KIA), killed in service (noncombat) (KIS), taken prisoner of war (POW), returned to duty (RTD), and wounded in action (WIA), with the number that died from injuries placed in parenthesis (DOI). The following definitions apply to some operations:

ABANDONED Crews took off, but not dispatched
CANCELLED Crews alerted, but not briefed
RECALLED   Crews took off, but ordered to return to base
SCRUBBED   Crew briefed, but did not take off

FON	GSN	DATE	TO	CS	DNR	BD	SAL	EVD	INT	KIA	KIS	POW	RTD	WIA	WIS	TARGET
65		22-Jun-43	21													DIVERSION
		23-Jun-43														Kerlin Bastard, France (RECALLED)
67	1	25-Jun-43	19	2	3					25		5				Bremen, Germany
	2	26-Jun-43	23	0												Le Mans, France
69	3	28-Jun-43	21	18											1	St. Nazaire, France
70	4	29-Jun-43	21	19												Le Mans, France
		TOTAL	105	39	3					25		5			1	
		2 Jul-43														Le Mans, France (SCRUBBED)

No.	Op	Date														Target
71	5	4-Jul-43	26	25	1	1										La Pallice, France
		8-Jul-43														La Pallice, France (SCRUBBED)
72	6	10-Jul-43	26	0	1			2								Le Bourget, France
		13-Jul-43														Le Bourget, France (SCRUBBED)
		14-Jul-43														Courtrai, France (SCRUBBED)
73	7	14-Jul-43	22	4		4	1							6		Le Bourget, France
		16-Jul-43														Courtrai, France (SCRUBBED)
		16-Jul-43	27				1				7				3	PRACTICE
74	8	17-Jul-43	22	0		4	1							2		Hamburg, Germany
		18-Jul-43														La Pallice, France (SCRUBBED)
		22-Jul-43														La Pallice, France (SCRUBBED)
75	9	24-Jul-43	24	20			1							2		Trondheim, Norway
76	10	25-Jul-43	24	15	1	11				6		4		1		Kiel (Warnemunde), Germany
77	11	26-Jul-43	20	16										1		Hannover, Germany
78	12	28-Jul-43	21	0		1								1		Oschersleben, Germany
79	13	29-Jul-43	21	14												Warnemunde, Germany
80	14	30-Jul-43	17	14		5										Kassel, Germany
		TOTAL	223	108	3	30	2	3		6	7	21		16	3	
		2-Aug-43														Bernay St. Martin, France (SCRUBBED)
		10-Aug-43														Regensburg, Germany (SCRUBBED)
81	15	12-Aug-43	21	20		4										Bonn (Wesseling), Germany
		13-Aug-43														Schweinfurt, Germany (CANCELLED)
		14-Aug-43														DIVERSION

FON	GSN	DATE	TO	CS	DNR	BD	SAL	EVD	INT	KIA	KIS	POW	RTD	WIA	WIS	TARGET
82	16	15-Aug-43	21	21		2				1						Merville-Lille Venderville, France
84	17	17-Aug-43	21	14	9	3		5	10	17		62	7	2		Regensburg, Germany
		18-Aug-43														Kassel, Germany (SCRUBBED)
. 85	18	19-Aug-43	7	0		1										Woensdrecht Gilz-Rijen, Germany
		20-Aug-43														Lille / Lesquin, France (SCRUBBED)
		22-Aug-43														DIVERSION (SCRUBBED)
86A	19	24-Aug-43	7	7		2								2		Everaux-Conches, France
86B	20	24-Aug-43	6	5												Bordeaux, France (return from Aug 17 Shuttle mission)
		26-Aug-43														Woensdrecht, Germany (SCRUBBED)
87	21	27-Aug-43	7	7		1										Watten, France
		30-Aug-43														Lille, France (SCRUBBED)
88	22	31-Aug-43	19	0												Lille Meulan, France
		TOTAL	169	74	9	13		5	10	18		62	7	4		
FON	GSN	DATE	TO	CS	DNR	BD	SAL	EVD	INT	KIA	KIS	POW	RTD	WIA	WIS	TARGET
		2-Sep-43														Kerlin Bastard, France (SCRUBBED)
90	23	3-Sep-43	21	17	5	10		11		17		12	10	2		Paris, France
		4-Sep-43														Paris, France (SCRUBBED)
91	24	6-Sep-43	21	10	3	3		1	9	4		12	1	1		Stuttgart, Germany
92	25	7-Sep-43	18	18										2		Watton, France
		9-Sep-43														Paris, France (SCRUBBED)
94	26	9-Sep-43	21	19												Paris France
95	27	15-Sep-43	20	19	1			7		1		1		1		Paris (Billancourt), France
97	28	16-Sep-43	19	17	1					1		9				Bordeaux (La Pallice), France
		17-Sep-43														Schweinfurt, Germany (SCRUBBED)
		20-Sep-43														Paris, France (SCRUBBED)
		20-Sep-43														Paris, France (SCRUBBED)

FON	GSN	DATE	TO	CS	DNR	BD	SAL	EVD	INT	KIA	KIS	POW	RTD	WIA	WIS	TARGET
		21-Sep-43														Paris, France (SCRUBBED)
100	29	23-Sep-43	23	16												Vannes, France
		24-Sep-43														Stuttgart, Germany
		24-Sep-43			1											PRACTICE
103	30	26-Sep-43	21	0												Paris, France (Citron)
104	31	27-Sep-43	20	17												Paris, France (Citron)
		28-Sep-43														Emden, Germany
		28-Sep-43														Lutzow, Germany (SCRUBBED)
		TOTAL	184	131	11	13		19	9	23	5	44	18	6		
FON	GSN	DATE	TO	CS	DNR	BD	SAL	EVD	INT	KIA	KIS	POW	RTD	WIA	WIS	TARGET
106	32	2-Oct-43	26	26												Emden, Germany
		3-Oct-43														Kassel, Germany (SCRUBBED)
		3-Oct-43														Wilhemshaven, Germany (SCRUBBED)
108	33	4-Oct-43	25	23	1	2		4				6				Hanan, Germany
		7-Oct-43														Bremen, Germany (SCRUBBED)
111	34	8-Oct-43	22	19	7	9	1	1		32		38	6	13 (1)		Bremen, Germany
113	35	9-Oct-43	16	13												Marienburg, Germany
114	36	10-Oct-43	14	12	12	1	1	1		38		83		2		Munster, Germany
		11-Oct-43														Emden, Germany (SCRUBBED)
		12-Oct-43														Emden, Germany (SCRUBBED)
		13-Oct-43														Emden, Germany (SCRUBBED)
115	37	14-Oct-43	8	8		1										Schweinfurt, Germany
		TOTAL	111	101	20	13	2	6	0	70		127	6	15 (1)		
		TOTAL	732	453	46	59	4	32	19	141	12	161	29	42 (1)	3	

APPENDIX B.
OPERATIONAL LOSSES,
JUNE 22, 1943–OCTOBER 14, 1943

Detailed chronologically are the operational losses of the 3rd Bombardment Division and its predecessor unit, the 4th Bomb Wing. The data identifies from left to right the aircraft tail number, group, aircraft nickname, pilot, and Aircraft Fate DNR (Did Not Return), DNR OW (over water), DNR MID (midair collision), DNR INT (B-17 interned in a neutral country). Also included are incidents such as premission activity (PMA), returning from operations (RFO), and take of assembly (TOA). Where possible, information is provided regarding crew members as to the number who evaded capture (EVD), interned in a neutral country (INT), killed in action (KIA), killed in service (KIS), prisoner of war (POW), returned to duty (RTD), wounded in action (WIA), and whose fate is yet to be determined (TBD). If available, the Missing Air Crew Report (MACR) number is provided.

SERIAL	GRP	NICKNAME	PILOT	FATE	EVD	INT	KIA	KIS	POW	RTD	WIA	UNK	MACR
22-Jun-43													
25880	94		John G. Sabella	DNR - Fighters					10				
230240	94	Black Kitten	2Lt. Jack R. McFarland	DNR -			3		7				
230211	95	Guess Who?	Capt. Joel W. Bunch	DNR - Fighters			2		8				4903
23284	96		Lt. Cyril (NMI) Morrison	DNR - Flak					10				
25877	96		2Lt. Harold C. Russell	DNR - Flak									
25-Jun-43													
23260	100	Angel's Tit	Lt. Alonzo P. Adams III	DNR OW - Fighters			9		1	9	1		271
229986	100		Capt. Oran E. Petrich	DNR OW - Fighters			10			8	2		269
230038	100	Bar Fly	Lt. Paul J. Schmalen- bach	DNR OW - Fighters			6		4	10			270
28-Jun-43													
23267	95		Lt. William K. Thomas	DNR OW -						9	1		

SERIAL	GRP	NICKNAME	PILOT	FATE	EVD	INT	KIA	KIS	POW	RTD	WIA	UNK	MACR
230284	95		Lt. Richard M. Smith	DNR OW -						8	2		
230286	95	*Spook V*	Lt. Robert F. Bender	DNR OW - Fuel						10			
4-Jul-43													
230051	100		Lt. Robert C. Pearson	DNR - Fighters Mechanical	1				9				655
10-Jul-43													
230105	95	*Slightly Dangerous*	Lt. James R. Sarchet	DNR - Fighters	2		6		2				4902
230050	100	*Judy E*	Lt. Charles L. Duncan	DNR - Fighters	2				8				268
14-Jul-43													
23071	94		Lt. Floyd B. Watts	DNR - Fighters	5		3		2				113
23190	94	*Mr. 'Five by Five'*	Capt. Ken H. Harrison	DNR - Fighters	6				4				114
23331	94	*"Naturals" Salty's Naturals*	Lt. Edward A. Purdy	DNR MID - Fighters	2		9						116
230243	94	*Good Time Cholly III Nip N' Tuck*	Capt. Willis T. Frank	DNR - Fighters	2				8				115
16-Jul-43													
230305	100	*Flak Shack*	Woodrow B. Barnhill	NOPS - Crashed			7	3					
17-Jul-43													
23219	94	*Dear Mom*	2Lt. Robrt B. Powledge	DNR - Fighters			10						93?
230304	95		Edward L. Lemke	RFO -			1						
24-Jul-43													
230418	95	*Piccadilly Commando*	George A. Tyler	RFO -							1		
25-Jul-43	100		Lt. Curtis Biddick	RFO - Crash landed						8	2		
230206	94	*Happy Day Happy Daze*	Lt. John F. Keelan	DNR OW - Flak			1			9			29
23277	95		2Lt. Lloyd L. Mauldin	DNR - Flak			9	1					194
25862	100	*Duration + 6*	Capt. Richard A. Carey	DNR OW - Flak			6	4					117
25907	388	*Wing and a Prayer*	2Lt. W. H. Fuller	DNR OW -			10						3120
26-Jul-43													
23280	94	*Cherokee Maid*	Lt. Gerald T. Smith	DNR OW - Fighters						10			

SERIAL	GRP	NICKNAME	PILOT	FATE	EVD	INT	KIA	KIS	POW	RTD	WIA	UNK	MACR
230174	94	Lady Luck 2 Lady Luck II Cherokee Maid Gorgeous Hussy	Lt. Robert F. Tessier	DNR - Flak & Fighters			1		9				90
230280	94		Lt. Ralph W. Holcombe	DNR OW - Fighters			1		10				2470
230450	94	Ramsbitch	Lt. Harold W. Alsop	DNR OW - Fighters			9		1				84
23264	95		Lt. Stanley (NMI) Foutz	DNR - Flak			10						193
23298	95		2Lt. Leroy A. Massey	DNR -			2						195
25893	95		Lt. Oliver V. Robichaud	DNR - Flak & Fighters			2						197
230304	95		2Lt. Henry S. Quirk	DNR -			5						196
23281	96	The Mary R	Lt. Frank L. Spino	DNR - Fighters					10				96
25895	385	Souse Family	Lt. Theo R. Harris	DNR OW - Fighters			4		6				191B
230279	385	Black Jacker	2Lt. Jack W. Daniel	DNR - Fighters			7		3				191C
230281	385		FO. Glenn F. Duncan	DNR -			10						191A
S/N?	388			DNR OW -						10			
230189	388	La Chiquita	2Lt. Jim B. Gunn	DNR OW - Flak			2		8				3067
230198	388		2Lt. Audrey M. Bobbit	DNR - Fighter			5		5				
230208	388			DNR - Flak			10						3142
230209	388		2Lt. Adalbert D. Porter	DNR OW -	3				7				
230224	388		2Lt. Earl P. Horn	DNR - Flak & Fighters			4		6				3130
230225	388	Mister Yank	Lt. John R. Denton Jr.	DNR - Flak			6		4				3131
27-Jul-43													
230356	96	Tarfu II		RFO - Salvaged						10			
28-Jul-43													
23282	95		Lt. James F. Rivers	DNR					10				118
25882	95	Spook III	2Lt. Francis J. Regan	DNR OW- Fighters			10						216
230150	95	Exterminator	2Lt. Fred D. Hodges	DNR - Fighters					10				214
230219	95		Lt. William K. Thomas	RFO - Crash Landed					3	7			
230377	95	Roger the Lodger II	Leslie B. Palmer	RFO -			1				1		
23326	96	Moore-Fidite II	Lt. Hugh L. Moore	DNR OW - Fighters			1						137

SERIAL	GRP	NICKNAME	PILOT	FATE	EVD	INT	KIA	KIS	POW	RTD	WIA	UNK	MACR
23343	96	Paper Doll	Lt. Ernest E. Deshotels	DNR OW - Fighters					10				137
230141	96	Liberty Belle	Capt. Milton C. Fulton	DNR OW - Fighters			10		1				140
230351	96	Alcohol Annie Excaliber	2Lt. Eugene (NMI) Wilcox	DNR OW - Fighters			5		·	5			
230355	96	Dallas Rebel	Lt. William B. Nance	DNR OW - Fighters			4		6				141
230394	96		Lt. Clarence (NMI) Covett Jr.	DNR OW - Fighters			4		6				
230401	96		Lt. Stephen W. Hettrick	DNR OW - Fighters			10						139
23316	385	Big Stinky Betty Boom	2Lt. William A. Storr	DNR OW -			10						189B
230179	385	Grim Reaper Murder Incorporated Murder Inc.	2Lt. Herman M. Gurgel	DNR - Flak			4		6				189A
230257	385	Lady Suzie II	2Lt. William M. Robbins	DNR OW - MID Flak			8		2				189C
230285	385	Roundtrip Ticket	2Lt. John H. Noel Jr.	DNR OW -			8		2				189D
230216	388	Johnnie	Lt. Ralph W. Swanson	DNR - Fighters					10				3128
230302	390	Calamity Jane		RFO - MID 306 BG 229974 Salvaged									
29-Jul-43													
230146		Down and Go! Cherokee	2Lt. Neal (NMI) Palmer	DNR - Mechanical			1		9				202
230370	96	Little Caesar	Lt. Cecil (NMI) Walters	DNR OW - MID 25908			10						144
30-Jul-43													
	385			DNR OW -						10			
25908	388		Lt. Heywood W. Collings Jr.	DNR OW - MID 230370			10						
230192	95		2Lt. Robert B. Jutzi	DNR OW - Flak			2		3	3	2		217
230183	96	Dry Run II Dry Run III	Capt. Andrew W. Miracle	DNR OW - Fighters						10			
230290	96	Lady Luck II	Lt. Camelo P. Pelusi Jr.	DNR - Fighters			5		5				145
230202	388		FO. Earl E. Pickard	DNR - Flak	1				9				3125
230210	388		2Lt. Charles H. Penn	DNR - Flak			3		7				3264

SERIAL	GRP	NICKNAME	PILOT	FATE	EVD	INT	KIA	KIS	POW	RTD	WIA	UNK	MACR
230238	388	*Wing and a Prayer Classy Chassy*	Lt. Frank F. Kelly	DNR - Flak & Fighters					10				3153
2-Aug-43													
25861	100	*Laden Maiden*	Lt. Owen D. Roane	NOPS - Crash Landed						10			
12-Aug-43													
230194	95	*We Ain't Scared*	Capt. Clifford B. Hamilton	DNR -	1		5		4				253
230418	95	*Piccadilly Commando*	Lt. Edward L. Lemke	DNR -					10				254
23299	390			RFO - Salvaged									
15-Aug-43													
230598	385		Lt. Edward S. Stone	DNR OW - Flak & Fighters			10						267
23306	390	*Phoenix*	2Lt. Billy C. Lawrence	DNR MID -	4		5		1				258
17-Aug-43													
230389	94	*Dear Mom*	Lt. Bernard W. Navovitz	DNR OW - Fighter	2		6		2				323
23194	95	*Little Hell*	Lt. Robert W. Hayden	DNR OW - Fighter			4		6				400
`230176	95	*Assassin*	Lt. John L. Sundberg	DNR OW - Fighter	4		1		5				401
230274	95	*Our Baby Our Bay-Bee*	Lt. Walter A. Baker	DNR OW - Fighter	3				7				402
230283	95	*Mason's Morons*	Lt. Robert C. Mason Jr.	DNR -					10				403
23232	100	*Flak Happy*	Lt. Ronald W. Hollenbeck	DNR - Fighters	2				8				676
25860	100	*Escape Kit*	Lt. Curtis R. Biddick	DNR - Flak			4		6				675
25867	100	*Alice from Dallas*	Lt. Roy F. Claytor	DNR - Fighters	5		2		3				678
230002	100	*The WAAC Hunter Damifino*	2Lt. Henry P. Shotland	DNR - Fighters	1				9				680
230042	100	*Oh Nau-sea!*	Lt. Glen S. Van Noy	DNR OW - Mechan-ical					10				682
230063	100	*Picklepuss*	Capt. Robert M. Knox	DNR - Fighters			6		4				677
230070	100	*Tweedle-O-Twill*	Lt. Ronald W. Braley	DNR - Flak & Fighters			1		9				679
230080	100	*High Life*	Lt. Donald K. Oakes	DNR INT - Fighters		10							683
230311	100	*Maybe*	2Lt. Thomas D. Hummel	DNR - Fighters			2		8				681
25886	385	*The Jolly Roger*	2Lt. Paul A. Sommers	DNR - Fighters	1		6		3				387A

SERIAL	GRP	NICKNAME	PILOT	FATE	EVD	INT	KIA	KIS	POW	RTD	WIA	UNK	MACR
25892	385	*Pregnant Porta*	Lt. John T. Keeley	DNR OW - Fighters			1			9			
25914	385	*"Sack Time" Roger Wilco*	Lt. Leslie L. Reichardt	DNR - Fighters					10				387B
23414	385	*Paddlefoot*	Lt. John W. Parker	DNR OW – Fuel						10			
23305	390	*Princess Pat Fertile Myrtle*	2Lt. Dale A. Shaver	DNR - Fighters	1				9				392
23310	390	*Blood Guts & Rust*	2Lt. Wade H. Sneed	DNR - Fighters						10			396
23333	390	*Purgatory Pete*	2Lt. Raymond A. Becker	DNR OW - Flak						10			389
230017	390	*All Shot to Hell*	2Lt. Ashbrooke W. Tyson	DNR - Fighters					10				388
230315	390	*Battle Queen "Peg of My Heart"*	2Lt. Stephen P. Rapport	DNR INT - Flak & Fighters		10							391
230316	390	*Madie*	2Lt. James R. Regan	DNR - Fighters			1		9				390
19-Aug-43													
230172	96	*Black Heart Jr.*		TOA - Fire Crash Landed						10			
230068	388		2Lt. B. (NMI) Howe	DNR - Flak & Fighters			8		2				
24-Aug-43													
230187	385	*Lulu Belle*	Major Presto (NMI) Piper	DNR OW - Fighters			4			6			961
230364	385		Lt. Wilmont C. Grodi	DNR - Fighters	6		3						395
230230	388	*Homesick Angel*		RFO Fuel - Crash Landed						10			
230308	388	*Hot Rocks*	Lt. Kenneth E. Daugherty	DNR OW - Mechanical			1			9			393
2-Sep-43													
	385			PMA - Explosion									
3-Sep-43													
25865	100	*Janie*	Lt. Victor E. Fienup	DNR - Flak	3		2		5				686
230035	100	*Torchy*	Lt. Charles B. Winkelman	DNR - Debris from 230059 and 230089 Midair Collision	7		1		2				

SERIAL	GRP	NICKNAME	PILOT	FATE	EVD	INT	KIA	KIS	POW	RTD	WIA	UNK	MACR
230059	100	Barker's Burdens	2Lt. Charles W. Floyd Jr.	DNR MID - Struck by 230089			8		2				685
230089	100	Sunny	Lt. Richard C. King	DNR MID - Struck 230059	1		6		3				684
230611	100	Horny	Capt. Henry M.Henington	DNR OW - Flak						10			
	390			TOA - Explosion									
23321	95	Kathy Jane II	Lt. Norman S. Rothchild Jr.	DNR - Flak							9	1	
6-Sep-43													
230161	95	Cuddle Cat	2Lt. John A. Cabeen	DNR -					10				547
230271	95	Bomboggie	2Lt. Glen F. Ransom	DNR - Fighters	5		1		4				545
230300	95	Hell-n-Back	Lt. George A. Tyler	DNR - Fighters					10				546
230057	100	Raunchy	Capt. Sam R. Turner	DNR INT - Fighters		9	1						689
230088	100	Squawkin Hawk II	Lt. Sumner H. Reeder	RFO -			1				3		
230335	100	Sans Finis	Lt. Walter J. Grenier	DNR - Flak Crash Landed			1		9				657
230402	100	The Poon-tang	Capt Edgar F. Woodward Jr,	DNR - Mechanical		1			9				688
23289	388	Wolff Pack	Lt. Edward A. Wick	DNR - Flak & Fighters			3		7				3066
23293	388	Slightly Dangerous	Lt. Demetrious Karezis	DNR - Fighters			5		5				3113
23378	388	Sky Shy Silver Dollar	2Lt. James A. Roe Jr.	DNR - Fighters			1		9				3114
23425	388	Silver Dollar II In God We Trust	2Lt. Richard N. Cunningham	DNR - Fighters	1				8				3115
25942	388	Sky Shy Wenatchee Special	FO. Myron A. Bowen	DNR - Flak			2		8				3121
230201	388	Shedonwanna? Tiger Girl	Lt. Earl S.Melville	DNR - Fighters			4		6				3124
230203	388	Shack-Up	Lt. Roy H.Mohr Jr.	DNR - Fighters			4		6				3126
230222	388	Lone Wolf	Lt. Alfreed (NMI) Kramer	DNR - Fighters	7		2		1				3129
230234	388		Lt. Lewis M. Miller	DNR - Fighters			7		3				3132
230349	388		2Lt. Ray T. Wilken	DNR - Fighters	2		8						2409

SERIAL	GRP	NICKNAME	PILOT	FATE	EVD	INT	KIA	KIS	POW	RTD	WIA	UNK	MACR
230478	388	*Impatient Virgin II*	Lt. William P. Beecham	DNR INT - Fighters		10							3136
9-Sep-43													
23353	96	*Tarfly Tar Fly*	2Lt. Edwin A. Noondrewier	DNR - Flak									
430362	388	*Wee Bonnie II*	Lt. Adelbert D. Porter	DNR - Flak	5				6				3134
15-Sep-43													
23266	95	*Sittin' Bull*	FO. Joseph H. Noyes	DNR OW -								?	616
23437	96		Lt. James V. Richardson	DNR - Flak			10						
230493	385		Lt. Ceril V. Reed	DNR - Flighters	1		9						727
230607	388	*Paty Hand*	2Lt. Kenneth E. Murphy	DNR - Flak			10						728
23452	100		2Lt. Arthur M. Veter	DNR - Flak	7		1		2				645
16-Sep-43													
230276		*Terry and the Pirates*	2Lt. Robert B. Jutzi	DNR -					10				615
230064	100	*Wild Cargo*	2Lt. Robert H. Wolff	DNR OW- Fighters			1		9				647
230601		*Mary Ellen II*		RFO MID - Salvaged			10						
25906		*Sondra kay*		RFO - Weather	1								
230030		*Old Iron- sides*	Lt. Henry J. Nagorka	DNR OW - Fuel			2		8				
25903		*Ascent Charlie*	Lt. Herbert T. Turner	DNR - Fuel			10						
23-Sep-43													
24-Sep-43													
230259	100	*Damifino*	2Lt. John G. Gossage	NOPS OW Practise sortie, Fighters				5		5			278
26-Sep-43													
23290	385	*Raunchy Wolf*	John T. Keeley	RFO MID - 230264			10						
230264	385	*The Dorsal Queen*	Paul M. Yannello	RFO MID - 23290			10			1			
27-Sep-43													
25888	94	*Elusive Elcy*	Lt. Hurley Roberts	DNR - Fighters			10		1				732
25989	94	*Marge H.*	Lt. Morris L. Hawkins	DNR - Fighter			10						5674
230454	94	*Reluctant Dragon*	Lt. John C. Thalman	DNR OW- Fighters			1		9				733
230792			FO. Alfred (NMI) Drab- nis	DNR - Flak			2		8				756
230270	94	*The Old Shillelagh*		DNR -									
2-Oct-43													
230421	388			DNR -			10						3135

SERIAL	GRP	NICKNAME	PILOT	FATE	EVD	INT	KIA	KIS	POW	RTD	WIA	UNK	MACR
4-Oct-43													
23538	94	Ten Knights in a Bar Room	Lt. Dennis T. Carlson	DNR – Flak & Fighters	6				4				771
23283	95	Yankee Queen	H. L. O'Neal	RFO - Salvaged						3	7		
230045	95	She's my Gal Fight'n 'n Bit'n	FO. Max L.Crowder	DNR OW -			1		9				744
230604	100	Bdger Beauty V	Capt. Harold B. Helstrom	DNR - Flak	4				6				843
23308	385		Lt. Carl W. Dawurske							10			
8-Oct-43													
230367	96	Flak Happy	2Lt. Edmund I. Boland	DNR - Fighter			7		3				852
230373	96	Lucky Lady III	Lt. Warren A. Jones	DNR - Flak			5		6				854
237752	96		2Lt. Paul A. Flahive	DNR - Fighter					10				853
23233	100	Our Baby	Capt. Bernard A. DeMarco/ Maj Gale Cleven	DNR - Flak					11				950
23386	100	Marie Helena	2Lt. Raymond J. Gromley	DNR MID - FW 190			10						949
23393	100	Just-A-Snappin'	Capt. Everett E. Blakely	DNR - Flak			1			6	3		
25864	100	Piccadilly Lily	Capt. Thomas E. Murphy	DNR - Flak			6		5				948
230154	100	War Eagle	2Lt. Arthur H. Becktoft	DNR - Flak			1		9				953
230358	100	Phartzac	Lt. Frank H. Meadows	DNR - Flak			8		2				947
230818	100	Salvo Sal	Capt. William H. McDonald	DNR - Flak	1		1		8				952
230840	100		2Lt. Herbert G. Nash Jr.	DNR - Flak			5		5				951
230275	385	The Vibrant Virgin Keep It Covered	2Lt. Ralph M. Jensen	DNR - Flak					10				825
230292	390	Pulsatin' Polly	Lt. Marshal M. Sheperd	DNR - Fighter			6		4				783
230318	390	The Devil's Daughter	Lt. Arlin (NMI) Rennels Jr.	DNR - Flak			1		9				781
230330	390	Blood, Guts, & Rust II	Capt. James C. Peterson	DNR - Flak			4		6				784
9-Oct-43													
230288	95	Louise II	J. P. Caspen	RFO - Crash Landed						10			

SERIAL	GRP	NICKNAME	PILOT	FATE	EVD	INT	KIA	KIS	POW	RTD	WIA	UNK	MACR
230377	95	*Roger the Lodger II*	Lt. Ralph W. Eherts	DNR OW -			10						854
23543	96	*Sack Time Suzy Sam*	FO. Rodney S. Greene	DNR INT - Fighters		10							946
230781	96		2Lt. William C. Hunt Jr.	DNR - Fighters			10						945
230336	385	*Miss No-nalee II*	Lt. Glyndon D. Bell	DNR - Mechanical	1				10				824
230214	388	*Iza Angel Iza Angel II*	2Lt. Henry J. Nagorka	DNR OW - Fighters			4		6				3141
230802	388	*Gynida*	2Lt. Henry Kinney Jr.	DNR OW - Fighters			1		9				3138
10-Oct-43													
23497	95		Lionel (NMI) Correia	DNR - Fighter			1		9				943
25986	95	*Brown's Mule*	Lt. John D. Riggs	DNR - Fighters			3		7				944
230272	95	*Fritz Blitz*	Lt. Eldon J. Broman	DNR - ?			1		10				1118
230273	95	*Patsy Ann III*	Lt. William E. Buckley Jr	DNR - ?			5		5				942
230817	95	*Miss Flower III*	Lt. John M. Adams	DNR - ?					10				1044
23516	96		2Lt. Daniel M. Williams Jr.	DNR - Fighters					10				893
23229	100	*Pasadena Nena*	Lt. John K. Justice	DNR - Flak z& Fighters	1		2		7				1021
23234	100	*Little Mike (Detached 390th BG)*	Lt. Robert Scheider 390th BG	RFO - Crash Landed									
23237	100	*Stymie*	Lt. John F. Stephen	DNR - Flak & Fighters					10				1030
23433	100	*Lena*	Lt. Robert P. Kramer	DNR - Flak			3		7				1024
230023	100	*Forever Yours*	Lt. Edward B. Stork	DNR - Flak & Fighters			2		8				1022
230047	100	*Sweater Girl*	Lt. Richard B. Atchison	DNR - Debris from 230723			4		6				1031
230087	100	*Shackrat*	Lt. Maurice E. Beatty	DNR - Flak & Fighters			8		2				1026
230090	100	*El P'sstofo*	Lt. Winton L. MacCarter	DNR - Fighters					10				1020
230723	100	*Sexy Suzy Mother of Ten*	Lt. William M. Beddow	DNR MID - Bf-109			6		4				1027
230725	100	*Aw-R-Go*	Capt. Charles B. Cruik-shank	DNR - Fighters			2		8				1028
230734	100	*Slightly Dangerous*	Lt. Charles H. Thompson	DNR Fighters			3		7				1023

SERIAL	GRP	NICKNAME	PILOT	FATE	EVD	INT	KIA	KIS	POW	RTD	WIA	UNK	MACR
230823	100	*Invadin' Maiden The Gnome*	Lt. Charles D. Walts	DNR Fighters			5		5				1025
230830	100	*M'lle Zig Zig*	Lt. John D. Brady/Maj John Egan	DNR - Fighters			1		10				1029
23539	385		Lt.William B. Whitlow	DNR - Fighters	3		3						826
26155	385		Lt. John F. Pettenger	DNR - Fighters					10				827
25898	385	*"Little Lass"*	Lt. Paul E. Williams	DNR OW - Flak & Fighters			1		9				3117
23302	390	*Rick-O-Shay*	Lt. Edward W. Weldon Jr.	DNR - Fighters					11				866
23328	390	*Miss Fortune*	Lt. Wade H. Sneed Jr.	DNR - Fighters			6		4				861
23415	390	*Miss Behaven*	2Lt. George E. Starnes	DNR MID - ?			9		1				859
23426	390	*Spider Kemy Jr. Kemy II*	Lt. William W. Smith	DNR - Flak			3		7				864
25915	390	*Cash & Carry*	Lt. Robert A. McGuire Jr.	DNR - Fighters					10				860
230262	390	*Tech Supply*	Lt. John G. Winant Jr.	DNR - Fighters			4		6				862
230265	390	*Pinky*	2Lt. Frank E. Ward	DNR - Fighters	1		1		8				865
230826	390	*Short Stuff*	Capt. Robert B. Short	DNR - Fighters			4		7				863
14-Oct-43													
23338	94		Lt. Sharman M. Dodge	DNR - Fighters			5		5				791
23453	94		2Lt. Silas S. Nettles	DNR - Fighters					10				831
25901	94	*Super-stitious Al-o-ysius*	Lt. Edward S. Reed	DNR - Fighters			1		9				789
230149	94	*Spare Parts*	Lt. James A. Mullinax	DNR - Fighters					10				790
230383	94	*Brennan's Circus*	Lt. Joseph X. Brennan	DNR - Fighters							10		
230453	94	*Thunder-bird*	Lt. Roy G. Davison	DNR - Fighters	3		1		6				831
230457	94	*Jimmy Boy II Jimmy Boy III*	Lt. Thomas W. Beal	DNR - Fighters	6		1		3				792
230135	95	*Trouble Shooter*	Capt. William R. McPherson Jr.	DNR -					10				855
23348	96	*Dottie J III*	2Lt. Raymond F. Bye	DNR - Fighters	4				6				833

SERIAL	GRP	NICKNAME	PILOT	FATE	EVD	INT	KIA	KIS	POW	RTD	WIA	UNK	MACR
23430	96	*Carolina Boomer-ang*	2Lt. Jack O. Horton	DNR - Fighters	2				8				835
23528	96		Lt. Marion F. Barnhill	DNR - Fighters			1		9				834
230040	96	*Wabbit-Twacks III*	Lt. Robert H. Harmeson	DNR - Fighters	4		1		5				837
230709	96		2Lt. Coles Goodner	DNR- Fight-ers					10				836
230806	96	*V-Packet*	2Lt. John J. Scarborough	DNR - Fighters					10				832
229991	390	*We'll Never Know*	McEwin	DNR - Fighters							10		858

APPENDIX C.
AIRCRAFT MARKINGS AND 100TH
BOMBARDMENT GROUP AIRCRAFT
HISTORY

Arranged by the aircraft tail number, information is provided for those B-17s assigned to the 100th between 22 June and 14 October 1943. Beneath this entry line, details are provided to the extent possible regarding squadron assignment as well as details regarding the aircraft's operational history.

CAMOUFLAGE AND MARKINGS

CREW POSITIONS

COM P	Command Pilot
P	Pilot
CP	Co-Pilot
N	Navigator
B	Bombardier
TT	Top Turret/Flight Engineer
RO	Radio Operator
BT	Ball Turret Gunner
LW	Left Waist Gunner
RW	Right Waist Gunner
TG	Tail Gunner

OPERATIONAL EVENTS

DNR	Aircraft Did Not Return
DNR - INT	Did Not Return, interned in a neutral country
DNR MID	Did Not Return, involved in a midair collision
DNR OW	Did Not Return, last seen over water
EVD	Crew member Evaded Capture or Escaped
INT	Crew member Interned
KIA	Crewmember Killed in Action
KIS	Crew member Killed in Service (non-operational)
MACR	Missing Air Crew Report
NOPS	Non-Operational Sortie
POW	Prisoner of War
REM	Returned Early, Mechanical reasons
REO	Returned Early, other than Mechanical reasons
RES	Returned Early, scheduled spare aircraft
RFO	Returned From Operational Sortie
TOA	Take Off or Assembly Incident
WIA	Wounded in Action
WIS	Wounded or Injured in Service (noncombat)

When the 100th Bomb Group flew its first operational sortie in June 1943, all B-17s had the upper surfaces painted in Number 41 Olive Drab and the lower surfaces in Number 43 Neutral Gray. The National Insignia was an Insignia Blue circle with a White five-pointed star; positioned on the upper-left and lower-right outer wing panels as well as on both sides of the waist forward of the waist window. The only visible means of identifying a bomber is the Insignia Yellow tail number, which was applied at the factory in the United States. Often, the last three digits of the serial number were used by the unit for record keeping. Thus B-17F 42-30062 had the number 230062 on either side of the vertical stabilizer, and the number 062 was often used in unit record keeping.

With the increased operational strength, VIII Bomber Command employed the RAF Bomber Command marking system to facilitate air-to-air identification. Each squadron received a two-letter code applied forward of the waist national insignia. The codes for the 100th Bomb Group were:

349th Bomb Squadron: XR
350th Bomb Squadron: LN
351st Bomb Squadron: EP
418th Bomb Squadron: LD

Each B-17 received an individual letter, also referred to as the R/T code. These codes were placed aft of the waist window and beneath the tail number on both sides of the vertical stabilizer. At this time, all codes were painted Bluish-Gray.

On June 29, 1943, the National Insignia was officially modified by adding a White rectangle to either side of the existing National Insignia. The entire insignia was surrounded with a Red border. It is unclear when all 100th B-17s carried the modified Star and Bar.

In late June 1943, VIII Bomber Command introduced geometric symbols so that bombers of one combat wing could distinguish B-17s from another wing. For aircraft of the 4th BW, which included the 95th, 100th, and 390th Bomb Group, the symbol was a White rectangle above the serial number and on the outer upper-right wing panel. Each group received an identifying letter—which, for the 100th, was an Insignia Blue D. Also, the individual aircraft letter was applied in Yellow beneath the serial number. Shortly afterward, efforts were taken to "dull" the reflective nature of the White portions of the National Insignia and the geometric symbol with Light Gray. Some of the White areas were not repainted but carried a mottled effect. Sometime before January 1944, this practice was reversed, and White was reinstated.

On August 14, 1943, the Insignia Red border outlining the Star and Bar was replaced with Insignia Blue.

On September 13, 1943, VIII Bomber Command reorganized into three bombardment divisions, with each division subdivided by combat wings, and each wing having three bomb groups. The 100th was part of the 13th Combat Wing along with the 95th and 390th Bombardment Groups.

23229	349 BS	XR * A	Pasadena Nina	
	1-Apr-43	Accepted into Inventory		
	2-Apr-43	Delivered-Cheyenne Municipal Airport-Cheyenne, Wyoming		
	28 May-43	Dow Field-Bangor, Maine		
	30-May-43	UNITED KINGDOM		
		100 BG-Thorpe Abbotts		
	28-Jun-43	REM-#2 and 3 engines failed		
	29-Jul-43	REO-waist gunner ill		
	15-Aug-43	RES		
	16-Sep-43	RFO-Honeybourne		
	9-Oct-43	REM-#1 engine oil line broke		
	10-Oct-43	DNR-Flak and Fighters-Harskamp-The Netherlands-MACR 1021		
	P	Lt. John K. Justice	EVD	
	CP	2Lt. John F. Shields	KIA	American Lake, Washington
	B	2Lt. William C. Brothers	POW	Birmingham, Alabama
	N	2Lt. Peter (NMI) Battisti	POW	Elmira, New York
	TT	T/Sgt. John T. McDonough	POW	Newark, New Jersey
	RO	T/Sgt. Richard E. Whitlock	POW	Terre Haute, Indiana
	BT	S/Sgt. Stanley S. Stopa	POW	Niagara Falls, New York
	LW	S/Sgt. Robert E. Bergendahl	POW	Eltingville, New York
	RW	S/Sgt. Harry (NMI) Hafko	POW	Barnsboro, Pennsylvania
	TG	S/Sgt. Gaetano D. Sportelli	KIA	Bridgeport, Connecticut
23232	350 BS	LN * V	Flak Happy	
	5-Apr-43	Accepted into Inventory		
	5-Apr-43	Delivered-Cheyenne Municipal Airport-Cheyenne, Wyoming		
	27-May-43	Dow Field-Bangor, Maine		
	29-May-43	UNITED KINGDOM		
	6-Jun-43	100 BG-Thorpe Abbotts		
	25-Jun-43	RE?		
	14-Jul-43	RE?		
	25-Jul-43	REM-Engine Trouble		
	28-Jul-43	REM-#2 fuel booster out		
	17-Aug-43	DNR-Fighters-Ghedi, Italy-MACR 676		
	P	Lt. Ronald W. Hollenbeck	POW	
	CP	FO. John L. Williams	POW	
	B	2Lt. Zeak M. Buckner Jr.	POW	
	N	2Lt. Harold L. Weintraub	POW	
	TT	T/Sgt. Rush S. Mintz	POW	
	RO	T/Sgt. Emile A. Reimherr	POW	
	BT	S/Sgt. Glen H. Keirsey	POW	
	LW	S/Sgt. John Q. Pachiotti	POW	
	RW	S/Sgt. William A. Rouse	POW	
	TG	Sgt. Thomas G. Flounders	POW	
		NOTE: 100 BG original cadre, Crew 14.		

23233	350 BS	LN * R	*Our Baby*		
	2-Apr-43	Accepted into Inventory			
	6-Apr-43	Delivered-Cheyenne Municipal Airport-Cheyenne, Wyoming			
	28-May-43	Dow Field-Bangor, Maine			
		UNITED KINGDOM			
	1-Jun-43	100 BG-Thorpe Abbotts			
	10-Jul-43	REM-Syphoning gas			
	14-Jul-43	FTO-Guns out, ball turret out			
	30-Jul-43	REO-Ball Turret Gunner ill			
	9-Sep-43	REM-Oxygen failure			
	8-Oct-43	DNR-Flak-Bremen, Germany-MACR 950			

	COM P	Major Gale W. Cleven	POW	Odessa, Texas
	P	Capt. Bernard A. DeMarco	POW	Mayfield, Kansas
	CP	FO. James F. Thayer	POW	Akron, Ohio
	B	Lt. Francis C. Harper	POW	Fairbanks, Alaska
	N	Lt. John W. Downs	POW	Provo, Utah
	TT	S/Sgt. Jerome K. Ferroggiaro	POW	
	RO	T/Sgt. Thornton Stringfellow	POW	Culpeper, Virginia
	BT	S/Sgt William J. Williams	POW	
	LW	S/Sgt. William R. Woodbury	POW	Alburn, Maine
	RW	T/Sgt. Benjamin J. Barr	POW	Houston, Texas
	TG	Sgt. Harry C. Calhoun	POW	Springfield, Massachusetts
		NOTE: 100 BG original cadre, Crew 15.		

23234	351 BS	EP * E	*Little Mike*
	2-Apr-43	Accepted into Inventory	
	6-Apr-43	Delivered-Cheyenne Municipal Airport-Cheyenne, Wyoming	
	26-May-43	Dow Field-Bangor, Maine	
		UNITED KINGDOM	
	31-May-43	100 BG-Thorpe Abbotts	
	28-Jun-43	REM-Internal engine failure, engine changed.	
	10-Oct-43	Crash landed-Wattisham-flew with 390 BG.	
	13-Oct-43	Salvaged	
		NOTE: 100 BG original cadre, Crew 26.	

23237	418 BS	LD * R	*Stymie*
	5-Apr-43	Accepted into Inventory	
	5-Apr-43	Delivered-Cheyenne Municipal Airport-Cheyenne, Wyoming	
	30-May-43	Dow Field-Bangor, Maine	
		UNITED KINGDOM-Podington	
	31-May-43	100 BG-Thorpe Abbotts	
	28-Jun-43	RES	
	17-Jul-43	FTO-Flat tire on takeoff.	
	28-Jul-43	REO-Could not locate formation.	
	8-Oct-43	REM-#1 engine leaking oil.	
	10-Oct-43	DNR-Munster-Flak & Fighters-Walten, The Netherlands-MACR 1030	

	P	2Lt. John F. Stephens	POW	Brookings, South Carolina
	CP	Lt. Hoyt L. Smith	POW	Raleigh, Tennessee
	B	2Lt. William J. Moore	POW	Roanoke Rapids, North Carolina
	N	2Lt. Randolph (NMI) Grum	POW	Detroit, Michigan
	TT	T/Sgt. John (NMI) Shay	POW	Fall River, Massachusetts
	RO	T/Sgt. Carl E. Battin	POW	Burlington, Iowa
	BT	T/Sgt. Max U. Drudge	POW	Wheatfield, Indiana
	LW	S/Sgt. William F. Young	POW	Sprague, Oregon
	RW	S/Sgt. George F. Knolle	POW	Sonoma, California
	TG	S/Sgt. Casmire A. Raczynski	POW	Milwaukee, Wisconsin

23260   349 BS   XR * K   *Angel's Tit*

- 12-Apr-43   Accepted into Inventory
- 16-Apr-43   Delivered-Lowry Army Airfield-Denver, Colorado
- 0-May-43   Dow Field-Bangor, Maine
- 4-Jun-43   UNITED KINGDOM
- 9-Jun-43   100 BG-Thorpe Abbotts
- 25-Jun-43   DNR OW—Fighters—Bremen. Germany; Ditched North Sea MACR 271

P	Lt. Alonzo Adams III
CP	FO. George Z. Drech
B	Lt. Nicholas Demchak
N	2Lt. James D. Gurley
TT	T/Sgt. John K. Sullivan
RO	T/Sgt. James B. Percell
BT	S/Sgt John C. Krurich
LW	S/Sgt Edmunde J. Walker
RW	Sgt. Norman Asbornsen
TG	S/Sgt. Bryan Hutchinson

23271   351 BS   EP * L   *Nine Little Yanks and a Jerk*

- 15-Apr-43   Accepted into Inventory
- 17-Apr-43   Delivered-Denver Lowry Army Airfield-Denver, Colorado
- 27-May-43   Presque Isle Army Airfield-Presque Isle, Maine
- 28-May-43   UNITED KINGDOM
- 5-Jun-43   91 BG, 401 BS
- 5-Jul-43   100 BG-Thorpe Abbotts from 91 BG
- 6-Sep-43   RFO-Dunnmsford
- 4-Oct-43   RFO-Ford
- 10-Oct-43   FTO-Engine trouble
- 7-Mar-44   Salvaged

23279   350 BS   LN * Z   *Badger Beauty*

- 20-Apr-43   Accepted into Inventory
- 21-Apr-43   Delivered-Lowry Army Airfield-Denver, Colorado,
- 21-May-43   Dow Field-Bangor, Maine
- 29-May-43   UNITED KINGDOM
- 2-Jun-43   Podington
- 9-Jun-43   100 BG-Thorpe Abbotts
-             TRN to 25 BG
- 29-May-44   DNR-Ditched off of Dingle Island

23307   351 BS   EP * N   *Skipper*

- 1-May-43   Accepted into Inventory
- 27-May-43   Delivered-Cheyenne Municipal Airport-Cheyenne, Wyoming
- 4-Jun-43   Dow Field-Bangor, Maine
- ?-Jun-43   UNITED KINGDOM
- 9-Jun-43   100 BG-Thorpe Abbotts
- 16-Sep-43   FTO-went off the runway, bogged down
- 10-Oct-43   REM-engine ran out of oil
- 24-Jan-44   TOA-Pilot Arch J. Drummond-1 KIA, 9 WIA
- 25-Jan-44   Salvaged

23386   351 BS   EP * H   *Marie Helena*

- 1-Jun-43   Accepted into Inventory
- 1-Jun-43   Delivered-Lowry Amy Airfield-Denver, Colorado
- 7-Aug-43   Presque Isle Army Airfield-Presque Isle, Maine
- 22-Aug-43   UNITED KINGDOM
- 23-Aug-43   100 BG-Thorpe Abbotts
- 8-Oct-43   DNR-MID with FW 190-Bremen, Germany-MACR 949

P	Lt. Raymond J. Gormley	KIA		Washington, D. C.
CP	Lt. Edward J. Fox	KIA		Norfolk, Virginia
B	2Lt. William J. Heath	KIA		Newport, Washington
N	2Lt. Peter T. Motta	KIA		Woodland, California
TT	T/Sgt. Jay B. McPhee	KIA		Wayne, Michigan
RO	T/Sgt. Dale A. Von Seggern	KIA		Layfayette, Indiana
BT	S/Sgt. Donald R. Hilton	KIA		Grandview, Michigan
LW	S/Sgt. William A. Avery Jr.	KIA		Benton Harbor, Michigan
RW	S/Sgt. Charles Presley	KIA		Chapman, Alabama
TG	S/Sgt. Clay E. Rife	KIA		Kansas City, Missouri

23393	418 BS	LD * Y	*Did You Say Ten Cents?*
			Blakely's Provisional Group
			Just-A-Snappin'
	1-Jun-43	Accepted into Inventory
	2-Jun43	Delivered-Dow Field-Bangor, Maine
	1-Jul-43	Dow Field-Bangor, Maine
	4-Jul-43	UNITED KINGDOM
	5-Jul-43	100 BG-Thorpe Abbotts
	16-Sep-43	RFO-Colerne
	8-Oct-43	RFO-Bremen-Crash landed-Ludham

COM P	Major John B. Kidd	RTD	Winnetka, Illinois
P	Capt. Everett E. Blakely	RTD	Seattle, Washington
CP	Lt. Charles A. Via Jr.	WIA	
B	Lt. James R. Douglass	WIA	
N	Lt. Harry H. Crosby	RTD	Rockford, Illinois
TT	T/Sgt. Monroe B. Thornton	RTD	Newport, Tennessee
RO	T/Sgt. Edmond C. Forkner	RTD	Tilsa, Oklahoma
BT	S/Sgt. William F. McClelland	WIA	
WG	S/Sgt. Lester W Saunders	WIA	Chicago, Illinois
WG	S/Sgt. Edward S. Yevich	WIA	
TG	S/Sgt. Lyle E. Nord	RTD	Superior, Wisconsin
12-Oct-43	Salvaged
15-Oct-43	Lester W. Saunders succumbed to injuries sustained on 8 Oct-43.

23413	350 BS	LN * V	*Hard Luck!*
	8-Jun-43	Accepted into Inventory
	17-Jul-43	Delivered-Love Field-Dallas, Texas
	18Aug-43	Dow Field-Bangor, Maine
	19-Aug-43	UNITED KINGDOM
	20-Aug-43	100 BG-Thorpe Abbotts
	16-Sep-43	REO-Landed-Castle Donington
	16-Sep-43	REO-Ball turret gunner unconscious
	30-Nov 43	REM
	11-Dec-43	RES
	13-Dec-43	RES
	14-Aug-44	DNR—Flak-Ludwigshaven—MACR 7899

P	2nd Lt Donald E. Cielewich
CP	2Lt. Lenard E. Moen
N	Lt. Clifford J. Brown
B	2Lt. John C. Cochran
TT	T/Sgt. Cyrenne L. Ropson
RO	T/Sgt. Benjamin M. Baldasano
BT	S/Sgt. John L. Funkhauser

		WG	S/Sgt. Herbert G. Klepp		
		TG	S/Sgt. Henry J. Sytnik		

23433	350 BS	LN * W *Lena*		
	17-Jun-43	Accepted into Inventory		
	12-Jun-43	Delivered-Lowry Army Airfield-Denver, Colorado		
	14-Jul-43	Dow Field-Bangor, Maine		
	17-Jul-43	UNITED KINGDOM		
	18-Jul-43	100 BG-Thorpe Abbotts		
	10-Oct-43	DNR-Flak-Munster, Germany-MACR 1024		

	P	2Lt. Robert P. Kramer	KIA	Fairport, New York
	CP	2Lt. Edward F. Connelly Jr.	POW	New Rochelle, New York
	N	2Lt. Hugh S. Geiger Jr.	POW	Tallahassee, Florida
	B	2Lt. Thomas B. Casey Jr.	POW	Portland, Maine
	TT	T/Sgt. Deanne O. Todd	POW	Oakland, California
	RO	T/Sgt. James A. Watkins	POW	Princeton, Indiana
	BT	S/Sgt. Donald M. Glass	POW	Gaston, Indiana
	LW	S/Sgt. Fred B. Moore	POW	Harglinton, Texas
	RW	S/Sgt. George A. White	POW	East Liverpool, Ohio
	TG	S/Sgt. Harvey F. Hames	POW	Jamestown, New York

23452	350 BS	LN * Z		
	23-Jun-43	Accepted into Inventory		
	24-Jun-43	Delivered-Cheyenne Municipal Airport-Cheyenne, Wyoming		
	17-Aug-43	Presque Isle Army Airfield-Presque Isle, Maine		
	19-Aug-43	UNITED KINGDOM		
	20-Aug-43	100 BG-Thorpe Abbotts		
	15-Sep-43	DNR-Paris-Flak-Lt Vetter Crew St. Just, France-MACR 645		

	P	2Lt. Arthur M. Vetter	EVD	South Payne, Idaho
	CP	2Lt. Donald G. Smith	EVD	Billings, Montana
	B	2Lt. James G. Bormuth	KIA	Baltimore, Maryland
	N	2Lt. Wendell K. McConnaha	EVD	Blair, Nebraska
	TT	T/Sgt. Orval L. Parsons	POW	Ann Arbor, Michigan
	RO	T/Sgt. John M. Wagner	EVD	Newport, Pennsylvania
	BT	S/Sgt. Edward W. Fontaine	EVD	Warwick, Rhode Island
	LW	S/Sgt. Edward M. Daly	EVD	
	RW	S/Sgt. Hobart C. Trigg	EVD	Glasco, Kentucky
	TG	S/Sgt. Warren O. Lush	POW	Atlanta, Nebraska

23474	351 BS	EP * B *King Bee*		
	? Jun-43	Accepted into Inventory		
	1-Jul-43	Delivered-Lowry Army Airfield-Denver, Colorado		
	10-Aug-43	Presque Isle Army Airfield-Presque Isle, Maine		
	30-Aug-43	UNITED KINGDOM		
	1-Sep-43	100 BG-Thorpe Abbotts		
	4-Oct-43	REM-#2 prop feathered		
	20-Oct-43	REM		
	13-Nov-43	REO		
	27-Dec-43	Landing accident with 26094 and 237772 on short runway.		

23508	418 BS	LD * F *Bastard's Bungalow II (first G model at Thorpe Abbotts) Jerry Lily*		
	13-Jul-43	Accepted into Inventory		
	14-Jul-43	Delivered-Lowry Army Airfield-Denver, Colorado		
	15-Aug-43	Scott Army Airfield-Belleville, Illinois		
	24-Aug-43	UNITED KINGDOM		
	25-Aug-43	100 BG-Thorpe Abbotts		

6-Mar-44	Berlin-battle damage-Lt Ferbrach Crew			
18-Mar-44	DNR-Munic-Fighters-Lt Robert Horn-MACR 3232			

P	Lt. Robert J. Horn	POW
CP	Lt. Bart E. Mahoney	POW
B	Lt. Charles E. Connor	POW
N	Lt. Wiliam A. Newell	POW
TT	Sgt. Albert J. Shubak	POW
RO	Sgt. Kenneth H. Mueller	POW
BT	Sgt. Russell A. Priester	POW
LW	Sgt. Aubrey Slimm	POW
RW	S/Sgt. Victor T. Seabye	POW
TG	Sgt. William E. Graser	POW

23534

349 BS BS	XR * L	*Ol' Dad*
23-Jul-43	Accepted into Inventory	
24-Jul-43	Delivered-Lowry Army Airfield-Denver, Colorado	
31-Aug-43	Dyersburg Army Air Base-Halls, Tennessee	
8-Sep-43	UNITED KINGDOM	
9-Sep-43	100 BG-Thorpe Abbotts (2nd B-17G assigned to the 100 BG)	
10-Oct-43	REM-Could not keep up with formation	
27-Apr-44	DNR-Flak-Ardoye, France-:Lt Winans C. Shaddix-MACR 1692	

P	Lt Winans C. Shaddix
CP	Lt George T. Sullivan
N	Lt Cole M. Dailey
TOG	T/Sgt Frederick H. Erb
TT	T/Sgt James H. Lee
BT	S/Sgt John B. Cortelletty
LW	S/Sgt Kenneth V. Hale
RW	S/Sgt William F. Cornelius
TG	S/Sgt Hugh Hamilton

25854

418 BS	
20-Mar-43	Accepted into Inventory
23-Mar-43	Delivered-Long Beach Army Airfield-Long Beach, California
15-April-43	Kearney Air Base-Kearney, Nebraska
2-May-43	Wendover, Field-Salt Lake City, Utah
27-May-43	Dow Field-Bangor, Maine
30-May-43	100 BG-Thorpe Abbotts
13-Jul-43	303 BG-Molesworth
NOTE: 100 BG Original Crew A-1	

25860

418 BS	LD * P	*Escape Kit*
26-Mar-43	Accepted into Inventory	
30-Mar-43	Delivered-Long Beach Army Airfield-Long Beach, California	
2-Apr-43	Denver Army Airfield-Denver, Colorado	
2-May-43	Wendover Field-Salt Lake City, Utah	
17-May-43	Hill Field-Ogden, Utah	
29-May-43	Dow Field-Bangor, Maine	
1-Jun-43	UNITED KINGDOM	
2-Jun-43	100 BG-Thorpe Abbotts	
17-Aug-43	DNR-Fighters-Regensburg, Germany-MACR 675	

P	Lt. Curtis R. Biddick	KIA	Kansas City, Missouri
CP	FO. Richard L. Snyder	KIA	Davis California
B	Lt. Dan B. McKay	POW	St. Joseph, Louisiana
N	2Lt. John C. Dennis	POW	Norwich, Connecticut

	TT	T/Sgt. Lawrence E. Godbey	KIA	Radford, Virginia
	RO	T/Sgt. Robert R. DeKay	KIA	Mt. Clemens, Michigan
	BT	S/Sgt. Walter (NMI) Halunka	POW	Berwyn, Illinois
	LW	T/Sgt. Howard J. Brock	POW	Lake Odessa, Wisconsin
	RW	S/Sgt. Clarence R. Bowlin	POW	Urbana, Illinois
	TG	S/Sgt. William M. Blank	POW	Memphis, Tennessee

25861   349 BS   XR * J   *Stud Duck*
                       Laden Maiden

26-Mar-43	Accepted into Inventory
30-Mar-43	Delivered-Long Beach Army Airfield-Long Beach, California
15-Apr-43	Kearney Air Base-Kearney, Nebraska
2-May-43	Wendover Field, Salt Lake City, Utah
22-May-43	Kearney Air Base-Kearney, Nebraska
6-Jun-43	Dow Field-Bangor, Maine
7-Jun-43	UNITED KINGDOM
8-Jun-43	100 BG-Thorpe Abbotts
2 Aug-43	NOPS-Crash Landed Lt. Owen D. Roane-10 RTD
23-Sep-43	REM-Could not keep up with formation.
30-Dec-43	DNR-Ludwigshaven-Lt Leininger-Fighters Liry, France, MACR 2020

P	Lt Marvin L. Leininger	KIA
CP	Lt Albert W. Witmyer	KIA
B	Lt Charles W. Compton	EVA
N	Lt Leonard D. McChesney	EVA
TT	T/Sgt Meyer M. Weintraub	KIA
RO	T/Sgt Marshall Banta	KIA
BT	S/Sgt Nicholas J. Matulik	KIA
LW	S/Sgt James W. Parham	KIA
RW	S/Sgt Eugene F. Latimer	KIA
TG	S/Sgt Charles J McGrogan	KIA

NOTE: 100 BG original cadre, Crew A-2

25862   350 BS   LN * T   *Duration + 6*

27-May-43	Accepted into Inventory
31-Mar-43	Delivered, Long Beach Army Airfield-Long Beach, California
2-Apr-43	Lowry Air Base, Denver, Colorado
15-Apr-43	Kearney Air Base-Kearney, Nebraska
2 May-43	Wendover Field-Salt Lake City, Utah
13-May-43	Dow Field-Bangor, Maine
29-May-43	UNITED KINGDOM
30-May-43	100 BG-Thorpe Abbotts
10-Jul-43	REM-feathered propeller
25-Jul-43	DNR OW-Kiel-Flak North Sea, MACR 117

P	Capt. Richard A. Carey	POW	Long Beach, California
CP	2Lt. William J. Styles	POW	Troy, New York
B	2Lt. Willian E. Griffith Jr.	KIA	San Francisco, California
N	2Lt. Calivin H. Defevre	KIA	Chicago, Illinois
TT	T/Sgt. Lester I. Berg	KIA	Pontiac, Michigan
RO	T/Sgt. Steven S. Kopoczewski	KIA	Jersey City, New Jersey
BT	S/Sgt. Norman C. Eddy	KIA	Hinsdale, Massachusetts
LW	S/Sgt. Charles J. Mayville	KIA	Pensacola, Florida
RW	Sgt. Robert D. Lepper	POW	Oakland, California
TG	S/Sgt. Maynard T. Parsons	POW	Portland, Oregon

NOTE: 100 BG original cadre, Crew 11

25863 350 BS   LN * V   *Paddlefoot's Proxy*
           27-Mar-43   Accepted into Inventory
           31-Mar-43   Delivered-Long Beach Army Airfield-Long Beach, California
           15-Apr-43   Kearney Air Base-Kearney, Nebraska
           2-May-43   Wendover Field-Salt Lake City, Utah
           30-May-43   Dow Field-Bangor, Maine
           31-May43   UNITED KINGDOM
           1-Jun-43   100 BG-Thorpe Abbotts
           28-Jun-43   RFO-Chivener
           26-Jul-43   REM—#3 engine out
           29-Jul-43   REM—oxygen leak in ball turret
           30-Jul-43   REO—battle damage by flak
           6-feb-45   Burtonwood-Salvaged
           NOTE: 100 BG original cadre, Crew A-5

25864 351 BS   EP * A   *Piccadilly Lily*
           29-Mar-43   Accepted into Inventory
           31-Mar-43   Delivered-Long Beach Army Airfield-Long Beach, California
           15-Apr-43   Kearney Air Base-Kearney, Nebraska
           2-May-43   Wendover Field-Salt Lake City, Utah
           30-May-43   Dow Field-Bangor, Maine
           31-May-43   UNITED KINGDOM
           1-Jun-43   100 BG-Thorpe Abbotts
           10-Jul-43   REM—blown exhaust stack
           17-Jul-43   REM—could not retract landing gear
           31-Aug-43   REM-#4 engine low oil pressure
           6-Sep-43   REM—could not catch formation
           24-Sep-43   REO—battle damage
           8-Oct-43   DNR-Flak, exploded—Bremen, Germany MACR 943

COM P	Capt. Alvin L. Barker	KIA	Sherman, Texas
P	Capt. Thomas E. Murphy	KIA	Waltham, Massachusetts
CP	2Lt. Marshall F. Lee	KIA	Rock Falls, Illinois
B	Lt. Floyd C. Peterson	POW	Cloquet, Minnesota
N	Lt. Charles C. Sarabun	POW	Bridgeport, Connecticut
TT	T/Sgt. John J. Ehlen	POW	Sioux Falls, South Dakota
RO	T/Sgt. Derrel C. Piel	KIA	Hinton, Iowa
BT	S/Sgt. Reed A. Hufford	POW	Homestead, Pennsylvania
LW	S/Sgt. Gerald O. Robinson	POW	Cedar Springs, Illinois
RW	S/Sgt. Elder D. Dickerson	KIA	McAlester, Oklahoma
TG	S/Sgt. Aaron A. David	KIA	Weleetka, Oklahoma

           NOTE: 100 BG original cadre s, Crew A-5

25865 351 BS   EP * H   *Janie*
           29-Mar-43   Accepted into Inventory
           31-Mar-43   Delivered-Long Beach Army Airfield-Long Beach, California
           15-Arp-43   Kearney Air Base-Kearney, Nebraska
           2-May-43   Wendover Field-Salt Lake City, Utah
           28-May-43   Dow Field-Bangor, Maine
           31-May-43   UNITED KINGDOM
           1-Jun-43   100 BG-Thorpe Abbotts
           14-Jul-43   RES
           25-Jul-43   REM-Engine trouble
           1 Sep-43   DNR—Flak-Evreux, France MACR 686

P	Lt. Victor E. Fienup	POW	St. Louis, Missouri
CP	2Lt. Eugene V. Mulholland	EVD	Hammond, Indiana
B	2Lt. Blanton G. Barnes	POW	Blackstone, Virginia

N	Lt. Paul (NMI) Pascal	EVD	Philadelphia, Pennsylvania
TT	T/Sgt. Roy A. Evenson	POW	Portland, Oregon
RO	T/Sgt. Blanton G. Barnes	POW	Blackstone, Virginia
BT	S/Sgt. Norman D. Kreitenstein	EVD	Evansville, Indiana
LW	S/Sgt. Charles T. Daniels	KIA	Evansville, Indiana
RW	S/Sgt. Robert H. Brown	POW	
TG	Sgt. Marvin E. Miller	KIA	New York City, New York

NOTE: 100 BG original cadre, CrewA-4

25867   350 BS   LN * O   *Alice from Dallas*

31-Mar-43	Accepted into Inventory
2-Apr-43	Delivered-Long Beach Army Airfield-Long Beach, California
15-Arp-43	Kearney Air Base-Kearney, Nebraska
2-May-43	Wendover Field-Salt Lake City, Utah
27-May-43	Dow Field-Bangor, Maine
29-May-43	UNITED KINGDOM
30-May-43	100 BG-Thorpe Abbotts
14-Jul-43	REM-Biggin Hill-oxygen failure
17-ul-43	FTO
29-Jul-43	REM—tachometer out
17-Aug-43	DNR-Flak, Langerloo, Belgium MACR 678

P	Lt Roy F. Claytor	EVD	Scottsboro, Alabama
CP	2Lt Raymond J. Nutting Jr.	EVD	Piedmont, California
B	2Lt Kenneth R. Lorch	POW	St. Paul, Minnesota
N	2Lt. Oscar C. Amison Jr.	POW	Palm Beach, Florida
TT	T/Sgt. John W. Burgin	EVD	Quitman, Texas
RO	S/Sgt. William M. Quinn	EVD	Spokane, Washington
BT	Sgt. William M. Hinton	KIA	New Park, Pennsylvania
LW	S/Sgt. Clifford R. Starkey	POW	
RW	S/Sgt. Charles K. Bailey	EVD	Wynnewood, California
TG	S/Sgt. Edward A. Musante	KIA	Ansonia, Connecticut

25878   350 BS   LN * W   *Badger Beauty*

10-Apr-43	Accepted into Inventory
14-Apr-43	Delivered-Long Beach Army Airfield-Long Beach, California
22 Apr-43	Smoky Hill-Salina, Kansas
2-May-43	Wendover Field-Salt Lake City, Utah
18-May-43	Wendover Field-Salt Lake City, Utah
27-May-43	Dow Field-Bangor, Maine
29-May-43	UNITED KINGDOM
30-May-43	100 BG-Thorpe Abbotts
26-Jul-43	REM-gas leak
12-Aug-43	REM-#4 supercharger out
18-Sep-43	Gained-381 Bomb Group

NOTE: 100 BG-original cadre, Crew 18

25957   349 BS   XR * D   *Horny II*

24 May-43	Accepted into Inventory
31-My-43	Delivered-Long Beach Army Airfield-Long Beach, California
5-Jul-43	Assigned-Gore Field-Spokane, Washington
20-Jul-43	Assigned-Dow Field-Bangor, Maine
25-Jul-43	Assigned-UNITED KINGDOM
29-Jul-43	100 BG-Thorpe Abbotts
6-Sep-43	RFO—Lt. Sumner H. Reeder-KIA, 1 RTD, 2 WIA
4-Oct-43	FTO-flat tire
9-May-44	Salvaged

25997	351 BS	EP * F	*Heaven Can Wait*
	11-Jun-43	Accepted into Inventory
	16-Jun-43	Delivered-Long Beach Army Airfield-Long Beach, California
	12-Jul-43	Smoky Hill-Salina, Kansas
	16-Jul-43	Dow Field-Bangor, Maine
	?-Jul-43	Assigned-UNITED KINGDOM
	17-Jul-43	100 BG-Thorpe Abbotts
	16-Sep-43	RFO-Honiley, UK
	27-Sep-43	REM-
	30-Dec-43	30-Dec-43 DNR-Ludwigshaven-Fighters-Les Rosiers,-Lt Frances Smith MACR 02019
	P	2nd Lt. Francis P. Smith
	CP	2nd Lt. James P. Law
	N	2nd Lt. Saul Hershkowitz
	B	2nd Lt. Clyde S. Manion
	TT	T/Sgt. John T. Amery
	RO	S/Sgt. John L. Swenson
	BT	Sgt. Alvin C. Little
	LW	Sgt. John W. Runcel
	RW	Sgt. Conrad P. Stumpfig
	TG	William Wertz
26087	418 BS	LD * Z	*Royal Flush*
			Harper's Ferry
			Aske's Angels
	11-Jun-43	Accepted into Inventory
	16-Jun-43	Delivered-Long Beach Army Airfield-Long Beach, California
	19-Jul-43	Cheyenne Municipal Airport-Cheyenne, Wyoming
	4-Sep-43	UNITED KINGDOM
	5-Sep-43	100 BG-Thorpe Abbotts
	10-Oct-43	Munster Ger, battle damage, 2 men SWA, Lt. Robert Rosenthal
	11-Aug-44	DNR—Villacoublay-Flak-Menlon Lt Alf Aske Crew-MACR 08074
26094	418 BS	LD * Q
	20-Jul-43	Accepted into Inventory
	20-Jul-43	Delivered-Long Beach Army Airfield-Long Beach, California
	23-Jul-43	Cheyenne Municipal Airport-Cheyenne, Wyoming
	17-Aug-43	Dalhart Army Airfield-Dalhart, Texas
	5-Sep-43	UNITED KINGDOM
	6-Sep-43	100 BG-Thorpe Abbotts
	23-Sep-43	REM-#3 supercharger failed
	10 Oct-43	REM-#2 low oil pressure
	27-Dec-43	Landing Accident with 23474 and 237772
	31-Jan-44	Salvaged
229738	350 BS	LN * U
	6-Feb-43	Accepted into Inventory
	11-Feb-43	Delivered-Cheyenne Municipal Airport-Cheyenne, Wyoming
	23-Feb-43	Walker, Roswell, New Mexico
	28-Mar-43	Smoky Hill-Salina, Kansas
	25-Apr-43	Kearney Air Base-Kearney, Nebraska
	2-May-43	Wendover Field-Salt Lake City, Utah
	21-May-43	Kearney Air Base-Kearney, Nebraska
	27-May-43	Dow Field-Bangor, Maine
	31-May-43	UNITED KINGDOM
	1-Jun-43	Podington
	9-Jun-43	100 BG-Thorpe Abbotts
	13-Jun-43	Assigned-303 BG became The Upstairs Maid

229931	418 BS	LD *	Jaybird
	10-Mar-43	Accepted into Inventory	
	13-Mar-43	Delivered-Cheyenne Municipal Airport-Cheyenne, Wyoming	
	28-Mar-43	Casper Army Air Base-Casper, Wyoming	
	10-Apr-43	Tinker Army Airfield-Del City, Oklahoma	
	16-Apr-43	Memphis, Tennessee	
	26-Apr-43	UNITED KINGDOM	
	9-Jun-43	100 BG-Thorpe Abbotts	
	13-Jul-43	Gained by 303 BG	

229947	351 BS	EP *	Target for Tonight (To Be Confirmed)
	15-Mar-43	Accepted into Inventory	
	17-Mar-43	Delivered-Cheyenne Municipal Airport-Cheyenne, Wyoming	
	28-Mar-43	Walla Walla, Washington	
	13-Apr-43	Smoky Hill-Salina, Kansas	
	4-May-43	Selfridge Field-Harrison Township, Michigan	
	6-May-43	Dow Field-Bangor, Maine	
	7-May-43	UNITED KINGDOM	
	8-May-43	Podington	
	9-Jun-43	100 BG-Thorpe Abbotts	
	6-Jul-43	TRN-91 BG	
	12-Jul-45	Returned to Zone of the Interior	
	14-Jul-45	Cincinnati	

229986	349 BS	XR * Q	Blue Bird "K"
	20-Mar-43	Accepted into Inventory	
	23-Mar-43	Delivered-Denver Army Airfield-Denver, Colorado	
	7-Apr-43	Cheyenne Municipal Airport-Cheyenne, Wyoming	
	16-Apr-43	Kearney Air Base-Kearney, Nebraska	
	2-May-43	Wendover Field-Salt Lake City, Utah	
	22-May-43	Kearney Air Base-Kearney, Nebraska	
	27-May-43	Baer Field-Fort Wayne, Indiana	
	3-Jun-43	Dow Field-Bangor, Maine	
	5-Jun-43	UNITED KINGDOM	
		100 BG-Thorpe Abbotts	
	25-Jun-43	25-Jun-43 DNR-OW Bremen-Fighters-North Sea MACR 269	

P	Capt. Oran E. Petrich	KIA	Sturgish, South Dakota
CP	2Lt. Bluford B. Mullins Jr.	KIA	Greenville, Mississippi
B	2Lt. Stanley O. Morrison	KIA	Lafayette, Indiana
N	Lt. Edward N. Jones	KIA	Shawnee, Oklahoma
TT	T/Sgt. Max P. Brim	KIA	Osceola, Iowa
RO	T/Sgt. Edward I. Zerblis	KIA	Melrose Park, Illinois
BT	S/Sgt. Henry H. Rutherford Jr.	KIA	
LW	S/Sgt. Joseph D. Bien	KIA	
RW	S/Sgt. Pete S. Villobes	KIA	Banning, California
TG	S/Sgt. James M. Strong Jr.	KIA	

230002	349 BS	XR * F	The WAAC Hunter
			Damifino
	24-Mar-43	Accepted into Inventory	
	1 Apr-43	Delivered-Cheyenne Municipal Airport-Cheyenne, Wyoming	
	15-Apr-43	Kearney Air Base-Kearney, Nebraska	
	17-Apr-43	Gore Field-Spokane, Washington	
	28-Apr-43	Hamilton Field-Novato, California	
	2-May-43	Wendover Field-Salt Lake City, Utah	
	12-May-43	Hill Field-Ogden, Utah	
	19-May-43	Wendover Field-Salt Lake City, Utah	

22-May-43 Kearney Air Base-Kearney, Nebraska
31-May-43 Dow Field-Bangor, Maine
2-Jun-43   UNITED KINGDOM
9-Jun-43   100 BG-Thorpe Abbotts
28-Jun-43 RFO-Lt Glenn Van Noy
10-Jul-43 FTO
14-Jul-43 REM-#4 engine rough
15-Aug-43 RES
17-Aug-43 FTR-Regensburg-Lt Shotland Crew, Fighters, Roxheim Ger MACR 00680

P	Lt. Henry P. Shotland	POW
CP	Lt. Charles R. Thompson	POW
B	Lt. William J. Harrison	POW
N	Lt. Thomas j. Doran	POW
TT	T/Sgt. Lloyd D. Field	POW
RO	T/Sgt. Edward M. Kussman	POW
BT	S/Sgt. Lawrence E. Capdeville	POW
LW	S/Sgt. John J. Keegan	POW
RW	S/Sgt. Roy L. Butler	POW
TT	S/Sgt. Foster Compton	POW

230023   349 BS   XR * M   *Forever Yours*
26-Mar-43 Accepted into Inventory
1-Apr-43   Delivered-Lowry Air Base-Denver, Colorado
27-Apr-43 Hill Field-, Ogden, Utah
19-May-43 Dow Field-Bangor, Maine
20-May-43 Presque Isle Army Airfield-Presque Isle, Maine
26-May-43 Geiger AAF-Spokane, Washington
28-May-43 Presque Isle Army Airfield-Presque Isle, Maine
4 Jun-43   UNITED KINGDOM
5-Jun-43   100 BG-Thorpe Abbotts
24 Jul-43 REM-#1 engine out
30-Jul-43 REO—tail gunner ill
19-Aug-43 RES
16-Sep-43 RFO-Exeter
26-Sep-43 REM—oxygen leak
4-Oct-43   REM—feathered prop
9-Oct-43   REM—lost ball turret door
10-Oct-43 DNR-Flak & Fighters, Munster, Germany—MACR 1022

P	2Lt. Edward G. Stork	POW	Ozone Park, New York
CP	2Lt. John S. Minerich Jr.	POW	Keewatin, Minnesota
B	2Lt. Arthur C. Twitchell Jr.	POW	Westhampton Beach, New York
N	2Lt. John J. Gibbons	KIA	Philadelphia, Pennsylvania
TT	T/Sgt. Laurence (NMI) Willey	POW	Bridgeville, Delaware
RO	T/Sgt. Stefan C. Palmer	KIA	Salem, Massachusetts
BT	S/Sgt. Paul M. Caveny	POW	Springfield, Illinois
LW	S/Sgt. Douglas C. Brown	POW	Bronx, New York
RW	S/Sgt. Gordon W. Shields	POW	Hudson Falls, New York
TG	S/Sgt. Ira G. Tuner	POW	Windon, Minnesota

230035   349 BS   XR * H   *Torchy*
28-Mar-43 Accepted into Inventory
3-Apr-43   Delivered-Cheyenne Municipal Airport-Cheyenne, Wyoming
15-Apr-43 Kearney Air Base-Kearney, Nebraska
4-May-43   Wendover Field-Salt Lake City, Utah
11-May-43 Hill Field-Ogden, Utah
16-May-43 Wendover Field-Salt Lake City, Utah

30-May-43	Dow Field-Bangor, Maine		
1-Jun-43	UNITED KINGDOM		
2-Jun-43	100 BG-Thorpe Abbotts, Gained from 94th Bomb Group		
24-Jul-43	REM-Oil cap loose		
31-Aug-43	REM-#4 engine rough		
3-Sep-43	DNR-Paris-Flak-Fighters instead of mid air		

P	Lt. Charles B. Winkelman	EVD	Des Plaines, Illinois
CP	2Lt. Ralph. D. Smith	EVD	London, Ohio
B	H. M. Harris	EVD	Elvde, New York
N	WIliam H. Booth	EVD	William H. Booth
TT	Thomas E. Combs	EVD	Chattanooga, Tennessee
RO	T/Sgt Jean E. Ray	POW	Newton, Iowa
BT	S/Sgt. Thomas L. Cuccaro	POW	New York City, New York
LW	S/Sgt. Michael F. Darcy	EVD	East Norwalk, Connecticut
RW	Sgt. Alfred J. Zeoli	POW	East Norwalk, Connecticut
TG	Ennis M. Bankhead	KIA	Paris Texas
	NOTE: 100 BG original cadre Crew 4		

230038   349 BS   XR * D   *Bar Fly*

28-Mar-43	Accepted into Inventory		
2-Apr-43	Delivered-Cheyenne Municipal Airport-Cheyenne, Wyoming		
15-Apr-43	Kearney Air Base-Kearney, Nebraska		
4-May-43	Wendover Field-Salt Lake City, Utah		
12-May-43	Hill Field-Ogden, Utah		
16-May-43	Wendover Field, Salt Lake City, Utah		
22-May-43	Kearney Air Base-Kearney, Nebraska		
27-May-43	Dow Field-Bangor, Maine		
29-May-43	UNITED KINGDOM		
30-May-43	100 BG-Thorpe Abbotts		
25-Jun-43	DNR-OW-Fighters—North Sea-MACR 270		

P	Lt. Paul J. Schmalenbach	KIA	Philadelphia, Pennsylvania
CP	FO. George W. Cox	KIA	Ranger, Texas
B	2Lt. Jack L. Clark	KIA	Houston, Texas
N	Lt. John F. Brown	POW	Oakland, California
TT	T/Sgt. Eugene M. Beck	KIA	Chicago, Illinois
RO	T/Sgt. Frank J. Podbielski	POW	Cleveland, Ohio
BT	S/Sgt. Norman C. Goodman	POW	Bradford, Massachusetts
LW	Sgt. Anthony J. Russo	KIA	College Point, New York
RW	S/Sgt. William C. Lucas	POW	Tulsa, Oklahoma
TG	S/Sgt. Lewis W. Priegal	KIA	Aurora, Illinois

230042   349 BS   XR * L   *Oh Nausea!*

28-Mar-43	Accepted into Inventory		
2-Apr-43	Delivered-Cheyenne Municipal Airport-Cheyenne, Wyoming		
15-Apr-43	Kearney Air Base-Kearney, Nebraska		
2-May-43	Wendover Field-Salt Lake City, Utah		
12-May-43	Hill Field, Ogden-Utah		
19-May-43	Wendover Field-Salt Lake City, Utah		
22-May-43	Kearney Air Base-Kearney, Nebraska		
29-May-43	Patterson Air Base-Dayton, Ohioi		
3-Jun-43	Detroit, Michigan		
6-Jun-43	Dow Field-Bangor, Maine		
-Jun-43	UNITED KINGDOM		
9-Jun-43	100 BG-Thorpe Abbotts		
17-Aug-43	DNR-OW Mechanical-Mediterranean	MACR 682	

P	Lt. Glen S. Van Noy	POW	Chelsea, Oklahoma
CP	2Lt. James B. Evans	POW	Bronx, North Carolina
N	Lt. Kenneth G. Allen	POW	Richmond, Maryland
TT	T/Sgt. William R. Stewart	POW	Stinesville, Indiana
RO	S/Sgt. James D. Gibson	POW	Des Moines, Iowa
BT	S/Sgt. Joe F. Hruskocy	POW	Whiting, Indiana
LW	T/Sgt. William W. Crab	POW	Madison, Wisconsin
RW	Col. William W. Kennedy	POW	
TG	S/Sgt. Samuel J. Cusmano	POW	Battle Creek, Michigan

NOTE: 100 BG original cadre, Crew 7

230047 350 BS LN * Q *Sweater Girl*

30-Mar-43	Accepted into Inventory
3-Apr-43	Delivered-Cheyenne Municipal Airport-Cheyenne, Wyoming
15-Apr-43	Kearney Air Base-Kearney, Nebraska
5-May-43	Hill Field-Ogden, Utah
1-May-43	Wendover Field-Salt Lake City, Utah
21-May-43	Kearney Air Base-Kearney, Nebraska
28-May-43	Dow Field-Bangor, Maine
1-Jun-43	UNITED KINGDOM
2-Jun-43	100 BG-Thorpe Abbotts
10-Oct-43	DNR—Munster, debris from a mid-air collsion between a Bf-109 and 230723

P	Lt. Richard B. Atchison Jr.	POW	Madera, California
CP	2Lt. Willard (NMI) Secor	KIA	Lexington, Massachusetts
B	2Lt. Sol (NMI) Goldstein	POW	Bronx, new York
N	2Lt. Kenneth (NMI) Baron	POW	Rochester, New York
TT	T/Sgt. Russell W. Bennett	POW	Anita, Wiscnsin
RO	T/Sgt. Elder E. Lisch	KIA	Appleton, Wisconsin
BT	S/Sgt. Clarence A. Coombs	KIA	Lisbon. Maine
LW	S/Sgt. Westley M. Field	KIA	Lexington, Massachusetts
RW	S/Sgt. Elliot O. Preble	KIA	Newburyport, Massachusetts
TG	S/Sgt. Van T. Write	POW	Phoenix, Arizona

230050 350 BS LN * X *Judy E*

30-Mar-43	Accepted into Inventory
3-Apr-43	Delivered-Cheyenne Municipal Airport-Cheyenne, Wyoming
15-Apr-43	Kearney Air Base-Kearney, Nebraska
2-May-43	Wendover Field-Salt Lake City, Utah
15-May	Hill Field—Ogden-Utah
18-May-43	Wendover Field-Salt Lake City, Utah
23-May-43	Kearney Air Base-Kearney, Nebraska
28-May-43	Dow Field-Bangor, Maine
28-May-43	UNITED KINGDOM
29-May-43	100 BG-Thorpe Abbotts
10-Jul-43	DNR-Flak & Fighters, Dieppe, France-MACR 268

P	Lt. Charles L. Duncan	POW
CP	2Lt Archibald L. Robertson	EVD
B	Lt. William H. Forbes	POW
N	2Lt. Oliver M. Chiesl	POW
TT	T/Sgt. Ernest DeLosSantos	POW
RO	Sgt. Edmund A. Oliver	POW
BT	S/Sgt. Bernard I. Hanover	POW
LW	S/Sgt. Gene F. Frank	POW
RW	Sgt. Parrish (NMI) Reynolds	EVD
TG	S/Sgt. William D. Whitley	POW

230051   351 BS   EP * J   *Nevada Wildcat*
          30-Mar-43   Accepted into Inventory
          3-Apr-43   Delivered-Cheyenne Municipal Airport-Cheyenne, Wyoming
          15-Apr-43   Kearney Air Base-Kearney, Nebraska
          2-May-43   Wendover Field-Salt Lake City, Utah
          15-May-43   Hill Field-Ogden, Utah
          18-May-43   Wendover Field-Salt Lake City, Utah
          28-May-43   Dow Field-Bangor, Maine
          31-May-43   UNITED KINGDOM
          1-Jun-43   100 BG-Thorpe Abbotts
          4-Jul-43   DNR-LaPallice-Mechanical—Il D'Olean, France MACR 685

          P   Lt. Robert C. Pearson   POW
          CP   2Lt. Melville G. Boyd Jr.   POW
          B   2Lt. John L. Dunbar   EVD
          N   Lt. Bruce T. Rinker   POW
          TT   T/Sgt. Jack M. Goss   POW   Bar Harbor, Maine
          RO   T/Sgt Randall G. Villa   POW   Los Angeles, California
          BT   S/Sgt. Everett J. Moore   POW
          LW   S/Sgt. John T. Westwood   POW   Munson, Pennsylvania
          RW   S/Sgt. Lonnie B. Rutledge   POW   Pendleton, Indiana
          TG   S/Sgt. Albert N. Purcell   POW   Greenfield, Oklahoma

230057   351 BS   EP * D   *Raunchy*
          31-Mar-43   Accepted into Inventory
          5-Apr-43   Delivered-Cheyenne Municipal Airport-Cheyenne, Wyoming
          15-Apr-43   Kearney Air Base-Kearney, Nebraska
          2-May-43   Wendover Field-Salt Lake City, Utah
          15-May-43   Hill Field-Ogden, Utah
          18-May-43   Wendover Field-Salt Lake City, Utah
          23-May-43   Kearney Air Base-Kearney, Nebraska
          28-May-43   Dow Field-Bangor, Maine
          31-May-43   UNITED KINGDOM
          9-Jun-43   100 BG-Thorpe Abbotts
          14-Jul-43   REM-Could not keep up with formation
          29-Jul-43   RES
          6-Sep-43   DNR-Stuttgart-INT, Fighters, Lake Constance, Switzerland-MACR 689

          P   Capt Sam R. Turner   INT   Orlando, Florida
          CP   Lt. William R. Freund   INT   Syracuse, New York
          B   Lt. Vance R. Bosdwell   INT   McMinnville, Oregon
          N   Lt. Morris (NMI) Weinberg   INT   Indianapolis, Indiana
          TT   T/Sgt Harold W. Smith   INT   Coklumbus, Ohio
          RO   T/Sgt. Carmine A. Gallo   INT   Brooklyn, New York
          BT   S/Sgt. Joseph F. Maloney   KIA   Boston, Massachusetts
          LW   Sgt/es E. Speakman   INT   Jonesboro, Arkansas
          RW   S/Sgt. Carter F. Thornton   INT   Elk City, Idaho
          TG   S/Sgt. DeWitt J. Weir   INT   San Antonio, Texas

230059   351 BS   EP * G   *Barker's Burdens*
          31-Mar-43   Accepted into Inventory
          5-Apr-43   Delivered-Cheyenne Municipal Airport-Cheyenne, Wyoming
          16-Apr-43   Kearney Air Base-Kearney, Nebraska
          2-May-43   Wendover Field-Salt Lake City, Utah
          16-May-43   Hill Field-Ogden, Utah
          21-May-43   Wendover Field-Salt Lake City, Utah
          28-May-43   Dow Field-Bangor, Maine

	31-May-43	UNITED KINGDOM
	9-Jun-43	100 BG-Thorpe Abbotts
	24-Aug-43	FTO-Lt. Alvin Barker.
	3-Sep-43	FTR-Paris-Hit by debris and exploded MACR 685

P	Lt. Charles W. Floyd Jr.	KIA	Memphis, Tennessee
CP	Lt. Jack C. Boyd	KIA	Indianapolis, Indiana
B	Lt. Frank C. Coon	KIA	Stilwell, Oklahoma
N	Lt. Robert M. Rosenburg	POW	Flushing, New York
TT	T/Sgt. Ohn M. Neal	KIA	Madison, Indiana
RO	T/Sgt. Theodore W. Price	KIA	Granville, Indiana
BT	S/Sgt. Earl (NMI) Griggs	KIA	Cameron, New Mexico
LW	Lt. Peter J. Theodore	KIA	Orange, New Jersey
RW	S/Sgt. Dale P. Huffer	KIA	Warsaw, Indiana
TG	S/Sgt. John K. Williams	KIA	Miseck, Wisconsin

230061 418 BS LD * Q *Wolff Pack*
Just-A-Snappin'

	3-Apr-43	Accepted into Inventory
	6-Apr-43	Delivered-Cheyenne Municipal Airport-Cheyenne, Wyoming
	15-Apr-43	Kearney Air Base-Kearney, Nebraska
	2-May-43	Wendover Field-Salt Lake City, Utah
	22-May-43	Kearney Air Base-Kearney, Nebraska
	16-May-43	Hill Field-Ogden, Utah
	30-May-43	Dow Field-Bangor, Maine
	1-Jun-43	UNITED KINGDOM
	9-Jun-43	100 BG-Thorpe Abbotts
	14-Jul-43	REM-Runaway prop
	10-Oct-43	REM-Could not test fire guns
	28-Jun-44	Returned Zone of the Interior
	17-Apr-45	Assigned-Brookley
		NOTE: 100 BG original cadre Crew 35

230062 418 BS LD * O *Bastard's Bungalow*
Terry n' Ten
T.N.T.

	3-Apr-43	Accepted into Inventory
	4-Jun-43	Delivered
	6-Apr-43	Cheyenne Municipal Airport-Cheyenne, Wyoming
	15-Apr-43	Gore Field-Spokane, Washington
	16-Apr-43	Kearney Air Base-Kearney, Nebrska
	2-May-43	Wendover Field-Salt Lake City, Utah
	18-May-43	Hill Field-Ogden, Utah
	22-May-43	Kearney Air Base-Kearney, Nebrska
	30-May-43	Dow Field-Bangor, Maine
	1-Jun-43	UNITED KINGDOM
	9-Jun-43	100 BG-Thorpe Abbotts
	22-Jun-43	RFO-Shipdam
	28-Jul-43	REO—At 6,000 feet parachute in nose area opened
	12-Aug-43	REM—Engine trouble
	9-Sep-43	REM—Supercharger went out
	16-Sep-43	RFO—Castle Donington
	26-Sep-43	REM—2 engines por governor out.
	4-Oct-43	REM-#1 engine oil leak, low oil pressure
	8-Oct-43	REM—3 generators failed
	9-Octo-43	FTO—bogged down off perimeter
	10-Feb-44	DNR—Brunswick-Fighters; 1 KIA, 9 POW,-MACR 2383

P	Lt. Arthur E. Scoggins	
CP	2nd Lt. Leslie R Patterson	
B	2nd Lt. William J. Cooney	
N	2nd Lt. Edward O. Davis	
TT	T/Sgt. William H. Queale	
RO	T/Sgt. Phillip Sheinfield	
BT	S/Sgt. Edward R. Gonzales	
LW	S/Sgt. Joseph F. Holp	
RW	S/Sgt. Earl B. Rutherford	
TG	S/Sgt. Willis H. Ray	

230063 418 BS   LD * X   *Picklepuss*

2-Apr-43	Accepted into Inventory
5-Apr-43	Delivered-Cheyenne Municipal Airport-Cheyenne, Wyoming
15-Apr-43	Kearney Air Base-Kearney, Nebraska
2-May-43	Wendover Field-Salt Lake City, Utah
22-May-43	Kearney Air Base-Kearney, Nebraska
29-May-43	Dow Field-Bangor, Maine
1-Jun-43	UNITED KINGDOM
2-Jun-43	388 BG, 561 BS-Paddlefoot
9-Jun-43	100 BG-Thorpe Abbotts
10-Jul-43	REO-Short one parachute
14-Jul-43	REM-Supercharger failed
25-Jul-43	REM-Turret and radio out
26-Jul-43	REM-Engine and radio out
29-Jul-43	REM-Top turret trouble
17-AUG-43	DNR-Regensburg-Fighters Exploded, Schmalgraf, ? MACR 677
	"Wheels Down Crew" Legend.

P	Capt. Robert M. Knox	KIA	Philadelphia, Pennsylvania
CP	Lt. John O. Whitaker	KIA	Wheeling, West Virginia
B	Lt. Edwin F. Tobin	POW	Newberry, California
N	Lt. Ernest E. Warsaw	POW	Chicago, Illinois
TT	T/Sgt. Glover E. Barney	POW	Portland, Oregon
RO	T/Sgt. Walter (NMI) Paulsen	POW	Belleville, New Jersey
BT	S/Sgt. Fank W. Tychewicz	KIA	Chicago, Illinois
LW	S/Sgt. Alexander W. Markowski	KIA	Utica, New York
RW	S/Sgt. Henry A. Norton	KIA	Enterprise, Alabama
TG	S/Sgt. Joseph F. Lospada	KIA	Buffalo, New York

230064 418 BS   LD * T   *Wild Cargo*

4-Apr-43	Accepted into Inventory
5-Apr-43	Delivered-Cheyenne Municipal Airport-Cheyenne, Wyoming
15-Apr-43	Kearney Air Base-Kearney, Nebraska
2-May-43	Wendover Field-Salt Lake City, Utah
22-May-43	Hill Field-Ogden, Utah
30-May-43	Dow Field-Bangor, Maine
1-Jun-43	UNITED KINGDOM
9 Jun-43	100 BG-Thorpe Abbotts
6-Sep-43	REM-oxygen leak9
9-Sep-43	REM-Supercharge went out
16-Sep-43	DNR-Bordeaux/LaPallice-Fighters—Ditched-MACR 647

P	Lt. Robert H. Wolff	POW	Verdes Estates, California
CP	Lt. Charles H. Stuart	POW	Shreveport, Louisiana
B	Lt. Frederic G. White	POW	Florence, Arizona
N	Lt. Lawrence K. McDonnell	POW	Seattle, Washington

TT	T/Sgt. Carl T. Simons	POW	Addington, Oklahoma
RO	T/Sgt. Ira F. Bardman	POW	Greenelane, Pennsylvania
BT	S/Sgt. William J. Casebot	POW	Osborn, Ohio
LW	S/Sgt. Arthur H. Eggleston	POW	New London, Connecticut
RW	S/Sgt. Willis F. Brown	POW	Maple Lake, Minnesota
TG	S/Sgt. Alfred M. Clark	POW	Charlton, Massachusetts

NOTE: 100 BG original cadre, Crew 23

230066 418 BS   LD * U   *Mugwump*

2-Apr-43	Accepted into Inventory
6-Apr-43	Delivered-Cheyenne Municipal Airport-Cheyenne, Wyoming
14-Apr-43	Gore Field-Spokane, Washington
16-Apr-43	Kearney Air Base-Kearney, Nebraska
2-May-43	Wendover Field-Salt Lake City, Utah
16-May-43	Hill Field-Ogden, Utah
22-May-43	Kearney Air Base-Kearney, Nebraska
30-Mau-43	Dow Field-Bangor, Maine
Jun-43	UNITED KINGDOM
2-Jun-43	Andrews Field-96 BG
9-Jun-43	100 BG-Thorpe Abbotts
17-Aug-43	Regensburg,Capt Cruickshank/Maj Egan Crew-Left in Africa
TBD	Aphrodite Project
30-Oct-44	-DNR-On Aphrodite Mission-Heligoland Island-U-Boat Pens, crashed in Sweden

230068 350 BS   LN * P   *Phartzac*

2-Apr-43	Accepted into Inventory
5-Apr-43	Delivered-Cheyenne Municipal Airport-Cheyenne, Wyoming
10-Apr-43	Gore Field-Spokane, Washington
15-Apr-43	Kearney Air Base-Kearney, Nebraska
2-May-43	Wendover Field-Salt Lake City, Utah
13-May-43	Hill Field-Ogden, Utah
23-Mau-43	Dow Field-Bangor, Maine
May 43	UNITED KINGDOM
29-May-43	Podington
9-Jun-43	100 BG—Thorpe Abbotts
28-Jun-43	RES
4-Jul-43	REM-Oxygen system out
?Jul-43	TRN 388 BG, 561 BS
19-Aug-43	DNR—Flak & Fighters, Lt. Ben Howe crew-388th BG

NOTE: 100 BG original cadre, Crew 13.

230070 350 BS   LN * S   *Tweedle-O-Twil*

2-Apr-43	Accepted into Inventory
6-Apr-43	Delivered-Cheyenne Municipal Airport-Cheyenne, Wyoming
15 Apr-43	Kearney Air Base-Kearney, Nebraska
-May-43	Hamilton Field-Novato, California
-May-43	Kearney Air Base-Kearney, Nebraska
-May-43	Dow Field-Bangor, Maine
—Jun-43	Podington
9-Jun-43	100 BG-Thorpe Abbotts
17-Aug-43	DNR-Regensburg,-Fighters MACR 0679

P	Lt. Ronald W. Braley	POW	Pasadena, California
CP	2Lt. Walter H. Trenchard	POW	New Orleans, Louisiana
B	Lt. Thomas D. Carlton	POW	Atlanta, Georgia
N	2Lt. John E. Fawcett	POW	Orville, Ohio
TT	T/Sgt. Joseph E. McGuire	POW	Seattle, Washington
RO	T/Sgt. James R. Blair	KIA	Terrace, Pennsylvania

BT	S/Sgt. Phil W. Ong	POW	Madison City, Missouri
LW	S/Sgt. Donald G. Ruggles	POW	Sabaraton, Iowa
RW	S/Sgt. Charles C. Grissom	POW	Malvern, Arkansas
TG	Sgt. Elmo E. White	POW	Coahoma, Texas

NOTE: 100 BG original cadre, Crew 16.

230071   418 BS

Brady's Crash Wagon
Skipper

2-Apr-43	Accepted into Inventory
6-Apr-43	Delivered
15-Apr-43	Cheyenne Municipal Airport-Cheyenne, Wyoming
2-May-43	Kearney Air Base-Kearney, Nebraska
21-May-43	Wendover Field-Salt Lake City, Utah
22-May-43	Hill Field-Ogden, Utah
30-May-43	Kearney Air Base-Kearney, Nebraska
9-Jun-43	Dow Field-Bangor, Maine
12-Jun-43	Gained by 96 BG
18-Apr-44	Crashed Landed,Salvaged with 96th BG

NOTE: 100 BG original cadre, Crew 32

230080   351 BS   EP * F   *High Life*

5-Apr-43	Accepted into Inventory
7-Apr-43	Delivered-Cheyenne Municipal Airport-Cheyenne, Wyoming
16-Apr-43	Kearney Air Base-Kearney, Nebraska
3-May-43	Westover—Chicopee, Massachusetts
16-May-43	Wendover Field-Salt Lake City, Utah
23-May-43	Kearney Air Base-Kearney, Nebraska
?-May-43	Dow Field-Bangor, Maine
31-May-43	UNITED KINGDOM
9-Jun-43	100 BG-Thorpe Abbotts
5-Jul-43	REM-prop feathered
17-Aug-43	DNR-Regensburg-INT-Fighters-Dubendorf, Switzerland

NOTE: 100 BG original cadre, Crew 19

P	Lt. Donald K. Oakes	INT	Riverside, California
CP	FO. Joseph C. Harper	INT	Brownwood, Texas
B	2Lt. Lloyd A. Hammarlund Jr.	INT	New York City, New York
N	2Lt. Hiram E. Harris Jr.	INT	Billings, Montana
TT	T/Sgt. George W. Elder	INT	
RO	T/Sgt. James P. Scott Jr.	INT	
BT	S/Sgt. Leslie D. Nadeau	INT	
LW	S/Sgt. Vincent E. McGrath	INT	
RW	S/Sgt. Nolan D. Stevens	INT	
TG	S/Sgt. Leonard P. Goyer	INT	

230086   351 BS   EP * B   *Black Jack*

5-Apr-43	Accepted into Inventory
16-Apr-43	Delivered-Cheyenne Municipal Airport-Cheyenne, Wyoming
2-May-43	Kearney Air Base-Kearney, Nebraska
16-May-43	Wendover Field-Salt Lake City, Utah
23-May-43	Kearney Air Base-Kearney, Nebraska
26-May-43	Dow Field-Bangor, Maine
1-jun-43	UNITED KINGDOM
9-Jun-43	100 BG-Thorpe Abbotts
17-Aug-43	Regensburg-Lt Victory Fienup Crew.
23-Sep-43	Salvaged

NOTE: 100 BG Original Crew 21

230087   351 BS   EP * M   *Shack Rat*

5-Apr-43	Accepted into Inventory
8-Apr-43	Delivered-Cheyenne Municipal Airport-Cheyenne, Wyoming
16-Apr-43	Kearney Air Base-Kearney, Nebraska
23-Apr-43	Hamilton Field-Novato, California
12-May-43	Wendover Field-Salt Lake City, Utah
23-May-43	Kearney Air Base-Kearney, Nebraska
31-May-43	Dow Field-Bangor, Maine
10-Jun-43	UNITED KINGDOM
11-Jun-43	Thorpe Abbotts
3-Sep-43	RRO-Took late could not catch formation
16-Sep-43	RFO Exeter
10-Oct-43	DNR-Flak & Fighters-Munster, Gremany-MACR 1020

P	2Lt. Maurice E. Beatty	KIA	Cove, Ohio
CP	2Lt. James B. Dabney Jr.	POW	Los Angeles, California
B	2Lt. Reid E. Griffiths	KIA	Salt Lake City, Utah
N	2Lt. Grady (NMI) Moyle	KIA	Albermarle, North Carolina
TT	T/Sgt. George C. Burgess	KIA	Richmond, Virginia
RO	T/Sgt. Alfred (NMI) Loguidice	KIA	Newburgh, New Jersey
BT	S/Sgt. Morton (NMI) Levine	KIA	Sommerville, New Jersey
LW	S/Sgt. Edward C. Karamol	POW	Toledo, Ohio
RW	S/Sgt. Angelo J. Licato	KIA	Brooklyn, New York
TG	S/Sgt. Smith J. Young	KIA	Newdale, North Carolina

230088   349 BS   XR * E   *Squawkin Hawk*

5-Apr-43	Accepted into Inventory
8-Apr-43	Delivered-Cheyenne Municipal Airport-Cheyenne, Wyoming
16-Apr-43	Kearney Air Base-Kearney, Nebraska
2-May-43	Wendover Field-Salt Lake City, Utah
12-May-43	Hill Field-Ogden, Utah
18-May-43	Wendover Field-Salt Lake City, Utah
22-May-43	Kearney Air Base-Kearney, Nebraska
27-May-43	Dow Field—Bangor, Maine
29-May-43	UNITED KINGDOM
9-Jun-43	100 BG-Thorpe Abbotts
17-Aug-43	RES
5-Nov-43	RFO—William R. Flesh-2 EVD, 1 KIA, 4 POW, 2 RTD.
17-May-44	RZOI (First 100 BG B-17 to complete 50 mission)
13-Dec-45	Walnut Ridge, Arkansas
	NOTE: 100 BG original cadre, Crew 9

230089   351 BS   EP * K   *Sunny*

7-Apr-43	Accepted into Inventory
9-Apr-43	Delivered Cheyenne Municipal Airport-Cheyenne, Wyoming
13-Apr-43	Gore Field-Spokane, Washington
22-Apr-43	Kearney Air Base-Kearney, Nebraska
30-Apr-43	Denver Lowry Army Airfield-Denver, Colorado Denver
2-May-43	Wendover Field-Salt Lake City, Utah
15-May-43	Hill Field-Ogden, Utah
28-May-43	
31-May-43	UNITED KINGDOM
9-Jun-43	100 BG-Thorpe Abbotts
3-Sep-43	DNR-Paris-Flak struck 230089 Beaumont, France-MACR 684

P	Lt. Richard C. King
CP	FO. George D. Brykalski
B	Lt. Howard H. Hovde

N	Lt. Ernest Anderson			
TT	T/Sgt. Trafford L. Curry			
RO	T/Sgt. Robert L. McKnight.			
BT	S/Sgt. Rudolph H. Harms			
LW	S/Sgt. James M. Sides			
RW	S/Sgt. Heber Hogge			
TG	S/Sgt. Donald E. Wise			

230090   **349 BS**   XR * B   *El P'sstofo*
                                             Mad House

6-Apr-43	Accepted into Inventory
8-Apr-43	Delivered-Cheyenne Municipal Airport-Cheyenne, Wyoming
16-Apr-43	Kearney Air Base-Kearney, Nebraska
2-May-43	Wendover Field-Salt Lake City, Utah
12-May-43	Hill Field-Ogden, Utah Hill
16-May-43	Wendover Field-Salt Lake City, Utah
22-May-43	Kearney Air Base-Kearney, Nebraska
28-May-43	Dow Field-Bangor, Maine
1-Jun-43	UNITED KINGDOM
2-Jun-43	385 BG—Great Ashfield
2-Jun-43	100 BG-Thorpe Abbotts
9-Jun-43	
23-Sep-43	REM-#3 Engine Failed
10-Oct-43	DNR-Munster-Fighters, MACR 1020

P	Lt. Winton L. MacCarter	POW	Holland Patent, New York
CP	FO. Daniel (NMI) Barna	POW	Clifton, New Jersey
B	Lt. George H. Ziegler	POW	Laramie, Wyoming
N	Lt. Harold L. Weachter	POW	Bartonville, Illinois
TT	T/Sgt. Jack C.Rogers	POW	Lynchburg, Virginia
RO	T/Sgt. Alexander F. Sawicki	POW	Three Rivers, Massachusetts
BT	T/Sgt. Robert W. Sandy	POW	Joplin, Missouri
LW	S/Sgt. Raymond J. Manley	POW	Malden, Massachusetts
RW	S/Sgt. Roy B. Graff	POW	Worthington, Massachusetts
TG	S/Sgt. Cosimo A. Demonica	POW	Jamaica, New York

NOTE: 100 BG original cadre, Crew 8.

230091   **418 BS**   LD * S   *Blivit*

6-Apr-43	Accepted into Inventory
9-Apr-43	Delivered-Lowry Army Airfield-Denver, Colorado
10-Apr-43	Gore Field-Spokane, Washington
27-Apr-43	Denver Lowry Army Airfield-Denver, Colorado
1-May-43	Tinker-Del City, Oklahoma
25-May-43	Great Falls Army Air Base-Montana
29-May-43	Kearney Air Base-Kearney, Nebraska
16-Jun-43	UNITED KINGDOM
17-Jun-43	100 BG-Thorpe Abbotts
21-Apr-44	NOPS-Crash landed at Eye, 2Lt Myron D. Richmond-10 KIC
5-May-44	Salvaged

230152   **418 BS**   LD * X   *Messie Bessie*

15-Apr-43	Accepted into Inventory
17-Apr-43	Delivered-Denver
24-Apr-43	Smoky Hill Army Airfield-Salina, Kansas
30-Apr-43	Walla Walla
20-May-43	Smoky Hill
28-May-43	Dow Field

31-May-43	UNITED KINGDOM	
1-Jun-43	Andrews	
12-Jun-43	Snetterton Heath	
25-Jun-43	REM #4 engines burned up	
16-Jul-43	Ridgewell	
	100 BG-Thorpe Abbotts	
25-Jul-43	REM-ball turret	
12-Aug-43	REM-Flap trouble	
17-Aug-43	RES	
16-Sep-43	FTO-#4 magneto out	
28-Apr-45	Salvaged	

230154 349 BS XR * H *War Eagle*

15-Apr-43	Accepted into Inventory
17-Apr-43	Delivered-Cheyenne Municipal Airport-Cheyenne, Wyoming
24-Apr-43	Smoky Hill Army Airfield-Salina, Kansas
19-May-43	Dow Field-Bangor, Maine
21-May-43	Presque Isle Army Airfield-Presque Isle, Maine
1-Jun-43	UNITED KINGDOM
Jun-43	Assigned 100th BG
6-Sep-43	REM
16-Sep-43	RFO Snetterton
23-Sep-43	REM-#2 engine failed
8-Oct-43	DNR-Flak-Bremen, Germany-MACR 953

P	2Lt. Arthur H. Becktoft	POW	Arlington, ,Virginia
CP	2Lt. Clifford M. Spencer	POW	Rapid City, South Dakota
B	2Lt. Robert L. Miller	POW	Louisville, Kentucky
N	2Lt. Walter (NMI) Nichols Jr.	POW	Birmingham, Alabama
TT	T/Sgt. Elmer J. Williams	POW	Truesdale, Missouri
RO	T/Sgt. Floyd A. Lowe	KIA	Carthage, New York
BT	S/Sgt. Charles E. Marengo	POW	Roxbury, Massachusetts
LW	Sgt. Edward J. Hoffman Jr.	POW	Struthers, Ohio
RW	S/Sgt. Henry T. Popielarski	POW	Detroit, Michigan
TG	S/Sgt. Andy P. Stanley	POW	Pennington Gap, Texas

230170 349 BS XR *G *Torchy 2*
Hot Spit
The Pride of the Century
Miss Carriage
Oh Nausea!
Ten Batty Boys

17-Apr-43	Accepted into Inventory
21-Apr-43	Delivered-Cheyenne
27-Apr-43	Tinker-Del City, Oklahoma
5-May-43	Smoky Hill Army Airfield-Salina, Kansas
28-May-43	Kearney Air Base-Kearney, Nebraska
7-Jun-43	Dow Field-Bangor, Maine
9-Jun-43	UNITED KINGDOM
10-Jun-43	100 BG—Thorpe Abbotts
17-Aug-43	Regensburg-Lt Barr/ Maj Veal Crew
15-Sep-43	RFO Lt Sammy Barr-1 WIA (Lt James Brown)
6-Mar-44	BERLIN FTR-Fighters-Colnrode, Germany MACR 3015

P	Lt. Coy I. Montgomery
CP	Lt. Robert F. Connaway
B	Lt. James W. Fulton
N.	Lt. Frank C. Laver

TT	T/Sgt. George W. Burton			
RO	T/Sgt.Wilbur I. Trembly			
BT	S/Sgt. Louis P Savell			
LW	S/Sgt. Junior L. Bucher			
RW	S/Sgt. Anthony E. Ruda			
TG	S/Sgt. Earl W. Ritter			

230184 **418 BS**   LD * Z   *"Muggs"*

20-Apr-43	Accepted into Inventory
24-Apr-43	Delivered-Cheyenne
5-May-43	Smoky Hill Army Airfield-Salina, Kansas
9-Jun-43	Dow Field-Bangor, Maine
	UNITED KINGDOM
10-Jun-43	100 BG-Thorpe Abbotts
10-Jul043	REM-#4 Oil Cooler failed
14-Jul-43	REM-Leaky oxygen
17-Jul-43	RFO-Fighters—Hamburg, Charles Cruikshanlk crew
5-Aug-43	Salvaged

230259 **349 BS**   XR * N   *Damifino II*

3-May-43	Accepted into Inventory
8-May-43	Delivered-Cheyenne
25-May-43	Smoky Hill Army Airfield-Salina, Kansas
27-May-43	Kearney Air Base-Kearney, Nebraska
7-Jun-43	Dow Field-Bangor, Maine
9-Jun-43	UNITED KINGDOM
10-Jun-43	100 BG—Thorpe Abbotts
4-Jul-43	RES
10-Jul-43	REM-Hatch came off Ball Turret
29-Jul-43	REM-Engine Trouble
15-Aug-43	RES
27-Aug-43	RES
24-Sep-43	DNR OW—North Sea—MACR 778

P	2Lt. John G. Gossage	RTD	Providence, Rhode island
CP	2Lt. William S. Grief	KIS	Knappton, Washington
B	2Lt. Theodore J. Don	RTD	Brookline, Massachusetts
N	2Lt. J. Ward Dalton Jr.	KIS	Vineland, New Jersey
TT	T/Sgt. William S. Humphrey	RTD	Grand Rapids, Michigan
RO	T/Sgt. Michael W. Gillen	RTD	
BT	S/Sgt. Francis J. DeCooman	KIS	South Range, Wisconsin
LW	S/Sgt. Clyde O. Lovell	KIS	San Angelo, Texas
RW	S/Sgt. Ralph Schulte	KIS	Delphos, Ohio
TG	S/Sgt. Bruce E. Alshouse	RTD	St. Paul, Minnesota

230305 **349 BS**   XR * D   *Flak Shack*

10-May-43	Accepted into Inventory
11-May-43	Delivered-Cheyenne
24-May-43	Gore Field-Spokane, Washington
25-May-43	Smoky Hill Army Airfield-Salina, Kansas
26-May-43	Kearney Air Base-Kearney, Nebraska
3-Jun-43	Presque Ilse, Maine,
24-Jun-43	305 BG-Chelveston
30-Jun-43	100 BG-Thorpe Abbotts
16-Jul-43	NCS TOA (training)-crashed Dickleburgh Rectory

P	Lt Woodrow B. Barnhill	KIS
CP	2Lt. Carl F. Hudson	KIS

B	Lt. Winfred L. Rucker	KIS	
N	Lt. William H. Carr	KIS	
TT	T/Sgt. Peter (NMI) Contos	KIS	
RO	T/Sgt. Edward D. Johnson	KIS	
BT	S/Sgt. Frank M. Opala	WIS	
WG	S/Sgt. Vincent S. Noel	WIS	
WG	S/Sgt. Newton E. Harris Jr.	KIS	
TG	S/Sgt. Peter S. Russell Jr.	WIS	

230311   350 BS   LN * T   *Maybe*

12-May-43	Accepted into Inventory
14-May-43	Delivered-Dallas
15-May-43	Gore
15-Juny-43	Love
19-May-43	Rapid City
22-Jun-43	Geiger AAF, Spokane, Washington
30-Jun-43	Grand Island Army Airfield-Grand Island, Nebraska
7-Jul-43	Dallas
23-Jul-43	Kearney Air Base-Kearney, Nebraska
26-Jul-43	Dow Field, Bangor, Maine
?-Aug-43	UNITED KINGDOM
?-Aug-43	100 BG—Thorpe Abbotts
17-Aug-43	DNR-Regensburg MACR 681

P	2Lt. Thomas D. Hummel	POW	Toledo, Ohio
CP	2Lt. Michael C. Doroski	POW	Cutchogue, New York
B	2Lt. Norman (NMI) Brewster	POW	Three lakes, Wisconsin
N	2Lt. Archie S. Depew	POW	Andice, Texas
TT	S/Sgt. Nelson G. Gunnar	POW	Des Moines, Iowa
RO	S/Sgt. Donald J. Meeker	POW	Chicago, Illinois
BT	S/Sgt. Gordon (NMI) Williams	POW	Ellicotville, New York
LW	S/Sgt. Kenneth T. O'Connor	KIA	Syracuse, New York
RW	Sgt. Richard E. Bowler	KIA	Meadville, Pennsylvania
TG	S/Sgt. Francis T. J. Stafford	POW	Carnegie, Pennsylvania

230335   350 BS   LN * Y   *Sans Finis*

14-May-43	Accepted into Inventory
18-May-43	Delivered
1-Jun-43	Gore Field-Spokane, Washington
2-Jun-43	Smoky Hill Army Airfield-Salina, Kansas
3-Jun-43	Grand Island Army Airfield-Grand Island, Nebraska
2-Jul-43	Dow Field, Bangor, Maine
2-Jul-43	UNITED KINGDOM
4-Jul-43	100 BG—Thorpe Abbotts
25-Jul-43	REM—Could not keep up with the formation
6-Sep-43	DNR Flak, crash landed Colmar, FRANCE. MACR 687

P	Lt. Walter J. Grenier	POW	Chicago, Illinois
CP	2Lt. Michael R. D'Amato	POW	Brooklyn, New York
B	2Lt. David H. Plant	POW	Tallahassee, Florida
N	2Lt. Saul (NMI) Trauner	POW	Brooklyn, New York
TT	T/Sgt. Howard Aufschlag	POW	Croyden, Pennsylvania
RO	T/Sgt. Carl H. Phillips	POW	Cushing, Oklahoma
BT	S/Sgt. Anthony J. Fusco	POW	Schenectady, New York
LW	S/Sgt. William I. Chang	KIA	Los Angeles, California
RW	S/Sgt. Francis X. Donnellan	POW	Somerville, Massachusetts
TG	Sgt. Robert N. Schrum	POW	San Diego, California

230358   350 BS   LN * X   *Phartzac*
            18-May-43   Accepted into Inventory
            23-May-43   Delivered-Cheyenne
            3-Jun-43   Grand Island Army Airfield-Grand Island, Nebraska Grande Ilse
            27-Jun-43   Dow Field-Bangor, Maine
            3-Jul-43   UNITED KINGDOM
            4-Jul-43   100 BG-Thorpe Abbotts
            17-Jul-43   REM—Nose and Tail guns inoperative
            17-Aug-43   RFO-Regensburg

            COM P   Major Gale W. Cleven   RTD
            P   Capt. Norman H. Scott   RTD
            CP   Lt. Kenneth I. Menzi   RTD
            B   Lt. Norris G. Norman   WIA
            N   Lt. Donald L. Strout   RTD
            TT   T/Sgt. James E. Parks   WIA
            RO   T/Sgt. Norman M. Smith   KIA
            BT   S/Sgt. Lewis D. Miller   RTD
            LW   S/Sgt. Jerome E. Ferroggiaro RTD
            RW   Britton. I. Smith   RTD
            TG   S/Sgt. Blazier (NMI) Paddy   PTD

            8-Oct-43   FTR-Bremen-flak, MACR 947

            P   Lt. Frank H. Meadows   KIA   San Francisco, California
            CP   2Lt. Lloyd W. Evans   KIA   Artesia, New Mexico
            B   2Lt. William C. Hubbard   POW   Crawfordsville, Indiana
            N   2Lt. Frank B. Bush   KIA   Minneapolis, Minnesota
            TT   T/Sgt. Harwold R. Jackson   KIA   Cushing, Oklahoma
            RO   S/Sgt. Robert H. Wussow   KIA   Milwaukee, Wisconsin
            BT   S/Sgt. Richard H. Agor   KIA   Shamokin, Pennsylvania
            LW   Sgt. Dexter B. Pate   KIA   Booneville, Mississippi
            RW   S/Sgt. James F. Ward   KIA   Woodside, New York
            TG   S/Sgt. Vincent D. Sapone   KIA   Schenectady, New York

230380   350 BS   LN * P
                        LN * W
            21-May-43   Accepted into Inventory
            24-May-43   Delivered-Cheyenne
            25-May-43   Gore Field-Spokane, Washington
            9-Jun-43   Kearney Air Base-Kearney, Nebraska
            27-Jun-43   Dow Field-Bangor Maine
            30-Jun-43   UNITED KINGDOM
            1-Jul-43   100 BG-Thorpe Abbotts
            6-Sep-43   REM-oxygen leak
            4-Oct-43   Squadron ID Letter changed from P to W
            5-Nov-43   REM
            22-Dec-43   REM
            31-Dec-43   FTO
            21-Jun-44   RZOI Homestead
            30-Jun-44   Tinker-Del City, Oklahoma
            19-May-45   RFC-Bush Field

230402   418 BS   LD * W   *The Poontang*
            ?-May-43   Accepted into Inventory
            28-May-43   Delivered—Cheyenne, Wyoming
            9-Jun-43   UNITED KINGDOM
            ?-Jun-43   100 BG-Thorpe Abbotts

15-Aug-43   Lt. Robert E. Dibble KIA (Capt Woodward Crew)
19-Aug-43   Woensdrecht , Belgium with S.R. Turner Crew
6-Sep-43   DNR—Stuttgart, MACR 688

P	Capt Edgar F. Woodward Jr.	POW	Brooklyn, New York
CP	FO. John H. Thompson	POW	Elk City, Idaho
B	Lt. Paul R. Englert	POW	Monticello, Indiana
N	2Lt. Emanuel A. Cassimatis	POW	
TT	T/Sgt. Frank (NMI) Danella	POW	Collingwood, New Jersey
RO	T/Sgt. Melvin E. Gaide	POW	Pueblo, Colorado
BT	S/Sgt. George A. Janos	POW	Charleston, West Virginia
LW	S/Sgt. Charles J. Griffin	POW	Oglesby, Texas
RW	S/Sgt Donald H. Fletcher	POW	Kansas, Missouri
TG	S/Sgt. William D. Brooks	POW	Waterloo, Iowa

230458   418 BS   LD * W
8-Jun-43   Accepted into Inventory
9-Jun-43   Delivered-Cheyenne, Wyoming
16-Jun-43   Assigned-Gore Field-Spokane, Washington
18-Jun-43   Kearney
1-Jul-43   Dow
3-Jul-43   UNITED KINGDOM
?-Jul-43   100 BG-Thorpe Abbotts
17-Jul-43   RFO Hamburg
24-Jul-43   RFO-Trondheim
23-Dec-44   RZOI
10-Dec-45   Salvaged
             NOTE: Only flew two missions with the 100 BG

230487   349 BS   XR * F   *Torchy 3rd*
                              Laden Maiden
8-Jun-43   Accepted into Inventory
9-Jun-43   Delivered-Dallas, Texas
11-Jun-43   Gore Field-Spokane, Washington
28-Jul-43   Love Field-Dallas, Texas
11-Aug-43   Scott Army Airfield-Belleville, Illinois
17-Aug-43   Presque Isle Army Airfield-Presque Isle, Maine
19-Aug-43   UNITED KINGDOM
20-Aug-43   100 BG-Thorpe Abbotts
2-Oct-43   REM-#2 engine failed
20-Oct-43   REM
20-Apr-44   RTO Flottemanville (NO BALL) gear collapsed upon landing , Lt Horne crew
28-Apr-44   Salvaged at 1st SAD at Honington.

230604   350 BS   LN * T   *Badger Beauty V*
25-jun-43   Accepted into Inventory
25-Jun-43   Delivered-Cheyenne
29-Jun-43   Gore Field-Spokane, Washington
22-Jul-43   Grand Island Army Airfield-Grand Island, Nebraska Isle
1-Aug-43   Walla Walla
9-Aug-43   Scott Army Airfield-Belleville, Illinois
17-Aug-43   Presque Ilse Army Airfield-Presque Isle, Maine
19-Aug-43   UNITED KINGDOM
20-Aug-43   Assigned 100th BG/350th BS
4-Oct-43   DNR—Flak—Pinky Helstrom, , Crash landed Caen, France MACR 843

P	Capt. Harold B. Helstrom	POW	Madison, Wisconsin
CP	FO. Hubert E. Trent	POW	Springville, Ohio

B	Lt. Hilbert W. Phillippe	POW	Crown Point, Indiana	
N	Lt. Harold H. Curtice	POW	Sacramento, California	
TT	T/Sgt. Robert G. Gilles.	EVD	Detroit, Michigan	
RO	T/Sgt. Carroll F. Haarup	EVD	Storm Lake, Iowa	
BT	S/Sgt. Thomas F. Mezynski	EVD	Pittsburgh, Pennsylvania	
LW	S/Sgt. Joseph (NMI) Shandor	EVD	Portage, Pennsylvania	
RW	S/Sgt. William D. Edwards	POW	Sacramento, California	
TG	S/Sgt. Charles C. Crippen	POW	Grants Pass, Oregon	

230611   349 BS   XR * D   *Horny*

28-Jun-43	Accepted into Inventory
30-Jun-43	Delivered-Seattle, Washington
14-Jul-43	Kearney Air Base-Kearney, Nebraska
18-Jul-43	Dow Field-Bangor, Mine
20-Jul-43	UNITED KINGDOM
?-Jul-43	100 BG-Thorpe Abbotts
17-Aug-43	Regensburg-Capt Henington Crew
3-Sep-43	FTR-Paris——Flak, Ditched in English Channel

P	Capt Henry M. Henington	RTD	
CP	Lt. Homer A. Tripp	RTD	
B	Lt. Alfred A Fahlstedt	SWA	
N	2nd Lt. Ward J. Dalton	RTD	
TT	T/Sgt. Russell G. Gilbert	RTD	BROKE LEG
RO	T/Sgt. Joe (NMI) Rodrick	RTD	
BT	S/Sgt. Nathan F. Holton	RTD	
LW	S/Sgt. Harold J. Janderup	RTD	
RW	S/Sgt. Joe L. Raff	RTD	
TG	S/Sgt. Rich Tangradi	RTD	

230723   351 BS   EP * D   *Holy Terror*
                                    Sexy Suzy Mother of Ten

15-Jul-43	Accepted into Inventory
17-Jul-43	Delivered-Dallas
8-Aug-43	Geiger
22-Aug-43	Pendleton
	UNITED KINGDOM
'31-Aug-43	100 BG-Thorpe Abbotts
27-Sep-43	FTO
10-Oct-43	DNR-Munster-collided with Bf 109 Lt Beddow Crew MACK 1027

P	2Lt. William M. Beddow	KIA	Burmingham, Alabama
CP	2Lt. Richard W. Brooks	POW	West Roxbury, Massachusetts
B	2Lt. Milton E. Harness	POW	Sulphur Springs, Texas
N	2Lt.Israel (NMI) Levine	KIA	Los Angeles, California
TT	S/Sgt. Dan Q. James	POW	La Follette, Tennessee
RO	T/Sgt. John L. Sullivan	KIA	Jersey City, New Jersey
BT	S/Sgt. Walkter E. Zoldak	KIA	Willimantic, Connecticutt
LW	S/Sgt. Robert J. Lynch	KIA	Winchester, Massachusetts
RW	S/Sgt. Samuel M. Hicks	KIA	Albuquerque, New Mexico
TG	S/Sgt. Richard E. Munger	POW	Phoenix, New York

230725   350 BS   LN * Z   *Aw-R-Go*

15-Jul-43	Accepted into Inventory
17-Jul-43	Delivered-Dallas
7-Aug-43	Love Field
8-Aug-43	Geiger
12-Aug-43	Pendleton
	UNITED KINGDOM

	3-Sep-43	100 BG-Thorpe Abbotts		
	10-Oct-43	DNR-Munster-fighter-Capt Cruikshank-MACR 1028		

P	Capt. Charles B. Cruikshank	POW	Everett, Massachusetts
CP	Lt. Glenn E. Graham	POW	Freedom, Pennsylvania
B	Lt. August H. Gaspar	POW	Oakland, California
N	Capt. Frank D. Murphy	POW	Atlanta, Georgia
TT	T/Sgt. Leonard R. Weeks	POW	Elkins, West Virginia
RO	T/Sgt. Orlando E. Vincenti	KIA	Carbondale, Pennsylvania
BT	S/Sgt. Robert L. Bixler	POW	Bisbee, Arizona
LW	S/Sgt. Donald B. Garrison	POW	El Dorado, Illinois
RW	S/Sgt. James M. Johnson	POW	Lmar, Oklahoma
TG	S/Sgt. Chalres A. Clark	KIA	ighland Park, Illinois

230734	351 BS	EP * G	*Slightly Dangerous*
		Accepted into Inventory	
	20-Jul-43	Denver, Colorado-Delivered	
	8-Aug-43	Long Beach, California	
	10-Aug-43	Geiger AAF, Spokane, Washington	
	19-Aug-43	Walla Walla, Washington	
		UNITED KINGDOM	
	9-Sep-43	100 BG-Thorpe Abbotts	
	10-Oct-43	DNR-Munster-MACR 1023	

P	2Lt. Charles H. Thompson	POW	Payson, Illinois
CP	2Lt. Ross (NMI) McEuen	POW	Miami, Arizona
B	2Lt. William J. Sprow Jr.	POW	Sandusky, Ohio
N	2Lt. Edward R. Jones	KIA	Jefferson City, Missouri
TT	S/Sgt. Richard E. Derby	POW	Elkhart, Indiana
RO	Sgt. Jack (NMI) Stern	POW	Brooklyn, New York
BT	S/Sgt. Jesse W. Cook Jr.	POW	Belew Creek, North Carolina
LW	S/Sgt. Floyd M. Cahall	KIA	Red Oak, Virginia
RW	S/Sgt. Charles L. Nessel	KIA	Philadelphia, Pennsylvania
TG	Sgt. Donald E. Leech	POW	Amber, Pennsylvania

230758	418 BS	LD * W	*"Rosie's Riveters"*
			Satcha Lass
	22-Jul-43	Accepted into Inventory	
	24-Jul-43	Delivered—Cheyenne,	
	7-Aug-43	Dyersburg	
	15-Aug-43	Dalhart	
	31-Aug-43	UNITED KINGDOM	
	31-Aug-43	Assigned 100 BG-Thorpe Abbotts	
	4-Feb-44	DNR-Frankfurt-Lt McPhee Crew-Flak-crash landed MACR 2344	

P	Lt. Ross McPhee
CP	Lt. Fred J. Nelson
B	Lt. Bernard B. Levins
N	Lt. Martin S. Keker
TT	S/Sgt. George C. Scarlett
RO	S/Sgt. Herbert Shope
BT	S/Sgt. Libero J. Bernagozzi
LW	S/Sgt. Blom H. Pate
RW	S/Sgt. David J. Shaw
TG	S/Sgt. James T. Delamar

230796	351 BS	EP * K	*Sunny II*
		EP * J	
	27-Jul-43	Accepted into Inventory	
	29-Jul-43	Delivered-Cheyenne	

	9-Aug-43	Grand Ilse	
	27-Aug-43	UNITED KINGDOM	
	28-Aug-43	100 BG-Thorpe Abbotts	
	?-Oct-43	Letter changed from K to J	
	12-Dec-43	RES	
	30-Dec-43	RFO-Crash Landed—Harleston, Lt. George Brannan	
	2-Jan-44	Salvaged	

230799	349 BS	XR * L *The Bigassbird II*	
	27-Jul-43	Accepted into Inventory	
	29-Jul-43	Delivered-Cheyenne	
	9-Aug-43	Gore	
	10-Aug-43	Scott	
	16-Aug-43	Presque Isle	
	20-Aug-43	Ground looped Gander, NEWFOUNDLAND UNITED KINGDOM	
	20-Aug-43	100 BG-Thorpe Abbotts	
	6-Mar-44	DNR—Berlin-Lt William Murray Crew-MACR 3017	

P	Lt. William B. Murray	
CP	Lt. Richard M. Lambiotte	
B	Lt. William G. Carr	
N	Lt. Orrin H. Heinrich	
TT	S/Sgt. Emory L. Brandt	
RO	T/Sgt. Fred C. Schillinger	
BT	S/Sgt. Jim Peace	
LW	S/Sgt. Nich F. Hamalak	
RW	S/Sgt. Palmer J. Hanson	
TG	S/Sgt. Mahlon A. Hall	

230818	350 BS	LN * S *Salvo Sal*	
		My Gal Sal	
	29-Jul-43	Accepted into Inventory	
	4-Aug-43	Delivered-Cheyenne	
	11-Aug-43	Grand Isle	
	24-Aug-43	UNITED KINGDOM	
	25-Aug-43	100 BG-Thorpe Abbotts	
	8-Oct-43	DNR Bremen-Flak-MACR 952	

P	Lt. William H. McDonald	POW	El Dorado, Arkandas
CP	2Lt. John L. James Jr.	POW	Yeardon, Pennsylvania
B	2Lt. Frank P. McGlinchey	POW	Brooklyn, New York
N	2Lt. Carl L. Spicer	POW	Mendon, Ohio
TT	T/Sgt. Charles W. Ashbaugh	POW	Leechburg, Pennsylvania
RO	T/Sgt.Fred (NMI) Pribish	POW	Joliet, Illinois
BT	S/Sgt. Ross W. Detillion	POW	St. Maries, Iowa
LW	S/Sgt. Douglas H. Agee	KIA	Saltillo, Texas
RW	S/Sgt. Victor P. Intoccia	POW	Brooklyn, New York
TG	S/Sgt. Paul G. Sears	POW	SomersetKentucky

230823	350 BS	LN * Y *Invadin' Maiden*	
		The Gnome (Stateside name)	
	30-July 43	Accepted into Inventory	
	4-Augu-43	Delivered-Dallas	
	5-Aug-43	Gore	
	8-Aug-43	Dallas	
	5-Sep-43	UNITED KINGDOM	

6-Sep-43	100 BG-Thorpe Abbotts			
26-Sep-43	REM-#2 Engine Oil Leak			
10-Oct-43	DNR-Munster-Fighters-Lt Walts Crew—MACR 1025			

P	2Lt. Charles D. Walts	POW	Georgetown, Indiana
CP	2Lt. Jerome H. Wallace	KIA	Robbinsdale, Minnesota
B	2Lt. Richard C. Dodson	KIA	Monroe, Georgia
N	2Lt. Louis H. Oss	POW	Cumberland, Maryland
TT	S/Sgt. Clyde M. Walker	KIA	Cement, Oklahoma
RO	T/Sgt. Travis D. Brumbeau	POW	San Antonio, Texas
BT	Sgt. Henry A. Gratzfeld	KIA	Galveston, Texas
LW	Sgt. Frank E. Fetherson	KIA	New York City, New York
RW	S/Sgt. Thomas F. Murphy	POW	Maynard, Massachusetts
TG	Sgt. William O. Higginbotham	POW	Decature, Georgia

230830	418 BS	LD * U	*M'lle Zig Zig*
			Mademoiselle Zig Zig
			M'lle Zig Zag (mistakenly identified in historical documents)
	31-Jul-43	Accepted into Inventory	
	4-Aug-43	Delivered-Cheyenne Municipal Airport	
	14-Aug-43	Grand Island Army Airfield-Grand Island, Nebraska	
	27-Aug-43	UNITED KINGDOM	
	28-Aug-43	Assigned-100th BG	
	10-Oct-43	DNR-Fighters-Munster, Germany-MACR 1029	

COM P	Major John C. Egan	POW	Manitowoe, Wisconsin
P	Capt. John D. Brady	POW	Victor, New York
CP	Lt. John L. Hoerr	POW	Baltimore, Maryland
B	Lt. Howard B. Hamilton	POW	Augusta, Kansas
N	Lt. David (NMI) Solomon	POW	San Francisco, California
TT	T/Sgt. Adolf (NMI) Blum	POW	Camillus, New York
RO	T/Sgt. Joseph E. Hafer	POW	
BT	S/Sgt. Roland D. Gangwer	POW	Bethlehem, Pennsylvania
LW	T/Sgt. George J. Petrohelos	POW	Chicago, Illinois
RW	S/Sgt. Harold E. Clanton	KIA	Tulsa, Oklahoma
TG	S/Sgt. James A. McCusker	POW	Niagara Falls, New York

230840	350 BS	LN * O	
	31 Jul 43	Accepted Into Inventory	
	5 Aug 43	Delivered-Cheyenne Municipal Airport, Cheyenne, Wyoming	
	13-Aug-43	Grand Island Army Airfield-Grand Island, Nebraska	
	24-Aug-43	UNITED KINGDOM	
	25-Aug-43	Thorpe Abbots	
	4-Oct-43	REO-crew member ill.	
	8-Oct-43	DNR-Bremen-Flak-Damme, Germany-MACR 951	

P	2Lt. Hubert G. Nash Jr.	KIA	Albania, West Virginia
CP	2Lt. Robert E. Speas	KIA	Sterling, Kansas
B	2Lt. Vernon N. Hogsett	POW	Longmont, Colorado
N	2Lt. John P. Hart	POW	Alloway, New Jersey
TT	T/Sgt. Patrick J. Neilon	KIA	San Antonio, Texas
RO	T/Sgt. Thomas B. Dilts	KIA	Cleveland, Ohio
BT	Sgt. Thaddeus L. Kirkpatrick	POW	Cellina, Tennessee
LW	Sgt. George D. Synder	POW	Akron, Ohio
RW	Sgt. Stanley Nowakowski	POW	Buffalo, New York
TG	S/Sgt. Joe (NMI) Bost	KIA	Newton, North Carolina

AIRCRAFT NAMES

25867	*Alice from Dallas*	23271	*Nine Little Yanks and a Jerk*
23260	*Angel's Tit*	230042	*Oh Nausea!*
230725	*Aw-R-Go*	23534	*Ol' Dad*
23279	*Badger Beauty*	23233	*Our Baby*
25878	*Badger Beauty*	25863	*Paddlefoot's Proxy*
230604	*Badger Beauty V*	23229	*Pasadena Nena*
230038	*Bar Fly*	230068	*Phartzac*
230059	*Barker's Burdens*	230358	*Phartzac*
230062	*Bastard's Bungalow*	25864	*Piccadilly Lily*
23508	*Bastard's Bungalow II*	230063	*Picklepuss*
230148	*The Bigassbird*	230402	*Poo Bah*
230799	*The Bigassbird II*	230402	*The Poontang*
230086	*Billy Jack*	230057	*Raunchy*
230086	*Black Jack*	230062	*Reilly's "Racehorse"*
23393	*Blakely's Provisional Group*	230758	*"Rosie's Riveters"*
230091	*Blivit*	26087	*Royal Flush*
230071	*Brady's Crash Wagon*	230818	*Salvo Sal*
230002	*Damifino*	230335	*Sans Finis*
230259	*Damifino II*	230758	*Satcha Lass*
23393	*Did You Say Ten Cents?*	230723	*Sexy Suzy Mother of Ten*
25862	*Duration + 6*	230042	*Shack Rabbits*
230090	*El P'sstofo*	230087	*Shack Rat*
25860	*Escape Kit*	23307	*Skipper*
23232	*Flak Happy*	230734	*Slightly Dangerous*
230305	*Flak Shack*	230088	*Squawkin Hawk*
230023	*Forever Yours*	25861	*Stud Duck*
230823	*The Gnome*	23237	*Stymie*
23413	*Hard Luck!*	230089	*Sunny*
26087	*Harper's Ferry*	230796	*Sunny II*
25997	*Heaven Can Wait*	230047	*Sweater Girl*
230080	*High Life*	229947	*Target for Tonight*
230723	*Holy Terror*	230062	*Terry'n ten*
230611	*Horny*	230035	*Torchy*
25957	*Horny II*	230170	*Torchy 2*
230170	*Hot Spit*	230487	*Torchy 3*
230823	*Invadin' Maiden*	230070	*Tweedle-O-Twill*
25865	*Janie*	230002	*The WAAC Hunter*
229931	*Jaybird*	230154	*War Eagle*
230050	*Judy E.*	230064	*Wild Cargo*
230061	*Just-A-Snappin'*	230061	*Wolff Pack*
23393	*Just-A-Snappin'*		
23474	*King Bee*		
230487	*Laden Maiden*		
25861	*Laden Maiden*		
23433	*Lena*		
23234	*Little Mike*		
230090	*Mad House*		
23386	*Marie Helena*		
230152	*Messie Bessie*		
230066	*M'lle Zig Zig*		
230311	*Maybe*		

APPENDIX D.
418TH BOMB SQUADRON
ORIGINAL AIRCREWS

This appendix reproduces that portion of the May 25, 1943, Special Order 103, detailing the original aircrew members and aircraft assigned to the 481st Bombardment Squadron. From left to right is information provided about the crew member's position. Rank and name, hometown, fate along with the date, and aircraft serial number. For the aircrew, information is also provided regarding the completion of their tour (CTD), killed in action (KIA), prisoner of war (POW), removed from flight status (RFS) transferred to another unit (TRN), wounded in action (WIA), and unknown (UKN).

POSITION	NAME and RANK	HOMETOWN	FATE	DATE	NOTES
Crew 28 – 230064 – *Wild Cargo*					
Pilot	Lt. Curtis R. Biddick	Kansas City, Kansas	KIA	17-Aug-43	25860
Co-Pilot	Lt. Hoyt L. Smith	Raleigh, Tennessee	POW	10-Oct-43	23237
Bombardier	Lt. Dan B. McKay	St. Joseph, Louisiana	POW	17-Aug-43	25860
Navigator	Lt. Paul S. Warner		RFS		
Top Turret	T/Sgt. Glover E. Barney	Portland, Oregon	POW	17-Aug-43	25860
Radio Operator	T/Sgt. Joseph P. Eigen	Old Forge, Pennsylvania	POW		
Ball Turret Gunner	S/Sgt. Roy L. Schellin		WIA	10-July-43	
Waist Gunner	T/Sgt. Ross H. Breckeen		UNK		
Waist Gunner	S/Sgt. John O. Stireman		WIA	10-July-43	
Tail Gunner	S/Sgt. Alfred J. Vickers		WIA	10-July-43	
Crew 29 - 23237 - *Stymie*					
Pilot	Lt. Ernest A. Kiessling		RFS		
Co-Pilot	2Lt. John F. Stephens	Brookings, South Dakota	POW	10-Oct-43	23237
Bombardier	Lt. David (NMI) Solomon	San Francisco, California	POW	10-Oct-43	23830
Navigator	2Lt. Stanley O. Morrison	Lafayette, Indiana	KIA	25-Jun-43	229986
Top Turret	T/Sgt. John (NMI) Shay	Fall, River, Massachusetts	POW	10-Oct-43	23237
Radio Operator	T/Sgt. Max U. Drudge	Wheatfield, Indiana	POW	10-Oct-43	23237
Ball Turret Gunner	S/Sgt. Frank S. Mazarka		RFS		
Ball Turret Gunner	S/Sgt Carl E. Battin		POW	10-Oct-43	23237
Waist Gunner	S/Sgt. William F. Young	Sprague, Oregon	POW	10-Oct-43	23237
Waist Gunner	S/Sgt. George F. Knolle	Sonoma, California	POW	10-Oct-43	23237
Tail Gunner	S/Sgt. Casmir A. Raczynski	Milwaukee, Wisconsin	POW	10-Oct-43	23237
Crew 30 – 230066 - *Mugwump*					
Pilot	Lt. William R. Flesh	PFF & CPT with 303rd BG	CTD		
Co-Pilot	FO. Richard L. Snyder	Davis, California	KIA	17-Aug-43	25860
Bombardier	Lt. Paul R. Englert	Monticello, Indiana	POW	6-Sept-43	230402
Navigator	2Lt. John C. Dennis	Norwich, Connecticut	POW	17-Aug-43	25860
Top Turret	T/Sgt. Lawrence E. Godbey	Radford, Virginia	KIA	17-Aug-43	25860

Radio Operator	T/Sgt. Robert R. DeKay	Mt. Clemens, Michigan	KIA	17-Aug-43	25860
Ball Turret Gunner	S/Sgt. Walter (NMI) Halunka	Berwyn, Illinois	POW	17-Aug-43	25860
Waist Gunner	S/Sgt. Charles F. Vielbig		UNK		
Waist Gunner	S/Sgt. William M. Blank	Memphis, Tennessee	POW	17-Aug-43	25860
Tail Gunner	S/Sgt. Clarence R. Bowlin	Urbana, Illinois	POW	17-Aug-43	25860

Crew 31 – 230062 – *Bastard's Bungalow*

Pilot	Capt. Charles B. Cruikshank	Everett, Massachusetts	POW	10-Oct-43	230725
Co-Pilot	Lt. Glenn E. Graham	Freedom, Pennsylvania	POW	10-Oct-43	230725
Bombardier	Lt. August H. Gaspar	Oakland, California	POW	10-Oct-43	230725
Navigator	Capt. Frank D. Murphy	Atlanta, Georgia	POW	10-Oct-43	230725
Top Turret	T/Sgt. Leonard R. Weeks	Elkins, West Virginia	POW	10-Oct-43	230725
Radio Operator	T/Sgt. Orlando E. Vincentl	Carbondale, Pennsylvania	KIA	10-Oct-43	230725
Ball Turret Gunner	S/Sgt. Robert L. Bixler	Bisbee, Arizona	POW	10-Oct-43	230725
Waist Gunner	S/Sgt. Donald R. Garrison	El Dorado, Illinois	POW	10-Oct-43	230725
Waist Gunner	S/Sgt. James M. Johnson	Lamar, Oklahoma	POW	10-Oct-43	230725
Tail Gunner	S/Sgt. Charles A. Clark	Highland Park, Illinois	KIA	10-Oct-43	230725

Crew 32 – 230071 - *Brady's Crash Wagon Skipper*

Pilot	Capt. John D. Brady	Victor, New York	POW	10-Oct-43	230830
Co-Pilot	Lt. John L. Hoerr	Baltimore, Maryland	POW	10-Oct-43	230830
Bombardier	Lt. Howard B. Hamilton	Augusta, Kansas	POW	10-Oct-43	230830
Navigator	2Lt. Harry H. Crosby		CTD		
Top Turret	S/Sgt. Adolf (NMI) Blum	Camillus, New York	POW	10-Oct-43	230830
Radio Operator	S/Sgt. Saul (NMI) Levitt		TRN	Yank Magazine	
Radio Operator	T/Sgt. Joseph E. Hafer		POW	10-Oct-43	230830
Ball Turret Gunner	S/Sgt. Ronald D. Gangwer	Bethleham, Pennsylvania	POW	10-Oct-43	230830
Waist Gunner	T/Sgt. George J. Petrohelos	Chicago, Illinois	POW	10-Oct-43	230830
Waist Gunner	S/Sgt. Harold E. Clanton	Tulsa, Oklahoma	KIA	10-Oct-43	230830
Tail Gunner	S/Sgt. James A. McCusker	Niagara Falls, New York	POW	10-Oct-43	230830

Crew 33 – 25860 - *Escape Kit*

Pilot	Capt. Edgar F. Woodward Jr.	Brooklyn, New York	INT	6-Sep-43	230402
Co-Pilot	FO. John H. Thompson	Elk City, Idaho	POW	6-Sep-43	230402
Bombardier	Lt. Robert E. Dibble		KIA	15-Aug-43	230402
Navigator	2Lt. Emanuel A Cassimatis		POW	6-Sep-43	230402
Top Turret	T/Sgt. Frank (NMI) Danella	Collingswood, New Jersey	POW	6-Sep-43	230402
Radio Operator	T/Sgt. Melvin E. Gaide	Pueblo, Colorado	POW	6-Sep-43	230402
Ball Turret Gunner	S/Sgt. George A. Janos	Charleston, West Virginia	POW	6-Sep-43	230402
Waist Gunner	S/Sgt. Charles J. Griffin	Oglesby, Texas	POW	6-Sep-43	230402
Waist Gunner	S/Sgt. Donald H. Fletcher	Kansas, Missouri	POW	6-Sep-43	230402
Tail Gunner	S/Sgt. William D. Brooks	Waterloo, Iowa	POW	6-Sep-43	230402

Crew 34   TBD Believe this is Crew 34

Pilot	LT JOHN T. RAY		KIC	20- Feb-43	25367
Co-Pilot	LT RICHARD H. REED		KIC	20-Feb-43	25367
Bombardier	LT HANS N. LEHNE ?		KIC	20-Feb-43	25367
Navigator	LT DAVID I. DUNNING		KIC	20- Feb 43	25367
Top Turret	T/SGT ALEXANDER DEC		KIC	20- Feb 43	25367
Radio Operator	T/SGT LLOYD L. BALL		KIC	20- Feb-43	25367
Ball Turret Gunner	S/SGT MILTON D. JOHNSON, JR		KIC	20 -Feb-43	25367
Waist Gunner	S/SGT WILLMER C. FANKHANEL		KIC	20-Feb-43	25367
Waist Gunner	S/SGT JOSEPH F. PERKINS		KIC	20-Feb-43	25367
Tail Gunner	S/SGT CLAUDE W. SEIFERT		KIC	20-Feb-43	25367

KILLED IN A TRAINING ACCIDENT AT WALLA WALLA. IT WAS THE ONLY FATALITIES THE 100TH EXPERIENCED ON TRAIN-ING PEROID. (NEARLY SIX MONTHS)

Crew 35 – 230061 - *Just-A-Snappin*

Pilot	Capt. Everett E. Blakely		CTD		
Co-Pilot	Lt. Charles A. Via Jr.		WIA	8-Oct-43	23393
Bombardier	Lt. James R. Douglass		RTD	8-Oct-43	23393
Navigator 2107024	Lt. Joseph H. Payne	Lexington, Kentucky	KIA	28-Apr-44	
Top Turret	T/Sgt. Howard J. Brock	Lake Odessa, Wisconsin	POW	17-Aug-43	25860
Radio Operator	T/Sgt. Edmund C. Forkner	Tulsa, Oklahoma	CTD		
Ball Turret Gunner	S/Sgt. John L. Olson		TRN	15-Jun-44	452 BG
Waist Gunner	T/Sgt. Monroe B. Thornton	Newport, Tennessee	RTD	8-Oct-43	23393
Waist Gunner 2107011	S/Sgt. Lyle E. Nord	Superior, Wisconsin	KIA	29-May-44	
Tail Gunner	S/Sgt. Lester W. Saunders	Chicago, Illinois	KIA	8-Oct-43	23393

Crew 36 – 230063 - *Picklepuss (Wheels Down Crew)*

Pilot	Capt. Robert M. Knox	Philadelphia, Pennsylvania	KIA	17-Aug-43	230063
Co-Pilot	2Lt. John O. Whitaker	Wheeling, West Virginia	KIA	17-Aug-43	230063
Bombardier	2Lt. Edwin F. Tobin	Newberry, California	POW	17-Aug-43	230063
Navigator	2Lt. Earnest E. Warsaw	Chicago, Illinois	POW	17-Aug-43	230063
Top Turret	T/Sgt. Carl T. Simon	Addington, Oklahoma	POW	16-Sep-43	230064
Radio Operator	T/Sgt. Walter (NMI) Paulsen	Belleville, New Jersey	POW	17-Aug-43	230063
Ball Turret Gunner	S/Sgt. Frank W. Tychewicz	Chicago, Illinois	KIA	17-Aug-43	230063
Waist Gunner	S/Sgt. Malcom K. Maddran		RFS	14-Oct-43	
Waist Gunner	S/Sgt. Henry A. Norton	Enterprise, Alabama	KIA	17-Aug-43	230063
Tail Gunner	S/Sgt.Joseph F. Laspada	Buffalo, New York	KIA	17-Aug-43	230063

APPENDIX E.
OPERATIONAL MATRIX—1943

Locating the 100th Bomb Group's J Form (takeoff and landing document), fuel consumption reports, formation charts, battle damage reports, and engineering reports make it possible to identify for a given mission which aircraft and where in the formation a pilot flew his assigned B-17. The following three tables represent what is known, but there are limitations. It is not possible to identify all the aircraft that flew on June 22 or identify every pilot participating on June 22; July 30; August 12, 24, 27, and 31; September 6, 7, 9, 15, and 24; as well as October 10 and 14. For all three tables, AugS represents those aircraft involved in the return mission from the August 17 mission to Regensburg. Information is included for the September 24 practice mission because German fighters attacked the formation, shooting down one B-17 and seriously damaging another.

The first table provides a matrix detailing which 100th Bomb Group B-17s participated on which operation. Events affecting the aircraft are:

A	Participated, received A category of damage (minor)
AC	Participated, received AC category of damage (major)
B	Participated, received B category of damage (severe)
CL	Crash Landed
DNR	Participated, did not return to England
E	Participated, declared beyond repair
FTO	Failed to Take Off
P	Participated, no reported battle damage
REM	Returned early, mechanical reason, credited sortie is possible
REO	Returned, other than mechanical reasons (i.e. crew member ill) , credited sorties possible
RES	Returned early, scheduled s Participated, received AC category of damage pare aircraft
SAL	Salvaged
TRN	Transferred to another unit

NOTE: SAL and TRN may represent approximate dates of the operational activity

The second table identifies which pilot flew which B-17 on a given date.

The third and last table in this appendix details which aircraft flew in what position in the formation. Roger A. Freeman's *The Mighty Eighth War Manual* (Coulsdon, UK: Jane's, 1984) traces the variety of formations employed by VIII

Bomber Command. For the period of June 22 through October 1943, there existed a twenty-one-plane formation. Each formation is referred to as lead, high, and low. Formation charts for the 100th also included a trail squadron, which usually contained aircraft that fill a slot in the formation. Below is an overhead view of the formation and the number system used.

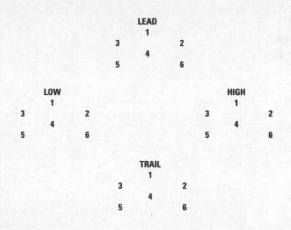

SERIAL	UNIT	Jun-22	Jun-25	Jun-26	Jun-28	Jun-29	Jul-4	Jul-10	Jul-14	Jul-17	Jul-24	Jul-25
23229	349 A			RES	REM							
23232	350 V		REM	REO		P	P		P	P	P	REM
23233	350 R		P		P	P	P	REM	FTO	P	P	P
23234	351 E				REM		P	P	A	RES	A	AC
23237	418 R	P		P	RES	P	P	P	P	FTO		
23260	349 K		DNR									
23271	351 L									A		A
23279	350 Z		RES	P	P	P	P	AC				
23307	351 N		RES	P	P	P	P	A		RES		AC
23386	351 H											
23393	418 Y											
23413	350 N											
23433	350 W											
23452	350 Z											
23474	351 B											
23508	418 F											
23534	349 L											
25854	418					P	P		TRN			
25860	418 P			P	P	P	P		A	P	P	P
25861	349 J	P				P	P	P	P	P	A	A
25862	350 T		A			P	P	P	REM	A	P	DNR
25863	418 V	A	RES	P	P					P	P	P
25864	351 A		A			P	P	A	P	REM	P	A
25865	351 B			P		P			RES		A	REM

25867	350 0		A	P	P		P		A	FTO	P	
25878	350 W		P	P								
25957	349 D-											
25997	351 F											
26087	418 Q											
229738	350 U			RES		P			TRN			
229931	418 ?			P		P		P	TRN			
229947	351 ?		RES			P		TRN				
229986	349 G		DNR									
230002	349 F							FTO	REM	P		
230023	349 M						P				REM	A
230035	349 H			P	P	P				P		
230038	349 D		DNR									
230042	349 L			REM			REM	P	REM	FTO	REO	A
230047	350 Q						P	P	REM	P	P	P
230050	350 X		P	P	P	P		DNR				
230051	351 J		P	P		P	DNR					
230057	351 D		P	P	P	P		P	REM	A	A	FTO
230059	351 G					P		A	REM	A		P
230061	418 Q	P		P	P			P	REM		P	P
230062	418 O	A		P	P			A			P	
230063	418 S			P	P		P	REO	REM	RES		REM
230064	418 T						P	P	AC			
230066	350 U		P	P	RES	P	REM	A		A		P
230068	350 P		P		P							
230070	350 S							AC				
230071	418											
230080	351 F						P	A				
230086	351 B		P	P	P		P	P	P	A	A	
230087	351 M		A	P		P						
230088	349 E					P	P	P	P	P	A	A
230089	351 K							A	A	A		A
230090	349 B							A				A
230091	418 S											
230152	418 X		REM							P	P	REM
230154	349 H											
230170	349 G							P			REM	A
230184	418 Z		RES	P	P		P	REM	REM	E		
230259	349 N	P	A	P	P		RES	REM	AC		A	
230305	349 D						P	P	P			
230311	350									P	REO	REM
230335	350 Y									REM	P	P
230358	350 N									P	P	
230380	350 P											
230402	418 W											
230458	418 X											
230487	349 F											
230604	350 T											
230611	349 D											
230723	351 D											
230725	350 Z											
230734	351 G											
230758	418 W											
230796	351 K											
230799	349 L											

SERIAL	UNIT											
230818	350 S											
230823	350 Y											
230830	418 U											
230840	350 O											

NOTE: July 10—230070 listed twice.

SERIAL	UNIT	Jul-26	Jul-28	Jul-29	Jul-30	Aug-12	Aug-15	Aug-17	Aug-19	Aug-24	Aug-24	Aug-27
23229	349 A		p	REO			RES	A			P	
23232	350 V	REM	REM	P		P		DNR				
23233	350 R	P	P	P	REO	P	P					
23234	351 E		P	FTO	P	P	P			P		A
23237	418 R	P	REO	P	A	P		AC			REM	
23260	349 K											
23271	351 L			P	P		P					
23279	350 Z											
23307	351 N						P		P			
23386	351 H											
23393	418 Y					P		A			P	
23413	350 N											
23433	350 W											
23452	350 Z											
23474	351 B											
23508	418 F											
23534	349 L											
25854	418											
25860	418 P	P	P		P		P	DNR				
25861	349 J	A	P					A			P	
25862	350 T											
25863	418 V	P	P	REM	P		P					
25864	351 A	AC				P		A			P	
25865	351 B	P	P	P	AC		P		P			P
25867	350 O			REM	P		P	DNR				
25878	350 W	REM	P			REM						
25957	349 D-											
25997	351 F											
26087	418 Q											
229738	350 U											
229931	418 ?											
229947	351 ?											
229986	349 G											
230002	349 F		P				RES	DNR				
230023	349 M	A	P		REO	P			RES			
230035	349 H						A	P				
230038	349 D											
230042	349 L	P				REM		DNR				
230047	350 Q	P	P	P			P					
230050	350 X											
230051	351 J											
230057	351 D		P	RES	P	AC				P		P
230059	351 G		P	REM		A		REM		AC		
230061	418 Q		P		P		A	P				
230062	418 O	P	REO	P		REM	P					

SERIAL	UNIT	Aug-31	Sep-3	Sep-6	Sep-7	Sep-9	Sep-15	Sep-16	Sep-23	Sep-24	Sep-26	Sep-27
230063	418 S	REM	P	REM	P	P		DNR				
230064	418 T											P
230066	350 U	P	REM	P	A	P		B				
230068	350 P											
230070	350 S							DNR				
230071	418											
230080	351 F			P	P		A	DNR				
230086	351 B	P		P	P	P		RES				
230087	351 M		P									
230088	349 E			P	A	P		RES	P	A		
230089	351 K	AC					AC		A	P		
230090	349 B	REM	P	REM		A						
230091	418 S											
230152	418 X	A		P		REM	P	RES				P
230154	349 H											
230170	349 G			P	REM	P	P	REM				
230184	418 Z											
230259	349 N		P	REM		A	RES		P			RES
230305	349 D					SAL						
230311	350						P	DNR				
230335	350 Y	P	P			P	P	A			P	
230358	350 N	P	P	P	P		P	A				
230380	350 P					AC						
230402	418 W						P		A	P		P
230458	418 X											
230487	349 F											
230604	350 T											
230611	349 D						P	A			P	A
230723	351 D											
230725	350 Z											
230734	351 G											
230758	418 W											
230796	351 K											
230799	349 L											
230818	350 S											
230823	350 Y											
230830	418 U											
230840	350 O											

SERIAL	UNIT	Aug-31	Sep-3	Sep-6	Sep-7	Sep-9	Sep-15	Sep-16	Sep-23	Sep-24	Sep-26	Sep-27
23229	349 A				P	P	P	P			P	P
23232	350 V											
23233	350 R			P		P	P	P	REM			P
23234	351 E			AC					P			
23237	418 R		REM	P	P	P	P					
23260	349 K											
23271	351 L	P	A	AC			P		P			P
23279	350 Z											
23307	351 N		A					FTO	P	P	P	
23386	351 H	P			P	P	P	P	P		P	
23393	418 Y	P		P	P	P	P	P				P
23413	350 N		P		P		P	P	REO	P	P	

SERIAL	UNIT	Aug-31	Sep-3	Sep-6	Sep-7	Sep-9	Sep-15	Sep-16	Sep-23	Sep-24	Sep-26	Sep-27
23433	350 W											
23452	350 Z			REO			DNR					
23474	351 B										P	
23508	418 F							P			P	
23534	349 L					P						
25854												
25860	418 P											
25861	349 J	P	A		P			P	REM	P	P	P
25862	350 T											
25863	418 V	P	A	AC								
25864	351 A	REM		REM	P	P	P			P	P	
25865	351 B	P	DNR									
25867	350 O											
25878	350 W								TRN			
25957	349 D-			P								
25997	351 F				P	P	P	P			P	REM
26087	418 Z								P			P
26094	418 Q								REM		P	P
229738	350 U											
229931	418 ?											
229947	351 ?											
229986	349 G											
SERIAL	UNIT	Aug-31	Sep-3	Sep-6	Sep-7	Sep-9	Sep-15	Sep-16	Sep-23	Sep-24	Sep-26	Sep-27
230002	349 F											
230023	349 M	P						P	P		REM	P
230035	349 H	REM	DNR									
230038	349 D											
230042	349 L											
230047	350 Q	P		REM			FTO	P	REM	P		REM
230050	350 X											
230051	351 J											
230057	351 D	P	A	DNR								
230059	351 G	P	DNR									
230061	418 Q											
230062	418 O	P	A		P	P	P	P	P	P	REM	
230063	418 S											
230064	418 T		P	REM	P	P	P	DNR				
230066	350 U											
230068	350 P											
230070	350 S											
230071	418											
230080	351 F											
230086	351 B								SAL			
230087	351 M		RES	REO		P	P	P	P	P	P	P
230088	349 E	P	A	P								
230089	351 K	P	DNR									
230090	349 B	P	A							P	REM	
230091	418 S	REM										P
SERIAL	UNIT	Aug-31	Sep-3	Sep-6	Sep-7	Sep-9	Sep-15	Sep-16	Sep-23	Sep-24	Sep-26	Sep-27
230152	418 X	P	FTO	P							P	P
230154	349 H			REM	P		P	P	REM	P		P
230170	349 G				P	P	P		P	P		P
230184	418 Z											

Serial	Unit											
230259	349 N	P	A							DNR		
230305	349 D											
230311	350											
230335	350 Y		A	DNR								
230358	350 N		A	A	P	P		P		P		P
230380	350 P			REM	P	P	AC				P	
230402	418 W	P		DNR								
230458	418 X											
230487	349 F			)		P	P		P	P		
230604	350 T				P	P		P			P	P
230611	349 D	P	DNR									
230723	351 D										P	P
230725	350 Z			REO	P	P						
230734	351 G									P	P	REM
230758	418 W								P	P		P
230796	351 K				P	A	P	P	P	P	P	P
230799	349 L						P		P	A	P	
230818	350 S		A	P	P	P	P	P		P	P	P
230823	350 Y									P	P	REM
230830	418 U			A			P	P	P	P	P	P
230840	350 O		P	A	A				FTO	P		P

SERIAL	UNIT	Oct-2	Oct-4	Oct-8	Oct-9	Oct-10	Oct-14
23229	349 A			P	REM	P	
23232	350 V						
23233	350 R			P			
23234	351 E				P	E	
23237	418 R			REM	P	DNR	
23260	349 K						
23271	351 L				P	FTO	P
23279	350 Z						
23307	351 N			FTO	P	REM	
23386	351 H			DNR			
23393	418 Y	P	P	E			
23413	350 N	P	P		RES	REO	P
23433	350 W		P	REM	P	DNR	
23452	350 Z						
23474	351 B	P	REM	AC			
23508	418 F	P	A				
23534	349 L				P	REM	P
25854	418						
25860	418 P						
25861	349 J		P				
25862	350 T						
25863	418 V						
25864	351 A		P	DNR			
25865	351 B						
25867	350 O						
25878	350 W						
25957	349 D-	P	FTO	A			
25997	351 F	P	P	AC			
26087	418 Q	P	A		P	AC	
26094	418 Q	P	P		P	REM	REM
229738	350 U						

229931	418 ?						
229947	351 ?						
229986	349 G						
230002	349 F						
230023	349 M		REM	REM	REM	DNR	
230035	349 H						
230038	349 D						
230042	349 L						
230047	350 Q			RES	P	DNR	
230050	350 X						
230051	351 J						
230057	351 D						
230059	351 G						
230061	418 Q					REM	
230062	418 O	P	REM	REM	FTO		
230063	418 S						
230064	418 T						
230066	350 U						
230068	350 P						
230070	350 S						
230071	418 -						
230080	351 F						
230086	351 B						
230087	351 M		P			DNR	
230088	349 E	P	P	A			REM
230089	351 K						
230090	349 B				P	DNR	
230091	418 S	P	P	A			
230152	418 X	P	P	A			
230154	349 H	P	P	DNR			
230170	349 G	P		A			
230184	418 Z						
230259	349 N						
230305	349 D						
230311	350						
230335	350 Y						
230358	350 N	P	P	DNR			
230380	350 P						P
230402	418 W						
230458	418 X						
230487	349 F	REM	P	P			
230604	350 T	P	DNR				
230611	349 D						
230723	351 D	P	P	P	P	DNR	
230725	350 Z	P	P			DNR	
230734	351 G		RES		P	DNR	
230758	418 W	P		A			
230796	351 K	P	P	AC			
230799	349 L				REM		
230818	350 S	P		DNR			
230823	350 Y	P	P		RES	DNR	
230830	418 U		P		P	DNR	
230840	350 O		REO	DNR			

Pilots

PILOT	Jun-22	Jun-25	Jun-26	Jun-28	Jun-29	Jul-4	Jul-10	Jul-14	Jul-17	Jul-24
A P. Adams III		23260								
? Anderson						23237				
R.B. Atchison										
A.L. Barker			230184	230086			230059	230059	230059	
W.B. Barnhill					25861	230305	230305	23005		
S.L. Barr		230152	230035	230035			230170		230042	230170
M.E. Beatty										
A.H. Becktoft										
W.M. Beddow										
A.R. Biddick			229931	230184	229931	230064	230064	230064		230458
E.E. Blakley			230061	230061	229947		230061	230061		230458
J.D. Brady			25863	25863				230063	25863	25863
C.A. Brooks										
R.W. Braley		25878	23232	230068	23232	25867	230070	230035	230358	230335
R.A. Carey			23279	23233		23233		25862		230047
M.E. Carnell		230068	23279	23279	23279	230047			230047	230047
R.F. Claytor		25862	25878	25862	25862	25862	25862	23582	23582	
G.W. Cleven		230068		23279			230047		25862	230358
C. B. Cruikshank			230062	230062	25854	230184	230184	230184	230184	230062
B.A. DeMarco							23233	23233	23233	23233
W.D. DeSanders		25867	25867	25867	232337	230070				25867
C.L. Duncan		230050	230050	230050	230050		230050			
G.W. Dye		230051	23307	23307	23307		230089	230089	230089	25865
J.C. Egan			230061			23237	230061			
A.E. Elton										
V.E. Fienup				230063				230061		
J. Flanigan										
W.R. Flesh			230066	230066	230066	230066	230066		230066	
R.E. Flesher		230087					230061		230047	
C.W. Floyd Jr.										
M.C. Fuller		230066	230042	23229						
Garcia						23307		230305		
R.J. Gormley										
J.G. Gossage										
W.J. Grenier										
J.T. Griffin										
N. Harding						23307		230305		
N.B. Helstrom					229738	23279	23279	25867	230335	
H.A. Hennington						230023	230002	230002	230002	230023
R.W. Hollenbeck		23232				23232	230042	23232	23232	23232
R.L. Hughes										
T.D. Hummel										
J.K. Justice										
H.E. Keel										
W.L. Kennedy										
J.B. Kidd			230063				23307			
E.A. Kiessing		23233	23237	23237	23237	23237	23237	23237	23237	
R.C. King		230086	23234	230051	23234	23234	23234			
R.T. Knight			230051		23307		230059			
R.M. Knox			230063	230063		230063	230063		230457	
R.P. Kramer										

PILOT									
W.G. Lakin									
B. Lay Jr.	25864			25864	25864	25864			
F.G. Lauro									
R.N. Lohof									
W.L. MacCarter							230042		230042
W.H. McDonald									
F.H. Meadows									
K. Menzie									
D.L. Miner									
D.M. Mitchell									
W.U. Moreno									230152
T. E. Murphy	25864			25864	25864	25864		25864	25864
H. G. Nash Jr.									
D.K. Oakes	230080	230086	230080	25865	230080	230080		23271	230080
R.C. Pearson		230051			230051				
A.C. Persons							230042		
O.E. Petrich	229986								
V. Reed				230035	230042	230090		230063	
S.H. Reeder				230088	230088	230088	230088	230088	230088
O.D. Roane					25861	25861	25861	25861	25861
R. Rosenthal									
P.J. Schmalenbach	230038								
N.H. Scott					23233	230047	230047		230358
H.P. Shotland									
J.F. Stephens									
E.G. Stork									
J.R. Swartout	230087	25865	25864	230087	23307	23307	25865		
C.H. Thompson									
O. Turner	230051		25864		23307				
S.R. Turner	230057	230057	230057	230057		230057	230057	230057	230057
G.S. Van Noy	230259	230259	230259		230259	230259	230259	25867	230259
W.W. Veal				25861	230305		230305		
A.M. Vetter									
C.B. Winkleman									
R.H. Wolff									
A.F. Woodward Jr.		25860	25860	25860	25860	229931	25860	25860	25860

July 10—two entries for 230070, R. W. Braley and W. D. DeSanders

PILOT	25 Jul	26 Jul	28 Jul	29 Jul	30 Jul	12 Aug	15 Aug	17 Aug	19 Aug	24 Aug	27-Aug
A P. Adams III											
? Anderson											
R.B. Atchison											
A.L. Barker		230089									
W.B. Barnhill											
S.L. Barr	230170		230259			230170	230170	230170			
M.E. Beatty											
A.H. Becktoft											
W.M. Beddow											
A.R. Biddick		230066	230066	230066			230402	25860			
E.E. Blakley	230061				23393			23393			

Name											
J.D. Brady	25863	25863	25863	25863	25863	230066	25863	23237			
C.A. Brooks											
R.W. Braley		23233	23233	230070		230070	230047	230070			
R.A. Carey	25862										
M.E. Carnell		230047	230047	230047							
R.F. Claytor						230380	25867	25867			
G.W. Cleven	230358	230358	230358								
C. B. Cruikshank	230063	230062	230062	230062	230061	230062	30062	230062			
B.A. DeMarco	23233		23233			23233		230335			
W.D. DeSanders	25862									23-380	
C.L. Duncan										230089	
G.W. Dye	230089	230089	25865	25865	25865	230089	230089		230089	230089	
J.C. Egan.	230061						230066				
A.E. Elton											
V.E. Fienup	23271	230086		230086	230086	230086	25865	230086			
J. Flanigan											
W.R. Flesh											
R.E. Flesher	230089										
C.W. Floyd Jr.	230059		230059	230059	230057	230059		30059	230035	230059	
M.C. Fuller			230002								
Garcia						230066					
R.J. Gormley											
J.G. Gossage											
W.J. Grenier											
J.T. Griffin											
N. Harding		230047				23393					
N.B. Helstrom	230335	230335	230335	25867	25867	230335	230335		230023		
H.A. Hennington		230023	230023		230023	230023	230611	230611			
R.W. Hollenbeck	23232	23232		23232		23232	23232	23232			
R.L. Hughes							23271				
T.D. Hummel	230047	25878	25878	23233	23233	25878	230311	230311			
J.K. Justice	230023		23229	23229		230042	23229	23229			
H.E. Keel											
W.L. Kennedy						230062		230042			
J.B. Kidd			230259					23393			
E.A. Kiessing	230066		23237	23237	23237	23237					
R.C. King	23307		23234	23234	23234	23234	23234		25865	23234	
R.T. Knight											
R.M. Knox		230063	230063	230063	230063	230062		230063			
R.P. Kramer											
W.G. Lakin											
B. Lay Jr.						230380		25864			
F.G. Lauro											
R.N. Lohof											
W.L. MacCarter	230042	230042		230259	230170				230259		
W.H. McDonald											
F.H. Meadows											
K. Menzie											
D.L. Miner											
D.M. Mitchell											
W.U. Moreno	230152	230152	230061	230152	230066	230152	230152	230152			
T. E. Murphy	25864	25864	230087	23271	23271	25864		25864			
H. G. Nash Jr.											
D.K. Oakes	230080	25865		230080	230080		230080	230080			

R.C. Pearson											
A.C. Persons											
O.E. Petrich											
V. Reed	230090	230090	230090	230090		230090					
S.H. Reeder				230088	230088	230088		230088	230088	230088	
O.D. Roane	25861	25862		230170			230035	25861			
R. Rosenthal											
P.J. Schmalen-bach											
N.H. Scott	230358	230358		230358	230358		230358	230358			
H.P. Shotland							230002	230002			
J.F. Stephens											
E.G. Stork											
J.R. Swartout							23307		23307		
C.H. Thompson											
O. Turner			25865	25865		230089					
S.R. Turner	25865		230057	230057		230057			230402	230057	
G.S. Van Noy	230088					230259	230259	230042			
W.W. Veal						230170	230170	230170			
A.M. Vetter											
C.B. Winkleman											
R.H. Wolff							230061	230061			
A.F. Woodward Jr.	25860	25860	25860		25860		25860			230402	

PILOT	27-Aug	31-Aug	3-Sep	6-Sep	7-Sep	9-Sep	15-Sep	16-Sep	23-Sep	26-Sep	27-Sep
A P. Adams III		23260									
? Anderson						23237					
R.B. Atchi-son								230062			
A.L. Barker											
W.B. Barnhill			230259								
S.L. Barr								25861	230154		
M.E. Beatty								230087	230087		
A.H. Becktoft								230154			
W.M. Beddow								25997			
A.R. Biddick											
E.E. Blakley								23393	230758		
J.D. Brady			25863					230830	230830		
C.A. Brooks									25861		
R.W. Braley											
R.A. Carey											
M.E. Carnell											
R.F. Claytor								23233	23333		
G.W. Cleven			230358								
C. B. Cruik-shank		x		x		230062			230062		
B.A. DeMarco								23233	23233		
W.D. DeSanders			230358						230380		
C.L. Duncan								230796			
G.W. Dye											

Name	1	2	3	4	5	6	7	8	9	10	11	12	13
J.C. Egan	23393		23393		23393								
A.E. Elton													
V.E. Fienup		25865											
J. Flanigan								233508	26087				
W.R. Flesh									230799				
R.E. Flesher									23307				
C.W. Floyd Jr.		230059											
M.C. Fuller													
Garcia													
R.J. Gormley								23386	23386				
J.G. Gossage									230023				
W.J. Grenier			230335										
J.T. Griffin								230358	230796				
N. Harding						230796	23393						
N.B. Helstrom		230335											
H.A. Hennington		230611											
R.W. Hollenbeck													
R.L. Hughes		23271											23271
T.D. Hummel													
J.K. Justice		230090										23229	230090
H.E. Keel													
W.L. Kennedy													
J.B. Kidd													
E.A. Kiessing													
R.C. King		230089											
R.T. Knight													
R.M. Knox													
R.P. Kramer													
W.G. Lakin									230823				
B. Lay Jr.													
F.G. Lauro													
R.N. Lohof													
W.L. MacCarter		230062						230023	230170				
W.H. McDonald		230818						230818	23413				
F.H. Meadows		230840						230047	230047				
K. Menzie													
D.L. Miner													
D.M. Mitchell		23413						23413					
W.U. Moreno		230152						230152	230162				
T.E. Murphy		23307	x				25864	230090					
H.G. Nash Jr.									230840				
D.K. Oakes													
R.C. Pearson													
A.C. Persons													
O.E. Petrich													

V. Reed											
S.H. Reeder		230088	230088								
O.D. Roane		25861									
R. Rosenthal											
P.J. Schmalenbach											
N.H. Scott											
H.P. Shotland											
J.F. Stephens											
E.G. Stork											
J.R. Swartout											
C.H. Thompson											
O. Turner											
S.R. Turner		230057	230057								
G.S. Van Noy											
W.W. Veal		230259									
A.M. Vetter		230087									
C.B. Winkleman		230035									
R.H. Wolff		230064									
A.F. Woodward Jr.		230402									

PILOT	Oct-2	Oct-4	Oct-8	Oct-9	Oct -10	Oct-14
A P. Adams III						
? Anderson						
R.B. Atchison	230062	230062		230062	230047	
A.L. Barker			25864			
W.B. Barnhill						
S.L. Barr				230799		
M.E. Beatty	230087	230796	23474	230723	230087	
A.H. Becktoft	230154	230154	230154			
W.M. Beddow	25997	25997	25997	23307	230723	
A.R. Biddick						
E.E. Blakley	23393		23393			
J.D. Brady		230830			230830	
C.A. Brooks	230088	230088				
R.W. Braley						
R.A. Carey						
M.E. Carnell						
R.F. Claytor						
G.W. Cleven	230604	230724	23233			
C. B. Cruikshank	23508	23508	230062	230830	230725	
B.A. DeMarco	23233		23233			
W.D. DeSanders		230725		23433		
C.L. Duncan						
G.W. Dye						
J.C. Egan					230830	
A.E. Elton						
V.E. Fienup						
J. Flanigan	26087	26087			26094	

W.R. Flesh		25861				
R.E. Flesher						
C.W. Floyd Jr.						
M.C. Fuller				23534		
Garcia						
R.J. Gormley	23386	23474	23386			
J.G. Gossage						
W.J. Grenier						
J.T. Griffin	230796		230796			
N. Harding				230830		
N.B. Helstrom	230604	230604				
H.A. Hennington	25957	25957	25957			
R.W. Hollenbeck						
R.L. Hughes	23271	23271		23271	23271	23271
T.D. Hummel						
J.K. Justice	230487	230487	23229	23229	23229	
H.E. Keel		230723	230723			
W.L. Kennedy						
J.B. Kidd			23395			
E.A. Kiessing						
R.C. King						
R.T. Knight						
R.M. Knox						
R.P. Kramer		23433	23433	23413	23433	
W.G. Lakin	230823	230823				
B. Lay Jr.						
F.G. Lauro	230758	23393				
R.N. Lohof			230088	230090		
J.H. Luckadoo			23474			
W.L. MacCarter	230170	230023			230090	
W.H. McDonald	230818		230818			
F.H. Meadows	230725	230840	230358			
K. Menzie		230358				
D.L. Miner	230091	230091	230091	26094		
D.M. Mitchell	23413	23413				
W.U. Moreno	230152	230152	230152			
T.E. Murphy	230723	25864	25864			
H.G. Nash Jr.	230358		230840			
D.K. Oakes						
R.C. Pearson						
A.C. Persons						
O.E. Petrich						
V. Reed						
S.H. Reeder						
O.D. Roane			230487			
R. Rosenthal			230758	26087	26087	
P.J. Schmalenbach						
N.H. Scott						
H.P. Shotland						
J.F. Stephens	26094	26094	23237	23237	23237	
E.G. Stork			230170	230023	230023	
J.R. Swartout	23474					
C.H. Thompson		230734		230734	230734	
O. Turner		25864				
S.R. Turner						

G.S. Van Noy						
W.W. Veal						
A.M. Vetter						
C.D. Walts	220047	230047	230823	230823		
C.B. Winkleman						
R.H. Wolff						
A.F. Woodward Jr.						

AIRCRAFT—FORMATION MATRIX

SERIAL	Jun 22	Jun 25	26 Jun	28 Jun	29 Jun	4 Jul	10 Jul	10 Jul	14 Jul	17 Jul	24 Jul
LEAD											
1		230087	230063	23279	25861	23307	230061		230305	230047	230061
2		230080	25863	23233	230035	23234	230063		230042	23233	230152
3		230086	229931	25862	230088	230080	230066		230002	230358	25863
4		230051	230061	230050	230087	230051	230184		230259	25862	230062
5		25864	23237	230068	25865	25864	23237		230088	23232	230458
6		230057	230066	25867	230051	230086	230064		25861	230335	25860
7			230062								
8			25860								
9											
HIGH											
1		230068	230051	230063	23279	23233	23307		230061	230042	230358
2		23232	23307	25863	230050	25867	23234		23237	230088	23233
3		25862	230057	25860	25862	25862	230080		25860	230002	230335
4		230050	230184	230061	23232	230047	230059	229931	230184	25867	230047
5		25867	230086	230062	23233	23279	230086	230170	230063	25861	23232
6		25878	25865	230184	229738	23232	25864	230070	230064	230063	25867
7		23233	230042	23237							
8			230035	230066							
			230259								
9											
LOW											
1		229986	23279	25864	23237	23237	230047	230305	25862	230089	25865
2		230038	230087	230080	229947	230063	23233	230002	23233	25864	230080
3		23260	25878	23234	229931	230064	23279	230090	230035	23271	23234
4		230152	230050	230086	25854	230184	230050	230259	230047	230059	25864
5		230259	23232	23307	230066	25860	230042	230088	23232	230057	230086
6		230066	25867	230057	25860	230066	230070	25861	25867	230086	230057
7				230035							
8				230259							
9				23229							
TRAIL											
1					23307	230305					
2					25864	230023					
3					230057	230042					
4						230259					
5						230088					
6						25861					
7											

July 10—230070 listed twice

SPARES	Jun 22	Jun 25	26 Jun	28 Jun	29 Jun	4 Jul	10 Jul	10 Jul	14 Jul	17 Jul	24 JUl
1		229947	229738			230259			25865	230063	
2		23307	23237							23307	
3		23279	230066							23234	
4		230184									
5		25865									
RETURN											
1		23232	23229			230066	230090		230002	230358	230042
2		230152	23234				230259		230042	25864	230170
3							23233		230047		230023
4							25862		23232		
5							23307		230057		
6							230063		23059		
7							230184		230061		
8									230184		
9									230063		
FTO											
1							230002		23233	230042	
2										25867	
3										23237	

SERIAL	25-Jul	26-Jul	28-Jul	29-JUl	30-Jul	12-Aug	15-Aug	17-Aug	19-Aug	24-Aug	24S-Aug
LEAD											
1	230089	230047	230259	25865	230061	23393	23307	23393	23307		
2	230059	23232	23229	230059	230063	230063	25865	230061	230035		
3	230080	23233	230090	23234	230066	230066	23234	23237	25865		
4	25864	230358	230002	23271	230062	230062	230089	230066	230089		
5	23307	25878	230023	230080	230152	230152	23271	230063	230088		
6	23271	230335	230066	230086	23237	23237	230080	25860	230402		
7									230259		
8											
9									230023		
HIGH											
1	230061	230062	230358	230358	25865	230089	230062	230170		230089	
2	25862	230063	23233	23232	230057	230059	230061	230611		230059	
3	25863	230066	230335	25867	230086	230057	25863	25861		230057	
4	230063	25860	230047	230047	23271	25864	25860	230042		230402	
5	230152	230152	25878	23233	230080	23234	230152	230002		230380	
6	230066	25863	23232	230070	23234	230086	230402	23229		23234	
7	230047	25865	230063		230088	230170	230170	25864		230088	
8	23232	230042	23237		230023	230023	230611	230259			
	25862		230061		230170	230088	230335	230080			
9											
LOW											
1	230170	230089	25865	230062							
2	230023	230086	230059	230063							
3	230090	25861	23234	25863							
4	230088	25864	230087	230066							
5	230042	230023	230057	230152							
6	25861	230090	25860	23237							
7		230062									
8		25863									
9											

TRAIL											
1	230358			230088							
2	23233			23229							
3	230335			230259							
4	25865			230090							
5				230057							
6				230170							
7											
SPARES											
1				230057			230259	230088	230023		
2							23229	230152			
3							230002	230086			
4											
5											
RETURN											
1	23232	230090		230259	230170	230042		230170			23237
2	230080	23232		23229	230023	255878		230059			
3	230152	25878		230090	23233	230062					
4	230063	230063		25867		230152					
5	230335			230059							
6	25865			25863							
7				230063							
8											
9											
FTO											
1	230059										
2											
3											

SERIAL	27 Aug	31 Aug	3 Sep	6 Sep	7 Sep	9 Sep	15 Sep	16 Sep	23 Sep	24 Sep	25 Sep
LEAD											
1		23393	230259	23393	230796	230796	23393	23233	23302		
2			25861					230818	23386		
3			230611					23413	230037		
4			230088					25861	23271		
5			230035					230023	23234		
6			230090					23229	230796		
7											
8											
9											
HIGH											
1			230358					23307	23233		
2			230818					25997	230823		
3			230840					26087	230840		
4			230335					230796	230380		
5			25863					230358	230047		
6			230062					23386	23413		
7			230402					230090	230154		
8			230064					230047	230023		
9			230152					230154	230170		

SERIAL										
LOW										
1			23307					23393	230758	
2			23271					230062	230830	
3			25865					23508	230152	
4			230089					230830	230062	
5			230059					230152	26087	
6			230057					230064	26094	
7										
8										
9										
TRAIL										
1			230087						23090	
2									230799	
3			30413						25861	
4			230087							
5										
6										
7										
SPARES										
1	230259		230087					230604		
2										
3										
4										
5										
RETURN										
1		230035		230154					23233	
2		25864		230725					230047	
3				230047					23413	
4				230380					230154	
5				230087					26094	
6				230064					230090	
7									25861	
8										
9										
FTO										
1							230047	23307	230840	
2								230152		
3										

SERIAL	26 Sep	27 Sep	2 Oct	4 Oct	8 Oct	9 Oct	10 Oct	14 Oct
LEAD								
1	230487	23357	230604	25864	23393	230830	230830	
2	23229	23229	230818	25997	230758	23237	26087	
3	230023	25861	23413	230796	23237	26087	26094	
4	230799	230170	23233	23271	230062	230723	230725	
5	25861	230047	230725	230723	230091	230090	230047	
6	230132	230154	230358	23474	230152	230023	23237	
7								
8								
9								

HIGH								
1	23307	23393	23393	230725	23233	23433	23307	
2	25997	230087	230758	230358	23433	230062	230723	
3	23386	26094	26094	23413	230840	26094	230734	
4	25864	230830	23508	230604	230818		23534	
5	230734	230758	230091	230840	230358		23229	
6	23474	230152	26087	230823	230047		23433	
7	230830	230604	230152	230830	230487		230087	
8	26094	230818	230062	23433	23229			
9	230062	230840	230796	230062	230154			
SERIAL								
LOW								
1	230604	230723	230487	23508	25864	230799	230823	
2	230818	23386	230088	26087	25997	23534	230090	
3	23413	26087	230170	26094	230723	23229	230023	
4	230380	23271	25957	230152	23474		230061	
5	230823	25997	230154	23393	230796	23271		
6	230725	230734	230825	230091	23386	230734		
7						23307		
8								
9								
TRAIL								
1		23233	23474	230487	25957			
2		230358	23271	230023	230088			
3	23508		230087	230088	230170			
4			230723	25987				
5			25997	230154				
6			23386	25861				
7								
SPARES								
1				230734		23413		
2				230047		230823		
3								
4								
5								
RETURN								
1	230023		230087	23474	23237	23229	23307	
2	230823			230023	23433	230023	23413	
3	230062			230062	230062	230799	23534	
4				230840			26094	
5							230061	
6								
7								
8								
9								
FTO								
1				25957	230830	230062	23271	
2					23307			
3								

September 27—23357 detached service from 482nd BG flown by Harding

APPENDIX F.
PERSONAL REPORT ON
THE REGENSBURG
MISSION, AUGUST 17, 1943

HEADQUARTERS
100TH BOMBARDMENT GROUP (H)
APO 634

U.S. Army Station 139
26 August, 1943

SUBJECT: Personal report on the REGENSBURG mission, 17 Aug 1943.
TO: Commanding Officer, 100th Bombardment Group (H).

1. This report does not attempt to render a complete summary of the mission. It is merely an eyewitness account of what was seen, together with certain recommendations pertinent thereto, during an ordeal in which the 100th Group fought its way to the target through fierce and prolonged enemy fighter attacks and accurately bombed a vital target.

2. When the 100th Group crossed the coast of Holland south of the Hague at 1008 hours at our base altitude of 17,000 feet, I was well situated to watch the proceedings, being co-pilot in the lead ship of the last element of the high squadron. The Group had all of its 21 B-17's tucked in tightly and was within handy supporting distance of the 95th Group, ahead of us at 18,000 feet. We were the last and lowest of the seven groups of the 4th Air Division that were visible ahead on a south-east course, forming a long, loose-linked chain in the bright sunlight—too long, it seemed. Wide gaps separated the three combat wings. As I sat there in the tail-end element of that many miles long

procession, gauging the distance to the lead group, I had the lonesome foreboding that might come to the last man to run a gauntlet lined with spiked
clubs. The premonition was well-founded. At 1017 hours, near Woensdrecht,
I saw the first flak blossom out in our vicinity, light and inaccurate. A few
minutes later, approximately 1025 hours, two FW-190's appeared at 1 o'clock
level and whizzed through the formation ahead of us in frontal attack, nick-
ing two B-17's of the 95th Group in the wings and breaking away beneath us
in half-rolls. Smoke immediately trailed from both B-17s, but they held their
stations. As the fighters passed us at a high rate of closure, the guns of the
group went into action. The pungent smell of burnt powder filled our cockpit, and the B-17 trembled to the recoil of nose and ball-turret guns. I saw
pieces fly off the wing of one of the fighters before they passed from view.

Here was early action, the members of the crew sensed trouble. There was
something desperate about the way those two fighters came in fast, right out of their
climb without any preliminaries. For a second the interphone was busy with admo-
nitions: "Lead more" . . . "Short bursts" . . . "Don't throw rounds away" . . . "There'll
be more along in a minute."

Three minutes later, the gunners reported fighters climbing up from all around
the clock, singly and in pairs, both FW-190's and ME-109's. This was only my
fourth raid, but from what I could see on my side, it looked like too many fighters
for sound health. A coordinated attack followed, with the head-on fighters coming in from slightly above, the 9 and 3 o'clock attackers approaching from about
level, and the rear attackers from slightly below. Every gun from every B-17 in
our group and the 95th was firing, criss-crossing our patch of sky with tracers to
match the time-fuse cannon shell puffs that squirted from the wings of the Jerry
single-seaters. I would estimate that 75% of our fire was inaccurate, falling astern
of the target—particularly the fire from hand held guns. Nevertheless, both sides
got hurt in this clash, with two B-17s from our low squadron and one from the
95th Group falling out of formation on fire with crews bailing out, and several
fighters heading for the deck in flames or with their pilots lingering behind under
dirty yellow parachutes. Our group leader, Major John Kidd, pulled us up nearer
the 95th Group for mutual support.

I knew that we were already in a lively fight. What I didn't know was the real
fight, the anschluss of 20 MM cannon shells, hadn't really begun. A few minutes later
we absorbed the first wave of a hailstorm of individual fighter attacks that were to
engulf us clear to the target. The ensuing action was so rapid and varied that I cannot
give a chronological account of it. Instead, I will attempt a fragmentary report of

salient details that even now give me a dry mouth and an unpleasant sensation in the stomach to recall. The sight was fantastic and surpassed fiction.

It was at 1041 hours, over Europe, that I looked out my copilot's window after a short lull and saw two squadrons, 12 ME-109s and 11 FW-190s climbing parallel to us. The first squadron had reached our level and was pulling ahead to turn into us and second was not far behind. Several thousand feet below us were many more fighters, with their noses cocked at maximum climb. Over the interphone came reports of equal number of enemy aircraft deploying on the other side. For the first time I noticed a ME-110 sitting out of range on our right. He was to stay with us all the way to the target, apparently to report our position to fresh squadrons waiting for us down the road. At the sight of all these fighters, I had the distinct feeling of being trapped—that the Hun was tipped off, or at least had guessed our destination and was waiting for us. No P-47's were visible. The life expectancy of the 100th Group suddenly seemed very short, since it already appeared that the fighters were passing up the proceeding groups, with the exception of the 95th, in order to take a cut at us.

Swinging their yellow noses around in a wide U-turn, the 12 ship squadron of ME-109s came in from 12 o'clock in pairs and in fours and the main event was on. A shining silver object sailed past over our right wing. I recognized it as a main exit door. Seconds later, a dark object came hurtling down through the formation, barely missing several props. It was a man, clasping his knees to his head, revolving like a diver in a triple somersault. I didn't see his chute open.

A B-17 turned gradually out of the formation to the right, maintaining altitude. In a split second the B-17 disappeared in brilliant explosion, from which the only remains were four small balls of fire, the fuel tanks, which were quickly consumed as they fell earthward. Our airplane was endangered by various debris, emergency hatches, exit doors, prematurely opened parachutes, bodies and assorted fragments of B-17s and Hun fighters breezed past us in the slip-stream.

I watched two fighters explode not far beneath, disappearing in sheets of orange flame, B-17s dropping out in every stage of distress, from engines on fire to control surfaces shot away, friendly and enemy parachutes floating down, and, on the green carpet far behind us, numerous funeral pyres of smoke from fallen fighters marking our trail. On we flew through the strewn wake of a desperate air battle, where disintegrating aircraft were commonplace and 60 chutes in the air at one time were hardly worth a second look.

I watched a B-17 turn slowly to the right with its cockpit a mass of flames. The copilot crawled out of his window, held on with one hand, reached back for his chute, buckled it on, let go and was whisked back into the horizontal stabilizer. I believe the impact killed him. His chute didn't open. Ten minutes, twenty minutes, thirty minutes, and still no let up in the attacks. The fighters queued up like a breadline and let us have it. Each second of time had a cannon shell in it. The strain of being a clay duck in the wrong end of that aerial shooting gallery became almost intolerable as the minutes accumulated towards the first hour.

Our B-17 shook steadily with the fire of the .50's and the air inside was heavy with smoke. It was cold in the cockpit, but when I looked across at Lt. Thomas Murphy, the pilot, and a good one, sweat was pouring off his forehead and over his oxygen mask. He turned the controls over to me for awhile. It was a blessed relief to concentrate on holding station in formation instead of watching those everlasting fighters boring in. It was possible to forget the fighters. Then the top-turret gunner's twin muzzles would pound away a foot above my head, giving a realistic imitation of cannon shells exploding in the cockpit, while I gave a better imitation of a man jumping six inches out of his seat. A B-17 of the 95th Group, with its right Tokyo tanks on fire, dropped back about 200 feet above our right wing and stayed there while 7 of the crew successively bailed out. Four went out the bombbay and executed delayed jumps, one bailed out from the nose, opened his chute prematurely and nearly fouled the tail. Another went out the left waist-gun opening, delaying his chute opening for a safe interval. The tail gunner dropped out of his hatch, apparently pulling the ripcord before he was clear of the ship. His chute opened instantaneously, barely missing the tail, and jerked him so hard that both his shoes came off. He hung limp in the harness, whereas the others had showed immediate signs of life after their chutes opened, shifting around in the harness. The B-17 then dropped back in a medium spiral and I did not see the pilots leave. I saw it just before it passed from view, several thousand feet below us, with its right wing a solid sheet of yellow flame.

After we had been under constant attack for a solid hour, it appeared certain that the 100th Group was faced with annihilation. Seven of our group had been shot down, the sky was still mottled with rising fighters and it was only 1120 hours, with the target time still 35 minutes away. I doubt if a man in the group visualized the possibility of our getting much further without 100% loss. I knew that I had long since mentally accepted the fact of death, and that it was simply a question of next second or the next minute. I learned first-hand that a man can resign himself to the certainty of death without becoming panicky. Our group fire power was reduced 33%, ammunition was running low. Our tail guns had to be replenished from other gun stations. Gunners were becoming exhausted and nerve-tortured from the prolonged strain, and there was an awareness on everybody's part that something must have gone wrong. We had been the aiming point for the Luftwaffe and we fully expected to find the rest primed for us at the target.

Fighter tactics were running true to form. Frontal attackers hit the low squadron and the lead squadron, while rear attackers went for the high. The manner of
their attacks showed that some pilots were old-timers, some amateurs, and that
all knew pretty definitely where we were going and were inspired with a fanatical
determination to stop us before we got there. The old-timers came in on frontal attacks with a noticeably slower rate of closure, apparently throttled back, obtaining
greater accuracy than those that bolted through us wide out. They did some nice
shooting at ranges of 500 or more yards, and in many cases seemed able to time
their thrusts so as to catch the top and ball turret gunners engaged with rear and
side attacks. Less experienced pilots were pressing home attacks to 250 yards and
less to get hits, offering point-blank targets on the break away, firing long bursts of
20 seconds, and in some cases actually pulling up instead of going down and out.
Several FW-190 pilots pulled off some first rate deflection shooting on side attacks
against the high group, then raked the low group on the break away out of a side-
slip, keeping the nose cocked up in the turn to prolong the period the formation
was in their sights.

I observed what I believe was an attempt at air-to-air bombing, although I
didn't see the bombs dropped. A patch of 75 to 100 gray white bursts, smaller than
flak bursts, appeared simultaneously at our level, off to one side. One B-17 dropped
out on fire and put its wheels down while the crew bailed out. Three ME-109s
circled it closely, but held their fire, apparently ensuring that no one stayed in the
ship to try for home. I saw Hun fighters hold their fire even when being shot at by
a B-17 from which the crew were bailing out.

Near the IP, at 1150 hours, one hour and a half after the first of at least 200
individual fighter attacks, the pressure eased off, although hostiles were in the vicinity. We turned at the IP at 1154 hours with 14 B-17's left in the group, two of
which were badly crippled. They dropped out soon after bombing the target and
headed for Switzerland, one of them, "042", carrying Col William Kennedy as tail
gunner, #4 engine was on fire, but not out of control. Major William Veal, leader
of the high squadron, received a cannon shell in his #3 engine just before the start
of the bombing run and went in to the target with the prop feathered.

Weather over the target, as on the entire trip, was ideal. The group got its
bombs away promptly on the leader. As we turned and headed for the Alps, I got
a grim satisfaction out of seeing a rectangular column of smoke rising straight
up from the ME-109 shops, with only one burst over in the town of Regensburg.

The rest of the trip was a marked anti-climax. A few more fighters pecked at us
on the way to the Alps. A town in Brenner Pass tossed up a lone burst of futile flak.
Col LeMay, who had taken excellent care of us all the way, circled the air division
over Lake Garda long enough to give the cripples a chance to join the family, and

we were on our way toward the Mediterranean Sea in a gradual descent. About 25 fighters on the ground at Verona stayed on the ground. The prospect of ditching as we approached Bone, short of fuel, and the sight of other B-17's falling into the drink, seemed trivial matters after the vicious nightmare of the long trip across Northern Germany. We felt the reaction of men who had not expected to see another sunset.

At 1815 hours, with red lights showing on all fuel tanks in my ship, the seven B-17's out of the group who were still in formation circled over Bertoux and landed in the dust. Our crew was unscratched. Sole damage to the airplane; a bit of ventilation around the tail from flak and 20 MM shells. We slept on the hard ground under the wings of our B-17, but the good earth felt softer than a silk pillow.

3. Recommendations:

A. That combat wings always comprise three groups, spaced close enough for mutual support, on deep penetrations and that the interval between combat wings be as close as is flying in order to cut down the overall distance from the head to the tail of the column. This should result in a more even distribution of fighter attacks with lower average loss per group. Enemy staff near their fuel limits did not try to catch preceding groups but concentrated on the tail or the long column we presented on the Regensburg mission.

B. That fighter escorts give particular attention to protection of rear groups on deep penetrations. I would judge that 17,000 feet, our base altitude, was too low—an awkward altitude for P-47's—even if fighter escort had covered us, which it didn't.

C. That emphasis on deflection shooting on the part of our gunners be continued and intensified. A B-17 group can put out tremendous fire power, and the 100th Group did some accurate shooting, but too many of the gunners were firing on targets that had just left.

D. That groups expecting to operate on the return trip from North African airdromes carry with them engine, gun, and radio compartment covers for protection against dust and mud.

E. That continued thought be give to further protective measures in the formation for the low squadron, which in our group, at least, was the A.P. for frontal attacks.

F. That better exchange of information be provided between air divisions. Even several days after a mission, groups in the 4th Air Division have little knowledge of what happened to the 1st Air Division, except through hearsay.

G. That 30 combat missions be reduced to 25 for crews that have engaged in deep penetration. It takes a rugged constitution to stand up to missions like Regensburg and even the toughest crew members were badly shaken by nearly two hours under persistent attack. The less phlegmatic were already potential candidates for the rest home when we landed in Africa. My four previous missions, in one of with our bombardier was killed, were pieces of cake in comparison to the 11 hour Regensburg show, and I doubt if 20 such normal missions would take the same amount out of a man as one stint to Regensburg.

4. Awards: The following suggested awards are recommended to the attention of the Group Commander:

A. Distinguished Flying Cross: To every combat crew member of the 100th Bomb Group who participated in the Regensburg mission, for courage and achievement in enabling the group to reach and successfully bomb a vital target against odds that could easily have resulted in 100% loss had it not been for the outstanding air discipline of the group as a whole. A tight formation was held, in spite of reshuffling of the group from consecutive losses, and cool judgment and self-control were exercised by individual crews under prolonged strain.

B. Distinguished Service Cross:

Major John Kidd group leader, for heroism and skill in his leadership of the group to target and final destination. This twenty-four-year-old officer carried out superbly an assignment above and beyond the call of duty for an officer of his age and experience. He had had only three previous combat missions.

Major William Veal, leader of the high squadron, for heroic and skillful leadership of his squadron. Just before turning in to the bombing run, a cannon shell hit his #3 engine, setting it on fire, and oxygen failure occurred. Instead of turning toward the safety of the Swiss border, approximately 65 miles distant, Major Veal feathered his #3 prop, a sure tip-off to the fighters in the vicinity, in order to regain position in the formation. He successfully bombed the target, extinguished the engine fire, crossed the Alps and several hundred miles of Mediterranean and reached base in North Africa, all on three engines.

C. **Lieutenant Robert Wolff,** a wing man in the lead squadron. The
undersigned did not have the opportunity to interview Lt Wolff or his
crew, but observed his ship hobbling along with the formation all the
way to North Africa in spite of what looked like the worst battle damage
of any airplane in the group. Appropriate investigation and award is
recommended.

D. CONGRESSIONAL MEDAL OF HONOR:

Major Gale W. Cleven, leader of the low squadron. Throughout approximately two hours of constant fighter attack, Major Cleven's squadron
was the principal focal point of the enemy's fire. Early in the encounter,
south of Antwerp, he lost his entire second element of three B-17's yet
maintained his vulnerable and exposed position in the formation rigidly
in order to keep his guns uncovered.

Approximately 30 minutes before reaching the target, his airplane received the following battle damage. A 20 mm cannon shell penetrated the
right side of the airplane and exploded beneath the pilot, damaging the
electrical system and injuring the top turret gunner in the leg. A second
20 mm shell entered the radio compartment, killing the radio operator,
who bled to death with his legs severed above the knees. A third 20 mm
shell entered the left side of the nose, tearing out a section of plexiglass
about two feet square, tore away the right hand nose-gun installation and
injured the bombardier in the head and shoulder. A fourth 20 mm shell
entered the cabin roof and severed the rudder cables to one side of the
rudder. A sixth 20 mm cannon shell exploded in the #3 engine, destroying all engine controls. The engine caught fire and lost its power, but the
fire eventually died out.

Confronted with structural damage, partial loss of control, fire in the air
and serious injuries to personnel, and faced with fresh waves of fighters
still rising to the attack, Major Cleven had every justification for abandoning ship. His crew, some of them comparatively inexperienced youngsters,
were preparing to bail out, since no other course appeared open. The
copilot pleaded repeatedly with Major Cleven to abandon ship. Major
Cleven's reply at this critical juncture, although the odds were overwhelmingly against him, was as follows, "You son of a _____ (bitch), You sit
there and take it." These strong words were heard over the inter-phone and
had a magical effect on the crew. They stuck to their guns. The airplane
continued to the target, bombed it and reached base in North Africa.
Sergeant Ferroggiaro, left waist gunner and veteran of the war in China
in 1932 and of seven months at the front in Spain in 1938, voiced the

opinion of the crew to the undersigned when he stated the completion of the mission was solely due to the extraordinary heroism and inspired determination of Major Cleven. The undersigned believes that under the circumstances which obtained, Major Cleven's actions were far above and beyond the call of duty and the skill, courage and strength or will displayed by him as airplane and squadron commander in the face of hopeless odds have seldom, if ever, been surpassed in the annals of the Army Air Forces.

5. It is requested that should any portion of this report be used for public relations purposes, the name of the undersigned be strictly withheld and that reference be made only to "an officer".

Signed
Beirne Lay Jr.
Lt. Colonel, Air Corps.

SELECTED SOURCES

Primary Sources
Documents

Air Force Historical Research Agency, various unit history files, Maxwell Air
Force Base, Montgomery, Alabama.

Aircraft Accident Reports, various report numbers. For additional information
concerning a "for fee" research service, contact the website Accident-Report.com.

National Air and Space Museum Library, Washington, D.C.

National Archives, Record Group 18, Records of the Army Air Forces, Tactical
Mission Folders, June 22, 1943–October 14, 1943, College Park, MD.

National Archives, Record Group 92, Records of the Office of the Quartermaster
General, Missing Air Crew Report (MACR), various numbers, College
Park, MD.

U.S. Army Air Forces, Eighth Air Force Tactical Development, August
1942–May 1945, issued July 1945, available from Paul Gaudette Books,
Tucson, AZ.

U.S. Army Air Forces, Informational Intelligence Report, No. 43-17, "German
Fighter Tactics Against Flying Fortresses," issued December 31, 1943,
available from Paul Gaudette Books, Tucson, AZ.

Correspondence, Interviews, and Personal Papers

Frank D. Murphy with Elfriede Rawe, Kattenvenne, Germany, 1983–1998.

Frank D. Murphy with Gerd Wiegand, München, Germany, October 27, 1991.
Wiegand was an Fw 190 fighter pilot, II Gruppen, Jagdgeschwader 26,
Lille-Nord, France (1942–1944), and was credited with thirty-one air
victories, including seven B-17s. He was shot down three times himself.

Frank D. Murphy with Gerda Berdelmann, Lienen, Germany, 1983–1998.

Frank D. Murphy with Heinz Hessling, Beckum, Germany, 1983–1989.

Frank D. Murphy with Heinz Knoke, Bad Iburg, Germany, 1983–1986. In October 1943, *Oberleutnant* Knoke was a Me 109 flight commander in 5 Staffel, Jagdgeschwader II, Marx airfield south of Jever station near Wilhelmshaven in northern Germany. He was shot down at Münster on October 10, 1943, but successfully crash-landed his aircraft at Twente, north of Münster, and was unhurt. He was one of Germany's leading fighter aces in the West. During four years of combat duty (1941–1945), Knoke was credited with fifty-two air victories over Allied aircraft.

Secondary Sources

Ambrose, Stephen E. *The Victors: Eisenhower and His Boys: The Men of World War II.* New York: Simon and Schuster, 1998.

Andrews, Paul M. *We're Poor Little Lambs: The Last Mission of Crew 22 and Piccadilly Lily.* Springfield, VA: Foxfall Press, 1995.

Andrews, Paul M., and William H. Adams. Project Bits and Pieces in four volumes, 1) *Heavy Bombers of The Mighty Eighth,* 2) *The Mighty Eighth Combat Chronology,* 3) *The Mighty Eighth Combat Chronology Supplement,* and 4) *The Mighty Eighth Roll of Honor.* Warrenton, VA: Eighth Air Force Memorial Museum Foundation, 1995.

Arizona Wing of the Confederate Air Force. *Sentimental Journey.* Phoenix, AZ, 1995.

Arnold, Henry H. *Airmen and Aircraft.* New York: Ronald Press, 1926.

Bell, Dana. *Air Force Colors, Vol. II: ETO & MTO 1942–1945.* Carrollton, Texas: Squadron/Signal Publications, 1980.

Bendiner, Elmer. *The Fall of the Fortresses.* New York: G. P. Putnam's Sons, 1980.

Bennett, John M. *Letters from England.* San Antonio, TX, 1986.

Bowers, Peter M. *Fortress in the Sky.* Granada Hills, CA: Sentry Books, 1976.

Bowden, Ray. *Plane Names & Bloody Noses: 100th Bomb Group (Heavy) United States Army Air Force, Thorpe Abbotts, England, 1943–1945.* Bridport, England: Design Oracle Partnership, 2000.

Bowman, Martin W. *Castles in the Air: The Story of the B-17 Flying Fortress Crews of the US 8th Air Force.* Sparkford, England: Patrick Stephens, 1983.

Bowman, Martin W. *Home by Christmas?: The Story of U.S. 8th/l5th Air Force Airmen at War.* Sparkford, England: Patrick Stephens, 1987.

Bowyer, Michael J. F. *Action Stations 1: Wartime Military Airfields of East Anglia, 1939–1945.* Sparkford, England: Patrick Stephens, 1979.

Boyne, Walter J. *Beyond the Horizons: The Lockheed Story.* New York: St. Martin's Press, 1998.

Brown, James R. *Combat Record of the Original 100th Bombardment Group (H): The Bloody Hundredth.* Privately printed, 1983.

Burgess, Alan. *The Longest Tunnel: The True Story of World War II's Great Escape.* New York: Grove Weidenfeld, 1990.

Caidin, Martin. *Flying Forts: The B-17 in World War II.* New York: Meredith Press, 1968.

Churchill, Winston S. *The Second World War,* vol. 1. New York: Life-Time, 1959.

Coffey, Thomas M. *Decision over Schweinfurt: The U.S. 8th Air Force Battle for Daylight Bombing.* New York: David McKay, 1977.

Coffey, Thomas M. *Iron Eagle: The Turbulent Life of General Curtis LeMay.* New York: Crown, 1986.

Corum, James S., and Richard R. Muller. *The Luftwaffe's Way of War: German Air Force Doctrine 1911–1945.* Annapolis, MD: Nautical & Aviation Publishing, 1998.

Crosby, Harry H. *A Wing and a Prayer.* New York: Harper Collins, 1993.

Crosby, Harry H., and Cindy Goodman, eds. *Splasher Six,* newsletter of the 100th Bomb Group, File Collection, 1983–1999.

Durand, Arthur A. *Stalag Luft III: The Secret Story.* Sparkford, England: Patrick Stephens, 1989.

Ethell, Jeffrey L. *Air War over Germany: The USAAF Bombing Campaign 1944–1945.* London: Arms and Armour Press, 1985.

Freeman, Roger A. *Airfields of the Eighth: Then and Now.* London: Battle of Britain Prints International, 1978.

Freeman, Roger A. *B-17 Fortress at War.* London: Ian Allan, 1977.

Freeman, Roger A. *Experiences of War: The American Airman in Europe.* Osceola, WI: Motorbooks International, 1991.

Freeman, Roger A. *The Friendly Invasion.* Lavenham, England: East Anglia Tourist Board, 1992.

Freeman, Roger A. *The Mighty Eighth: A History of the U.S. 8th Army Air Force.* London: Jane's, 1970.

Freeman, Roger A. *The Mighty Eighth in Color.* Forest Lake, MN: Specialty Press, 1992.

Freeman, Roger A. *Mighty Eighth War Diary.* London: Jane's, 1981.

Freeman, Roger A. *Mighty Eighth War Manual.* London: Jane's, 1984.

Freeman, Roger A. *The Mighty Eighth Warpaint & Heraldry.* London: Arms and Armour Press, 1997.

Freeman, Roger A. *U.S. Strategic Airpower Europe 1942–1945*. London: Arms and Armour Press, 1989.

Girbig, Werner. *Six Months to Oblivion: The Eclipse of the Luftwaffe Fighter Force*. New York: Hippocrene, 1975.

Gardiner, Juliet. *"Overpaid, Oversexed, & Over Here": The American GI in World War II Britain*. New York: Canopy, 1992.

Goodman, Cindy, and Jan Riddling. *The Forgotten Man—The Mechanic: The Kenneth A. Lemmons Story*. Little Rock, AR: CinJan Productions, 1999.

Hawkins, Ian L. *The Münster Raid: Before and After*. Trumbull, CT: FNP Military Division, 1999.

Held, Werner. *Battle Over the Third Reich*. Walton-on-Thames, England: Air Research Publications, 1990.

Holles, Everett. *Unconditional Surrender*. New York: Howell Soskin, 1945.

Jablonski, Edward. *Double Strike: The Epic Air Raids on Regensburg/Schweinfurt*. New York: Doubleday, 1974.

Jablonski, Edward. *Flying Fortress: The Illustrated Biography of the B-17s and the Men Who Flew Them*. New York: Doubleday, 1965.

Jeffery, P. H. *East Anglian Keeps, Castles, and Forts*. Gillingham, England: Old Orchard Press, 1986.

Johnson, Brian. *The Secret War*. London: British Broadcasting Corporation, 1978.

Kahn David. "The Intelligence Failure at Pearl Harbor," *Foreign Affairs*, winter 1991/92.

Kaplan, Philip, and Rex Alan Smith. *One Last Look: A Sentimental Journey to the Eighth Air Force Heavy Bomber Bases of World War II in England*. New York: Abbeville Press, 1983.

Keller, Henry. *North Africa: Gateway to the Barbed Wire Front*. Apollo, PA: Closson Press, 1994.

Knight, Lucian Lamar. *Georgia's Landmarks, Memorials, and Legends, Vol. II*. Atlanta: Byrd Publishing, 1914.

Knoke, Heinz. *I Flew for the Führer*. London: Evans Brothers, 1979.

Lande, D. A. *From Somewhere in England*. Osceola, WI: Motorbooks International, 1990.

Le Strange, Richard, with James R. Brown. *Century Bombers: The Story of the Bloody Hundredth*. Diss, England: 100th Bomb Group Memorial Museum, 1989.

Lockheed Horizons, issue 14, 1983.

McKee, Alexander. *Dresden 1945: The Devil's Tinderbox*. New York: E. P. Dutton, 1984.

McLachlan, Ian. *Final Flights: Dramatic Wartime Incidents Revealed by Aviation Archaeology*. Sparkford, England: Patrick Stephens, 1989.

McLachlan, Ian, and Russell J. Zorn. *Eighth Air Force Bomber Stories: Eye-Witness Accounts from American Airmen and British Civilians of the Perils of War.* Sparkford, England: Patrick Stephens, 1991.

Middlebrook, Martin. *The Schweinfurt-Regensburg Mission.* London: Allen Lane, 1983.

Nilsson, John Ryan. *The Story of the Century.* Privately printed, 1946.

O'Hearn, Robert E. *In My Book You're All Heroes.* Privately printed, 1984.

Philpott, Bryan. *Fighters Defending the Reich.* Sparkford, England: Patrick Stephens, 1988.

Piekalkiewiez, Janusz. *Luftkrieg 1939–1945.* Munich, Germany: Sudwest, 1978.

Price, Alfred. *Battle Over the Reich.* New York: Charles Scribner's Sons, 1973.

Price, Alfred. *Instruments of Darkness.* London: Macdonald and Jane's, 1977.

Price, Alfred. *Pictorial History of the Luftwaffe.* New York: Arco, 1969.

Putney, Diane T., ed. *ULTRA and the Army Air Forces in World War II.* Washington, D.C.: Office of Air Force History, 1987.

Rand McNally Encyclopedia of Military Aircraft 1914–1980. New York: Military Press, 1983.

Rich, Ben, and Leo Janos. *Skunk Works.* New York: Little, Brown, 1994.

Ries, Karl. *Luftwaffe: A Photographic Record 1919–1945.* Blue Ridge Summit, PA: Aero, 1987.

Roane, Owen D. *A Year in the Life of a Cowboy with the Bloody 100th.* Dallas, TX: Minuteman Press, 1995.

Rust, Kenn C. *Eighth Air Force Story.* Temple City, CA: Historical Aviation Album, 1978.

Saward, Dudley. *"Bomber" Harris.* London: Buchan & Enright, 1984.

Sellers, Robert C. *Flying Control in the Air War Over Europe.* Minnesota: Flying Control Veterans Association, 1990.

Sheridan, Jack Walrath. *They Never Had It So Good: The Personal Unofficial Story of the 350th Bombardment Squadron (H), 100th Bombardment Group (H), USAAF, 1942–1945.* San Francisco, CA: Stark-Raith, 1946.

Speer, Albert. *Inside the Third Reich, Memoirs by Albert Speer.* New York: Collier, 1999.

Stadtmuseum Münster. *Bomben auf Münster.* Münster, Germany, 1983. This is a catalog that accompanied an exhibit held at the Stadtmuseum between October 10, 1983, and April 29, 1984.

Steinbeck, John. *Bombs Away: The Story of a Bomber Team.* New York: Paragon House, 1990.

Steinhoff, Johannes. *The Last Chance: The Pilots' Plot Against Göring 1944–1945.* London: Arrow Books, 1977.

Stephens, Glenn A. *Kriegies, Caterpillars and Lucky Bastards.* Anaheim, CA: Robinson Typrographics, 1987.

Sweetman, John. *Schweinfurt: Disaster in the Skies.* New York: Ballantine, 1971.

Taylor, Michael J. H., ed. *Jane's Encyclopedia of Aviation.* New York: Crescent, 1993.

Terraine, John. *Time for Courage: The Royal Air Force in the European War.* New York: Macmillan, 1985.

Toland, John. *The Last 100 Days.* New York: Bantam, 1985.

USAAF. *Contrails: My War Record: A History of the World War II as Recorded at U.S. Army Air Force Station No. 139 Thorpe Abbots, Near Diss, County of Norfolk, England.* New York: Callahan, 1947.

USAAF. *ULTRA and the History of the United States Strategic Air Force in Europe vs. the German Air Force.* Frederick, MD: University Publications of America, 1980.

Varian, Horace L. *The Bloody Hundredth: Missions and Memories of a World War II Bomb Group.* Privately printed, 1979.

Weems, P. V. H. *Air Navigation.* New York: McGraw Hill, 1931.

Williamson, Murray. *Luftwaffe.* London: George Allen & Unwin, 1985.

Willis, Steve, and Barry Holliss. *Military Airfields in the British Isles 1939–1945.* Wellingborough, England: Woolnough Bookbinding, 1987.

Wright, Arnold A. *Behind the Wire: Stalag Luft III South Compound.* Privately printed, 1993.

INDEX

ABOUT THE AUTHORS

FRANK MURPHY survived months in a German POW camp after being shot out of his B-17 Flying Fortress. His bravery earned him the Distinguished Flying Cross, the Purple Heart, and the Air Medal. The incredible stories of Murphy and his Eighth Air Force's 100th Bomb Group will be featured in the upcoming Steven Spielberg and Tom Hanks TV series, *Masters of the Air*.

CHLOE MELAS is an entertainment reporter for CNN, covering breaking celebrity news, industry analyses, and in-depth investigations. She currently resides in New York with her husband and two sons.

ELIZABETH MURPHY holds a masters of art in English Literature from Northern Arizona University and is the author of numerous children's books. She currently resides in Atlanta, Georgia, where she was born and raised.